Books *by* HOPE LAMPERT

Behind Closed Doors: Wheeling and Dealing in the Banking World (1986)

Till Death Do Us Part: Bendix vs. Martin Marietta (1983)

Behind
Closed Doors

Behind Closed Doors

Wheeling and Dealing
in the
Banking World

Hope Lampert

New York Atheneum 1986

Library of Congress Cataloging-in-Publication Data

Lampert, Hope.
    Behind closed doors.

    Bibliography: p.
    Includes index.
    1. Banks and banking—United States—Case studies.
I. Title.
HG2481.L34   1986   332.1'0973   86-47683
ISBN 0-689-11747-7

"After all," mumbled J. P. Morgan when accused of doing secret deeds behind closed doors, *"that is what doors are for."*

Acknowledgments

This book could not have been written without the moral support of Jennifer Seymour, Kimberly Brown, Kevin Ward, Danny McNevin, and Werner Disse. Marty Lipton and Jay Higgins encouraged me to begin work on a second book and helped me to figure out what I wanted the book to be. Lee Kimmel, Ken Wilson, Steve McLin, Ken Brody and Shelley Floyd offered assistance well beyond the call of duty. Art Merrick, Katie Weiss, Helen Braun, Joan Horvich, Dick Howe, Mel Adams, Phil Thomas, Bill Dillman, Bill Greenhill, Marcia Roth, Naomi Rosenfeld, Warren Vieth and Dan Harrison answered hundreds of questions that must have seemed irrelevant. Jennifer Seymour patiently read and commented on various drafts of the manuscript. Susan Leon of Atheneum edited with clarity. Charlotte Sheedy, my agent, never let me doubt that I would finish, and when I did, skillfully shepherded the book from typewriter to bookstore.

Contents

Behind
Closed Doors

Introduction

First National City Bank

"Go to Hell"

Charles E. "Sunshine Charley" Mitchell had flair. A big heavyset man with a square jaw, Mitchell worried about his weight, so every morning he walked the three and a half miles from his elegant town house in Manhattan's East Seventies to National City Bank headquarters at 55 Wall Street. Mitchell was an optimist; even in 1929, falling stock prices didn't trouble him. "Things have never been better," he told a reporter the day he and his wife departed for a month's vacation in Europe. "Be a bull on America." Many people took Mitchell's word as gospel. Mitchell was known around the world as "the banker of bankers, the salesman of salesmen, the genius of the New Economic Era." He had, after all, changed the way America banked.

Charley Mitchell was born in Boston and worked his way through Amherst by giving lessons in public speaking. When he graduated in 1899, Mitchell landed a job at Western Electric in Chicago. Studying commercial law and bookkeeping at night, he quickly became company credit manager. In 1911, Mitchell set up an investment house in New York and made a name as the best salesman in the business. Five years later, he got an offer he couldn't refuse. He closed his shop and took over the brokerage operations of National City Bank, the world's largest bank.

When Charley Mitchell started to work there, the bank had just

3

launched a daring bid for the consumer: it had opened a network of branches across Manhattan, pressed New Yorkers to open checking accounts, and offered them the first unsecured personal loan—a loan that required no collateral. The bank also sold stock, the most popular investment of the 1920s. Although banks were formally forbidden to sell stock, in 1911, National City had circumvented the law by setting up a "nonbank" subsidiary called National City Company.

Under Mitchell, the company quickly became the biggest stock brokerage in America with 1,900 employees, 69 branch offices and sales of $1.5 billion a year. National City salesmen sold from their offices; they sold on railroad cars; they sold door-to-door. National City stock salesmen urged National City depositors to get their money out of savings accounts and into stocks and bonds; they offered clients special "call" loans to buy stock with just a 10 percent down payment; call loans aren't a bargain: they have to be repaid whenever the bank decides it wants its money back. A lot of the stock that the National City salesmen sold was worthless—companies didn't then have to tell investors even the most basic financial information, so investors didn't know that their U.S. Steel stock had been watered or that their Peruvian bonds would never be redeemed by the already bankrupt government—but no matter: the salesman got a bonus for high volume and the bank made money.

The stock-selling business was so good that by 1927 Mitchell had borrowed $25 million from the government's New York Federal Reserve Bank at 5 percent to relend to stock-buying clients at 8 to 20 percent.

In early 1929, the Fed announced that banks should not borrow money from the government to make call loans; call loans were bad banking.

"Go to hell," said Mitchell, now chairman of National City Bank, and borrowed more.

While Mitchell was building up a brokerage, he was also pushing National City into underwriting, contracting with a company to sell to the public an entire issue of stocks or bonds for a set price. Underwriting was risky: National City couldn't sell shares to savvy investors unless they thought the price was right—and guessing

4

the right price meant forecasting the ups and downs of the stock market. If National City guessed right and investors bought, the bank made a handsome 15 percent commission almost overnight. If National City guessed wrong, then the bank had to buy the stock itself, at a big loss. Mitchell didn't like losses, and he found a way to avoid them: he sold the bad stock that National City Bank had underwritten to naïve National City Company clients.

Selling and underwriting stocks and bonds weren't the only new ways that Mitchell found to make money. Mitchell used cash in National City customer accounts to play the stock market: he bought stock in a company whenever the company's top executives gave him tips; he poured cash into pools to manipulate the price of stocks like Anaconda Copper and National City Bank.

On Black Thursday, October 24, 1929—two weeks after Mitchell and his wife returned from their vacation in Europe—the stock market crashed.

The price of U.S. Steel stock skidded from $205½ to $193½ a share.

Montgomery Ward dropped from $83 to $50.

General Electric fell by $32.

As stock prices collapsed, "call" loans to small investors went sour. Savers got scared that the bad call loans would break the banks, so they rushed to the teller window to get their cash; many banks couldn't pay: they *had* been broken by the bad loans—and their own bad speculation; a bank that couldn't pay was bankrupt, and as bank after bank collapsed, depositors got so frightened that no bank seemed safe enough.

The runs began.

In August 1930, every bank in Toledo but one failed.

In September, thirty-nine banks in Philadelphia went bust.

Three hundred and five banks failed in September 1931.

Five hundred and twenty-two failed in October.

By 1933, bank failures since the Crash hit 5,738. Depositors lost more than $3.5 billion. State governor after state governor had declared a banking "holiday" to keep the panic from getting worse. Franklin Delano Roosevelt made the holiday national as soon as he was sworn in as president March 4, 1933; when the holiday ended four days later, the runs stopped, but many banks survived only with loans from the federal government. The Continental Illinois National Bank & Trust Company, the kingpin bank of the Midwest, had to borrow $50 million.

In his inaugural address, Roosevelt had promised to drive the money changers out of the temple, and Charley Mitchell was clearly at the top of the list. At the end of March, Mitchell was called to Washington to explain to Congress just what had been going on. Certain unsavory details had to be spelled out. There was the lost depositor money. There was the stock manipulation. There was the $10,020 "loan" to the general manager of the Port Authority of New York just before National City won a $66-million bond deal.

Then someone asked just how much the chairman of National City made.

Mitchell explained that he earned more than $1 million a year: $25,000 in salary plus a $1-million bonus.

The government's share of that?

"Well, zero," said Mitchell. In 1929, he had paid no income taxes.

The IRS started an investigation. Mitchell was indicted for evading $573,312.81 in taxes in 1929 and forced to resign his post at the bank.

By the time Mitchell lost his job, National City had lost its freedom. National City had been regulated for more than a hundred years, but the old rules were loose and largely irrelevant. In 1933, Congress passed the Glass-Steagall Banking Act that tightened the noose. A commercial bank, defined as an institution that accepts consumer deposits and makes corporate loans, was henceforth forbidden to underwrite securities and sell stock; banks were no longer allowed to have nonbank subsidiaries; commercial banks could no longer compete with each other for deposits by raising interest rates because Congress would set the maximum interest rates; all commercial bank savings accounts up to $2,500 were now insured by the new Federal Deposit Insurance Corporation (FDIC).

Congress also set new rules for investment banks. An investment bank was allowed to use only its own money—not customer money—to underwrite; an investment bank could only sell stock and bonds that were "registered" with the government Securities and Exchange Commission (SEC); investment bankers and company officials were forbidden to buy and sell stock on the basis of secret "inside" information about company plans; anyone who owned more than 5 percent of the stock of a company had to file an official statement with the SEC explaining just why he had bought so much.

Banking would never be the same again.

(1)

Bank of America

"A Branch Within a Mile and a Half of Almost Every Californian"

"What do you think about this one?" asked Harry Mullikin. He pointed to a name on the list in front of him.

Dick Cooley leaned back in his chair. "He's a smart man," he said. "But I'm not sure he's the right man for you." Cooley stared out the window of his office at the traffic on Los Angeles' South Flower Street. "Seafirst is sick—you lost $56 million in the second quarter and you're going to lose another $60 million this quarter. That's a fourth of your capital. This guy is a senior vice president at a big bank; he hasn't had experience handling your kind of problems."

Mullikin frowned. "What about this one?" He pointed to another name.

Cooley looked across the round table and wrinkled his brow. "He'd be better," he said. He paused. "It might be tough to convince him to take the job: he's chairman of a healthy small bank. Seafirst is in so much trouble that only someone really young and aggressive is going to be willing to take the job, someone who wants to earn his spurs. You'd probably never convince one of my Wells Fargo deputies to risk tainting his record with Seafirst."

Mullikin sighed. He twisted his pearl tie tack and then folded his hands in his lap. "Do you think anyone can rescue Seafirst?" he asked. "I wish I understood banking better. It's not like running Westin Hotels."

"Sure, someone can save Seafirst," said Cooley. "Seafirst is a good bank. You got into trouble because you got too aggressive with the oil and gas loans. That's behind you. Now you've got to focus on doing what you do best. There will be a couple of bad years for earnings, but you'll survive."

Mullikin nodded.

"Unless there's a wire run," said Cooley. "If the big investors start to telex their money out, the bank could go bankrupt in a couple of hours."

Mullikin looked horrified.

"Don't worry," said Cooley. "That won't happen as long as earnings don't drop too far. It won't be a problem."

"I hope not," said Mullikin. "Seafirst has always been a bank that Seattle could be proud of. I've always been proud to be a director." He paused. "I just bought five hundred shares." That brought his stake to 3,975 shares. "I figured it was cheap at $23."

Cooley laughed.

"We're running out of time," said Mullikin. "We fired Jenkins in August. I've been looking for a new chairman for three months already. We've got to have a man by mid-December—and it's already Thanksgiving."

"You'll find someone," said Cooley. "You've got a list of finalists."

"I can't believe you've given me so much help," said Mullikin. "You've got enough to do running Wells Fargo."

Cooley looked at Mullikin for a minute. "I just told my board that I'm going to resign next year," he said. "I've been chief executive officer of Wells Fargo for long enough." Cooley paused. "I've always said I was going to retire when I turned sixty. I'm fifty-nine now."

Mullikin had heard Cooley say that he was going to retire at sixty, but he'd never quite believed it. "What are you going to do?" he asked. "I can't imagine you sitting still."

"I've talked to a headhunter," said Cooley. "I told him to find me something completely different. Something definitely non-banking. A new challenge." He paused. "And out of San Francisco."

Mullikin nodded. Cooley had just gotten through his second · messy divorce. He had remarried again; his ex-wife lived in San Francisco.

"But you know," said Cooley. "I'm worried about starting over in a new industry. I know banking. I wish there were a banking job that looked right."

"I've got one for you," said Mullikin. He played with the white sheet of paper in front of him. "Chairman of Seafirst."

Cooley stared.

"I was joking," said Mullikin. He paused. "Let's get back to the list."

Cooley leaned back in his chair again. "Running Seafirst would be a new challenge," he said.

"No kidding," Mullikin agreed. He fiddled with the white sheet of names.

"I might be interested," said Cooley.

Mullikin was startled. "You're interested?" he said.

"I'm ready for a new challenge," said Cooley.

Mullikin stared. "If you're really interested," he said, "why don't you come up to Seattle and talk to the board?"

Cooley looked straight at Mullikin. "I'll do that," he said. "Next week."

Later that afternoon, Mullikin put in a call to each of the seventeen members of the Seafirst board of directors. "Dick Cooley is interested in taking the job as chairman of Seafirst," he said. "He's coming up to see the books and meet the staff." Mullikin paused. "I hope he takes the job. If anyone can save the bank, Dick Cooley can."

Dick Cooley is in constant motion. At fifty-nine, he looks thirty-nine—tall, slender with light brown hair and glittery gray eyes—and he attacks his work with the zip of a man just turned nineteen. He skis in the winter, boats in the summer and reads escape fiction all year round: he says he reads too much nonfiction on the job. He never gives up. Cooley lost his right arm at the shoulder when his fighter plane was shot down by the Germans during the Second World War; he wears a hook as a right hand, and he refuses to let that crimp his style: he still plays squash; he still plays golf; his handicap is 21. He has a huge ego; at Wells they call him "Richard P."

Cooley was born in Dallas and majored in industrial engineering at Yale. He studied hard, but he played harder; he won letters in football, tennis and squash. After he graduated in 1944, Cooley joined the Air Force; back in the States, he signed on at American Trust Company in San Francisco. He had wanted to be an engineer, not a financier—he joined a bank in 1949 because he needed a job—but he turned out to be quite a banker. He was named a vice president in 1957, a senior vice president in 1964 and president of Wells Fargo, new owner of American Trust, in 1966. He was forty-three years old.

Dick Cooley quickly pushed what had been a small and sleepy bank into Southern California and Latin America, into real estate and modern marketing. Cooley's Wells was the first bank to offer shorter lines and pampered service to big depositors, and the first bank to offer a check with a pretty pattern on the background instead of plain blue stripes; Wells was the brains behind MasterCard, the only bank card that held its own against the BankAmericard. The Wells loan portfolio leapt from $4.2 billion in Cooley's first year to $24 billion in 1982; at the same time, profits skyrocketed from $16.8 million to more than $100 million.

Lots of people asked Cooley for help; he was one of the West Coast's most esteemed bankers. Naturally he had heard about Seafirst.

"See Seafirst First." For more than a hundred years, the Seattle-First National Bank had been the premier bank in the Pacific Northwest. It was the bank where Washington banked: half the households in the state had an account at Seafirst; two thirds of the "middle market" companies—the business customers bigger than mom-and-pop stores but too small for the Fortune 1000— did their banking at Seafirst. Banking experts called Seafirst far-sighted, well managed, a model for even the country's largest banks. Seafirst was a pioneer: the bank boasted the first automated teller machines, the first single-statement account, and the first bank debit card, good for everything from the cash machine to groceries at the Safeway. In 1981, the bank proudly announced its twentieth straight year of increased earnings; by then, the loan portfolio totaled $800 million; Seafirst was the nineteenth-largest bank in the country, on the way to being number ten.

Seafirst got its start in 1854 when Dexter Horton opened a general store with the unique feature of a money-keeping service for prospecting goldminers. Horton soon dropped the cornmeal and coffee beans to concentrate on banking. It was rocky going, but by the turn of the century, Dexter Horton was the largest bank in the state. In 1929, Dexter Horton merged with banks number two and three, and soon Seattle-First National had branches all across the state. By 1960, the client list included Western giants like Carnation, Weyerhaeuser, Boeing, Westin Hotels and Pacific Car and Foundry (Paccar).

In 1961, Seafirst bought the First National Bank of Everett, Washington, and two years later, William M. Jenkins, president of Everett, became chairman of Seafirst. Jenkins wanted Seafirst to keep growing, and he wanted to stabilize earnings; he opened seven domestic and foreign branch offices and encouraged Seafirst to lend to national companies and to South American countries. In 1979, as part of Jenkins' diversification program, Seafirst started to make energy loans. At first, the bank lent money to large oil companies on the West Coast and in Alaska. Then Seafirst opened a branch in Oklahoma City. Most oil banks have an engineering staff. Not Seafirst. The oil and gas division was headed up by a thirty-nine-year-old corporate loan officer named John Boyd. Boyd was Bill Jenkins' protégé.

The well-established Texas banks had a lock on loans to reputable independents. That mean that Seafirst had to lend to less credit worthy borrowers: gas drillers in Oklahoma, wildcatters in Texas, small refiners like NuCorp Energy and Good Hope Refineries. The loans were risky, of course, but the interest rates were high. If things went right, Boyd figured he'd hit pay dirt; if things went wrong, Seafirst could lose every penny.

At first, things went right and the money rolled in. Boyd liked the profits so much that he couldn't make energy loans fast enough. So he bought loans. Buying loans isn't itself unusual—the law says that a bank can lend no more than 10 percent of its capital to a single borrower, so when a small bank lands a big loan, it has to sell "participations" to other banks—but the Seafirst purchases were somewhat odd. Four hundred million dollars worth came from the Penn Square Bank of Oklahoma City.

Penn Square had a reputation in the financial world. Bill Patterson, the executive vice president who ran the oil and gas division, had been seen drinking beer out of a cowboy boot. Sometimes he showed up for work in a Nazi uniform; other days he wore his Mickey Mouse hat. Patterson like to sell his loans blind—the bank that bought the participation had to promise not to investigate the borrower and not to tell the borrower that it had bought the loan. The buying bank had to rely on the credit check done by Penn Square. In fact, Penn Square didn't do much credit checking, and it didn't keep careful records. Most banks shied away from Penn Square.

Not Seafirst. Seafirst wanted to grow, and besides, John Boyd, loan buyer, and Bill Patterson, Penn Square's loan seller, were personal friends. They were drinking buddies and hunting partners. Patterson gave Boyd an antique gun. Boyd lined up a $1.4-million loan from Seafirst so that Patterson could buy stock in Penn Square. Patterson helped Boyd get a Penn Square loan to buy a car.

Boyd approved the loans that Seafirst bought from Penn Square.

Between the end of 1978 and early 1981, the Seafirst energy portfolio grew from $11 million to more than $300 million. That was so fast that it raised a red flag even at fast-growing Seafirst.

"My staff is worried that Seafirst isn't keeping tabs on loan quality," the chief financial officer told Bill Jenkins. "We're worried that Penn Square is going to go belly up. I've checked around. No one else has limits on lending in a particular industry, but I think it makes sense for us and oil."

"I agree," said the vice chairman.

"So do I," said the president.

"Not yet," said Jenkins. He trusted Boyd.

"We don't have a choice," said the chief financial officer. "Our oil loans aren't good banking."

Jenkins nodded. At the end of 1981, Jenkins slapped a limit on the energy portfolio—maximum exposure: $700 million or 150 percent of the bank's capital.

The limit didn't work. Boyd could authorize energy loans up to $10 million without approval from his boss. He kept authorizing. His boss, the head of the world banking division, could authorize energy loans up to $25 million without approval from his boss, the president of Seafirst; he kept authorizing. In November and December of 1981, Boyd bought $350 million of loans from Penn Square. That brought the total energy loans to $1.2 billion. By March, energy loans were $1.3 billion, 12 percent of all Seafirst loans.

Boyd's boss was transferred. His new boss was the old chief financial officer, the man who had insisted on a limit to energy loans. "Come upstairs," the new boss told Boyd. "We've got to talk."

Boyd came up.

"What's going on down in the energy department?" asked the boss.

Boyd evaded.

"Too risky," said the new boss. "There will be no more loans to Penn Square."

Boyd called his friends into his office. He passed out paper cups full of grape juice. "Jonestown has just struck in this bank," he toasted.

Boyd's boss called again a few weeks later. "We've been looking through your files for loan papers," he said. "There aren't any. There aren't even confirmations that Seafirst has bought loans from Penn Square."

"Don't worry," said Boyd. "Patterson has sent a couple of shoe boxes full of documents from Penn Square. There's more paper in Oklahoma City."

The boss frowned.

The president of Seafirst flew down Oklahoma City to investigate. There were stacks of documents on the floor, but not much in the files. There didn't seem to be a loan approval system. The president was shocked.

"Don't worry," said the chairman of Penn Square. "I'm tightening up."

He wasn't.

Oil prices collapsed in June. Seafirst borrowers started to go bankrupt.

Penn Square missed its first payment on Seafirst's bought loans that month.

The bank failed over the Fourth of July weekend.

Boyd's new boss ran to the files. He called Oklahoma City. Then he called Bill Jenkins. "We're in trouble," said Boyd's new boss. "We don't know how much we bought; we don't know how much we lost. Boyd didn't keep good records. The Penn Square records have been seized by the government."

Jenkins held a crisis meeting in his office.

The president of the bank held a crisis meeting in his office.

Boyd's new boss held a crisis meeting in his office.

Boyd held a crisis meeting in his office.

The stories began to trickle out: the shoe boxes, the hunting trips. Someone said that Seafirst had made a multimillion-dollar loan to a man who had been an assistant in a funeral parlor and now wanted to drill for oil; it wasn't clear that the funeral assistant had done any drilling, but he did have a big ranch complete with a helicopter pad.

Boyd's new boss called Bill Jenkins. "You've got to fire John Boyd," he said. "You've got to fire Boyd's old boss."

Jenkins balked. Then he changed his mind. Two weeks after Penn Square failed, Jenkins fired both John Boyd and John Boyd's old boss.

"We've got a big problem," Jenkins told the board at the July meeting. "We bought a lot of loans from Penn Square; Penn Square is bankrupt and the Penn Square loans are bad, but we don't know much more than that. We don't know what we bought—we're not even sure how much—and we don't know what we lost, but we know it's big. I think we lost $65 million, but I'm going to call it $125 million just in case. That makes our loss for the quarter $56 million." Seafirst lost just $44 million in bad loans for all of 1981.

"How did this happen?" asked Harry Mullikin. Jenkins had never mentioned Penn Square at board meetings. Mullikin didn't think that he'd ever heard of Penn Square until he read about the bank in the newspaper. "How do we know it won't happen again?"

"I've fired the two men who made the problem," said Jenkins. "Everything is going to be all right."

Mullikin wasn't so sure. So he called his friend Dick Cooley, chairman of Wells Fargo. "Seafirst has to retrench," Cooley told him. "The bank has to sell off all the loans out of the Pacific Northwest and cut costs to the bone. I always had a lot of respect for Jenkins, but I guess he encouraged his officers to take too many risks."

Mullikin nodded. Now he understood: Jenkins had to go. He got the ax at the August board meeting, effective December 31. Harry Mullikin, the hotel man, was named head of the committee to find a new chairman. First, Mullikin called a headhunter. Then he called Cooley.

"Jenkins is out," he said. "I'm chairman of the executive committee. I'm in charge of finding a new chief executive officer for Seafirst. I'm not sure what kind of a banker I want. Can we talk?"

"Sure," said Cooley. "Come down to my office."

Mullikin flew down to Los Angeles.

They talked for four hours.

Mullikin flew to Los Angeles again in the middle of November. By then, he had a list of finalists. As it turned out, none got asked. That was the meeting where Cooley told Mullikin that he'd told the Wells board that he was going to resign and Mullikin told Cooley he ought to think about Seafirst.

Which he did.

While Mullikin courted Cooley, Seafirst coasted. Every day more Penn Square loans went bad. Every day the Seafirst losses ballooned. Jenkins, lame duck chairman, did what he could: cut staff, cut costs, sold loans.

"We're not getting interest on the Penn Square loans," Jenkins told Bill Pettit, the chief financial officer, just after Thanksgiving. "We may have another loss this quarter. We've got to raise capital or the Comptroller will close the bank down." The Comptroller of the Currency set a minimum ratio of bank capital—cash in the bank's own account—to bank deposits; that was supposed to guarantee that the bank could cover its bad loans out of its own pocket. "We need $100 million."

Pettit nodded. "We can't raise that money ourselves," he said. "I'll call our investment banker."

"Make sure that he knows that this assignment is coming from me," said Jenkins.

Pettit called Salomon Brothers in New York. "Do you know

16

anyone who wants to sink $100 million in the biggest bank in Washington State?" he asked Lee Kimmel, the partner who specialized in finding cash for commercial banks. "Bill Jenkins says it can't wait."

"I think I can find someone," said Kimmel. "There are a lot of regional banks that want to invest in other regionals to form a national regional. Regional banks make most of their loans to local and national companies and consumers; money center banks lend to multinational companies and countries."

"Fine," said Pettit.

"How serious is this?" asked Kimmel. "Are you talking about putting the bank on the market? You can't sell Seafirst to an out-of-state bank unless you're almost bankrupt."

"We don't need to sell the bank," said Pettit. "We've got a problem. We're nowhere near bankrupt."

"Okay," Kimmel said. Just a $100-million investment. "I'll make some calls."

Soon the results began to come in:

Northwest Bankcorp, a holding company in Minneapolis. Maybe.

First Bank System, another Minneapolis bank. Maybe.

First Interstate, an eleven-state bank based in San Francisco. No.

In the middle of December, Kimmel called Steve McLin (pronounced *Mack*-lin), head of strategic planning at Bank of America. "Have you thought about an investment in Seafirst?" he asked. "It's a nice strategic play: if you are later able to buy the rest of Seafirst, you'll become the biggest bank in two states."

McLin laughed. "I don't think Sam is interested," he said. Sam Armacost is president of the Bank of America. "Seafirst is a very sick bank."

"The retail part of the bank is healthy," replied Kimmel. "The problem is the energy loans, and they have that under control now."

McLin laughed again. The idea was preposterous. He suggested another bank.

"A couple of banks are interested," Kimmel told Pettit later that afternoon. "Let's start negotiating."

Then Kimmel got a call from Harry Mullikin.

"I hear you're trying to find an investor to put $100 million into Seafirst," he said. "I don't know who hired you, but you're fired. I've just hired Dick Cooley as chairman of Seafirst. He starts on the job January 1, and he's going to solve the Seafirst problems by himself."

Sam Armacost looked down the fairway. "I wish I weren't so busy," he said. "I'd like to get in a game every week, not just on the day before Christmas Eve." He swung his iron. "My game is slipping. I have a seven handicap, but I've been hitting like I'm a fifteen."

Steve McLin laughed. "Seven is a lot better than my twelve," he said.

"True," said Armacost. "I'll bet you two, two, and four."

"Okay," said McLin. They shook hands and strolled down the green to the next hole.

Armacost gave his putter to his caddie. He turned to McLin. "What kind of wild ideas have you been looking at back there in your corner office?" he asked.

Steve McLin didn't answer at first. He took the 3-wood from his caddie and weighed it in his hand. "I've got a lot of ideas for what the Bank of America ought to be doing," he said.

Armacost raised an eyebrow.

"I've been running acquisition studies," said McLin.

"On what?" asked Armacost.

"Banks with a big market share," said McLin. "A big percentage of their state's accounts."

Armacost nodded. He teed off. McLin teed off. They walked down the fairway.

"What banks are you looking at?" asked Armacost as they passed the sand trap.

"Well," said McLin. "A couple of different banks."

"Like what?" said Armacost.

"Well," said McLin. He took a practice swing with his 5-iron. "Like Seafirst."

Armacost frowned. "Seafirst?" he laughed. "Haven't I been reading about that bank? Didn't Seafirst buy a lot of loans from Penn Square?"

"Seafirst used to be the premier bank in the Northwest," said McLin. "It would be a perfect extension for the Bank of America. If we have the daring to buy it."

"You've got to be kidding," said Armacost.

"I'm serious," said McLin. "The fit is good. Buying Seafirst would start to lock up the West Coast."

Armacost looked at him. "I'll buy the drinks when we're done," he said.

McLin looked down the fairway. "Seafirst is a good strategic play."

"Let's just play golf," Armacost said.

"Your shot," said McLin.

They walked down the fairway.

"Seafirst," mumbled Armacost. "What next?"

McLin puffed on his pipe.

Armacost shot a 73 that day. McLin shot an 84.

"You lose the bet," said Armacost. "That'll cost you six bucks. Let's get some drinks."

"Okay," said McLin.

They walked to the clubhouse.

Armacost bought the drinks.

Samuel Armacost is conscientious. At forty-four, he's six feet tall, with a round face, brown hair and brown eyes. He's a natty dresser, a rock-'n'-roll dancer and a race car fiend. Until he was named president of the bank, he zipped around in a 280ZX. Recently he's been forced to use the company's limousine to get to the office in the morning: he's got so much to do that he needs the extra hour to read his memos. He used to be a bit overweight, the result of too many five-course meals with clients—so he went on a crash diet and lost fifteen pounds. He still makes a point of counting calories; he orders light when he has to eat lunch out and when he doesn't, Armacost lunches on a cup of coffee at his desk. No one walks into Armacost's office without an appointment; and getting an appointment isn't easy: Sam books a year in advance. Yet he's got a lighter side. At a cocktail party once, Mrs. Armacost introduced Sam as an employee of the Bank of America.

"You are?" said the new friend.

"I am," said Sam. He didn't mention that he was president. "Would you like to open an account?"

Armacost grew up in Newport News, Virginia, and Redlands, California. He went to Denison University in Ohio and, to the dismay of his college president father, spent more time chasing girls than hitting the books. In 1961, Armacost got a job at the Bank of America as a credit trainee in the San Bernardino office. He took two years off to get an M.B.A. at Stanford and returned to the bank as a junior lending officer. From the start, it was clear he was on the fast track. He rose through the ranks in California and was sent to London for seasoning. After a stint in Chicago as head of the bank's midwestern division and a tour in San Francisco running the corporate office, Armacost was named head of the overseas divisions. Two years later, in 1979, he was cashier, the number three job at the bank. In 1981, Armacost was promoted to president and chief executive officer. He was forty-one years old.

Although the bank Armacost inherited was foundering, it had once been one of America's proudest banks. Bank of America still boasted "A Branch Within a Mile and a Half of Almost Every Californian." BoA was a consumer bank: 40 percent of all Californians had an account at one of the eleven hundred branches. It had had a tradition of being progressive—and aggressive. It was the first U.S. bank with branches instead of just a headquarters office, one of the first banks to cross state lines. Bank of America pioneered the TimePlan installment credit system and popularized the bank credit card with its BankAmericard, now called Visa. Bank of America bankrolled farmers, vintners, movie producers, aerospace giants and Silicon Valley start-ups. In the 1970s, Bank of America lent more money to students for college tuition than any other bank in the world.

It had always been a bank with a philosophy. A. P. Giannini, son of an Italian immigrant fruit merchant, made his first fortune as a produce wholesaler and then decided to become "the little fellow's banker," so in 1904, he founded the Bank of Italy headquartered on Montgomery Street. Established bankers laughed that Giannini's bank was sure to fail, but in 1906, San Francisco was hit by the Great Earthquake. While the city's leading banks were covered in rubble, Giannini salvaged the cash from his vault and set up a tent office on the waterfront. In less than a week, he had won scores of new and faithful clients, and after that he never looked back. Soon Transamerica Corporation, Giannini's holding company, controlled insurance companies, finance companies, real estates companies. Transamerica's 645 bank branches in California, Oregon, Nevada, Arizona and Washington together held 41 percent of all deposits and 50 percent of all the loans in the five states.

Regulators who thought big banks were bad got scared. By the 1940s, many of the states Bank of America wasn't in had passed "Giannini" laws to keep Bank of America out. Now the Federal Reserve Board insisted that Giannini dismantle Transamerica. Transamerica sold its stake in Bank of America and spun off the out-of-California branches into a new bank now called First Interstate. To keep Giannini from rising again, Congress then passed a law forbidding a bank to open branches outside its established home state.

Giannini died in 1949, and Bank of America lost its touch. It kept banking the way it always had. Personnel policy was: no pink slips and no raises. Decisions were made—or rather weren't made— by committee. Bank of America stopped taking risks, and it didn't react when Congress passed a law deregulating interest rates on its bread-and-butter passbook savings accounts. While other banks experimented with variable-rate loans, Bank of America built branches; while other banks tried out savings certificates and cash management accounts, Bank of America pushed fixed mortgage loans. BoA refused to tinker with glittery technology: at the beginning of 1981, it had only a handful of automated teller machines; three years later, the bank still hadn't got around to buying automatic envelope stuffers: canceled checks were put into return mailers by hand. The mistakes hit hard on the bottom line. Market share plummeted. Loan losses surged. The bank had had seventy-two consecutive quarters of increased earnings, but now earnings dropped by $199 million in 1981, $52 million in 1982, $5 million in 1983. By the end of 1982, Bank of America wasn't the world's biggest bank anymore, or the most profitable. Citibank had $9 billion more in assets, and twice the earnings.

In 1981, Sam Armacost began to kick the bank back to life. He raised salaries; he bought modern computers and automated teller machines; he tried to win back accounts with an advertising blitz. And he did the undoable: he hired new, aggressive executives away from American Airlines, IBM, and American Express, and he began to close Bank of America branches. That helped Bank of America to catch up. But Armacost knew that if it was to become America's premier bank, it had to have imagination. So three months after he was named chairman, Armacost promoted Steve McLin, then vice president, to be the chief planner. McLin's assignment: dream up a way to put Giannini's empire back together again.

Stephen McLin is cerebral. At thirty-six, he's tall, balding and decidedly unbankerly. Although he usually wears pinstripes, he doesn't own a tuxedo; and he isn't on the San Francisco social circuit. McLin's an avid reader, from Shakespeare to Alexander Pope to John MacDonald and Len Deighton. McLin collects California wines, smokes $125 worth of MacBaren's tobacco a year and zips about town in a 280ZX, the same model that Sam Armacost drives, but with power windows—Armacost laughs that he can "roll his own windows down." McLin spends his holidays hiking around Angels Camp, his wife's home town in the heart of the California Gold Country.

McLin's an Army brat, born in St. Louis and raised at a dozen Air Force bases around the country. He went to college at the University of Illinois and set his sights on being a petroleum engineer. Armed with a degree in chemical engineering, he landed a job at Atlantic Richfield in Los Angeles in 1968, where he helped analyze the first barrel of crude oil pumped from the North Shore of Alaska. A year at Arco convinced McLin that he didn't want to be an engineer, but deal making looked fun. He went to Stanford for a master's in mechanical engineering and an M.B.A. in finance. After a stint at the First National Bank of Chicago, he joined Bank of America as an assistant vice president in the cashier's division. Seven years later, Armacost made him chief planner.

McLin's biggest coup had been engineering the acquisition of Charles Schwab & Company, the largest discount broker in America.

In 1978, three years before the Schwab deal, McLin stumbled

on a way to get Bank of America back into interstate banking. By a quirk in the banking laws, Bank of California is allowed to have full consumer branchs in three states: California, Washington and Oregon. BankCal hadn't opened a branch out of California in years; BankCal was in deep financial trouble. McLin thought that there might be a way for Bank of America to buy the BankCal charter without buying the California branches. He'd talked to a top executive at BankCal who said that it was interested in selling. McLin pressed forward. He looked at banks in Oregon and Washington and noticed Seafirst. Like Bank of America, it was retail oriented. But it was even more aggressive.

"Our price is $10 million," said the man from BankCal.

"I was thinking $2 million," said McLin.

The deal didn't get off the ground.

McLin thought he'd never get a chance to buy Seafirst again.

Then Penn Square failed. Seafirst looked weak. Late in September 1982, he called a staffer into his office. "Put together a study of Seafirst," said McLin. "The bank isn't for sale yet, but it might come on the market soon. Seafirst is the biggest bank in Washington, so if it is going to be bought, the buyer is going to have to be out of state. Buying Seafirst might be a good strategic move for the Bank of America." Interstate banking is illegal, with one exception: when a bank fails, the Federal Deposit Insurance Corporation sometimes arranges a shotgun wedding to keep the doors open. If the local legislature approves, the groom can come from another state.

The staffer started the study.

McLin didn't mention the idea to Sam Armacost; that was premature.

When he got the call from Lee Kimmel of Salomon Brothers just after Thanksgiving, McLin called the staffer working on the Seafirst study. "Seafirst is indeed looking for a buyer," he said. "If the bank gets sicker, the price might be right."

Seafirst got sicker. Kimmel called again. "I don't think so," said McLin. "Sam might not like the risk."

The day before Christmas Eve, McLin went golfing with Sam Armacost. He mentioned Seafirst, but Armacost only laughed. McLin went to the Gold Country for Christmas. The day he got back to the office, the staffer who was doing the Seafirst study walked into McLin's office. "Dick Cooley has just been named chairman of Seafirst," he said. "I want to stop working on this study. Cooley isn't going to sell the bank."

"Keep working," said McLin. "We can use the study even if Cooley doesn't sell the bank. It'll help our business loans office in Seattle. When Seafirst fails, we'll know how to capture all the business in Washington."

The day after he accepted the job of chairman at Seafirst, Dick Cooley drove his family to the Sierras for a week of skiing.

On his first day on the job, he called a staff meeting. "It's good to be here," he began. "We're going to be a great team." He paused. "We'll get the problems under control. It seems to me that the biggest problem at this bank isn't bad loans, it's morale," he said. "And I'm going to do something about that. We're going to get a new slogan—'Expect Excellence'—and everyone's going to wear it on his lapel." He looked at the head public relations man.

"The pins are on order," said the man. "They'll be in later this month."

Cooley nodded. "We're getting rid of the square table in this conference room," he said. "Henceforth, we're using a round table. No one can sit at the head of a round table." He motioned to the office across the hallway, Jenkins' throne room. "That's going to be a conference room," he said. "My office is going to be in here." The president's office, the place for the man on the way up. "I don't think there's enough communication at this bank. Decisions always seem to be made in secret closed-door meetings; henceforth, we're going to have a regular morning staff meeting. Just walk into my office when you have a question. Or sit down with me in the executive lounge for a chat." He paused. "Any questions?"

No.

"Great," said Cooley. "Let's get to work. There's a lot to do. I've got to write the 1982 annual report." He didn't want to do it; 1982 had been Bill Jenkins' disaster. But Cooley had no choice.

A couple of days after the staff meeting, the treasurer of Seafirst walked into Cooley's office. "Dick," he said. "We've got a problem."

Cooley looked up. The 1982 results were spread across the desk. "We've got lots of problems," he said. "These 1982 numbers are terrible. Seafirst lost at least $80 million."

The treasurer studied the numbers. The year had indeed been horrible. He looked at Cooley. "The big depositors are starting to worry that Seafirst is going to collapse," said the treasurer. "They are closing their accounts. If this keeps up, we're going to have to call loans to pay up. We may not be able to call loans fast enough."

A wire run—the one thing that Cooley knew could break the bank. He stayed calm. "I'll call the big depositors," said Cooley. "I think I can talk them into staying."

"They're jittery," said the treasurer. "That might not be enough."

Cooley thought for a minute. "I'll put together a loan for us from the big New York banks," he said. "If the depositors know that we're ready and able to borrow to pay out their cash, they won't run."

The treasurer nodded.

"How much do we need?" asked Cooley.

"One-point-five billion," said the treasurer.

"That's not going to be easy," said Cooley. "No one is going to want to lend to Seafirst."

The treasurer nodded again.

"If I can't get a loan commitment, I'll get an overnight line of credit," said Cooley. "A safety net isn't as good as a loan, but it will help." He looked at the papers on his desk. "I don't have a lot of time. If I announce a big loss before I have the safety net, we're going to have a wire run."

The treasurer was silent.

"I'll see what I can do," said Cooley. "I've got some contacts."

The treasurer walked back to his office.

Cooley picked up the telephone. He called one of his New York banking buddies. "Seafirst is in trouble," he said.

The buddy laughed. "Everyone knows that," he said. "You lost $30 million in the first three quarters."

"Big trouble," said Cooley. "We lost more than that in the fourth quarter. There's going to be a wire run if we don't have a safety net by the end of the month."

"It's that bad?" said the buddy.

25

"It's that bad," said Cooley.

"You think a safety net will do it?" said the buddy.

"Yes," said Cooley. "If Seafirst has a stand-by line of $1.5 billion from a consortium of big banks, there won't be a run. The depositors will know that we can pay." He paused. "Can you do that for me?" he asked.

"I'll try," said the buddy. "It isn't going to be easy."

"Thanks," said Cooley.

Cooley had scheduled a press conference the day of the January board meeting to announce the 1982 results. By noon that day, he still didn't have a safety net. He went into the board meeting. "We're going to have to slash the quarterly dividend from thirty-six cents a share to twelve." This was the first dividend cut ever. "I've hired an auditor to look over our energy loans. We need to get a handle on these losses." He paused. "We've got to have a $1.5-billion safety net lined up before this meeting ends. Otherwise the $80-million loss will trigger a run on the bank. So far, I don't have any safety net commitments."

Cooley's secretary buzzed. "There's a banker on your line," she said. "He says it's urgent." Cooley walked out of the board room to his office. He picked up the phone. It was the buddy in New York.

"Do the banks have to sign papers on this safety net?" asked the banker.

"Signing makes it solid," said Cooley.

"The banks don't want to sign," said the banker.

Cooley hesitated. "Okay," he said. "A gentleman's agreement is good enough."

"Then you've got your money," said the banker. "One and a half billion."

"Thanks," said Cooley. He walked back into the board meeting. "That was New York," he said. "We've got our safety net. There's still a chance that the bank will live."

Seafirst had bought some time.

But Cooley wasn't sure how much time. "I'm going to call all the big depositors," he told the treasurer. "I'm going to explain that the bank is solvent as long as they don't call their deposits."

The treasurer nodded. "I hope that works."

First Cooley called the big Seattle companies—Boeing, Paccar, Safeco, Weyerhaeuser. "You've got a lot of money at Seafirst," he reminded each chairman. "Our life is in your hands. I hope you believe that Seafirst is going to survive. I do."

"We'll keep the money where it is," said one chairman after the next. "At least for now."

Then Cooley called money managers around the country. "I hope you plan to leave your deposits here," he said. "Seafirst is going to survive."

"Sure," said one after the next. "We're putting our cash somewhere else."

At the beginning of February, Cooley flew to London and Tokyo to talk to foreign depositors. "Seafirst is going to survive," he said.

"We are moving our money," said the depositors.

When he got back to Seattle, Cooley called all the big depositors again. Then he looked over the January results. They were horrible. Cooley stood up and strolled down the hall. He stopped at the coffee urn in the lounge and poured himself a cup; Cooley had bought the earthenware mugs with his own money as inspiration for the staff. He sipped. He walked around the corner and popped his head into Bill Pettit's office.

"Got a minute?" he asked.

Pettit looked up. "Sure, Dick," he said.

"We lost $80 million last year," said Cooley.

"I know that," said Pettit.

"We've got to replace that capital," said Cooley. "Otherwise the government is going to close the bank down." Seafirst was still losing money; soon it would not have enough capital to support deposits. "I meant to get to this sooner, but I had to stabilize deposits. We need that money by the time we announce this quarter's results—the annual meeting—there's not much time."

William Pettit is steadfast. He has piercing blue eyes and a square chin. Pettit is short and muscular; one of his front teeth is chipped; although he's only thirty-two, he's almost bald. He's got a Western way of looking at the world. Pettit hates the dirty air and street noise in New York; he has orange juice and cold cereal for breakfast; he's got a loud, boisterous laugh and he laughs a lot. He's a family man, with two sons ages one and three. He lives an hour from his offices in the Seafirst Building, and no matter how late he has to work, he doesn't take a room at a Seattle hotel. Long ago, he promised his wife that whenever he was in town, he'd spend the night at home—even if it meant driving to the house after midnight and leaving again at 6 A.M.

Pettit grew up in New Jersey, and when he graduated from Princeton in 1971, he decided to head west. He didn't want to live in New York City; he didn't want to work for a big company. Pettit and a partner started a small real estate finance company in Salem, Oregon. When the partner quit, Pettit landed a new job in the mortgage division of the Seattle-First National Bank. By the time he turned thirty, Pettit was running the mortgage company; then he was asked to do a strategic study of Seafirst for the vice chairman. His conclusion: Seafirst couldn't compete with banks like Bank of America unless it joined a regional alliance with, say Wells Fargo and a half a dozen other Western banks. A month after Penn Square went bankrupt, Pettit was named Seafirst's chief financial officer. A month after that, Pettit was the most senior officer in the corporate division: the chairman, the vice chairman, the president, Boyd's old boss and his new boss had all been fired or had resigned. Two months after that, Pettit was reporting to Dick Cooley.

At first, Pettit didn't like Cooley much. Dick was always personable, but whenever Pettit came into his office with some advice, Cooley called a friend in New York to check it out, while Pettit watched. After a while, Cooley stopped doing that—apparently his friends in New York kept telling him that Pettit was right— and when Cooley popped his head into Pettit's office to say he needed capital, Pettit figured he'd finally won his spurs.

"I've done everything I can to cut costs," said Cooley. "I cut staff. I slashed expenses. I got the bank out of things it didn't know how to do. When I took this job, I thought it was going to be enough to cut costs and reorient strategy, but I didn't understand how bad Penn Square was."

Pettit nodded. "No one did." He paused. "No one does."

"Can we sell more loans?" asked Cooley. If Seafirst had fewer loans, then it needed less capital.

Pettit shook his head. "We've already sold off all the loans outside the Pacific Northwest," he said. "If we sell any more, we're selling our core business."

"Our options aren't very attractive," said Cooley. "We can't sell stock or bonds to the public. The price is so low now that that doesn't make sense. Besides, no one would buy our securities."

Pettit nodded.

"Can't we sell some assets?" said Cooley.

"The headquarters building is on the market already," said Pettit. "It might fetch $100 million. Even if it does, we don't clear much: we still have to rent office space. We could sell some of our branches, but they are Taj Mahals, not very valuable as bank branches or anything else."

"That means we have just one choice: find an investor," said Cooley.

"Salomon Brothers put out some feelers in November and December," said Pettit. "A couple of banks were interested, but things are a lot worse now."

"I have a lot of contacts," said Cooley. "I can find an investor. We've still got time."

"Should I call Salomon Brothers?" asked Pettit.

"No," said Cooley. "Not yet. I want to handle this myself."

Pettit nodded. "Just tell me if you change your mind," he said.

"I will," said Cooley. He walked back to his office. He started to make some calls. No luck. He was beginning to get frustrated when one Lou Ferris called.

"I represent Clint Murchison," said Ferris. Murchison, the oil magnate with a personal net worth estimated at $250 million. "Murchison already owns a bank group. We're interested in buying Seafirst to be our flagship. We want you to stay as chairman."

Cooley was excited. Murchison's price—$150 million for 80 percent of the stock—seemed possible.

Ferris called with questions and he came up to look over the Seafirst books. Cooley kept asking him for a firm price.

But Ferris didn't want to commit himself. And Cooley was worried that Murchison couldn't really save Seafirst. Cooley didn't doubt that Murchison could provide $100 million of capital; but capital was just one problem: Cooley wasn't sure Murchison could borrow the money to fund the Seafirst loans, and that meant he might not be able to protect the bank from a wire run. A big bank like Bank of America could. If the Murchison deal fell apart—right now that looked likely—Cooley needed an alternative rescue line. He didn't have one, and Seafirst was losing money fast.

At the end of February, Cooley called Pettit. "It looks like we're going to have another bad quarter," said Cooley.

"If the losses keep up, the government is going to close the bank," said Pettit. Seafirst would have too little capital to pass the operating test. "If anyone gets wind of that, there will be a wire run first."

"I'm going to New York next week to talk to the banks in the safety net," he said. "Make me an appointment at Salomon Brothers."

"Okay," said Pettit. He hesitated. "I'm not sure that $100 million in capital is going to be enough any more."

"It's not," said Cooley. "We need $200 million."

"Two hundred million is just about what it would cost to buy all the stock in Seafirst on the market," said Pettit.

"I know," said Cooley. "We may have to sell the bank to stay alive."

"The law says that an out-of-state bank can't buy Seafirst," said Pettit.

"I know," said Cooley. "Even if the federal regulations okay a shotgun wedding, we still have to convince Washington State. I'll talk to our chief lobbyist. Maybe we can get the state law changed without letting anyone know that Seafirst might have to use it."

"Salomon Brothers didn't have much luck in the fall," said Pettit.

"I know," said Cooley. "We have to try again."

"Okay," said Pettit. "I'll set up a date."

Cooley flew to New York. "I want to hire Salomon Brothers to find an investor in Seafirst," Cooley told the Salomon Brothers managing partner John Gutfreund. He paused. "Look, I know I once fired Salomon Brothers when I was at Wells Fargo. I thought you weren't paying enough attention to me then. Well, I was wrong. I've grown up since then. My financial staff likes you. I think you're the best investment bank for this job."

Gutfreund smiled. "We're happy to oblige," he said.

"You may have to sell Seafirst to raise that rescue money," said Kimmel. "Two hundred million is close to the market price of the Seafirst stock."

"I know that," said Cooley.

"It's *illegal* for an out-of-state bank to buy Seafirst," said Kimmel. "There isn't a bank in the state big enough to do it."

Cooley hesitated. "I know. I've talked to my chief lobbyist. He thinks we can get the state to change the banking laws."

"Last fall, Salomon Brothers was talking to regional banks and Bank of America," said Kimmel. "This time we're just going to call big banks. Your problems are too big for a regional."

"I know," said Cooley.

Gutfreund shook Cooley's hand. "We'll keep in touch," he said.

Later that afternoon, Kimmel began to make his calls.

Security Pacific, the second largest bank in California. No.

Citibank. No.

Industrial Bank of Japan, one of the big Japanese banks—Kimmel figured that a Japanese bank might like Seattle better than a European. No.

Dai-Ichi Kangyo Bank, another Japanese giant. No.

Barclays, the biggest British bank. No.

The Midland Bank, the British bank that owns Crocker Bank in San Francisco. Maybe.

Hong Kong and Shanghai Bank. Maybe.

In the middle of March, Kimmel called Steve McLin at Bank of America.

"I don't think Sam is interested," said McLin. "Seafirst is a black hole."

Kimmel kept calling. Surely someone wanted to buy Seafirst.

Steve McLin, of course, did have his eye on Seafirst. At the beginning of March, two weeks before Lee Kimmel's call, McLin brought it up in a weekly meeting with Armacost. "Seafirst is up for sale. Why don't we think about making a bid?"

Armacost raised an eyebrow. He knew all about Seafirst. He'd read the newspapers. "My God," he said. "We've got enough to do in California. We don't need to buy someone else's problems."

31

"It makes good strategic sense," said McLin. "Seafirst has 40 percent of the Washington market."

"I don't like the energy losses," said Armacost.

"I like the retail franchise," said McLin. "One of my staffers just did a study. I want to take a closer look."

Armacost wasn't quite sure why McLin was pushing Seafirst so hard, but he figured that this was a passing fancy; he could humor Steve. "Go ahead," he told McLin.

McLin walked back to his office. He pulled out his papers on Seafirst. He looked at the numbers again. He was sure that buying a first was a smart move for Bank of America; the problem was risk. How could Bank of America bound the Seafirst losses? McLin was pondering a way to do that when the phone rang. It was Kimmel.

"What about Seafirst?" he asked.

"I don't know," said McLin. "If the Bank of America buys Seafirst, the Bank of America is responsible for keeping Seafirst capital up to minimum. Seafirst is losing money fast. And we don't have a lot of extra capital." Since Bank of America has a higher percentage of consumer deposits than any other big bank, bank regulations require it to have a lower percentage of capital, because most consumers don't move their money often. "Seafirst losses will be Bank of America losses—and you keep telling me you don't know how big those losses will be."

"They won't be bigger than $1.3 billion," laughed Kimmel. "That's what you'd lose if all the energy loans went bad." He paused. "Seriously, the losses aren't going to be more than a couple of hundred million, and whatever the losses are, they won't kill the Bank of America."

"I don't know," said McLin. "What if there's a run on Seafirst?"

"There won't be a run on the Bank of America," he said. "The Bank of America can always borrow on the market. You're ten times as big as Seafirst."

"Isn't there a way that we could pay for Seafirst with a Bank of America stock that changes value as the Seafirst loan losses increase," asked McLin. "A shrink to fit stock would protect us."

Kimmel was silent for a minute. "That's a smart idea," he said. "I hadn't thought of that. No one has ever done that."

"It's my idea," said McLin. "Don't you go suggesting it to other bidders. I don't want to see someone else buy Seafirst with a shrink to fit stock."

"I won't shop the idea," promised Kimmel. "Are you going to make a bid?"

"I can't commit myself," said McLin. "Keep in touch."

By now, McLin was worried that time was running out. He figured that Seafirst would collapse after the annual meeting in April. If Bank of America was going to bid, it had to bid soon. "What about mentioning Seafirst to the board?" asked McLin at the end of his weekly strategy meeting. "You've got a session on Monday. Why don't you float the idea now in case we decide we want to negotiate before the April meeting?"

Armacost looked across his desk at McLin. Telling the board that Bank of America was looking at a Seafirst merger was definitely inappropriate. McLin was looking, not Sam Armacost. "No," he said.

McLin didn't argue. It hadn't been that kind of no.

But McLin didn't give up. He had to have a sponsor for his project, but that didn't have to be Armacost. There were three other top offices that would do: Lee Prussia, the chairman; Jim Wiesler, the vice chairman in charge of retail banking; and Bob Frick, executive vice president and cashier. McLin would try them all.

Two days after meeting with Armacost, McLin talked to Lee Prussia, chairman of Bank of America. "I've been looking at Seafirst," explained McLin. "I think it's a good strategic fit. The board meets Monday, and Sam ought to mention bidding for Seafirst. Can you suggest it to him?"

"I'll give it a try," said Prussia.

That should do it, thought McLin. He walked back to his office.

Lee Prussia called. "Sam doesn't want to hear about Seafirst," he said. Prussia didn't offer to bring up Seafirst with the board himself.

Sam Armacost didn't mention Seafirst at the March board meeting.

Two days after the meeting, Steve McLin made a presentation on interstate banking to Wiesler's retail strategy council. "I'm looking for banks like the Bank of America," said McLin. "We want to buy other buys with strong consumer franchises. Banks like Valley National in Arizona or Michigan National in Michigan." He paused. "We might want to look at Seafirst," he said.

"I'm interested in Florida and Texas," said Wiesler, "not Washington State."

"This is an interesting opportunity," said McLin.

"No thank you," said Wiesler.

McLin shook his head. He called Bob Frick's office and made an appointment. Frick was his last chance.

"Seafirst is a good strategic fit," said McLin. "I know that it isn't number one on Wiesler's list of states, but Washington has potential."

"That's a crazy idea," said Frick. Frick calls all of McLin's ideas "crazy," and he says that he expects just one in five of them to pan out. "But this is a crazy idea that might make sense. Might." He paused. "I've got two questions," he said. "First, management: Cooley is first rate, but what about the other officers? Seafirst has fired a dozen or so already. Is there anyone left? Second, the loan portfolio: are the commercial and local loans any better than the energy loans?"

"I don't know," said McLin. "I won't know until I talk to Seafirst. Sam isn't ready to do that. Sam isn't even ready to mention the idea to the board. But Seafirst has got serious problems. And I think I can figure out a way to limit our risk if we make a bid."

McLin handed Frick his staffer's memo. Frick tossed it into his "In" box. "Keeping working on this," he said. "I'll handle Sam."

McLin walked back to his office. Later that afternoon, Kimmel called from New York. "You'd better send a team up to Seattle to look at Seafirst," he said. Seafirst wouldn't let its internal documents out of the bank. "Other interested banks are sending teams. I've been talking to Citibank."

"Oh?" said McLin. Citibank was a sore point for McLin, and Kimmel knew it. When Fidelity Savings, the fifteenth-largest thrift in California, had gone bankrupt the year before, McLin had told Armacost that Bank of America had to keep Citi out of California; BoA couldn't buy Fidelity—it was too big to be allowed to do that—but McLin had tried to line up the financing for another bidder. The Bank of America–sponsored deal had fallen apart;

34

Citibank had bid and won and changed the name to Citicorp Savings. Now Citi was stealing customers from Bank of America. McLin wasn't going to let Citibank get hold of another bank.

"Are you coming to look?" asked Kimmel.

"Yes," said McLin. "I'm sending a man up. I'd go myself, but I'll be away on business."

"Seafirst is a good bank," said the investigator when he sat down with Sam and McLin in the north conference room just down the hall from Sam's office a few days later. "It's a good strategic fit."

McLin nodded. He didn't say a word: he wanted Sam Armacost to hear about Seafirst from someone else.

"What can you tell me?" asked Armacost. "Good Northwestern loans? Good people? Good computer systems?"

"Good loans," said the investigator. "Good people. Okay computer. It's a good bank if you ignore the oil loans."

"Are you ready to bid?" asked McLin.

"I'm not sure," said Armacost. "You still haven't convinced me that buying Seafirst is a good idea."

"What do we have to do to convince you?" asked McLin.

Armacost turned to McLin. "You keep saying that Seafirst is like us: a retail-based bank with a good middle-market postion," he said. "I haven't heard you say that there's bottom to the potential losses."

"There may not be," said McLin. "We can try to find out."

Armacost nodded.

"I think you ought to tell the board that we're looking at Seafirst," said McLin. "The April 5 meeting is next week."

"I don't think this is the right time," said Armacost.

"What about Salomon Brothers?" asked McLin. "Can I invite them out to make a presentation on Seafirst?" A presentation might make Sam change his mind.

"Okay," said Armacost. It couldn't hurt to listen.

McLin scheduled that meeting the day before Bank of America's April board meeting. Unfortunately Armacost wasn't in a great mood that day. "Why the hell should I buy this bank?" he asked Kimmel as soon as the banker had sat down. "It's sick."

"Seafirst is really two banks," he said, as he handed Armacost a booklet of numbers that he'd put together on Seafirst. "A very sick $1-billion energy bank and a healthy retail bank. It's a logical extension for Bank of America, more logical than it would be for, say, Citibank."

Armacost was skeptical. "When is this bank going to be profitable again?"

"Three years," said Kimmel.

"That's not soon enough," said Armacost. "And I think you're being optimistic." He looked at the booklet that the banker had given him. "Where do these numbers come from?"

"Look," Kimmel said. "This bank used to be a money machine. It made some bad loans. The cancer is contained. It's going to be profitable again."

Armacost scowled. "I'm not sure I like this," he said. "We've got problems of our own."

McLin started to get worried. The whole project was going to fall apart. Armacost was going to tell McLin to stop looking at Seafirst; he wasn't going to mention the idea to the Bank of America board the next morning.

Armacost looked at his watch. He asked a couple of questions. Then he got up to leave. "You guys can keep talking," he said. "But the numbers don't look good. I've got another meeting."

Dick Cooley called Lee Kimmel at the end of March. He was starting to worry. "How are you doing?" he asked Kimmel. "Do you have an investor lined up for us?"

"No one is solid. There are three possibles, though: Bank of America, Marine Midland and Crocker. The Bank of America is the best bet."

"When are they going to commit themselves?" asked Cooley. "There isn't much time."

"I don't know," said Kimmel. "I call to check every day."

"You've go to know soon," said Cooley. "It looks like we're going to have another big loss this quarter. If I announce that at the annual meeting on April 21 without also announcing a rescue deal, there will be a wire run. We'll go bankrupt in minutes."

"I'll do what I can," said Kimmel.

Cooley put down the phone. There was only one option left: a

Federal bailout. He picked up the receiver again and dialed Washington.

Two weeks later—just eight days before the Seafirst annual meeting, Cooley and Pettit flew to Washington to pay their calls.

"We've been talking to a couple of banks about a big investment in Seafirst. Marine Midland. Crocker. Clint Murchison. Bank of America," said Cooley over lunch with R. Todd Conover, the Comptroller of the Currency, the government's bank policeman. "It might turn into a sale. What do you think?"

"Maybe," said Conover. "I don't want to commit myself."

So far so good; it looked like Conover wouldn't oppose a merger.

In the afternoon, Cooley and Pettit went to the Federal Deposit Insurance Corporation, the government agency that insures bank deposits, to talk to William "Wild Bill" Isaac, the chairman.

"Look," said Cooley. "Our annual meeting is next Thursday. We've been talking to investors, but the bank is going to be in trouble if we don't have some good news fast. Can you give us a hand if we don't have a buyer lined up in time? We'll need a loan of $250 million."

"Relax," said Isaac. "You don't have anything to worry about. You are a perfect guinea pig for DGNB."

"What?" asked Cooley.

"Deposit Guaranty National Bank," said Isaac.

"What's that?"

"The FDIC has just developed a procedure for handling a major bank collapse," said Isaac. "We'll take over. We'll cancel all the stock. We'll close the bank on Friday and reopen it on Monday as Deposit Guaranty National Bank. Then we'll run the bank. We'll straighten out the problems and pocket the profits. It will be an FDIC investment, not a bailout."

Cooley was so surprised he didn't know what to say.

"We'll keep you as chairman," said Isaac. "We'll keep the whole management team. The people who made this mess are already gone."

"What about the stockholders?" Cooley finally asked. Cooley's job was protecting the shareholders.

"The shareholders will get zero," said Isaac. "There will be no government money if shareholders get a penny."

Cooley sighed. He couldn't accept a deal to keep the bank alive that gave the shareholders nothing, even if the deal meant that he kept his job. The shareholders owned the bank; they would get more than zero if he simply closed the bank and auctioned the assets. Cooley would be the laughing stock of the business world if he sold out to the FDIC just to keep his job. "We'll keep in touch," he said.

Late in the afternoon, Cooley and Pettit met Kimmel at the Jefferson Hotel.

First, Cooley told him about Isaac and the DGNB.

Kimmel laughed. "Do you know the difference between a vulture and a Jewish wife?" he asked.

Cooley didn't answer. He had five days left to find a rescue for his bank, and this investment banker was cracking jokes.

"A vulture waits until you're dead to eat your heart."

Cooley and Kimmel went on to talk about the alternatives for a few minutes. Then they went to the restaurant to meet Lou Ferris, Murchison's representative. Cooley wanted to nail down a price.

"We're still talking $150 million for 80 percent of the bank," said Ferris. "I'm ironing out some details."

"Like what?" asked Cooley.

"Oh," said Ferris. "Odds and ends."

"When are you going to have a solid offer?" asked Cooley.

"Soon," said Ferris. "A couple of days."

Cooley went back to the hotel. He sat on the bed. The air conditioning was broken, the room was dingy.

Kimmel came in. He'd stayed behind to try to find out why Ferris seemed to be stalling. "Do you want me to keep negotiating?" he asked.

"No," said Cooley. "It isn't going to work. He probably doesn't have the money." Now he knew that Seafirst couldn't stay independent; there were no investors. He wasn't even sure that Seafirst could survive as an institution. There might be no buyers either.

Cooley flew back to Seattle the next morning. Pettit caught a cab to the Federal Reserve headquarters. "Will you make an emergency loan to stop a wire run on Seafirst?" asked Pettit.

"You've got $65 million of eligible collateral," said the chief bank supervisor. "We'll lend to the limit."

"That's not going to stop a run," said Pettit. "It's not enough."

The man shrugged. "We'll lend to our limit. That's the rule."

"Okay," sighed Pettit. He knew the limit wasn't enough.

When he got to Dulles Airport to catch his flight back to Seattle, Pettit called Cooley. "The Fed will only lend to the limit," he said. "They won't make a special loan."

Cooley sighed. "We still don't have a buyer. We don't have a government bailout." He paused. "Look, Bill," he said. "I've been counting on negotiating this myself, but if something comes up now, I won't have time. I've got to run this annual meeting. I've got to keep the big deposits from running."

Pettit didn't say anything.

"I want you to handle the talks," said Cooley. "You're good. You know the bank. I trust you. Fly to New York first thing Monday morning. I want you to be there if a bidder surfaces."

Pettit nodded. "I'll be there."

Cooley spent the weekend talking to big depositors in Seattle. Tuesday morning he headed to New to talk to the safety net banks: Seafirst might have to borrow later in the week. Late in the afternoon, Cooley was chatting with Donald Platten, chairman of Chemical Bank, when Platten's secretary buzzed.

"Sam Armacost of Bank of America is calling for Dick Cooley," she said.

Tuesday, April 5, two weeks before the call to Cooley, Sam Armacost and Steve McLin sat on the Bank of America jet headed to Los Angeles for the Bank of America board meeting. McLin looked out the window; Armacost had been so negative at the meeting with Salomon Brothers the afternoon before that McLin was afraid to mention Seafirst.

Armacost turned to McLin. "Can you put together a quick list of talking points on Seafirst for me?" he asked. "I'm going to tell the board that we're taking a look."

"Sure," said McLin. He got out a yellow legal pad and started to write. He didn't dare ask what had changed Armacost's mind.

"Thanks," said Armacost as they got off the plane. "This should do it."

McLin wasn't invited into the meeting to talk about Seafirst. He waited outside the board room with Bob Frick, the cashier.

"Who else do you think is looking at Seafirst?" asked Frick.

"Well," said McLin, "I think Citibank is."

Frick didn't say anything. Frick knew what had happened with Fidelity Savings.

"Crocker sent up a team," said McLin. "I think Barclays is looking. I think Northwest Bankcorp is interested."

Frick nodded.

"If the board doesn't veto this, we're going to need an improvement banker," said McLin. "Maybe I can find out who else is bidding." McLin picked up the telephone. Salomon Brothers, First Boston, and Goldman, Sachs handle most bank deals. Salomon Brothers was representing Seafirst. "We might be doing a deal," he told the president of First Boston. "If I were to ask, would you be able to represent Bank of America in a bid for Seafirst?"

"Well," said the man, "we have a commitment, but I think we can get out of it."

Good. If First Boston could get out of its commitment, it wasn't representing Citibank. McLin called Goldman, Sachs. "Would you be able to represent Bank of America in a bid for Seafirst?" he asked.

"We'd be happy to take the assignment," said the Goldman banking partner.

Good. Goldman wasn't representing Citibank either. McLin looked at Frick. "Citibank isn't bidding," he said.

Frick nodded.

Armacost walked out of the meeting. He thumbed up. Buying Seafirst was on. The directors had liked the fit, but they had a lot of questions. They wanted him to report back for approval before he made an offer.

As soon as they got back to San Francisco Armacost barked out the orders. Six credit officers raced to Seattle with questions. The cashier's office crunched the numbers through the computer.

McLin called Armacost.

He talked to Prussia.

He talked to Frick.

He talked to the team in Seattle.

Late Friday afternoon, April 15, McLin finished his income tax forms. Just before midnight, his wife drove him to Rincon Annex, San Francisco's all-night post office, to mail the return.

Over the weekend, he put the finishing touches on his proposal for paying for Seafirst. McLin was in meetings with Armacost all day Monday. McLin and Armacost met again on Tuesday morning at eight o'clock. The Bank of America executive committee of directors was scheduled to meet at eleven o'clock to decide whether or not to bid for Seafirst, and Armacost wanted to go over the numbers one last time. When they'd finished the run-through, McLin and Armacost walked into the west conference room.

Lee Prussia called the meeting to order.

"I want to propose that the Bank of America bid for Seafirst," said Armacost. "It's a good strategic fit. The price is right."

McLin stood up. "I've worked out a 'shrink to fit' stock that we're going to use for payment," he began. Some of the directors looked puzzled. "This piece of paper will be redeemable for cash in five years. How much cash will depend on how much money Seafirst has lost by then. The maximum will be $125 million. The minimum will be $10 million."

"Are you sure that will work?" asked a director.

McLin nodded. "No one has ever done this before, but it makes good sense. It protects us against some of the losses."

"Is Washington a good state?" asked a director.

"Oh, yes," said Armacost. "And Seafirst is the bank in Washington."

The directors kept asking questions. McLin was terribly afraid the directors would veto the idea.

Armacost looked at his watch: twelve-thirty. "Let's vote," he said. It was unanimous: Bank of America would send a team to New York to make an offer for Seafirst.

Dick Cooley caught a cab from the meeting at Chemical Bank to La Guardia for his flight back to Seattle. Just before takeoff, Cooley called Bill Pettit, who was at Salomon Brothers headquarters. "I talked to Sam Armacost," he said. "He told me that he was sending a team to negotiate for Seafirst. Have they arrived? What's the price?"

"They aren't here yet," said Pettit. "But Steve McLin just called to say that he's on the way."

"I'll call again when I change planes in Chicago," said Cooley.

"They still aren't here," said Pettit when Cooley called again. "I can't figure out what's going on. I hope that they didn't change their minds."

"They are coming," said Cooley.

"They had better get here soon," said Pettit. "We don't have much time."

At eleven o'clock, Steve McLin called Bill Pettit. "We're at La Guardia. We got delayed," he said. "We're getting in a cab now. We want to talk tonight."

As soon as the Bank of America team got to Salomon Brothers, the bankers got down to business.

"I speak for Bank of America," Bob Frick said. Armacost wanted his cashier, a nuts-and-bolts man, to lead the negotiating, not McLin, the thinker. "I've brought my investment banker." The man from Goldman, Sachs. "He's going to make the offer."

"Bank of America is here to present an offer, not to negotiate," said the investment banker. He looked at Pettit. "If you don't like the price, we're back on the plane," he said.

Pettit shifted in his seat. He couldn't figure out why Bank of America was being so hostile. Not only were they sitting like the enemy, lined up along one side of the table, they were talking like the enemy too. Pettit didn't need an ultimatum.

"The price is $400 million," said the BoA investment banker. "It's in three pieces: $150 million in capital; $125 million in cash; $125 million in special shrink-to-fit stock." The special stock that would be worth less as Seafirst losses increased.

"That's not a $400-million offer," said Pettit. "You know that as well as I do. The $150 million of capital isn't payment, it's money shifted from one Bank of America pocket to another. That makes that a $250-million offer. It might even be a $135-million offer if that special stock turns out to be worth the minimum of $10 million."

"Let's caucus," said the BoA investment banker.

Pettit called Cooley.

It was ten-thirty in Seattle. Cooley had just gotten home from the airport.

"It's $250 million, half in cash," said Pettit.

"Twice as much as Ferris had offered," Cooley said. "Much more than Seafirst could get by trying to sell off all its assets."

"I don't think the board is going to understand that this is a good deal," said Pettit. "I don't think they understand that the bank is almost bankrupt." He paused. "I was hoping for $250 million, all cash."

"You're right about the directors," said Cooley. "We need more."

"It isn't going to be easy," said Pettit. "They're pretty hostile."

"Keep fighting," said Cooley. "Stall. Make them think you're talking to someone else."

Pettit came back to the negotiating room. The air conditioning had gone off at five o'clock and the place was roasting. By now, it was so full of cigar smoke that he could hardly see across the table. "I want more money," said Pettit. "We need the whole $250 million in cash."

The Bank of America investment banker shook his head. So did Bob Frick.

"We need more money," said Pettit.

Now Frick took over as the Bank of America negotiator. "We can't pay more cash," he said. "But I'm willing to haggle over the terms of the stock."

"We need a more valuable piece of paper," said Pettit.

"We can't give much," said Frick.

Pettit and Frick argued.

"That's not enough," said Pettit when Frick finally sweetened the terms. "I need more cash. I need a promise that the Bank of America will back Seafirst deposits starting the minute this deal is signed." That would guarantee that there wouldn't be a wire run.

"No," said Frick. "No backing of deposits."

"We need a better offer," said Pettit.

Frick wouldn't budge. "What kind of talks have you had with the regulators?" asked Frick. "Have you looked at the possibility

43

of help from the FDIC? That could change our offer."

McLin looked at Frick. On the plane they'd decided that if the government was willing to give Bank of America money to buy Seafirst, then Bank of America would raise its offer. The government had put up money to rescue failing banks before, so it was possible that there was money for Seafirst.

"The FDIC isn't going to help," said Pettit. "Bill Isaac wants to run Seafirst himself."

McLin laughed. "Isaac can't be serious," he said. "Seafirst is a black hole." He turned to Frick. "Seafirst isn't talking to any other bidders," he whispered. "Bank of America is the only girl on the dance floor. Seafirst has to accept the Bank of America offer. We don't have to raise our bid."

Frick nodded.

Pettit scribbled a note to Kimmel. "Bank of America is hot to buy Seafirst. If they were serious about not negotiating, they wouldn't have sent a team to New York to start talks at midnight— and the team would have left long ago."

They kept talking. They didn't settle any of the terms.

"I've got to make a call," said McLin at a little after three in the morning; it was midnight in California. He had to brief Armacost, and he was worried about using the Salomon Brothers phone. He considered dashing outside to use a pay phone—but then he'd have to explain why the phone at Salomon Brothers wouldn't do.

"We're still stuck on the terms," said McLin. "But it looks like we'll have a deal by sometime tomorrow. Seafirst is ready to concede."

"I need to know the new Seafirst numbers," said Armacost. "What was their first-quarter loss? How does that change the model we showed the executive committee on Tuesday?"

"I don't know how much Seafirst lost," said McLin. "Pettit hasn't said."

"He's got to know," said Armacost. "Seafirst's annual meeting is on Thursday. Cooley is going to announce the number then."

"I've asked," said McLin. "I'll ask again."

"We've got to settle the order of the board meetings," said Armacost. "It's important that they meet first to approve our offer

44

and then we meet." Armacost had never made a major proposal to the board. He was scare that Seafirst would turn him down after he'd put his neck out in front of his own board. If the Seafirst board met first, that couldn't happen.

"No problem," said McLin.

McLin walked back to the negotiating table. "We need to have Seafirst's first-quarter results," he said.

"I don't have the exact numbers," said Pettit. "I've got some estimates."

"You've got to make the announcement Thursday," said McLin. "I don't believe you still just have estimates."

"We're having trouble figuring out which energy loans are bad," said Pettit. He read off the numbers.

McLin wrote them down. "I'll need the extra numbers as soon as you can get them," he said.

"We've got to settle the terms of the merger," said Kimmel. "We want more cash."

But Frick wouldn't give a penny.

Steve McLin didn't leave Salomon Brothers until eight the next morning. Bob Frick had gone to the hotel at four—he was starting to feel sick and he wanted to lie down. "I'll be back at noon," McLin told his investment banker as the two walked to the elevator. "I've got to get some sleep."

"Don't go to sleep," said the investment banker.

"What?" said McLin. "I'm tired. I'm going to lie down for a couple of hours. I'll feel better after a nap."

"Don't sleep," said the investment banker. "You'll just feel worse. Take a shower instead."

McLin caught a cab to the Inter-Continental Hotel on Forty-eighth Street. McLin showered. He went down to breakfast and picked up a *Wall Street Journal*. He skimmed the paper until a headline caught his eye.

Wells Fargo Looks at Seafirst.
Wells Fargo & Co. yesterday joined the ranks of possible investors in troubled Seafirst Corp., Carl E. Reichart, Wells Fargo's chairman, president and chief executive officer said.

Mr. Reichart said that he spoke by telephone yesterday with Richard P. Cooley, Seafirst's chairman. Messrs. Reichart and Cooley worked together at Wells Fargo until Mr. Cooley took early retirement as Wells Fargo's chairman and chief executive to take the top job at Seafirst.

McLin knew that Reichart was a close friend of Dick Cooley. He figured that Cooley had planted that rumor to put pressure on Bank of America. If Wells were really looking at Seafirst, Reichart wouldn't have announced it.

As soon as he finished breakfast, McLin caught a cab downtown.

Pettit and Frick were still arguing. They settled some technical points. Finally, late in the afternoon, the lawyers finished up a handwritten draft of the agreement.

Pettit left to take a nap.

McLin called Sam Armacost. "I think we've got a deal," he said.

"What about those Seafirst first-quarter numbers?" asked Armacost.

"I'll get them," said McLin.

"What about the board meeting?" asked Armacost.

"I'll settle that right now," said McLin.

When he got off the line, McLin called Bill Pettit. "Have you got first-quarter results yet?" asked McLin. "We need them to plug into our model."

"The numbers aren't ready yet," said Pettit.

"Goddammit, we've got to have numbers," said McLin. "I've got to write a memo for the Bank of America board."

"These are close," said Pettit. "That's the best I can do."

McLin scribbled them down. "You have to get board approval for this merger first," he said. "After your board approves, Sam will present the merger to our board."

"That doesn't make sense," said Pettit. "We can't approve an offer until you make it."

"You have to approve first," said McLin.

Pettit signaled to Kimmel. They caucused in the corner. "This is ridiculous," said Pettit. "Why do I care which board meets first? Why does McLin care?"

"I don't know why McLin cares," said Kimmel. "Probably Sam

46

cares. Whatever the reason, it's good bargaining leverage. It's about the only leverage we've got."

Pettit walked back to the table. "The Bank of America board meets first," he said. "Seafirst can't accept an offer that hasn't been made."

"No," said McLin. He sounded edgy.

McLin and Pettit argued.

Pettit walked down the hall to Kimmel's office. "We've got to get more money," he said.

"It isn't going to be easy," said Kimmel.

"Maybe we can use this board meeting thing to force them," said Pettit. "Why don't we have Cooley call Armacost and say he thinks that the board is going to veto the deal unless he gets more cash."

"It can't hurt to try," said Kimmel.

Pettit called Cooley. "The price is too low," he said. "You've got to call Sam Armacost."

Cooley thought for a minute. "I don't really know Armacost," he said. "We've met at parties and conferences, of course, but Sam and I are from different generations of bankers."

"The board isn't going to take this proposal," said Pettit. "There isn't enough cash."

"You're right about the Seafirst board," said Cooley. "We've been in meetings all day, and they don't like the Bank of America price. They want more cash. They really are talking about vetoing the deal."

"I get the sense from McLin that Armacost is worried about his board," said Pettit. "He's afraid that they'll be mad if Bank of America makes an offer and we turn it down."

"I'll call tonight," said Cooley. "You're doing just fine."

"They're being intransigent," said Pettit. "They know that there isn't anyone else interested in making a bid."

"You know, Carl Reichart of Wells Fargo called me Monday about an investment in Seafirst," said Cooley. "I told him to send a team up to Seattle."

"That's where the *Journal* story came from," said Pettit.

"I guess that's right," said Cooley.

Pettit hung up.

Cooley called Armacost at about four that afternoon. "I understand your team in New York is being intransigent," said Cooley. "You have to be a little more flexible. The Seafirst board doesn't like your offer at all."

That was exactly what Armacost had been worried about. "I want to be flexible," he said.

"We need more money," said Cooley.

"I'll talk to my team in New York," said Armacost. "I want to get a deal done."

Armacost called McLin. It was eight in the evening. "I've just talked to Cooley," said Armacost. "Don't you think that we should give him more money?"

"We don't need to give," said McLin.

"I think we should," said Armacost. "We can afford more." Bank of America earned almost as much in a quarter as it was proposing to pay for Seafirst. "The Seafirst board has to okay the deal."

"Let me talk to the investment banker," said McLin. "He knows negotiating strategy. You call Frick. I'll call you back."

The investment banker had gone home. McLin called him there.

Armacost called Frick at the hotel. Frick sat on the corner of the bed and listened.

"Cooley says you're being intransigent," said Armacost.

Frick laughed. "If that's what Cooley told you, we're doing a good job," he said.

"I told Cooley we could be flexible," said Armacost. "I want to do a deal. I think we can give a little."

"No," said Frick. "We've got all the cards. We don't have to give. And I don't think you should negotiate with Cooley. Then you'll become a court of appeals."

When McLin talked to the investment banker, he agreed with Bob Frick.

Two hours later after that, Frick called Lee Kimmel.

"I understand you're going to be a bit more flexible," said Kimmel. "That's what Armacost told Cooley."

"We're not changing our offer," said Frick. "We're not raising the price. The negotiations are going on here in New York. Don't you try to do anything behind my back."

* * *

Pettit had gotten a couple of hours of sleep that night. The draft had been typed overnight and first thing Thursday morning he got the new copy. He look over the pages.

"What's this clause?" Pettit asked Kimmel. He pointed to the place in his text.

Kimmel looked at it. Bank of America was free to drop out of the agreement if there was a "material and adverse change" in the condition of Seafirst. "That's not unusual," he said. "Most contracts have a 'material and adverse change' clause. The idea is to protect the buyer from some kind of natural disaster."

"Maybe so," said Pettit, "but in this case that clause isn't appropriate. Seafirst is up for sale precisely because it has experienced a material and adverse change in its condition, and including a clause that said the contract is void if there is a further change is ridiculous. Bank of America could back out just because Seafirst loses some of its big deposits or announces more losses from Penn Square." Pettit paused. "Both of those things are going to happen."

Kimmel read the text again. "You're right," he said. "The way this is written, the Bank of America can drop out of the deal any time it wants to."

"Some binding contract," said Pettit. "This isn't going to help Seafirst one bit. When we announce a deal that says in black and white that Bank of America is so worried that Seafirst will go belly-up that even they won't commit themselves, we're going to have a wire run. Then Bank of America will back out and there won't be anything left to sell."

"We've got to get that clause out," said Kimmel. "We need a firm offer."

Pettit called Bob Frick at Bank of America's law office to say he and Kimmel were coming over to talk about it.

"What's this clause about material and adverse change?" he asked.

"What?" said Frick.

"Material and adverse change," said Pettit.

"That's boiler plate," said Frick. "If an earthquake hits Seattle, Bank of America has to have the option to back down."

49

"The Seafirst board won't approve the offer if it has that clause in it," said Pettit. "With that clause, we don't have an offer at all."

"The Bank of America board isn't going to okay any deal without it," said Frick.

Pettit sighed; he couldn't believe that today, the very day of the Seafirst shareholder meeting and the day they needed to wrap up a deal, he couldn't rescue his bank just because of a legal technicality. He glared at Frick. "This is supposed to be a friendly merger," he said. "You're talking as if it's a hostile takeover." And he thought, Bank of America had been acting hostile since they began negotiating.

All this time McLin had been listening without saying anything. "Wait a minute," he said. "Calm down, you two. Bank of America wants to buy Seafirst. We negotiated in good faith—we've got a deal. Stop fussing over legal technicalities."

"Maybe we could put some parameters on what you mean by a material and adverse change," suggested one of the lawyers. He looked at Frick. "Make me a list of what you're worried about. We'll write those things into the agreement."

"No," said Frick. "What I'm worried about is the unknown. If I make a list of everything I can think of, I'll leave out the one change that will cost the bank $100 million."

Pettit signaled to Kimmel. They caucused in the room down the hall.

"This won't work," he said. "The Seafirst annual meeting is going to start in a couple of minutes. There isn't anyone else interested in buying Seafirst."

"Let's give them one last try," said Kimmel. "If that doesn't work, we'll have to have Cooley call Armacost again."

"I'm not sure that will help," said Pettit.

"We don't have a lot of choice," said the investment banker. "As it is, we don't even have a handshake. Maybe Cooley can get Armacost to give him that."

"Okay," said Pettit. "As soon as the annual meeting is over, I'll call Frick. If Frick won't change, I'll tell Cooley to call Armacost."

Someone brought in a copy of the Dow wire. The shareholder meeting had started. A few minutes later, the phone rang. It was a Salomon Brothers trader. "You won't believe this," he said. "Dick

Cooley just told shareholders that Seafirst is talking to potential investors. He said that the board would be willing to consider selling the bank. The stock price is soaring."

"Oh, no," said Pettit. He looked at the investment banker.

"What's the price?" asked the investment banker.

"Fourteen and three quarters," said the trader.

"We're still okay," said the banker. "Barely. Bank of America is offering $15 a share. If the stock goes above that, the deal is dead."

"And so is Seafirst," said Pettit.

Kimmel nodded.

Pettit stared out the window at New York Harbor.

The trader called again. "An institution just bought 100,000 shares of Seafirst at $15.75 a share," he said.

"Now what?" asked Pettit.

"Wait," said the investment banker. "Maybe the stock will drop again."

Pettit waited. Finally the stock dipped below $15. Pettit called the Stock Exchange. "Suspend trading in Seafirst," he said. "We're going to make an announcement." The price was frozen. Pettit called Steve McLin. "We've got to talk about material and adverse change," he said.

McLin didn't want to talk about material and adverse change. That was a legal technicality. He had a deal. "I thought we'd settled that," said McLin.

"We've got to talk about it again," said Pettit.

McLin thought Pettit sounded mad. The last thing McLin needed now was to have Pettit put Cooley up to calling Armacost. Armacost already thought that the team in New York was being too stubborn. Maybe if McLin talked to Pettit once more, Pettit would realize that he was being ridiculous. "Come on over," said McLin.

Pettit and McLin and Frick argued for hours. At nine o'clock, Pettit played his trump card. "Cooley's got to talk to Armacost," he said.

McLin shook his head. "I don't think that's necessary," he said.

Pettit glared.

McLin looked at his watch. It was ten o'clock in New York. Bank of America was closed. "I'm not even sure where Armacost is right now," said McLin.

"You don't know?" asked Pettit.

"I'll try to find him," said McLin. "His secretary probably knows how to reach him."

McLin went into another room. He didn't have the secretary's home number so he dialed information. "I've got to find Sam," said McLin when he got the secretary.

"He's in Fresno," she said. "He's at the Piccadilly Inn. Here's the number."

McLin scribbled it down. "Thanks," he said.

"What's up?" asked Armacost when McLin finally got him on the line.

"Dick Cooley is going to call you," said McLin. "Don't give an inch. Just tell him you've got a deal."

"Okay," said Armacost.

Dick Cooley called half an hour later. "My people in New York tell me that you aren't going to sign a binding contract," said Cooley. "I guess it's too late to convince you on that—but before I take this to my board, I want to know something. Do we have a deal?"

"Yes," said Armacost. "The Bank of America is going to buy Seafirst."

It was midnight. Steve McLin stuffed his papers into his brief-case. He had a deal. Bill Pettit packed his papers too. Someone offered him a ride on the Bank of America jet, but he turned it down. He didn't want to see anyone from Bank of America right now. He was flying to Seattle by himself, first-class.

Pettit had checked out of his hotel. His flight to Seattle left at nine the next morning. He decided to go to the airport. He'd wait in the United Airlines Red Carpet Club. Pettit caught a cab. He walked to the United section. The door of the Red Carpet Club was locked; the lounge didn't open until six in the morning. Even the coffee shop was closed.

Pettit walked back to the Red Carpet Club. There was a plastic chair outside the door. Pettit sat down. He had clenched the merger agreement. He'd only had two hours' sleep since Tuesday. It wasn't until the next morning that Pettit finally got a nap.

Early in the afternoon he drove to his office.

"You did a good job," Cooley told him. "We couldn't have gotten more."

Cooley's secretary buzzed. Sam Armacost was on the line. "The Bank of America board has just approved the deal," he said. "The offer is good until midnight."

The Seafirst directors were waiting. "We've been talking about an offer from the Bank of America for three days now," said Cooley after he called the meeting to order. "We talked at board subcommittee meetings on Wednesday, at the directors' dinner Wednesday night, at the board meeting Thursday afternoon, over the phone this morning. Sam Armacost just called me to make it formal." He paused. "I know that you don't like the price. I wish it were more, and believe me I tried. But no one wants to buy the loans we bought from Penn Square. I know you don't want to sell the premier bank in the Pacific Northwest. I don't either. But this is much more favorable for our shareholders than a takeover by the FDIC."

The directors talked.

"The price is low," said one. "Very low."

"This bank used to be the pride of Seattle," said another.

"I've known Sam Armacost for years," said a third. "I can't believe he's doing this."

"We don't have much choice," said a fourth.

An hour later, Dick Cooley called for a vote. It was unanimous: Seafirst would accept the offer from Bank of America.

Cooley adjourned the meeting. He drove home and went to bed. Cooley had been working nonstop for almost six months and he was exhausted. Sam Armacost could wait until morning.

Saturday, Dick Cooley told Sam Armacost the good news, and Armacost called Steve McLin. "The deal's on," he said.

McLin sighed. "Cheers," he said. "The Bank of America has just about locked up the West Coast."

The word went out on the wires that afternoon at five-fifteen: Bank of America had signed an agreement to buy Seafirst for $125 million in cash and $125 million in shrink-to-fit stock.

McLin had had just eight hours' sleep in the past four days. He was exhausted, but he had to celebrate. McLin walked down to his wine cellar. He pulled a bottle of 1974 Mondavi Reserve Cabernet. He'd been wanting to open it for years. Now he had an excuse.

Dick Cooley had thought that the merger would save Seafirst, but ironically it almost killed the bank. Suddenly Seafirst's less sophisticated depositors understood that Seafirst had been about to collapse, and they withdrew their money. A week after the rescue announcement, Seafirst had had to borrow both from the Federal Reserve Bank and the safety net.

A month later, the Seafirst shareholders approved the merger into Bank of America. They had no choice.

Now the Bank of America owned Seafirst. Cooley could worry about market share instead of survival. Market share had plummeted compared to a year before. Cooley held a month-long loan "sale" and quickly won back most of Seafirst's business. Seafirst earned $12 million in 1984 and $29 million in 1985.

The Seafirst energy loans have gotten worse instead of better. A year after that final call from Cooley to Armacost, Seafirst used the last penny of its original capital to protect depositors from loan losses. If Dick Cooley had not accepted Sam Armacost's offer, Seafirst would now be bankrupt.

Sam Armacost has his hands full running Bank of America. Since he bought Seafirst, Armacost has shaken his bank to the roots. Bank of America is focusing on well-heeled customers who want more than just a basic checking account. Many banks offer upscale clients plush offices and special fast-banking lines, but, true to the Giannini spirit, Bank of America refuses to do that. "We don't want anyone to feel that he isn't special," explains one of the bank's strategic planners. Bank of America has also pioneered an at-home computer with which its customers can transfer funds and pay bills. In the summer of 1983, the bank began to reorganize its branch network as a hub-and-spoke system of full-service branches in key locations and smaller deposit-only branches at most outposts. In December 1983, Armacost announced that the bank would close 140 branches and let the payroll shrink 3,600 by attrition.

Bank of America earnings are still down, but Armacost insists that earnings have bottomed out and will start to rise in a quarter or two.

Steve McLin has been to Seattle just once since the negotiations to buy Seafirst: he attended the shareholder meeting to approve the Bank of America offer. Then he turned his attention back to strategic planning. He's looking at other ways to bank out of state, and he's intrigued with the idea of buying a big brokerage house—if it were only legal.

In July 1983, McLin's wife, Cathy, had a six-pound eleven-ounce son. McLin carried a snapshot of Scott in his wallet, and he pulls it out to show admirers as often as he can. The baby is his second-proudest achievement. The first, of course, was orchestrating the acquisition of Seattle-First.

(2)

Morgan Guaranty Trust Company

*"Only First-Class Business, and
That in a First-Class Way"*

"Three hundred million is a lot of money," said Tom Kellogg.

"Morgan raised $125 million for us on this project in 1978," said Rick Schile. "You can do $300 million now."

Kellogg took a pack of cigarettes out of his pocket. "I don't know," he said. "Raising money for an Indonesian gas project could be a problem now," he said.

"Why?" asked Schile. He shuffled through the papers on his desk. "Oil prices have tripled in the past five years." Up from $12.70 a barrel in early 1978 to $34 a barrel by July 1982. "Capacity at the Badak plant is about to double. We've got sales contracts with the Japanese."

"Oil prices are soft," said Kellogg. He lit a cigarette. "The quota system that OPEC set up in March to stabilize them isn't working. Nigeria is over quota. Libya is over quota. Indonesia is over quota. Iran is producing double its quota. And there's price cutting on the spot market. The posted price is going to fall."

Schile frowned. He was just getting started on the Allied 1983 financial plan, and he was counting on $300 million.

"Mexico is having problems," said Kellogg. "Argentina is having problems. The banks are nervous about making any LDC loans." Loans to less developed countries.

Schile nodded.

"Indonesia is pinched," said Kellogg. "The government is going to have to borrow at least $1 billion. You don't want to be the kind of company that competes with the government for loans. You want to be a good corporate citizen."

Schile looked at Kellogg. That was true.

"I'm not saying that Morgan can't do a loan," said Kellogg. "We can. It probably won't be $300 million."

"What about an interest rate?"

"A point and a quarter over Libor," said Kellogg. Libor, the international equivalent of the prime rate. "Maybe more."

"We had a point and a quarter over Libor last time," said Schile. "There's less risk now."

Kellogg shrugged.

"Couldn't we secure the loan by selling the LNG [liquefied natural gas] to the banks?" asked Schile. "Using the LNG as collateral ought to cut our interest rate."

"That won't work," said Kellogg.

"Why not?" asked Schile. "That's how the Japanese banks structured their Badak loans."

"Those loans were different," said Kellogg. "Those were loans to the Japanese utilities to pay for gas-processing equipment. The utilities own the gas they buy—and they can use it as collateral. Allied is a project operator. You never own the gas."

Schile frowned.

Kellogg stood up to go. "Let's keep talking," he said. "Morgan will think of something."

At forty-six, Thomas P. Kellogg is tall, pin-striped and gruff. He gets to the office before nine every morning, and works into the night. There's a golf club leaning against the wall behind his desk. Kellogg practices putts for two minutes every morning. That's helped his game—Kellogg's handicap is down to six—and it's made him friends. Everyone in the petroleum department wants to try it, even the night cleaning lady.

Kellogg grew up in Waterbury, Connecticut, and studied history at Princeton. In 1960, after two years in the Navy, Kellogg landed a job at Morgan Guaranty's financial analysis department, making loans in the Midwest and putting together merger and acquisition deals. In 1968, he was assigned to Morgan's merchant banking affiliate in Melbourne, Australia. Kellogg's job was helping put together lending packages for big Australian companies, but between corporate finance calls, Kellogg got a chance to watch the project team put together loans to finance coal mines, nickel mines and dozens of other natural-resource-processing facilities. Three years later, Kellogg was back in New York screening the project loan applications that came in to Morgan Guaranty International, and in 1973, Kellogg was assigned to the energy, minerals and construction department as one of three vice presidents supervising all petroleum loans. Kellogg's territory was Texas and Louisiana; his clients included Shell, Tenneco, Union Texas Petroleum and Roy M. Huffington Inc.

"Only first-class business," J. P. Morgan, Jr., once said. "And that in a first-class way." The Morgan Guaranty Trust Company has clout. The parent J. P. Morgan & Company is the only bank-holding company rated AAA. Morgan makes fewer loans than most other banks, it makes less risky loans, and yet it makes more money. The secret: tradition and talent and an emphasis on detail. A vault clerk once uncovered $1.9 million worth of counterfeit J. C. Penney bonds when he noticed that a certificate he was carrying felt funny. Morgan is famous for its financial sophistication; the bank not only pioneered interest-rate and currency swaps, it also held the first foreign "treasury" auction for the Kingdom of Sweden and designed the first private company Eurobond issue—backed by a guarantee from Aetna—for the Rockefeller Group. Morgan raises money in more currencies than any other bank in the world; its trust department manages more money; its stock transfer department registers more shares. Morgan is so profitable that it can afford to be choosy. Morgan joins syndicates only as a manager. It eschews small accounts; "corporate" means Fortune 500; "personal" means an interest-free minimum balance of $5,000. The Morgan client list reads like a corporate social register: Du Pont, Peugeot, British Petroleum, and the governments of England, France, Indonesia, and Brazil.

John Pierpont Morgan founded J. P. Morgan & Company in 1860 as the U.S. agent bank for his father's London merchant bank. The New York office quickly overshadowed the British parent. By the turn of the century, Pierpont was the world's premier dealmaker: he lined up $1.4 billion to form United States Steel from Andrew Carnegie's mills—and billions more to put together General Electric, International Harvester and Western Union. The bank was always ready to come to the rescue at the height of an economic crisis. Pierpont Morgan raised $65 million to bail out Uncle Sam when gold runs drained the Treasury in 1895; he engineered a $100-million rescue for Teddy Roosevelt in 1907. When asked what was the driving force in the lending business, Morgan answered: "The first thing is character...a man I do not trust could not get money from me on all the bonds in Christendom."

Pierpont Morgan died in 1913, and the top job went to his son Jack. Morgan remained the house that financed gilt-edged companies and backstopped the U.S. government. When stocks opened down on Black Thursday, October 24, 1929, Thomas Lamont, a senior Morgan partner, organized a syndicate said to control $240 million and sent his broker to support the market by buying U.S. Steel, Westinghouse and GE. Two hundred and forty million was the best that even Morgan could get, but this time Morgan's best wasn't enough.

The market crashed.

The Depression began.

In 1933, Congress decreed that banks would be either "commercial" or "investment." The Morgan partners opted for commercial: Morgan's outstanding loans totaled $430 million, more than the entire $400 million of stocks and bonds that all banks had underwritten that year. Needless to say, Morgan, commercial bank, was the bank with status. For thirty years, the Morgan executives sat behind their old partners desks and lent money the way Pierpont had. Then in 1959, Morgan began to change. It merged with the Guaranty Trust Company, the sixth-largest trust company in New York (Morgan was already number ten) and pushed overseas. In 1960, Morgan had just three non-American branches: London, Paris and Brussels. By 1975, Morgan operated more than twenty offices in Europe, the Far East and South America, and owned stakes in half a dozen banking-related companies around the world. When New York City teetered on the brink of bankruptcy in late 1974, Morgan didn't pull its lines; the other banks did, and soon the city faced a crisis. Ellmore Patterson, Morgan chairman, was named head of the private-sector rescue team. Patterson helped put together a rescue plan—by then the crisis had spread to New York State—and when the city offered the first $1 billion of "Big MAC" bonds in July 1975, Morgan was coagent of the deal.

By then, Morgan had made a name as one of the top oil and gas banks in the world. Morgan got into the game late—Chase had long been associated with the Rockefellers of Standard Oil, Mellon Bank with the Mellons of Gulf—but Morgan's lending team was topflight. The assignments poured in. Morgan offered competitive rates, and better ideas. In 1972, Morgan put together a $900-million "production payment" loan for British Petroleum; the loan would be paid as BP sold oil it hoped to pump from the yet undeveloped Forties field in the North Sea. The BP loan was the first bank loan to an oil project that hadn't yet been started. It was also the biggest loan on record.

Morgan's oil and gas executives were still talking about the feat when Tom Kellogg got transferred to the department a year later. After spending the first couple of months getting to know his new clients, he got a call from Roy Huffington, operator of the Huffco gas exploration partnership in Indonesia.

"We're short $25 million to pay our share of development at Badak," he said. "Can you line up a loan?"

"I'll look," said Kellogg. He wasn't optimistic. Morgan didn't usually make loans to oil field ventures that weren't yet flowing. But Indonesia was the eighth-largest oil producer in the world.

Indonesia had been on the international oil map ever since 1880 when a Dutch tobacco plantation superintendent accidentally found oil at Telaga Said in northern Sumatra. Soon after, his Royal Dutch exploration company hit oil in the Badak region on the island of Borneo and built a four-inch pipeline through a hundred miles of jungle to the port of Balikpapan. In 1944, Caltex, a joint venture of California Standard and Texaco, discovered the giant Minas field in central Sumatra and for the next twenty years, Indonesia was a playground for the international oil giants.

The banks followed the drilling rigs. The companies refused to

back their oil searching units and since lending millions to subsidiary foraging for oil in the Sumatran jungle was clearly riskier
than lending to Standard of California, the banks charged stiff
rates for "project" money, and they demanded "step in shoes"
rights to the oil in the ground if the project went belly up.

Despite the high bank rates, Indonesia was soon dotted with oil
projects.

And soon it became obvious that although Indonesia was rich
in oil, it was richer in natural gas. In 1971 Mobil discovered the
massive 35.5-square-mile-field at Arun on the northeast coast of
Sumatra. The next year, Huffco, a small Texas exploration partnership, found a slightly smaller field at Badak. It's harder to make
money on gas than oil—gas has to be liquefied to be transported
and sold—but with oil barren Japan right across the East China
Sea, liquefied natural gas looked like a winner.

In 1973, Pertamina, the Indonesia government oil company,
signed contracts with a group of Japanese electric companies. Indonesia would sell them fixed cargoes of LNG from Arun and
Badak, and the Japanese would line up $1 billion to build a gas
liquefication plant at Bontang Bay in Indonesia, and regasification
plants in Japan. But instead of paying Indonesia directly for their
LNG, the Japanese utilities would send the money to a trust account at the Continental Illinois National Bank & Trust Company.
The bankers dubbed the Continental account "the spigot" because
that was where the Badak money came out. Continental first paid
the Japanese banks, and then divided up the remaining cash among
Pertamina and the Badak and Arun operators. Accepting the Spigot
was a huge concession. The Indonesian government owned the
Badak gas but instead of getting paid for shipments, it was forced
to let a more trustworthy bank collect the proceeds and pay the
bills—and forward the remaining profits later.

The Japanese billion wasn't enough to get the LNG flowing.
The fields had to be drilled and piped. The project operators—
Mobil and Huffco—had to pick up the tab for that.

Money wasn't a problem for Mobil. Soon crawler tractors and
pipe layers were rolling across Arun.

But Huffco didn't have Mobil's deep pockets. To raise money,
Huffco founder Roy Huffington sold shares in Badak to five part-

ners. After the partners kicked in their portions of development dollars, costs came in over budget. The other partners anted up, but Huffco was short $25 million to pay its share.

Roy Huffington called Tom Kellogg about a loan.

Morgan sent a team to the site to "kick the tires," and back in New York, the oil and gas experts pored over the Badak papers.

The loan didn't seem promising.

"The technology is a little risky," Kellogg told his boss. There had been only two liquefied natural gas projects before Badak. The Huffco liquefication system would be the most modern Bechtel had ever made; it might not work. "And there's a problem with collateral." Just about the time that Huffco hit gas, the Indonesian government had unveiled a new concession system. Until then, when an oil company bought a "contract of work" concession, it owned everything on it: the rigs, the refineries, the oil in the ground. Now everything on Indonesian soil would belong to Indonesia. A company that wanted to pump Badak gas got just cost plus 35 percent of the profits. Pertamina would pocket the rest.

But Kellogg knew that there were good reasons to go ahead. The project would be such a big moneymaker for the Indonesian government that Jakarta had agreed to the Spigot—that made the collateral problem less serious—and the Japanese banks had already committed more than $1 billion. Huffco was talking just $25 million.

Kellogg's boss agreed.

Tom Kellogg called Roy Huffington. "We'll do it," he said.

Morgan made a bridge loan of $10 million.

Before the rest of the money came through, all Indonesian loans went on hold; the Pertamina crisis had begun.

Since 1967, when the president of Indonesia had named a flashy medical doctor, Ibnu Suwoto, to run the government oil company, Pertamina had been an "international glamour stock." Production had soared to over a million barrels a day, and the empire included a chain of hotels and a fleet of airplanes. Pertamina borrowed millions to pay the bills; it didn't keep track of how much.

Then, in 1974, the Franklin National Bank went bust.

The big banks got jittery about all their LDC loans. And Pertamina looked like trouble. By that time, oil production was below target—and the debt was clearly huge.

In February 1975, Pertamina missed a payment on a small loan from the Republic Bank of Dallas. If Pertamina didn't find the cash, Republic said it would declare a default. And Pertamina knew that one default would trigger the cross-default clauses on all of what the banks guessed was Pertamina's $6.2 billion of loans—and disaster for Indonesia's $7.3 billion international debt.

Something had to be done. Fast.

Morgan had never done much in Indonesia—in 1974, there was just one Indonesian loan on the Morgan books and it was guaranteed by the U.S. government's Export-Import Bank—but if Morgan was going to do anything, it seemed to Indonesia that this was the time. The governor of the Indonesian Central Bank called Morgan's executive vice president in charge of international banking.

"We'll send a team," he said.

"The Indonesian technocrats are impressive," the head of the team told the executive vice president back in New York. "They are Western-educated. They are sincere. They understand that they will have to tighten the belt."

That was what he wanted to hear. "We'll help," he told the governor of the Central Bank.

Soon Morgan put together $850 million of rescue money.

That was the beginning of a close banking relationship. The Indonesian government had just embarked on a massive development program and it wanted to raise money for its new projects at the best possible rate. Jakarta depended on Morgan to help figure out when which project should raise how much.

That meant that Morgan was the only bank the Indonesian government ever asked to put together a syndicate.

Soon after the bailout, Morgan approved the $25-million loan to Huffco for Badak field development.

The Badak gas wasn't yet flowing when Kellogg handed Roy Huffington his $25-million check, and Kellogg had some bad nights worrying that something would go wrong. But his sleeplessness had been for naught.

Badak began to operate on July 7, 1977, and ship after ship of LNG sailed for Japan.

Huffco called to ask for a second loan for the project in 1978, and that gave Kellogg an idea. If Huffco could raise money for Badak, so could its other consortium partners.

Kellogg's team called.

Mobil wanted a loan.

Superior wanted a loan.

"We're interested in $125 million," said the treasurer of Allied-Chemical. "But we don't want a loan backed by the full faith and credit of Allied. If we pledge our name, the debt shows up on our balance sheet." Under the new Indonesian concession system, Allied didn't have assets in Indonesia to use as collateral; Huffco had gotten around that problem by using its own name, but too much debt on the balance sheet would hurt Allied's credit rating. "This has to be a project loan." A loan secured just by Badak. That wouldn't be an Allied credit; it wouldn't show up in the same category on the balance sheet—or affect the credit rating the same way.

"That's going to be tricky," said Kellogg. "We'll have to try a measuring rod, with recourse just to Allied's share of the Badak cash as measured by the Spigot." Cash flow would be computed by a formula based on Badak output and the price of Minas crude.

It was a very unusual loan.

Morgan put together a syndicate.

Tom Kellogg gave out deal mementos at the closing dinner in September 1978: dark blue silk ties dotted with gold Spigots.

Now that Badak was on-stream, there were just two things that could go wrong: oil prices and Indonesia. If oil prices fell, so would Badak cash flow. If Indonesia had credit problems—because oil prices and income fell or because of a revolution—then Badak would have credit problems too.

For the next three years, everything went right.

In 1979, OPEC hiked the price of oil; Indonesian Minas went from $13.55 to more than $30. Badak revenues doubled, and so did Indonesian revenues.

With its new dollars, the Indonesian government stepped up its already ambitious development program. It began building steel mills, petrochemical plants and an aluminum facility.

OPEC hiked prices again. By the end of 1980, Indonesian Minas was up to $31.50.

Higher prices notwithstanding, the Japanese wanted more gas. Pertamina lined up new contracts with the Japanese companies for larger annual shipments. LNG commitments doubled.

Mobil began to expand the processing plant at Arun, and Huffco laid new gas piping and ordered two new liquefication plants for Badak.

Then suddenly things began to go awry.

For the first time in history, it looked like the price of Minas was going to fall.

OPEC's price hikes in 1979 and 1980 had cut the demand for OPEC crude. To keep the price of Saudi light oil steady, the cartel slashed production from 31 million barrels a day in 1979 to 22.5 million barrels a day in 1981.

At the beginning of 1982, spot prices—the price of oil on the free market—began to slide: Saudi light dipped from $34 a barrel in January to $31.75 a barrel in mid-February to $29.50 a barrel at the beginning of March; Indonesian Minas slid from $34.10 to $32. A decline in the spot price almost always meant a decline in the official price. Soft spot prices could hurt Badak later on—and they could mean a cut in Indonesia's revenue and in the country's credit rating.

Spot prices kept sliding.

Big OPEC customers began to cancel orders and buy spot.

The cartel had two options. It could cut prices to lure orders back, or it could slash production to shore up the price.

Saudi Arabia, OPEC's largest member, was awash in dollars; it wanted to cut prices to keep customers. Indonesia, overwhelmed by its development bill, wanted to keep prices up by slashing Saudi Arabian production: shaving just one dollar off the posted Minas rate would cost Indonesia almost $500 million a year.

The thirteen OPEC oil ministers scheduled an Extraordinary Conference in Vienna at the beginning of March. They decided to cut production. Total OPEC output would drop to just 17.5 million barrels a day. Indonesia's quota would be down 19 percent to 1.3 million barrels a day.

Prices firmed; Saudi light climbed from $28.10 on spot markets in late March to $33.90 in the middle of May; Indonesian Minas, from $31 in March to a high of $35 at the end of April.

Then the cheating began.

Nigeria needed cash to pay for food imports. Nigeria dropped prices on its top-quality oil, and at the same time production of Bonny light jumped to 1.3 million barrels a day, 200,000 barrels a day above the quota.

Libya needed cash to buy weapons. Production of Zueltina light ran double the 900,000-barrel-a-day quota.

Iran needed cash to pay for its war against Iraq. The unofficial price was slashed to $26 a barrel; output soared 63 percent to 2.5 million barrels a day.

Indonesia needed cash for its key development projects: it looked like Jakarta would be short $6 billion for 1982, and more for 1983. By summer, Pertamina was pumping 200,000 barrels a day above quota to raise cash.

In July, Rick Schile, assistant treasurer of Allied, called Tom Kellogg.

"We're thinking about a new loan for Badak," said Schile. "The $125 million you did in 1978 has amortized down to $60 million. Oil prices have tripled. Capacity is going to double. We can raise much more than $60 million against cash flow."

"Maybe," said Kellogg. "I'll think about it."

While Kellogg thought, the price war escalated.

By August, Saudi light was down to $31 a barrel spot, Indonesian Minas to $32.

At the end of the month, Mexico, the world's fifth-largest oil producer, announced that it could no longer pay interest on its debt.

By then, Venezuela, oil producer number six, was teetering.

Nigeria, number nine, had no more cash to pay for food.

Rick Schile called Kellogg again in early September 1982.

Kellogg made an appointment to see him at Allied's Morristown, New Jersey, headquarters at the end of the month.

A couple of days before their meeting, Rick Schile called. "I've got to cancel," he said. "We just bid $1.9 billion for Bendix." Schile didn't have time to think about financing Badak.

That was okay with Kellogg. Morgan had put Badak on hold too.

* * *

Mike Dacey looked through his window on the fifteenth floor of the Bankers Trust Company headquarters at the Colgate-Palmolive Building next door. It was sizzling hot out there. Dacey's air conditioner banged. He pressed the receiver to his ear.

"You know Allied is going to want to refinance Badak," said Tom Hardy from Bankers Trust in Houston. "The loan will have amortized down to less than $60 million by October. We ought to think about putting together a proposal."

"Well," said Dacey. "Maybe."

"Badak is a proven project," said Hardy. "The spreads are good. We've never led a syndicate in Indonesia. Badak would give us a foot in the door."

Dacey raised an eyebrow. "Indonesia is going to be tough to crack," he said. "That's Morgan territory. I don't think anyone besides Morgan has ever led an Indonesian loan."

"This looks like our chance," said Hardy. "We're underexposed in Indonesia. Morgan may be overexposed. We think Morgan has been having problems raising money for this project." He paused. "Huffco has been talking to us about switching to Bankers Trust for its next deal."

"Morgan is adviser to the Indonesian government," said Dacey. "Morgan led the syndicate last time. If Morgan isn't involved, we'll have trouble getting banks to join up: everyone will say 'If Morgan is backing out, so will I.'"

"Morgan doesn't have to be the lead," said Hardy. "Citibank just won a loan bid."

Dacey thought. "An Allied bank loan could be important to us," he said. "It will solidify our relationship with Allied—and leading a syndicate would be a big step for the Indonesian desk." He paused. "Beating Morgan is going to be tough, but we've got a chance. Allied is sharp-penciled."

"We've done well on other Allied projects," said Hardy.

Dacey looked out the window again. Maybe Badak was Morgan's soft underbelly. "Let's give it a try," he said. "I'll call Rick Schile."

* * *

Michael Dacey is debonair. At thirty-eight, he's tall and silver-haired. He wears yellow suspenders and a gold pocket watch. Dacey's schedule is so unpredictable that he says it makes sense for him to mark his pocket calendar in pencil. But he could never remember to carry a pencil with him. This year he bought an appointment book at Harrod's with a minipencil in the spine. That means that Dacey always has a pencil, and it means he has a new problem. The Harrod's lead got blunt by February, and it doesn't fit into his pencil sharpener.

Dacey grew up in New Jersey. He studied philosophy at St. Peter's College and got a master's in sociology at New York University. In 1969, after a three year stint as an Army recruiter, Dacey signed on at Bankers Trust as a junior lending officer. His first assignment: Delancey Street. Making loans to mom-and-pop stores wasn't Dacey's idea of banking, but it was good training. "If you can lend money on Delancey Street and get it back," said the boss, "you're ready to lend anywhere." After two years, Dacey was switched to the credit card division; the Chase Manhattan Bank had just decided to offer customers the BankAmericard, and Bankers Trust, until then the only BankAmericard bank in New York City, had decided to fight to protect its turf. The bank quickly put together a team to call on every BankAmericard merchant in Manhattan. Dacey covered 125th Street from the East River to the Hudson. Walking through Harlem with a big briefcase seemed risky, so Dacey started his rounds at seven each morning and stuffed BankAmericard literature under the doors. The shopkeepers weren't up then, but neither were the thugs.

In 1972, Dacey finally got a more traditional assignment: a desk in the corporate division and a list of clients in the Southwest and later in the West. In 1978, Dacey was made head of the eastern division, covering clients like Nabisco, Du Pont, and Allied Chemical.

Dacey was in the right place at the right time. Nineteen seventy-five was the year that Alfred Brittain became bank chairman. Under his leadership, the bank stopped floundering for corporate and commercial accounts—in just ten years, it had become Morgan Guaranty's closest rival. And by 1982, it was competing with the big investment banks like Morgan Stanley and Salomon Brothers. The head of the investment banking division liked to remind the troops that Goldman, Sachs spent months unsuccessfully trying to steal his entire swap team. The emphasis at Bankers is on trading. It has the biggest private placement department of any commercial bank in America, the biggest interest rate and currency swap department, and the biggest tax-based leasing department. When the Navy, a nontaxpayer, realized that it could make a bundle selling $2.5 billion of its ships to investors as a tax shelter, Bankers Trust lined up sale-and-leaseback deals for $1.3 billion worth of tankers, more than any other bidder.

At the turn of the century, only trust companies were allowed to provide their customers money management services. The banks wanted to offer their customers all services under one roof, and so in 1903, a Citibank vice president named Henry Pomeroy Davison resigned his job to found the Bankers Trust Company, to wholesale account management services to commercial banks. The company was a big success: Bankers Trust deposits soared from $10 million at the end of the year to more than $300 million in 1917. When Congress lifted the wall between banks and trust companies, Bankers Trust began taking corporate deposits and making commercial loans. The bank braved the Great Depression without government help, and after the Second World War, Bankers Trust decided to grow. The only way to get more money to lend was to have branches, so Bankers quickly added a "Chevrolet" retail division to its "Cadillac" wholesale department. In 1955, Bankers Trust, America's ninth-largest commercial bank, bought the Public National Trust, number forty-three. Soon Bankers Trust boasted 220 branches across New York State offering products like no-minimum-balance checking to home and auto loans and a Christmas club.

The retail department was never a big earner: business was mediocre and costs, including the cost of buying branch buildings, were high. Earnings dragged in the early seventies, and the problem didn't seem to have an answer. Citi had twice as many branches— and lower processing costs. As the retail problems got worse, the real estate market collapsed: by 1975, Bankers' shaky loan total was $1.2 billion.

"We are selling the branches," announced chairman Al Brittain in 1978. "Henchforth, Bankers Trust will be a wholesale-only bank."

Bank stock watchers were speechless; there was only one wholesale bank: Morgan Guaranty.

Becoming a wholesale bank wasn't easy. Step One: Build up the bond-trading desk. That was the only way to learn to buy money cheap, and without a retail system to collect lendable deposits, Bankers would have to buy.

Five years and a $15-million trading room later, Bankers had just fifty-four retail offices, and it made more of its money buying and selling bonds than any other bank in America.

Then came Step Two: leverage the commercial banking and trading contacts into a sales network for a variety of new investment products. Brittain planned to diversify into everything that he could legally sell.

The first "new" product: commercial paper, the ninety-day credit that had all but replaced short-term loans. Cracking the commercial paper market was slow: "CP" was dominated by investment banks like Goldman Sachs and A. G. Becker.

"We'll be the agent on your paper issue," Brittain told one CEO. "The fee will be $1 million."

"Hell," said the man. "We'd pay Goldman that."

Brittain kept trying.

In 1983, Bankers boasted twenty-two commercial paper clients, including Coca-Cola, ITT and Fluor Corporation. Then Bankers went a step further: it sold a $70-million registered bond issue for Louisiana Land and Exploration Company.

By then, Bankers was brokering loans, lining up interest rate and currency swaps, and trading futures. By the end of 1983, *Fortune* magazine reported that when four hundred companies were asked where they went for investment banking services, Bankers Trust was ranked number eleven, ahead of every other commercial bank, including Morgan Guaranty.

Eleven was good, but it wasn't good enough. Brittain wanted Bankers Trust to be "top tier." To get there, Brittain put together a client company hit list. He called the regional managers into his office and passed out a sheet of names. "You've got to talk to someone at each of these companies at least two hundred times a year," he said. Just about once every business day. "They have to know what Bankers Trust can do."

Mike Dacey, head of the eastern division, nodded. Thirty-five of the targets were in his territory. And at the top of the list was Allied Corporation.

Allied was exactly the kind of client Brittain wanted. Allied generated lots of commercial banking activity—the corporate revolver, oil and gas projects for the Union Texas Petroleum subsidiary—and even more investment banking business—debt for equity swaps, interest rate and currency swaps, real estate sale and leasebacks, stock and bond issues, half a dozen acquisitions.

Dacey was confident that he could seal Allied's relationship with Bankers. After all, Bankers had a foot in the door: it was one of the banks on Allied's $2-billion revolver. Dacey called the account officer in New York. "Keep a close eye on Allied," he said. "Go out to Morristown. Pitch a tent in their front yard and live there until Allied believes we're serious. And listen. We need to know when Allied is thinking about selling commercial paper, when they are thinking about a swap, when they are raising money for a project. And we want Allied to know about us. We want them to know about our private placement services, about our merger advisory service. Every Allied problem is a Bankers Trust opportunity."

"I'll get on it," said the man.

Dacey called Houston. There were already two men on Union Texas Petroleum (UTP), the Allied subsidiary that owned a share of Badak. "We've got to call on UTP at least once a month," said Dacey. "I'd like to call every day. We need to prove that we mean business."

The extra attention worked.

At the beginning of 1982, Bankers called to ask if Allied wanted to buy Apollo Laser. Allied did—and Bankers helped negotiate the $10-million deal. Then Allied called to ask for bids on project loans to the Allied-Sedco jack-up rig in the Mediterranean; the Allied-Occidental Petroleum joint venture at the Piper and Claymore fields in the North Sea, and the Allied–Cities Service partnership near Mendoza, Argentina.

So in August 1982, when Dacey got the call from Tom Hardy

in Houston saying that UTP was thinking about refinancing Badak, Dacey knew that Bankers would have trouble running a deal in Indonesia without support from Morgan Guaranty, but he was ready to bid. He dialed Rick Schile, the assistant treasurer at Allied. "What about Badak?" he asked. "We'd like to be on the bidding list."

"We're going to talk to a couple of banks," said Schile. "This spring. I've got my hands full with Bendix right now."

"Can we take a look?" asked Dacey.

"Sure," said Schile. "Why don't you put together a presentation."

Dacey smiled. That was what he liked to hear: a five-track race with Bankers Trust on the inside lane.

Tom Kellogg was worried about oil prices. And about a Badak deal.

"Spot prices were stable this month, but we're still pessimistic," said the oil and gas economist in September.

Spot oil prices stayed steady through October, but then they began to skid: Saudi light sunk from $33.50 in mid-October to $29.75 by the end of November; Indonesian Minas, from $34 to $32.

"Clearly there will be a cut in the posted price," said the economist. "The only question is whether it will be coordinated or competitive." The economist paused. "There's been wild talk: that we'll see $20-a-barrel crude; that the price of oil will gyrate for months; that oil prices will never be stable again."

Kellogg shook his head. Any of those changes would affect the economics of Badak, and the credit rating of Indonesia.

"OPEC is meeting in Vienna next week," said the economist. On December 19. "I'm betting on a single official cut to $28.50 a barrel."

The OPEC ministers couldn't agree in Vienna.

They met again in Geneva in January. Still no agreement. They scheduled a third meeting in London for March 2.

"If OPEC doesn't strike an agreement soon," said the oil and gas economist, "market confidence will collapse. Prices will freefall."

Kellogg shook his head. Free-falling prices would be a disaster for Badak—and for every other oil project in the world.

In the meantime, though, Indonesia looked like it was getting back on track. At the beginning of January, Jakarta called its advisers—the International Monetary Fund; Lehman Brothers, Kuhn Loeb; Lazard Frères; and S. G. Warburg—to help design an austerity package. The fiscal 1984 budget cut food and energy subsidies to the bone. Austerity was good for Indonesia: it meant its credit rating wouldn't fall. Austerity might be a problem for Morgan, though. Total Indonesian borrowings had to slow down—even as government borrowing rose—and that meant that Morgan, official adviser to the government, would have to help figure out which projects—and which Morgan clients—would get the money.

At the beginning of February, oil prices slid again.

The Soviet Union cut the price of Urals crude from $32.20 a barrel to $29.35.

Great Britain slashed the official price of Brent crude by $3 a barrel.

Nigeria retaliated by breaking with OPEC and cutting the official price of Bonny light $5.50 a barrel.

The spot price of Saudi light slumped to $29.50; spot Indonesian Minas hit $31.30.

The Indonesian oil minister flew to Kuwait for a series of secret meetings. OPEC's third negotiating summit was coming up. Word was that the Arab members of OPEC were scheming to force a price cut.

Tom Kellogg called Brian Weight. "It's time to talk to Allied about Badak," said Kellogg. "Give Rick Schile a call."

At thirty-three, Brian Weight has brown hair, brown eyes and a bristly mustache. He's got a sophisticated sense of humor, a sharp wit and a quick tongue. Weight's a British hsitory buff, and an occasional contributor to several British periodicals. He has a passion for music. As a boy, Weight was a chorister in the Salisbury Cathedral Choir and later with the Trinity College Choir in Cambridge. He says that his most uplifting experience—aside from the birth of his two daughters—is to attend choral evensong sung by a cathedral choir.

A native of Bath, Weight read English and European literature at Cambridge. He had considered getting a Ph.D., but decided to forgo the "ivory towers" to get involved in the "real world." He joined Morgan in London after graduating and spent three years as an account officer, lining up financings for clients like Marks and Spenser. Weight was transferred to project finance in 1976. Morgan had just set up a London project department, and Weight seemed to have the right kind of mind. He quickly became an old hand at putting together lending consortiums. In 1978, Weight was transferred to Singapore as project finance coordinator for the Southeast Asia Pacific area (Thailand, Malaysia and Singapore). He was also country coordinator for Indonesia, where he helped steer the Huffco, Superior, and Allied Badak loans through Jakarta's Ministry of Finance. At the end of 1982, after a stint in Sydney as project finance coordinator for Australasia, Weight was transferred to Morgan headquarters in New York. His new assignment: covering oil companies headquartered in Texas, such as Union Texas Petroleum.

Tom Kellogg's desk was next to Brian Weight's, and from Weight's first day on the job, the two had talked about the loan. At the beginning of February they brainstormed for hours about whether to go ahead with it. Weight called the senior vice president for Southeast Asia Pacific for the okay.

When he talked with Rick Schile on March 3, he said Morgan was looking at approximately $200 million.

"We need $275 million to $300 million," said Schile. "Think about it."

The next day, Rick Schile called Brian Weight. "We want to keep thinking about Badak," he said. "We've asked two other banks for estimates on how much they can raise."

Weight raised an eyebrow. He hadn't expected the Badak loan to be competitive.

As soon as Rick Schile gave Bankers Trust the go ahead to look at Badak in September, Mike Dacey called the Allied lending team into his office. "It's time to get the ball rolling," he said. "We've got a head start on Badak. We need to put together a proposal."

The team set to work and by January it had put together four proposals.

The man in Houston set up a meeting at Union Texas headquarters for the middle of the month.

The Bankers Allied account officer flew down from New York, but Mike Dacey stayed home. This was a grass-roots meeting for the Houston team and Union Texas; Dacey didn't belong at that.

One of the New York bankers talked about Bankers Trust.

The banker from Houston talked through the financing proposals.

"We're worried that the market for Indonesian projects is drying up," said one of the Union Texas executives. Indonesia was overextended. It would have to scale back imports.

"This isn't an Indonesian project," said the banker from New York. "This is an oil and gas project."

"Oil prices are headed down," said the man from UTP. Recently, Saudi Arabia had cut its output by more than half to keep prices up—that could go on indefinitely.

"Don't look at why we can't do it," said the man from Bankers Trust. "Let's talk about how we can."

Mike Dacey called Rick Schile just after the team came back. UTP was interested, but it was Allied, as parent company, who made the borrowing decisions.

"Badak is on hold," said Schile. "I'm busy with Bendix."

"Bankers is ready when you are," said Dacey.

On March 4, the day after his meeting with Brian Weight, Rick Schile called Mike Dacey. "The bidding for Badak is on," he said. "We need your proposal."

Dacey called the account officer. He called Houston.

Everything looked good.

Except oil prices.

That week, the OPEC oil ministers were meeting at the Inter-Continental Hotel in London to settle on a cut. So far, there had been no announcement, but if the cartel lowered prices, the Badak numbers would change.

Dacey watched the wires.

75

No news.

Day after day, the thirteen ministers flew into their suite over-looking Buckingham Palace; day after day, the meetings broke without an agreement.

By the end of the week, Dacey was worried.

Moscow cut the price of Urals crude $1.75 a barrel to $29.25, the second cut in six weeks.

The OPEC ministers kept arguing.

The Bankers man in Houston called Mike Dacey. "We've got a proposal," he said. "Five hundred million. At one and a quarter over Libor, the same interest rate as Allied paid on the $125-million 1978 loan."

Dacey dialed Rick Schile and they made an appointment for March 14.

The wires looked worse and worse.

The British hinted that they would shave another dollar off the price of Brent crude.

That meant that Nigeria would slide too: the oil minister had pledged to match British cuts "cent for cent."

Word leaked from the OPEC meeting that Algeria and Venezuela were pushing for a production ceiling of 14 million barrels a day and a price of $32 a barrel; the Saudis were holding out for $29 a barrel, and a ceiling of 17.5 million barrels a day. Whatever the price, Iran wanted a bigger quota. So did Venezuela. So did Indonesia.

OPEC still hadn't reached an agreement when the Bankers team drove to allied headquarters in Morristown on March 14.

"Five hundred million looks good," said Schile.

"I've got to tell you," said the Bankers officer. "We're eager to lead this syndicate, but Morgan has to be involved. Morgan and Indonesia are like this." He held up his hand; his first two fingers were crossed.

Schile nodded. "We'll get back to you. We're still waiting for the bids from the other banks."

"Allied is interested," the officer told Dacey when he got back to New York.

"Good," said Dacey.

Bankers had a shot at being manager. Bankers could beat Morgan yet.

*   *   *

Brian Weight heaved a sigh of relief. He'd been watching the OPEC negotiations in London from his Morgan office for two weeks, and he'd been worried.

But on Monday morning, March 14—the very day the Bankers Trust team had gone to Morristown—the word had come across the Reuters wire:

> OPEC announced today it had cut its crude-oil reference price by about 15 percent from $34 to $29 a barrel, the first cut since it started fixing prices during the 1973 Arab oil embargo against the West. OPEC's communiqué said it had also set itself an overall production ceiling of 17.5 million barrels a day for the rest of 1983 to try to erase surpluses from the market and keep the price from falling again. Saudi Arabia, the biggest and wealthiest oil exporter, took no individual quota but would act as a "swing producer."

Twenty-nine dollars a barrel was almost exactly what the Morgan oil and gas economist had predicted. Weight skimmed the communiqué. Indonesian Minas would go for $29.53, high enough to keep Badak well in the black.

It was time to put together a bid.

Weight dialed John Lane, the head of the Middle Atlantic group. Ten minutes later, Weight, Lane and Breck Denny, the Allied account officer, were sitting in the armchairs behind Lane's desk.

"OPEC finally agreed to cut the price of crude," said Weight. "We're ready to move on Badak."

"Work it out with Breck," said Lane.

Breck Denny is sober. At thirty-five, he has brown eyes and thinning brown hair. His sense of humor is wry: when he was stuck on the Brooklyn Bridge for two hours behind an overturned chemical truck, he didn't complain. "It could have been worse," he said. "What if it had been the tunnel?" Denny has been to every state of the Union except North Dakota, Mississippi and Hawaii inspecting mines and plants for Morgan Guaranty. He doesn't mind the travel—especially where the fly fishing is good. One of Denny's proudest moments was watching his six-year-old daughter catch her first fish, a twenty-inch pike.

Denny grew up on Long Island and majored in American history at Vanderbilt University. He taught economics to high school seniors to help pay the way, and when he graduated in 1970, Denny signed on as a Morgan trainee. After four years doing legwork on New England accounts, Denny was transferred to the Fifth Avenue office to cover New York City corporate clients. Two years later, he was back at 23 Wall Street as an in-house consultant specializing in the heavy-equipment industry. Denny helped account officers evaluate loan proposals; he put together studies and located targets for the mergers and acquisitions department. In 1979, he was made head of the financial analysis department's basic-industries group, overseeing steel, forest products, chemicals, mining and heavy industry. Seven years seemed like long enough to be a consultant, so when Denny came up for reassignment in 1983, he asked for a job as an account officer. In February the assignment came through: the Middle Atlantic group—corporate clients headquartered in Pennsylvania and New Jersey—with a focus on New Jersey.

Two weeks before he was scheduled to start the new job, the outgoing Allied account officer called. "I've set up a dinner for you," she said. "To celebrate the passing of the baton." Allied's treasurer had just been promoted to vice president for planning; the vice president for tax had been promoted to treasurer. Denny was taking over the Allied account at Morgan. "And we've got tickets to the Virginia Slims tournament afterward. Tom Kellogg and John Lane from our office will be there too. They all want to talk about Badak."

Thursday, March 24, Denny, Kellogg and Lane caught a cab to Woods, the restaurant on Thirty-fourth Street. Brian Weight, the Union Texas account officer, should have joined them, but he was in Houston for a loan signing.

"We've been looking over the numbers for Badak," said the Allied treasurer.

"We might be able to put together $225 million," said Tom Kellogg.

"That's ridiculous," said the Allied tax vice president. "You did $125 million last time. Oil prices have quadrupled. You can raise a lot more than $225 million."

"We're comfortable with $225 million," said Kellogg. "With benchmark crude at $29 a barrel, $225 million seems about right."

"Prices are stable," said the treasurer. "We're about to double output. We've been talking to another bank about this—and the number they're quoting is a lot more."

"Indonesia is having problems," said Lane. Who was Allied talking to? Chase? Chase hadn't been keen on the structure of the first Allied Badak loan and had refused to join the syndicate. How much was a lot more? Three hundred and fifty million? "Jakarta has to cut back borrowings. It looks like the market is going to be crowded with project loans. You'll have to get by on the smallest loan possible, not the biggest."

The tax vice president frowned. Lane had a point. Allied wanted to be on the right side of the Indonesian government.

"Timing could be a problem," said Lane. "We think you're okay if you close by May 31. Otherwise you're going to bump into the government jumbo." A second loan. "You don't want to do that. The government is a better credit." The government is the best credit in any country. "You don't want to be the kind of company that sabotages government deals."

That made sense. "We'll keep thinking," said Schile.

On April 1, Denny moved to his new desk. Three days later, he got a call from Rick Schile. "We're ready for bids on Badak," he said. "We need your proposal."

"We'll get moving," said Denny. This was a key loan for Morgan: the first Allied loan since Allied bought Bendix.

"Indonesia looks less risky," said the senior vice president for East Asia when Denny called that afternoon. Just five days ago, Indonesia had announced a 28 percent devaluation of the rupiah; exports would be 28 percent cheaper and imports would be 38 percent more expensive. The government made it clear that there would be other major reforms. "I don't think there is going to be a balance-of-payments problem after all. I'm comfortable making a bid."

Denny called Brian Weight. "We've got to get moving on Badak," he said. "Schile wants a bid. Olds says okay." John Olds, the senior vice president.

Weight called Morgan's man in Jakarta. "Allied wants to raise $275 million for Badak," he said. "Sound out the Indonesian government."

The next morning, Weight and Denny and the oil and gas engineer on the project sat down to talk over the proposal.

"I've done the sensitivity analysis," said Weight. "The worst-case scenario we want to test is that oil prices drop to $20 a barrel. If that happens, a $225-million loan is still comfortable."

"The coverages look good," said the oil and gas engineer. The project should earn several times its total yearly payments. This was well below Morgan's usual cutoff: it generally leads to international oil projects whose base-case scenario cash flows are over two times principal plus interest.

"LNG no longer trades at a premium to condensate," said Weight. Condensate, another gas-liquid fuel, is a by-product of an oil refinery. "How does that change the way we look at this?"

"Do you think the Japanese are likely to switch the kind of fuel they use?" asked Denny. "Could they cartelize purchasing to push down the price? What about coal from Australia?"

"The Japanese are committed to LNG," said Weight. "They own the ships and the gasification plant."

"What about competing projects?" asked Denny. That was a big worry. Morgan was sure that half a dozen other Indonesian projects were going to market in the next few months; that meant that there would be stiff competition for money—and interest rates would get bid up.

"Let's talk about trends we're seeing in gas projects around the world," said the oil and gas engineer.

They kept talking for eight hours.

Jakarta called the next morning. "We checked with the government," said the Morgan representative. "A Badak deal for Allied is fine. Badak is a big earner. They want to know what capital expenditures will be."

The team talked about timing.

They kept talking all day Wednesday and all day Thursday.

Finally the bid was set.

80

Breck Denny called Rick Schile Friday afternoon, April 8. "We're proposing $225 million at one and a quarter over Libor," he said. The same amount he'd mentioned at Woods two weeks ago. "The loan has to close no later than May 31. We need a response from you soon."

"Come on out," said Schile. "We need to talk."

Denny and Kellogg drove out to Morristown Monday morning. Weight was in Dallas for the day on another project.

"Two hundred twenty-five isn't enough," said Schile. "We need $275 million."

"We'll think about it," said Denny.

"The other bank we're talking to is quoting much more," said Schile.

Denny shook his head. How much was Chase talking about?

"There's flexibility," said Schile.

"Allied wants to do what's good for Indonesia," said Denny. "Raising $275 million might not be appropriate."

Schile frowned. Denny had a point.

Denny called the senior vice president for Southeast Asia Pacific as soon as he got back to his office. In the SVP's office, the team talked through the parameters once again. "We need to talk about Badak," he said.

By Thursday morning, April 14, they had agreed to raise the bid to $275 million.

Brian Weight, back from Dallas, went back to his office to draft an official offering letter. He had just finished when the telephone rang.

It was Rick Schile. "One of the two Badak liquefication trains just exploded," he said.

Mike Dacey almost dropped the telephone. "You're kidding," he said.

"No," said the Bankers Trust officer in Houston. "Huffco just called to say that Badak Train B exploded."

"I can't believe it," said Dacey.

"It's still not clear what happened," said the man in Houston.

Dacey frowned. If the train had exploded because of a design error, then all four of the trains used to transport LNG from Badak would have to be fixed; that would be expensive and it would change the project's technology risk. If it had been sabotaged, then the whole risk profile of the project changed. The only hope was that the accident had been a quirk. In that case, financing would be delayed but nothing else would change.

"I'll keep you posted," said Houston.

Dacey dialed Rick Schile. "Our bid is on hold," he said. "We can't do anything more until we know just why that train exploded."

Schile didn't say much. There wasn't much to say.

The news trickled in.

By mid-May, just a month after the explosion, Huffco seemed to have the answers, and things didn't look as bad as they had at first.

Train B had been down for routine maintenance. After the maintenance technicians derimed the refrigeration system—dried it out—then left the block valve closed. It should have been open. When high-pressure deriming gas was pumped into the exchanger, the pressure built up. Half an hour later the exchanger exploded.

The exchanger was shattered, but Huffco had ordered a new one. High-pressure warning bells would henceforth be added to all the trains. And although the repairs would cost $75 million, most of that was covered by Huffco's insurance. Huffco would have to pay only $6 million. And thanks to a loan of a spare exchanger from Mobil's plant at Arun, Huffco's train would be back on stream by November. The man from Huffco assured Bankers that the project would be at full capacity in ninety days. That was good. The project wouldn't lose revenues.

Mike Dacey called Rick Schile at the end of May. "Let's talk about our offer," he said. "Bankers Trust is ready to get moving."

"We haven't decided which loan proposal is best," said Schile. "We've got a bid from you and a bid from Morgan. We're considering having three comanagers. We want a Japanese bank in on the deal. Are you willing to be one of three?"

"Sure," said Dacey. Being one of three was still a victory.

"Which Japanese bank makes most sense?" asked Schile.

"Let me call Tokyo," said Dacey.

* * *

Brian Weight called Rick Schile on April 18, the Monday after the explosion. "We'll send our bid for $275 million," said Weight. The offer that Weight had been drafting when Schile had called to tell him about the explosion. The only difference was that the deadline had been pushed back to September. "But it isn't firm. Not until we know what happened."

"I understand," said Schile. "Send me the bid."

Weight put the envelope in the mail on Monday.

By Wednesday the Mobil loaner looked likely.

"We like the proposal you sent," Schile told Weight. "Let's keep talking."

Breck Denny called Rick Schile in the middle of May. "We need to have a meeting," he said. Morgan had to keep its edge in the Badak bidding. And it looked like Allied might want a loan for its share of the Sean field in the North Sea.

"Morgan is very interested in Badak," said Denny when they met in Morristown. "We're just waiting for news."

"I know," said Schile. "We like your offer. We're still thinking."

Denny shook his head. Why wouldn't Allied commit?

A couple of days after the meeting, Brian Weight called Breck Denny. "Oil prices seem to have stabilized," he said. "Jakarta just announced that it will 'rephase' some development projects." Delay them indefinitely. The government claimed that rephasing forty-seven projects would save $10 billion over the next few years.

"Good. The market won't be cluttered with loans," said Denny.

By the middle of June, when it was clear the accident had been a quirk, Breck Denny called Rick Schile. "Let's talk about Badak," he said. "We're ready to go."

Denny and Weight drove out to Morristown on Monday, June 20.

"We need a firm offer for $275 million," said Schile.

Denny frowned. He could get that.

"You guys have to improve your interest rate," said Schile.

"Badak is risky," said Denny. "The rate has to be a premium."

Schile frowned. "If you don't cut the rate, we'll give you less collateral."

"We'll take another look," said Denny.

"We want Bankers Trust as a comanager," said Schile.

Denny raised an eyebrow. So Bankers was the other bidder, not Chase. Morgan was lead manager; Morgan had won.

The Morgan team met back in New York in the conference room behind Brian Weight's desk to talk through the offer one more time. Two days later, they agreed on a firm $275 million.

Denny walked back to his desk to read through the offering letter that Weight had drafted that afternoon. He looked at the clock. Half past five.

The telephone rang.

It was Dennis Ruggles, Rick Schile's assistant.

"Did we tell you that we wanted to fix the rate on a big piece of this loan?" asked Ruggles.

Denny's jaw dropped. "What?" he asked. Allied couldn't fix a project loan. Project finance wasn't done at fixed rates. Projects were so risky that the banks lent to them only at rates pegged to prime or Libor, the benchmark market rates that changed every day.

"Fix the rate," repeated Ruggles. "We don't want to risk paying 20 percent on all of this $275 million if rates spiral up again."

"Fix the rate on how big a piece?" asked Denny.

"We haven't decided," said Ruggles. "Maybe a hundred million."

Denny didn't think that was possible. "I'll see what I can do," he said.

First thing the next morning, Denny dialed Barbara Austell, the officer in international finance who covered New Jersey. "I've got a problem on an Allied project loan," he said. "I've got to fix the interest rate on a big piece, maybe $100 million."

"Come on up," said Austell. "We'll think of something."

At twenty-eight, Barbara Austell is short, with wavy brown hair and brown eyes and big tortoise-shell glasses. She lives in a one-hundred-year-old farmhouse in Ridgewood, New Jersey, with her husband, an advertising executive, and their one-and-a-half-year-old daughter. Austell spends weekends renovating the house—she recently designed a new kitchen that her husband built—and reads the *New Yorker* on the train to work. Austell has two thousand mystery novels stashed in the attic of her house. Two years ago she submitted her own novel to the Scribners mystery competition. She didn't win, but she hasn't given up.

Austell was raised in upstate New York and majored in economics at Williams. She spent the summer between her junior and senior years working at a bank where the officers kept talking about how much they wished their bank banked as well as Morgan. So when she graduated in 1975, Austell decided to get a job at the bank that banked the best. Austell's first assignment at Morgan: doing legwork on upstate New York accounts like Kodak, Gannett and Corning Glass. After a year, Austell traded accounts with the officer at the next desk. Among her new names: Allied Corporation. In 1979, she was part of the team on a $600-million loan to finance Allied's acquisition of the Eltra Corporation. After a four-month maternity leave in 1981, Austell was back at the bank teaching new officers how to evaluate oil companies and other credits. Austell liked training, but she missed calling on clients. When her name came up for a new assignment a year and a half later, Austell asked for international financial management. Working on big Euromarket and corporate finance transactions sounded exciting.

It was. Austell lined up sophisticated financings like interest rate and currency swaps, defeasance deals and long-term dated forwards.

In the fall of 1982, Austell asked Allied if it was interested in a swap. It wasn't. Austell spent the next six months lining up complicated financings for other clients on her list.

Then in mid-June, Breck Denny called to ask about fixing the rate on the loan to Allied. "If the fixed piece is going to be as big as $100 million, it will have to be amortized," said Denny. "Allied made it clear that the fixed loan has to be part of the project package. The $275 million can't be for the Allied account. Neither can the $100 million."

"Okay," said Austell. "We could do a private placement." Morgan could sell shares of a $100-million fixed-rate loan to sophisticated investors like bank trust departments, insurance companies and endowment funds. The Allied loan was unusual though; it might be difficult to syndicate.

"We don't have time for a private placement," said Denny. "The loan has to close by September. The Indonesian government is coming to market with a jumbo after that." A private placement could take months to negotiate, particularly for an oil project in Indonesia. Because insurance companies, the biggest placement lenders, have quotas for how much of the portfolio they can invest in oil paper, project paper and foreign paper, no insurance company could buy a big piece of Badak.

"Well," said Austell. "Then you'll have to do an interest-rate swap."

Denny frowned. He understood swaps. An American industrial company wanted fixed-rate money but could get cheap floating-rate money on the commercial paper market: a European bank wanted floating-rate money but could get cheap fixed-rate money on the Eurobond market. If the company and the bank both borrowed where money was cheapest and then swapped interest payments, both came out paying less than they would have just borrowing what they wanted. But swaps were a new way to finance projects. Allied might not want to be a guinea pig. "I know how an interest-rate swap works, but this is a syndicated loan," he said. "Morgan can't take on the swap alone. How can we syndicate a swap?"

"Look," said Austell. She drew boxes and arrows on her yellow legal pad to show how the money flowed.

Denny nodded. That was clear.

"This is an unusual swap," said Austell. "The Allied loan is unusual. It sounds to me like the swap is going to have to be amortizing." Amortizing loans are paid back a little at a time. "Eurobonds are sold as bullets—they come due all at once. I can only think of two amortizing issues."

Austell and Denny walked over to the private placement department. They talked to the two bankers who weren't on the telephone.

"Maybe we can do this," said one. "But it won't be easy. A lot of lenders will have problems with the risk. We might be able to do it in two months. We might get 125 over treasuries." Competitive with a swap if a syndicated swap could be done.

"What about backing the placement with a letter of credit?" asked Austell. A guarantee that Morgan would pay if Allied didn't.

"A letter of credit won't help much," said the placement man. "Insurance companies look at letters of credit, but they base their decisions on their assessment of the project."

Austell looked at Denny. Two months—or even six weeks—wouldn't do. It was already mid-June. The loan had to close in September. Besides, a private placement wouldn't dovetail with a syndicated loan; a placement meant two separate loans, a $100 million fixed-rate loan by a group insurance companies and a $175 million floating-rate loan by the banks. A swap would be much simpler. One syndicate would raise the cash and process the swap payments.

Denny took the elevator back to his desk.

Austell walked to her desk. "I've got a client looking for a swap in August or September," she told her counterpart at Morgan Guaranty Ltd. in London. "What's the outlook?"

"It depends on the market," said London. "You know the Europeans. They're opportunistic."

Banks were cool on swaps right now. Floating-rate loans were relatively cheap. Fixed-rate loans were expensive—the seven-year treasury note was paying 10.84 percent, up from 10.05 percent in May, and the highest rate since October 1982. Austell couldn't count on a European bank.

Maybe there was a Japanese bank. The Japanese government regulates the bond market; to keep things orderly, only one bank is allowed to sell bonds at a time. Each bank gets a two-week selling period, and there is almost always a Japanese bank in the market for a bond deal.

Austell dialed Tokyo to find out which banks were selling in August and September.

"This is for a project finance in Indonesia," said Austell. "Maybe one of the banks in the current syndicate wants to swap."

"We'll check," said Tokyo. "A plain vanilla swap is going for 70 over treasuries right now." A swap with no complications costs 70 basis points or .7 of a percentage point over treasuries, the rate the U.S. Government pays on treasury bonds. "This swap is strange. The rate is going to be higher, maybe 100 over treasuries."

Austell called London again.

"Allied would have to pay 70 over treasuries for seven-year

bonds," said the man. A swap would cost Allied a couple of million more each year, but the bonds would go on the balance sheet as long-term debt; the swap, as part of a project finance, wouldn't.

Austell called Denny. "The swap is the best alternative," she said. "The rate will probably come in about 100 basis points over treasuries."

Breck Denny dialed Rick Schile. "We're ready to make a new proposal," he said.

Schile marked down an appointment.

Mike Dacey put down the receiver. He couldn't believe that Rick Schile wanted to fix the interest rate on a project loan. Banks didn't do that. Or hadn't. Dacey called the team into his office. If there was a way to make the rate fixed, Bankers Trust would find it.

"There are two obvious ways to fix a rate," said the account officer. "There's a traditional fixed-rate loan."

"We're never going to be able to syndicate that," said Dacey. Badak was too risky.

"What about hedging?" suggested someone. "Couldn't we do something on the futures market?"

"That won't work," said Dacey. Futures were new then and the market wasn't very deep. "You can't buy seven year futures."

"True," said the loan officer. "What about an interest rate swap?"

"No," said Dacey. "This is an amortizing loan. Swaps conventionally are bullets." As far as Dacey knew, no one had ever done an amortizing swap.

"Is there some way to break up the swap?" suggested the loan officer. "We could do five swaps." Each for $20 million, coming due in three, four, five, six and seven years respectively.

"We don't have time to do five swaps," said Dacey. Twenty-million-dollar swaps are tricky to set up: banks don't sell bond issues that small.

"Couldn't we do a private placement?" asked David Smith, the junior man on the Bankers team. Bankers Trust has the largest private placement department of any commercial bank in the world.

"Not by September," said Dacey.

"What about a placement backed by a letter of credit," said Smith. A Bankers Trust guarantee.

Dacey raised an eyebrow. Traditionally letters of credit are used to finance trade: a bank in Abu Dhabi won't make a loan to a banana exporter in Uruguay unless a major bank vouches for the payments.

"Badak paper backed by a letter of credit is really Bankers Trust paper," said Smith. "Bankers Trust paper will sell overnight."

The bankers talked.

"A letter of credit sounds good," Dacey told Smith at the end of the meeting. "Flesh out the details."

Smith walked back to his desk. He called the private placement department. "We're thinking about doing a $100-million private placement backed by a letter of credit," he said.

The placement expert asked some questions.

Smith answered.

"Sure, we can sell that," said the placement man. "We can sell it fast. The rates will be quite competitive." He flipped through the papers on his desk. "Somewhere around 11 percent."

Smith called Dacey.

Mike Dacey called Rick Schile the third week in June. "We've got some ideas about fixing the rate on that $100 million," he said.

"Morgan is working on a swap," said Schile.

"We're working on a private placement," said Dacey. "We'll have a formal proposal ready for you in a couple of days."

Breck Denny and Brian Weight met with Rick Schile in Morristown on Thursday, June 30. Barbara Austell would make the presentation on interest-rate swaps, but she'd be flying in from Pittsburgh, where she'd had a dinner meeting with a client the night before; she'd promised Denny that she'd get up at five to catch USAir's seven o'clock flight to Newark.

"We're ready to raise to $275 million," said Weight right off. "The rate is one and a quarter over Libor."

"You've got to shave your interest rate," said Schile. "One and a quarter over Libor is awfully conservative. Bankers Trust is talking about twice this much money at the same rate."

"We'll take another look," said Denny. Brian Weight would have to call the senior vice president for Southeast Asia Pacific again.

The door to the conference room opened. Barbara Austell walked in. "Sorry I'm late," she said. She sat down in the chair next to the door. "Let's talk about the swap."

Weight shifted in his seat. He'd never met Austell before, and he wasn't sure that he liked the idea of this syndicated swap. Morgan might not be able to put the deal together fast enough. And timing was critical.

"A swap is easier to understand with a diagram," said Austell. She got out a yellow legal pad. "Here's the project," she said. She drew a box. "Here's a foreign bank." She drew another box. She talked through the borrowing and payment-swapping system. She drew the arrows just as she had for Denny a couple of days before.

Schile watched. He asked a few questions. Then he smiled. "That's very simple," he said.

Austell nodded. It was—on paper. In practice, it might not be. Austell wasn't quite sure that Morgan could sell a bond issue with amortization payments that matched the Badak loan payments. She wasn't sure that she could syndicate the swap.

"Can you do a swap quickly?" asked Schile. "An amortizing swap?"

"I can do a plain vanilla swap in a couple of hours," said Austell. Austell wasn't sure that she could find a bank that wanted to do an amortizing project swap at all. "Why don't you just do a bullet swap for Allied and allocate it to this transaction?" she suggested. Swapping an Allied loan for a bond would be a snap. Allied is rated A by Standard & Poor's; a swap is most attractive to companies rated BBB or lower.

"No," said Schile. "The Badak financing has to be self-contained. The $100-million fixed loan has to be $100 million of project debt. It has to be amortized like the rest of the loan."

Austell frowned.

"What about a private placement?" asked Schile. That was what Bankers Trust was going to try.

"A private placement doesn't work with your timetable," said

Austell. "A private placement is complicated. You'll have to negotiate with a new group of lenders. You'll have to put together
more documents. You'll probably have to change the terms on the
rest of the loan. It isn't a simple answer."

The bankers talked.

Denny and Weight and Austell were all chainsmoking. By the
middle of the afternoon, the room was filled with smoke. There
were no windows—and no fan.

"We're sure that interest rates are going to fall," said Schile.
"We're worried that we'll fix a rate now and then see the market
drop a hundred basis points."

"If you're positive rates are going to fall, you might want to
think about deferred rate setting," said Austell. An innovation that
Morgan had just introduced on a $100-million Eurobond issue
for Citicorp. "We fix your spread over treasuries the day of the
swap." The interest rate premium. "You choose your treasury yield
any day in the next six months." Morgan didn't lose money by
letting Allied choose the day to set the rate; to hedge a $100-
million deferred swap, the bank would buy $100 million worth
of treasury notes the day that it set the spread; Morgan would
resell the bonds the day Allied chose its treasury yield; if rates
were down, the value of the bonds would be up.

"We'll think about it," said Schile.

"We've got to shave our rate," said Denny when the team caucused in the conference room behind Weight's desk the next day.

The bankers talked.

Indonesia had just announced a second round of austerity mea-
sures. It looked like the country credit rating wouldn't fall after
all.

Weight called the senior vice president for Southeast Asia Pacific.
He was in Hong Kong on business.

"I'm much more comfortable about Indonesia now," said the
senior vice president. "We can cut to one percentage point over
Libor for the first two years and one and an eighth after that."

Weight called Schile the next morning. "We've just put together
a new offer," he said. He read the terms. "Timing is very important." They had been over timing again and again; Allied had
to go to market before the Indonesian government did. "If we

91

don't get an answer from you by mid-July, the schedule is out the window." Allied had ignored the deadline in every other Morgan offer; Weight was starting to worry that he wouldn't have time to put together a syndicate.

"We're considering the alternatives," said Schile.

After he told Rick Schile that Bankers Trust was working on fixing the interest rate in a private placement, Mike Dacey called David Smith into his office. "Put together a proposal to fix the rate on that $100-million private placement," said Dacey.

Smith walked back to his desk. He took out a legal pad and started to scribble. After two years of grace, Allied would pay $13.75 million of principal every quarter—$55 million a year—for seven years. Smith studied his numbers. Bankers Trust would sell pieces of the loan to investors. The pieces didn't have to fit together—the pieces of a swap did—and that meant that Allied could fix whichever payments it wanted to. "I need estimates on some rates," Smith told the head of the capital market groups.

The man looked at Smith's sheet. He scribbled an estimated interest rate under each principal number.

Smith watched. "How long will this take to sell?" asked Smith.

The man looked over the numbers. "Two weeks," he said.

Just having interest rate estimates wasn't enough. Smith sat down at his desk to polish up a proposal. He worked on the pages for hours.

The secretaries left.

The cleaning lady came to vacuum the carpet around Smith's desk.

Finally the proposal was done.

Smith walked into Dacey's office to go through the numbers.

Dacey was working on a big loan to the Hercules Chemical Company. He looked up. "This makes sense," he said. "Check off with Mogan." Terrence Mogan, the senior vice president in charge of credit for the world corporate department.

It was nine o'clock at night. Smith took the elevator to Mogan's office on the sixteenth floor.

Mogan looked up from his papers.

92

"We've got a problem," explained Smith. He outlined the Allied deal. "We need a $100-million letter of credit to make the private placement fly."

Mogan asked a couple of questions. "Okay," he said. "Check off with MacDonald." The head of the world corporate department. Even Mogan couldn't sign off on a letter for $100 million.

Smith rode up to the seventeenth floor to see Ralph MacDonald. No problem.

Smith worked out a few loose ends. He finally took the elevator down to Park Avenue at eleven o'clock.

First thing the next morning, Friday, July 9, Smith Rapifaxed the bankers proposal to Allied.

Early that afternoon, Rick Schile called Mike Dacey. "We've decided to give Morgan the mandate for the $275-million loan," he said. "Bankers Trust will be comanager."

Dacey grinned. Bankers had pushed Morgan aside—and just making Morgan share the pedestal was a victory of sorts.

"We still haven't decided how to handle the $100 million at a fixed rate," said Schile.

Maybe Bankers could win that too.

Breck Dacey could hardly believe it. How could Morgan have won the mandate on the $275-million allied loan but not the $100-million rate fixing? He dialed Barbara Austell.

"That sounds odd," she said.

"Schile says that Bankers has its own idea that's different from ours," said Denny.

"I wonder what they're proposing," said Austell. "We looked at all the options. A swap is clearly the best."

"I don't know," said Denny.

"I'll talk to Schile," said Austell.

First, she had to figure out exactly how the swap would work. Austell sat at her desk. She got out a legal pad and a pack of cigarettes; she was trying to quit, but that could wait until after this deal. Austell drew four columns down the page. She filled in the expected project revenues. She marked down the amount of each Allied amortization payment. She thought. Eurobonds only paid interest once a year so a quarterly amortization wouldn't work. The match would have to be annual.

"I've gone through a whole pack of cigarettes," she told Denny and Weight later in the afternoon. "But I think I've got it. Allied wanted the swap to match the loan quarterly. That was too complicated. But I have a match year by year."

"That's probably okay," said Denny.

"There's still a problem," said Weight. "Every year Allied will make one fixed-interest payment on the counterparty's bonds. Every year the counterparty will make two payments on Allied's loan. There's a risk that the project will take the six-month floating payment from the counterparty but default on its annual interest come year-end."

Austell and Weight sat down in a conference room on the petroleum floor to brainstorm. They went through page after page on the legal pad; they lit cigarette after cigarette.

"What about an escrow account?" suggested Weight. Banks frequently insist that projects make payments into an escrow account because cash flow is so uneven.

"That might work," said Austell. She scribbled some numbers. She fiddled.

It worked. Instead of paying Allied twice a year, the swapping bank would make its half-year payment into an escrow account. The money would earn interest for six months. Morgan would swap interest payments with Allied once a year.

First thing next morning, Barbara Austell called Breck Denny. "I've got it," she said. She explained how the escrow account worked. "I'm going to 'fax' the proposal to Schile right now," she said. "We'll talk it through later today."

"This swap fits right into our structure," Schile told Austell that afternoon. "I like the deferred rate-setting mechanism too."

They talked through the nuts and bolts for a few minutes.

"Has anyone ever done a swap on a project before?" asked Schile.

"Well, no," said Austell. "But we can do it."

"We'll see," said Schile. He didn't commit.

Rick Schile called Breck Denny on Monday, July 18. "I talked to Bankers on Friday about fixing the rate with a private placement," said Schile.

So that was what Bankers Trust had proposed. Denny shook his head: the Morgan private placement team had said that a placement wouldn't work.

"I want your team to sit down with the Bankers team to talk about the Bankers idea," said Schile. "If you bankers all sit down together, you can work out the best solution."

Denny was silent for a minute. He'd never heard of a bank presenting its idea to the competition; Allied must be leaning toward Bankers. "Okay," he finally said. He didn't have much choice.

Rick Schile's Friday meeting with Bankers Trust was held in a basement conference room. It was hot outside but the room was freezing cold—and filled with smoke. David Smith thought that it was the most uncomfortable room he'd ever been in, even worse than the narrow, windowless one on the fourth floor where Schile usually held meetings.

"Let's go through this placement," said Schile. By now he had settled on fixing $100 million, amortized.

"Here's how it works," said Smith. He got out the yellow sheets that listed the amortization payments. "You can decide which payments you want to fix," he said.

Schile looked at the sheets. He started to circle payments.

Smith watched. Schile wanted to fix the long-term pieces.

"What's the rate?" asked Schile. He pointed to a payment.

Smith pointed to the estimate that the placement man had penciled in.

"How long will a private placement take?" asked Schile.

"Two weeks," said Smith.

"Is adding a private placement going to change the rest of the loan?" asked Schile. "I don't want to do reams of extra paperwork."

"There will be a little extra paperwork," said Smith. "Not reams. We'll have to include a description of Bankers Trust in the information memorandum since Bankers will be guaranteeing the payments."

"Has this ever been done before?" asked Schile.

"Yes," said Smith. "We sell paper backed by letters of credit all the time."

95

"Project paper?" asked Schile.

"You can sell almost any paper with a letter of credit," said Smith.

Schile nodded. "We'll have a decision soon," he said.

Smith drove back to Manhattan.

First thing Monday morning, Rick Schile called David Smith. "I want you to explain this idea to Morgan Guaranty," he said.

Smith was stunned. Banks don't explain their ideas to other banks. It was like Macy's talking to Gimbels. They don't.

"I'll set something up," Schile said.

Late that afternoon, Smith and the head of the Bankers private placement department caught a cab to Morgan headquarters at 23 Wall Street.

Denny and Austell and Weight were sitting in a conference room on the fifth floor.

Austell introduced herself.

The Bankers man from Houston walked in. He had never met the placement man. They introduced each other. Then they shook hands with the team from Morgan.

Everyone sat down.

Smith and Austell chatted about Allied. They chatted about the general problem of fixing the interest rate on a project loan.

"I understand that you're talking about a private placement," said Austell.

"Yes," said Smith. He didn't volunteer any details. "I understand that you're talking about an interest-rate swap." He hoped that Austell would tell him just how Morgan planned to make the swap payments amortized.

Austell didn't volunteer any details.

"Won't a private placement make the loan riskier to the banks in the syndicate?" asked Austell. The Morgan team had spent Friday night preparing a dozen questions to ask Bankers, and risk seemed to be the key. Since there were more lenders with a private placement, there was more chance that something would go wrong.

Smith wasn't sure how to answer. He didn't want to tell Austell that Bankers was planning to back the placement with a letter of credit; the letter would solve the risk problem. "I don't think we need to worry about the risk," he said.

Austell frowned. It sounded as if Smith hadn't thought about risk at all. Austell repeated the question.

Smith wouldn't answer.

"How quickly can you line up a placement?" asked Austell.

"Two weeks," said Smith.

Austell raised an eyebrow. The Morgan placement experts were sure that it would take at least six weeks.

Someone brought in a platter of sandwiches.

The bankers kept talking.

"I can't figure out why Allied called this meeting," said Smith two hours later. "Allied has to make this decision, not the banks."

"That's right," said Weight. "And Allied has to make a decision soon. Allied is running out of time."

Smith nodded. The loan had to be syndicated by September. That was only a month and a half away. Lining up a $100 million syndicated swap would take time.

The meeting broke up.

Weight and Denny and Austell walked back to Weight's desk.

"A swap fits better with the loan structure," said Austell. "I didn't hear anything at that meeting that made me change my mind."

"I wonder what rate Bankers told Allied it could get on the placement," said Weight. Smith hadn't volunteered.

"It must be close to our rate," said Austell. Otherwise Schile wouldn't be interested.

"We've got to call Schile," said Denny. "I promised we'd call as soon as the meeting was over."

Denny and Weight and Austell walked into the conference room behind Weight's desk. Denny switched on the speaker phone. He dialed Allied. "We've talked to Bankers Trust," said Denny.

"Well?" asked Schile.

"A private placement will work," said Austell. "But we don't think that a placement is a good answer. We are convinced that a swap is the best alternative."

"How do you know that a swap will work?" asked Schile.

"We've done lots of swaps," said Austell.

"But you said that no one had ever done one for a project," said Schile. "Have you ever done one with amortization?"

"I haven't," said Austell. "But it has been done." Once or twice. "A private placement won't mesh well with the rest of the Badak package. You want the financing to be self-contained. The swap is the best alternative."

Schile kept asking questions.

Austell started to get worried. Very worried. It sounded like Allied was leaning toward Bankers.

"Can you guarantee a fixed rate on the swap?" asked Schile.

"No," said Austell. The rate depended on the rate that the swapping bank got for its Eurobonds. That depended on the bond market in September. "I don't know what the markets will be like. Right now a plain vanilla swap is going at 80 above treasuries. You'd have to pay a premium."

"How high could that go?" asked Schile.

"Twenty-five basis points," said Austell. A quarter of a percentage point.

"Are you sure?" asked Schile.

"That's my best guess," said Austell. "Look, I can't make a promise, but you guys know me." She had worked on the Allied account on and off for six years. "You can trust me. I'm not going to tell you 100 if it's going to be 150. That's not the way I operate. That's not the way Morgan operates."

"We can get fixed-rate money at 70," said Schile.

Austell knew that. "But money you get by selling bonds at 70 over treasuries won't be project money," she said. "Bonds will be for the Allied account."

"True," said Schile. That might put pressure on the credit rating. "I'll get back to you."

Austell put the receiver in the cradle. "We've got to do something," she said. "Allied is moving away from the swap."

"What can we do?" asked Denny.

"Maybe we should talk to Roberto," suggested Austell. Roberto Mendoza, then the senior vice president in charge of merchant banking. "Roberto could talk to Allied."

"I'll ask," said Austell.

The meeting broke up.

Austell took the elevator back to the fourth floor. Mendoza happened to be walking by when Austell got to her desk. "You may have to call Allied about this swap," she said. "I think it would help if you told them that a swap is a routine transaction. We've done hundreds of them. It's nothing to worry about. It makes sense."

On Wednesday morning Mendoza hadn't yet gotten through. Then Rick Schile called Barbara Austell.

"We're going with the swap," said Schile.

Austell smiled. Mendoza didn't have to call after all. Morgan had won.

Now that Morgan had the mandate for the swap, Barbara Austell was under the gun. There was only a month to line up the counterparty. And the market for swaps was even worse than it had been in late June when Denny had first asked her how Allied could fix a rate. A U.S. government bond due in seven years was now paying 11.89 percent, the highest since September 1982.

Austell spent the day working on details. She didn't get home until almost ten that night.

At ten-thirty, the phone rang. Tokyo. Ten-thirty at night in New York is twelve-thirty in the afternoon in Tokyo.

Austell sat down at the kitchen table. "We got the mandate to do the Allied amortizing swap," she said. "Which banks are going to be interested?" She read off the first name from the queue list.

"Well," said Tokyo. He sounded skeptical. "Maybe. I'm not sure that they are going to be interested in an amortizing bond."

"What about this one?" asked Austell. The next name.

"I don't think they'll like the amortization either," said Tokyo.

"Maybe I should concentrate on Europe," said Austell.

That ruffled Tokyo. "The Europeans aren't going to like the amortization either," he said.

Austell and Tokyo kept talking. Austell didn't get to bed until well after midnight.

London called Austell in her office first thing Thursday morning. "I got your message," he said. Austell had put a note in the overnight "missile" to London before she left Wednesday. "We can't do anything right now. We might be able to find a bank that wants to do an amortizing swap, but we won't know until the week they go to market."

No surprise. Austell had talked to London about banks before.

Austell was on the phone to London and Tokyo all day. By Friday afternoon, she had pared the list down to six big banks: four Japanese and two European.

"We called the Bank of Tokyo and the Industrial Bank of Japan," said Tokyo. The two Japanese banks that were already in on the Allied Badak syndicate. "They liked the idea of a swap, but neither one has a September spot in the square."

"Then they're both out," said Austell. "Allied is adamant that the swap be done by October, just after the loan closes."

The list was down to five.

"This amortization schedule doesn't really fit our book," said one.

The list was down to four.

"What is the amortizing schedule going to do to our interest rate?" asked another.

The list was down to two.

Tokyo called Barbara Austell. "We've set up a meeting with one of the Japanese banks for next Wednesday," he said. August 10, the very day that Brian Weight had scheduled the key syndication meeting. Every bank that had been invited to join would send a representative to Houston to hear the details of the loan package, which Weight had already settled with Schile.

When the bankers sat down in the Grand Salon Ballroom at the Inn on the Park, Weight talked through the mechanics of the $275-million loan. He reviewed the risks.

Someone from Union Texas talked about the project.

An engineer made a report on the accident.

Austell stood up to make a slide presentation on the swap. She was very nervous: she had never spoken to a group before. The lawyers who had coached her told her not to write out a speech, just to jot down a few notes right before she walked onto the stage.

It was time for questions.

"Is there an insurance policy on Train B?" asked a banker.

"Yes," said the man from UTP. "Insurance pays everything but $5 million in costs and the $1-million deductible."

"Are the Japanese likely to try to renegotiate prices?" asked a third.

"Maybe," said Weight. "The Japanese are tough when it comes to negotiating oil and gas prices."

The room was silent. The bankers would ask the rest of their questions one-on-one; the others didn't need to hear.

"Okay," said Weight. "We're doing this syndication on a tight time schedule. You've only got until the fifteenth to make a decision." Two working days plus a weekend. Normally a bank gets two weeks.

A banker raised his hand. "We need an extra day to make a decision," he said.

"The fifteenth is the deadline," said Weight.

"The senior officers at my bank are on vacation," said another banker. "We can't make a decision until they get back."

"We need a decision," said Weight.

The meeting broke up.

A foreign banker walked up to Austell. He didn't speak English well. "I'm sure that was all very interesting," he said. "But maybe..." His voice trailed off. "The swap?"

Austell got out a sheet of paper and drew two boxes. She talked through the swap again.

The foreign banker seemed to understand.

Austell handed him her card. She wrote her home phone number on the back. "Call me if you still have questions," she said.

By then, a dozen bankers had gathered around. They all had questions about the swap. Austell thought that some of them had never heard of a swap before. She handed out business cards. She kept writing down her home number.

Finally the last banker left.

Austell went back to the hotel room.

It was four-thirty in Houston, six-thirty in the morning in Tokyo. Austell dialed.

"It went well," said the man in Tokyo. "We'll have an answer in a couple of days."

First thing next morning, Austell flew back to New York. Months ago, she and her husband had decided to spend that Friday with Austell's in-laws at their summer house in Pennsylvania. Austell had given her secretary the Pennyslvania number, and said to forward all calls regarding Badak.

Just after the Austells arrived, the in-laws' phone rang. It was a banker with a question about the swap.

Austell sat down at the dining room table. She started to explain.

101

The banker kept asking questions.

Austell was sure that he had never heard of a swap before. She talked through the mechanics.

Finally he understood.

Austell hung up.

The phone rang again.

It was another banker with a question about the swap.

Austell spent the whole day in the dining room talking to bankers about the swap. She kept talking to bankers about the swap all weekend.

Two days later, Austell got a call from Tokyo.

"That bank we talked to last week decided to pass on the swap," said the man. "They have to go to market now. They can't wait for Allied."

There was just one Japanese bank left: Sanwa, the sixteenth-largest bank in the world.

"Sanwa's queue week is in the middle of September," said Tokyo.

"Perfect," said Austell.

"We've got an appointment this Friday," said the man. August 19.

Austell marked her calendar.

Tokyo called right after the meeting. "Sanwa seemed interested," he said. "They like the amortizing swap; it balances their maturities."

Austell called London. If Sanwa fell through, she would have to find a European swap partner.

"We've been talking to two banks," said the man. "I think they're both interested."

Austell might have a backstop.

Tokyo called Tuesday morning.

Sanwa would swap.

"Great," said Austell.

The queue week would start Monday, September 12.

By then, Brian Weight had put together a syndicate. Just about everyone on the invite list wanted to join. Chase stayed out: Chase didn't like the collateral. Citi stayed out: its Indonesian book was full.

The market was off on Monday, the first day that Sanwa could sell. Interest rates on seven-year treasury notes rose to 11.49 percent.

"The market is bad," said the man in London. "Sanwa can't float $100 million worth of bonds. Not at 12⅜ percent. It will be closer to $80 million."

Allied needed $100 million. Austell would have to find another bank to swap the last $20 million. That was a problem, because banks don't usually sell bond issues so small. Fortunately, Morgan had done a $65-million cross-currency interest-rate swap earlier in the summer and hadn't been able to match $20 million of five-year bonds. Austell could swap that for $20 million of the Allied loan.

The market was bad on Tuesday too. Rates rose to 11.57 percent.

Wednesday rates fell.

Sanwa sold the bonds. The rate came in at 12⅜ precent.

Austell called Roger Matthews, Allied's director of finance; Rick Schile was on vacation.

"We're sure rates will fall," said Matthews. "We want the deferred rate-setting option."

"Okay," said Austell. "Tell me when you want to unwind." There would be a lot of paperwork.

Matthews hung up.

Austell and several officers talked about the deferred rate-setting procedure. Then Austell took the elevator up to the government bond desk. "Remember that $100 million deferred rate set that we talked about," she said. "We're going ahead."

"Okay," said the man.

Rates bounced up and down all week.

Matthews called on Monday, September 20. "We're worried," he said. "We think interest rates will come down, but we're not sure how far."

Austell read off a list of dates when key economic statistics would be released, and Morgan's estimates of what the numbers would be.

On Wednesday, September 22, interest rates started to rise.

Matthews called again. "I didn't realize how much this deferred rate setting would worry me," he told Austell. "I don't want to miss the low rate."

103

"We're watching," said Austell.

"We've thought about this," said Matthews. "If we can save an eighth of a percentage point, we're happy."

"You're nowhere near there," said Austell.

"No," said Matthews. "What I'd like to do is give you an order. If rates hit our number, we want to unwind."

"Okay," said Austell. Seven-year government bonds had been trading at 11.64 percent the day that Sanwa went to market. An eighth below that was 11.52 percent.

"We're a long way from there," said the head bond trader a little after lunch. "The seven-year treasury is at 11.67 percent."

Austell called Matthews.

"Let's see what happens," said Matthews. "You've got our order."

The bond market was flat most of the afternoon. At a little after three, prices began to rally.

The head bond trader called Barbara Austell. "We're still eight basis points over your target," he said. "But the rate is coming down."

"Doesn't the market close at four?" asked Austell.

"I can keep trading as long as there is someone to trade with," said the bond dealer.

Austell waited.

At four o'clock, the trader called again. "Sit tight," he said. "It looks like rates are going to come down more."

"I've got to visit a friend in the hospital tonight," said Austell. No one was going to bid for $100 million worth of treasury bonds after the market closed.

"Stick around," said the head trader.

Austell sat at her desk. The deal wouldn't go tonight.

At a quarter after five the trader called again. "We're four basis points off," he said. "Sit tight."

"Can you really sell bonds now?" asked Austell.

"Sure," said the man. "If I can find a buyer, I'll sell."

Austell waited.

At five thirty-five the trader called again. "One basis point off," he said.

Austell waited. She wouldn't get the rate tonight. No one traded after six. Certainly not $100-million blocks.

At a quarter to seven, the phone rang. It was the bond trader. "We just sold $100 million of treasuries at your rate," he said.

Austell called Allied. "You got your eighth of a point," she said. Morgan had done it.

After the Badak deal, Allied continued to generate bank assignments. In April 1985, Allied announced that it was selling half of Union Texas Petroleum to Kohlberg Kravis Roberts, a private conglomerate that specializes in leveraged buy-outs, for $1.7 billion. To line up the financing, Kohlberg had to pledge Union Texas assets as collateral—and that meant that the Badak loan had to be paid off. Rick Schile called Tom Kellogg, and Morgan quickly unwound the swap. Interest rates had dropped since Allied had fixed its rate, and Schile didn't want to be locked into the old payment schedule. Then, only a month later, Allied announced that it would merge with the Signal Companies; the $5-billion price made the merger the biggest nonoil combination in history.

In September, just after the Badak closing, Morgan hosted a dinner in honor of the Badak deal at the bank's suite at the Galleria on East Fifty-seventh Street. Rick Schile was there. Brian Weight and Breck Denny and Barbara Austell were there. So was Mike Dacey and his team.

There was lots of champagne.

There were a dozen toasts.

A couple of weeks later, Morgan sent Bankers a bill. As co-manager, Bankers got half the credit for the deal—and paid half the expenses.

Mike Dacey just laughed at the bill. He was busy with other things. Just after the Badak closing, he'd been promoted to senior vice president and reassigned to a dozen key Bankers Trust accounts including Allied, Coca-Cola, Nestlé and Reynolds Metals. The assignments poured in: a commercial paper deal for Coke, a fleet leasing for Xerox, financing for the Nestlé-Carnation merger, a Eurobond sale for Nabisco, financing for a Reynolds bauxite mine.

Meanwhile, Bankers Trust pressed forward in its campaign to

become a merchant bank. By the end of 1985, Bankers ranked fifteenth in the Eurobond-underwriting totals. By then, the bank had begun to sell shares of loan to investors just the same way companies sell "shares" of debt. But just after Bankers Trust began selling commercial paper in 1981, the Securities Industry Association sued the bank for violating Glass-Steagall, the law that forbids banks to underwrite stock. In the winter of 1984, the Supreme Court upheld the SIA on a technicality and remanded the case to the lower court. A year later, the Federal Reserve announced that distributing commercial paper was not underwriting and that Bankers Trust was not underwriting. The Bankers CP staff was jubilant, and Mike Dacey is sure that Bankers Trust can beat Wall Street yet.

But Bankers may not be able to beat Morgan. During 1984 and 1985, Morgan unveiled one innovative deal after another: morning to midnight defeasance, undated floating rate notes convertible into four year FRNs, long-term warrants with a call option, floaters sold by auction. Morgan was clearly the bank to reckon with in the Eurobond market—1984 underwritings totaled thirty-three deals worth $5 billion—and so the bank shifted emphasis from capital markets to mergers and acquisitions.

Tom Kellogg is still working on oil loans. In the spring of 1985, Brian Weight was transferred to London to supervise Morgan's lending to oil and gas projects in the North Sea. Breck Denny has his hands full calling on Allied and other New Jersey clients. Barbara Austell began a second maternity leave in July 1985—in August, she had a ten-pound baby boy named Robert—and although she enjoys the baby and the mystery writing, she was happy to get back to work. She missed the excitement of being at the bank that's the envy of the financial world.

(3)

Goldman, Sachs & Company

"And That's What Makes Goldman Sachs, Goldman Sachs"

"I can't believe Gulf is backing out of the merger," said Geoff Boisi. He pulled the telephone cord around his shoulder and sat down on the kitchen counter. "Fortune 50 companies don't do that."

"I know," said Steve Friedman. It was eleven o'clock Saturday morning, August 7, 1982, about the time that Friedman usually called to talk to Boisi about merger opportunities.

"It couldn't have come at a worse point," said Boisi. "We're in the depths of a recession. The stock and bond markets are already jittery."

"I just talked to Bob Rubin," said Friedman. "He says that Cities stock might fall to $22 a share." From $53. "We didn't have a big investment. We'll just get a kick in the shins." He paused. "Some traders had a lot of stock, though. There are going to be some big losses, and that's going to hurt the market."

"I know," said Boisi.

"Both Bob and I have had calls from a lot of people on the Street," said Friedman. "They sure would like to see us pull this one out."

Boisi looked out the kitchen window. The sun was shining. He hadn't spent a Saturday in Port Washington in weeks, and it sounded like he was going to spend this one on the phone to his partners instead of in the backyard with the kids. "We thought Gulf's price was high from the start," he said.

"You know," said Friedman. "Given what's happened, I'll bet a bidder could get Cities for a lot less than Gulf was offering. Cities is in a tough situation. The traders want to sell."

"Finding a buyer isn't going to be easy," said Boisi. "Boone Pickens said he was going to bid for Cities in May. Gulf didn't come in until the middle of June. There were more than two weeks when another company could have made an offer. No one did. Gulf says that it backed out because of pressure from the FTC. But people are saying that's not the real reason. There are rumors that Cities had overstated its reserves; there are rumors that the Cities people were proud and would be hard to work with. Still, one of the majors might bid for Cities if the price were right."

"Is a major really going to buy Cities with all those gas stations?" asked Friedman. "Couldn't we put together a group of smaller companies that could raise the $3 billion and divide Cities among themselves?"

"We could probably do that," said Boisi. "But not fast enough. Negotiating a breakup might take months. At the right price, Cities is going to go quickly. A smaller buyer has a chance only if he is very decisive. The first company to put a bid on the table has an advantage. Majors don't like bidding contests or bidding against each other."

"There's got to be an answer," said Friedman. "Cities has some valuable assets."

Boisi thought for a minute. "Maybe we could find a small company that's willing to buy Cities as an asset play: keep the oil and gas fields and sell the gas stations and the coal fields and the copper mine to raise cash," he said. "A deal like that could pay for itself."

"Who would be willing to do that?" asked Friedman.

"Probably not a major oil company," said Boisi. "Oil company executives are conservative. I'm not sure that they'd buy the concept, much less be willing to try." He paused. "But there's someone who might: David Murdock."

Friedman thought. Murdock was a long-time Goldman client, a close friend of Armand Hammer and Occidental Petroleum's largest shareholder.

"Murdock is very sophisticated, he's asset-oriented and he has a lot of money," said Boisi. "He's also on the Oxy board. Between them Murdock and Oxy can afford Cities."

"Why don't we try," said Friedman. He paused. "Of course, Oxy's not going to be the first name on the Cities list."

"In a raid situation, what a company likes and what it takes are two different things," said Boisi. "Given the circumstances, Cities may find Oxy a very friendly port."

Geoffrey Boisi is determined. He's thirty-five, with green eyes and wavy black hair. He's a workhorse, so devoted to doing deals that he's usually on the road four days a week; whenever he can, Boisi spends weekends coaching his two sons' soccer teams and antique hunting with his wife. Boisi is nervous about publicity— he refuses to be listed in *Who's Who* and turns down most interviews, but he's supercompetitive. Until he severed his Achilles tendon playing quarterback for the mergers and acquisitions department's touch football team, he had a no-holds-barred tennis game. He's hard-nosed. Once Boisi locked the door of the negotiating room and pocketed the key; no one was leaving until there was a deal.

Boisi grew up on Long Island and worked his way through Boston College selling real estate. After he graduated in 1969, Boisi headed to Wharton for an M.B.A. He landed a summer job at Goldman Sachs in New York as an investment-banking associate. In those days, the entire investment-banking division was on the same floor, and that meant that Boisi got a chance to watch the young, athletic four-man merger team line up deals in the corner. Boisi liked doing deals, and he thought he'd rather deal in companies than real estate. At the end of the summer, he took the youngest M&A associate to lunch. That did it. Boisi knew he belonged in M&A—and that he belonged at Goldman Sachs.

Goldman Sachs is known for its quality, not for its daring. The product focus: transactions so big that the CEO has to get involved. At Goldman, business comes first; one young associate was told that he ought to think about a honeymoon that was not contiguous with his wedding—otherwise he might not be able to finish an

109

important project on time. The emphasis: teamwork. For years, two partners shared the chairmanship; two partners run the investment-banking division; partners from different departments cooperate to put together any deal. Goldman won't raise money for casinos; it won't sell stock that has no voting rights; it won't shop merger bids.

The good-guy approach works. In 1982, Goldman was the largest partnership in the investment banking business with seventy-six partners, $478 million in capital and a return on equity of 40 percent. By then, Goldman boasted the biggest commercial paper business in the world; it handled 20 percent of the block trades on the New York Stock Exchange, and it claimed to have brokered more corporate marriages than any other banking firm in America.

Marcus Goldman, formerly a door-to-door ribbon salesman, started his commercial paper business in 1869. Early each morning he trekked from his office at 30 Pine Street in the heart of New York City's financial district to Maiden Lane to buy short-term notes from jewelry merchants; late in the afternoon, he resold the notes to the big commercial banks for a small profit. Goldman's son-in-law Samuel Sachs joined the firm in 1882, and soon Goldman, Sachs & Company had clients in Boston, Hartford and Philadelphia and an array of short-term products from commercial paper to letters of credit to foreign currency exchange. By the turn of the century, Goldman's commercial paper clients wanted long-term cash, so the firm tried its hand at underwriting stock. That was a big success, and soon Goldman's stock-issuing list included most of America's biggest merchants: United Cigar; Woolworth; Sears, Roebuck; and Brown Shoe.

When the stock market crashed on Black Thursday, Goldman Sachs' reputation crashed too. At the end of 1928, the firm had launched its "Goldman, Sachs Trading Co." mutual fund. Shares opened at $104 each and soon rose to $232. By 1933, the price had fallen to less than $2 a share, and Eddie Cantor, one of the big investors, soon made the debacle famous: a stooge in his vaudeville routine squeezed a bone-dry lemon and announced that he was "the margin clerk for Goldman Sachs."

Goldman wasn't on its back for long. Sidney Weinberg, the managing partner, had an unparalleled network of friends—General Electric chairman Charles E. Wilson, New York Stock Exchange president Keith Funston, U.S. President Franklin Delano Roosevelt—and uncanny financial savvy. He garnered new business from Woolworth and Sears; he lured General Electric from Morgan Stanley; he signed on the Ford family when Ford Motor first sold stock in 1956. By then, Weinberg was known around the world as "Mr. Wall Street," with seats on the boards of thirty-one client companies.

Weinberg liked to boast that he had made Goldman into a financial department store: clients could buy everything from underwriting muscle to merger and acquisition advice. For years, Goldman had been the only investment bank with a merger department. The team specialized in selling family-owned companies to public corporations, and running sealed-bid auctions. In 1974, Inco, the classy Canadian nickel refiner, staged a raid on ESB, the Philadelphia battery manufacturer and Goldman client. Overnight, raids became the rage, and Goldman Sachs was in on the ground floor.

Goldman quickly became the power to reckon with in the corporate defense business. The firm adopted a policy of never representing hostile raiders and of never shopping bids—never telling one company what another has already bid in order to raise the first company's bid. One of Goldman's specialties was finding a "white knight" company to ride to the rescue with a high friendly bid. The secret: Goldman's massive new business department files on five thousand giant American companies. In 1982, Goldman put together sixty-nine deals, thirty-four worth over $100 million, more than any other firm on the Street. "And that," goes the slogan, "is what makes Goldman Sachs, Goldman Sachs."

The defense business hadn't yet taken off when Geoff Boisi got his summer job in 1970, and in those days, the firm had a strict policy of keeping new hires out of M&A: mergers were for veterans. Boisi negotiated his way into the job and quickly proved his mettle. In 1978, Boisi, then thirty-one, became Goldman's youngest partner.

In the spring of 1981, Boisi got a call from a Goldman new-business vice president. "I'm going to see the chief financial officer of Cities Service," he said. Cities Service was the nineteenth-largest oil company in America, and a company that Goldman Sachs had been courting for years. "The chairman of Cities thinks his company is vulnerable to a takeover, and the CFO wants to talk to you about defenses. Can I make an appointment?"

"Sure," said Boisi. Boisi's father, the vice chairman of Morgan Guaranty, happened to be a director of Cities Service, and that meant that Boisi paid particular attention to the company. The merger department had been watching Cities ever since Charles Waidelich (pronounced *Way*-delick) had been named chairman that April.

Charles Waidelich is meticulous. At fifty-two, he's dapper, with clear blue eyes and wavy silver hair. Waidelich fishes in the summer, hunts quail and pheasant in the winter, and runs two miles a day at the Oral Roberts Center in Tulsa after work. He's an American history buff—lately he's been reading up on Thomas Jefferson—and he likes to spend vacations driving through New England, Colorado and the Texas plains. When a reporter asked about his low public profile, Waidelich snapped that he wasn't a "P. T. Barnum."

Waidelich grew up in Ohio and graduated from Purdue University with a degree in civil engineering in 1951. He spent two and a half years designing pipelines for Cities Service; then he logged two years in the Army's photomapping department. As soon as he got out of the service, Waidelich was back at Cities directing petroleum transportation. He headed the team of Cities executives that supervised construction of the Colonial pipeline from Houston to New York Harbor and later ran the industrial chemical division; two years later, he was Cities executive vice president for operations, and in 1970 was named president. In 1981, he was promoted to chief executive officer.

The Cities Waidelich inherited had big problems. During the 1970s, the company had diversified into half a dozen nonoil ventures—plastics, coal, chemicals, even a copper mine—and many of the ventures hadn't panned out. Cities' oil and gas reserves had fallen by 21 percent over the past five years, despite a 21 percent-a-year increase in the annual exploration budget. Waidelich thought that the problem was that looking for oil took capital and Cities didn't have enough capital to look for oil—along with all the other projects Cities had started. So he put the copper, coal and chemicals operations up for sale and wrote off the plastics business. That made sense, but it left Cities vulnerable. The write-down pushed the company $49 million into the red in 1981.

In the summer of 1980, when Waidelich was still just president of the company, the chairman of Cities Service got a call from Boone Pickens, chairman of tiny Mesa Petroleum. Pickens was known in the oil patch for his pot shots at industry management.

"Are you interested in a merger with Mesa?" asked Pickens.

"No," said the chairman. "Definitely not."

The chairman thought that no meant no, but not to Pickens. Pickens figured he could buy the Cities cheap and manage it himself. He put in a big order for Cities Service stock.

The chairman found out. He called Pickens. "I'm not interested in a merger," he repeated. "I already told you that."

Trading in Cities stock surged. The Cities executives figured that Pickens was buying.

In late April 1981, the week Charles Waidelich was named Cities chief executive officer, one of his assistants called. "Guess who else is buying our stock?" said the assistant. "Nu-West." The Canadian oil company. Waidelich had never heard the name.

Someone from Nu-West called the next day to say that the company owned 7.2 percent of Cities stock. It wanted to swap the stock for Cities' Canadian properties.

"No way," said Waidelich.

Meanwhile, Conoco, America's ninth-largest oil company, was on the market. Waidelich wondered if Cities Service could be far behind. He sent his chief financial officer to New York to find out.

The chief officer called on half a dozen investment bankers. One of them was Goldman Sachs.

"What do you think is going to happen to Cities Service?" asked the CFO when he sat down in Boisi's office that afternoon. "Are we more vulnerable with that block in the hands of Nu-West? Should we buy it back?"

Boisi hesitated. It wasn't quite clear why the CFO was asking.

Was Cities unhappy with the advice of First Boston Corp., its investment banker, and looking for someone new? Or was the CFO trying to find out if Goldman was representing a potential bidder? Or did he just want some free advice? "Look," Boisi finally said. "I can tell you what I think, but I don't want you to tell me anything confidential about Cities Service." If the CFO gave Boisi confidential information, then Goldman couldn't represent a white knight or arbitrage a Cities deal.

The CFO nodded. He figured if Boisi was being so careful, Cities' future must be bleaker than he had thought.

"Cities is in a precarious position," said Boisi. "Boone Pickens has given you a high profile. The Nu-West block is a problem. Nu-West wants to make money on that stock. They can make money by selling the block back to you at a profit, by swapping the block for some of your assets or by selling the block at a premium to someone who wants to buy all of Cities."

"What can we do?" asked the CFO.

"There are a lot of possibilities," said Boisi. "You can buy your stock back, you can start a self-tender, you can file legal action, you can sell treasury stock to a 'big brother,' you can make a defensive acquisition." He talked through each alternative. "If a bidding war starts, you can find a white knight."

The CFO nodded. He hoped it wouldn't come to that. "What if we do nothing?" he asked.

"Nu-West will threaten to sell the block to someone who will bid for the whole company, or they'll bid for Cities themselves," said Boisi.

In August, Boone Pickens announced that he had bought 3.9 percent of Cities stock and that he wanted to buy the Nu-West stake.

Waidelich lined up a $3.5-billion loan. He used part of the money to buy back Nu-West's Cities stock. Cities paid $306 million, $51 a share, and $24 million over market. Cities didn't buy the Pickens stock. They had bought back enough.

The chairman of U.S. Steel called. "We're interested in oil," he said.

"What about buying a block of Cities Service?" asked Waidelich. "We're looking for a 20 percent investor." A big brother.

But before Waidelich could put together a deal, Mobil bid $5.1

billion for Marathon, the nation's sixteenth-largest oil company. U.S. Steel, represented by Goldman, charged to the rescue at $6 billion. Word was that Cities was next on the Mobil hit list.

Waidelich called around a bit. He tried the chairman of R. J. Reynolds and the chairman of General Electric. But neither seemed enthusiastic about buying a block of Cities stock.

Then, at the end of May 1982, Waidelich picked up a rumor that Pickens was putting together a group of investors to buy Cities.

Waidelich called First Boston, which was spearheading the defense.

The team huddled.

By the end of the week, they had settled on a strategy: Cities would bid for Mesa, Pickens' company.

Before Cities could launch the bid, Pickens called.

"I'm about to launch a bid," he said. "Will you tell the board?"

"No," said Waidelich. "If you want to bid, you have to put your offer in writing."

Hours later, the word was on the tape: Cities had bid for half of Mesa at $17 a share, 25¢ a share over market.

Pickens announced a bid for 15 percent of Cities for $45 a share. Cities was then trading at $35.50.

Waidelich raised his offer to $21 a share.

Pickens hung tight.

Geoff Boisi smelled business. He asked the oil and gas specialist in the merger department to do a valuation study of Cities Service. The numbers were ready by the end of the week: $52 to $58 a share. Boisi looked at a list of oil companies: Mobil, unsuccessful raider of first Conoco and then, a year later of Marathon, was now a rumored suitor of Cities Service; Texaco, said to have lined up $5.5 billion to buy Conoco the previous summer; Allied Corporation, oil and chemical conglomerate that was said to have looked at Conoco and Marathon; Gulf, seventh-largest oil company in America, known to be on the lookout for U.S. reserves.

In the middle of June, Boisi called the executive vice president of Gulf.

"Cities Service?" said the executive vice president. He sounded evasive. "Well, I don't know. I'm going on vacation. I'll give it some thought."

Boisi hung up. Gulf didn't seem very interested.

The executive vice president hadn't been leveling with Boisi; he *was* interested in Cities but not in hiring an investment banker. He cut his own deals. In fact, several days before the Gulf EVP got the call from Boisi, one of Cities' directors got word of Gulf's interest. The director called Waidelich. Then the Gulf EVP had called Martin Lipton, the ace takeover lawyer from Wachtell, Lipton, Rosen & Katz, who was representing Cities.

"We think Cities is a good fit," the EVP had said. "Antitrust isn't going to be a problem."

Then, a couple of days after Boisi's approach, the chairman of Gulf called Waidelich from Canada. "They're hawking your company," he said. The investment bankers. "Why don't we talk."

"Cities is bidding for Mesa," said Waidelich.

Gulf kept calling.

Waidelich decided to find out what the chairman had in mind.

By June 17, the deal was done: Gulf would buy Cities for $63 a share, 40 percent higher than Mesa's bid, a total of $5 billion. Cities and Mesa had agreed to drop the bids for each other; as part of the deal, Pickens would sell his Cities stocks to Cities for $55 a share, $11 a share more than he had paid.

The arbitrageurs, aka "arbs," traders who specialize in takeover situations, borrowed millions to buy Cities stock. It looked like easy money. The shares were trading at $55 each; Gulf would buy them back for $63.

Ivan F. Boesky Corporation bought a million shares.

O'Connor Associates bought a million shares.

Bache bought shares. Merrill Lynch bought shares. Bear, Stearns bought shares. Goldman bought shares.

Soon 85 percent of the stock was sitting in the bank, ready for Gulf to buy.

Oil prices slid. By the end of July, U.S. wellhead prices were down $3 a barrel; OPEC members were cheating on their quotas.

The rumors started. Gulf was going to back out. Cities had fudged its numbers. The Gulf directors belatedly realized that Pickens couldn't have raised his bid to more than $50 a share—and that Gulf could have won Cities for $53 a share, not $63.

The arbs laughed. Fortune 50 companies didn't back out once a contract had been signed. Fortune 50 companies kept their promises.

Before Gulf and Cities could merge, they needed to have the go-ahead from the government trust busters. Since both companies were in the oil-refining and -marketing businesses, Gulf would have to sell some of Cities' gas stations, pipelines and maybe the refinery before the Federal Trade Commission (FTC) would give the all clear. The merger automatically went on hold for twenty days while Gulf and the government negotiated about what had to go. The talks started. Gulf stalled. On Thursday, July 29, the FTC got a temporary restraining order blocking the merger for an extra ten days—they still hadn't reached an agreement.

Gulf called an emergency board meeting.

Waidelich flew from his Tulsa office to Pittsburgh to attend the meeting, but the chairman of Gulf wouldn't let him in. "Don't worry," the chairman said. "I'll tell the directors how you feel."

A couple of days later, Waidelich found out what was causing the FTC delay: Gulf didn't want to sell the Cities refinery. Waidelich dialed Gulf.

"We might be willing to shave the price if you have to sell the refinery," he said. A couple of dollars a share.

"We'll think about that," said the Gulf chairman. "Let me figure out how much we're going to lose."

The chairman called Waidelich again the next morning. "We're reviewing all the FTC demands," he said. "We'll try to figure out how much the losses total."

"When I said we'd adjust the cost, I was talking about just a refinery," said Waidelich. He wasn't sure he wanted Cities to pay Gulf's losses so Gulf could meet every FTC demand.

The chairman of Gulf didn't call again until Friday, August 6. "We've just had a board meeting," he said. "We're going to make an announcement shortly." The chairman of Gulf paused. "We're pulling out," he said. "We're not going to buy Cities Service."

Waidelich was stunned. "That's terrible," he said.

"I know," said the chairman of Gulf. "I feel terrible."

That afternoon, Geoff Boisi got a call from Bob Freeman, the senior Goldman arb. "Did you see the wire on Gulf?" asked Freeman.

"No," said Boisi.

"Take a look," said Freeman.

Boisi punched up the news on his Quotron screen:

Gulf Oil Corp. said that it has exercised its right to terminate its tender offer for Cities Service. Over the past two weeks, Gulf Oil said, it has made detailed proposals to resolve the antitrust objections of the Federal Trade Commission. As a result of discussions with the FTC this week, Gulf said, it has become clear that the FTC is unwilling to accept the Gulf proposals.

Boisi couldn't believe it.

And he knew the timing couldn't have been worse. The past six months had been one disaster after the next. At the beginning of April, Argentina had declared war on Great Britain and the British had frozen Argentine bank assets. Then Braniff Airways had gone bankrupt. In May, the Chase Manhattan Bank had lost $137 million when Drysdale Securities went broke. In July, the Continental Illinois Bank had lost $150 million when the Penn Square Bank of Oklahoma City went belly-up. Mexico was near bankrupt. International Harvester was near bankrupt. The economy was in the throes of the worst recession since the 1930s. The Dow Jones Industrial Average was at 784, the lowest level in twenty-seven months. And now Gulf had left Cities Service hanging.

"The word is that the FTC problems are a smoke screen," said Freeman. "Antitrust wasn't a problem except that Gulf wanted it to be. This pull out could be a disaster."

Unless a white knight stepped in. Cities was a sitting target. The arbs owned the stock. And they wanted to sell.

Saturday morning, Steve Friedman, head of the Goldman investment-banking department, called Geoff Boisi to talk about opportunities. Friedman and Boisi agreed to contact David Murdock about a bid from Oxy Pete. Boisi knew Murdock: he'd represented Iowa Beef Processors, then controlled by Murdock, when Oxy bought it in 1981 for $746 million in stock.

By Sunday night, Boisi had an answer. "The Doctor is interested," said the partner who had called Murdock. Dr. Armand Hammer, chairman of Oxy Pete. "He's asked David to orchestrate this."

118

* * *

Armand Hammer is mercurial. At eighty-four, he has a hawkish nose and piercing dark eyes. A personal friend of U.S. Senator Charles Percy, he's so chummy with the Russians that Leonid Brezhnev gave him a plush apartment in Moscow and OXY 1, Hammer's 727, is one of the few private planes allowed in Soviet air space. He's known for his collection of art masterpieces and ninety-four-horse stable. His philosophy: "When you see an opportunity, grab it by the forelock."

Hammer has an iffy reputation in financial circles. He's forever announcing a big deal that doesn't pan out. He's been in trouble with the Securities and Exchange Commission three times, and in 1975, he was indicted for illegal personal political contributions. Hammer keeps Oxy in the black by selling assets—and he's so famous for firing Oxy presidents that company executives are in awe of him. The company president had to lie when Hammer demanded an explanation for what had caused a sudden rise in Oxy's stock price: the president didn't dare say that the stock jumped on the rumor that Armand Hammer had just died.

A native of the Bronx, the son of an impoverished Russian immigrant radical, Hammer was a student at the Columbia medical school when he stepped in to manage the failing family drug company. He lined up a boarder to take lecture notes, and spent his days straightening out company finances and buying "medicinal" whiskey; by the time he graduated in 1921, Hammer had made his first million, mostly by selling liquor under the noses of prohibition agents. Then he was off to Russia to spend six months studying the typhus epidemic. But Hammer never got around to that; he soon made friends with V. I. Lenin and agreed to line up a wheat deal with the U.S. government. Soon Hammer was head of a thriving trading company.

In 1924, when Lenin's successor, Joseph Stalin, cracked down on foreign businessmen, Hammer fled to the U.S. with his collection of Russian art masterpieces. During the next twenty years, he made millions in whiskey distilling, beer barrel manufacturing and Black Angus cattle breeding. In 1956, Hammer liquidated his extensive holdings and announced that he planned to live a quiet retirement in Los Angeles. Like many millionaires, he was on the lookout for a tax break, and later that year, Hammer sank $50,000 into a near-bankrupt oil company called Occidental Petroleum.

Oxy Pete didn't perform as planned. Instead of turning in quarter after quarter of tax losses, Oxy struck oil. Hammer, bored by retirement, decided to go back to work as president of Occidental. He didn't know anything about oil and gas, but he did know about negotiating. When Libya struck oil in 1961, Hammer flew to Tripoli and convinced King Idris to grant Oxy a concession. Then Hammer bought a company called Hooker Chemical & Plastics Corporation and schemed to swap Florida phosphate for Soviet potash.

By 1969, Oxy was the sixth-largest international oil production company, topped only by consortiums like Aramco and governments like Kuwait. Then Muammar al-Qaddafi overthrew the Libyan monarchy. Qaddafi needed more oil revenue, and Oxy, with only one source of crude, was the weakest driller. Qaddafi threatened to stop the flow if Oxy didn't grant him better terms. It did, and the balance of power in the oil world suddenly shifted. Now it was the oil-producing countries, later formally organized as OPEC, that called the shots.

Hammer was determined never to be squeezed again. He drilled in the North Sea, in Venezuela, in Nigeria and in Peru. And struck it rich. At the same time, Hammer diversified. He bought Island Creek Coal Inc., the third-largest coal producer in America; he bought Iowa Beef Processors, America's largest fresh-meat-packing company; he made a raid on the Mead Corporation, the forest products giant. When he lost the Mead battle, he vowed never again to try a hostile deal.

The wheeling and dealing raised eyebrows on Wall Street—what was Occidental Petroleum doing mining coal in China? or trying to mint coins for the Moscow Olympics?—and it didn't make the company less vulnerable. Oxy earnings were highly cyclical and profits were risky. Libya could cut back crude quotas; Britain could raise taxes on the North Sea take; the U.S. government could pressure Hammer to stop selling fertilizer to the Russians. Risk meant that Oxy Pete got bad debt ratings, and that meant that Hammer couldn't raise money cheap. What Hammer needed was stability, and the most logical way to get that was to find American oil. Or better yet, to buy a company that had it.

Hammer flipped through annual report after annual report. Nothing seemed quite right. Companies with big fields were out of Oxy's price range.

In June 1982, just after Boone Pickens and Cities launched their raids on each other, Hammer flew to New York to talk to stock market analysts. After the presentation, Pickens' investment banker pulled the Oxy president aside. The president said that Oxy was indeed interested in Cities, but that Oxy didn't make hostile bids.

Saturday morning, the day after Gulf dropped its offer, Chuck Waidelich drove to the Southern Hills Country Club in Tulsa to watch the PGA golf tournament. Waidelich doesn't play golf himself, but he needed a break. He figured he couldn't do anything about the Gulf pull-out until Sunday anyhow. He watched the first couple of rounds. Then he headed home.

"New York called," said Waidelich's wife when he came in the door.

Waidelich dialed.

"We've picked up the word that some traders are peddling their blocks of Cities stock for as little as $30 a share," a Cities executive vice president told him. Two EVPs had flown to New York as soon as the Gulf announcement crossed the wire. "The traders could sell control of the company for a song. We've got to stop that. We've got to do something before the market opens on Monday."

Waidelich caught the next flight.

The Cities executives huddled with Martin Lipton, their lawyer, in Waidelich's suite at the Helmsley Palace Hotel on Saturday night.

First thing Sunday morning, Waidelich met the investment bankers for a briefing.

The next morning the Cities Service board met at its offices in the ITT building on Park Avenue.

"I don't understand what happened," said Waidelich. "I offered to talk about cutting the price. Gulf didn't seem interested."

"There's no excuse for what Gulf did legally or ethically," said the Cities general counsel. "We're considering suing for breach of contract. We're going to ask for $3 billion in damages."

"The word is that Gulf dropped because we overstated oil reserves," said the chief financial officer. "That isn't true, and it's very disturbing. We may have trouble finding another buyer."

"The arbs own 25 percent of our stock," said the investment banker. "If they all sell, the price will collapse to $20 a share."

"If the price falls to $20, a raider will be able to pick us off for less than $40 a share," said Lipton. "That will be a disaster for our shareholders."

"You can keep the price up by buying your own stock and at the same time announce that the company is for sale," said the investment banker. "Arbs will hold their stock to sell to the new buyer—and the new buyer will have to pay a premium price. If a buyer doesn't surface, we'll liquidate the company. Over a period of two years, we can get a good price for all your assets."

"I'm not sure buying our stock is a good idea," said Waidelich. "We already bought back the Nu-West stake and the Pickens stake. We've just purchased 12 percent of the company. We don't want to shrink our equity by buying another 20 percent."

"Buying our own stock is a waste of money," said a director.

The investment banker kept insisting that buying stock was a smart move.

"Well, maybe," one director finally said. "But it doesn't make sense to pay more than $30 a share."

"I'm not eager to liquidate the company," said Waidelich. "And I don't think we'll have to. I think we'll find a buyer. The chairman of Allied has already called. He's interested."

The directors talked.

Waidelich called for a vote. The board unanimously endorsed the two-point plan, which Waidelich summarized for waiting reporters from the *Wall Street Journal* and the *New York Times* as soon as the meeting broke up.

"We're now looking for a buyer that will come as close to the Gulf deal as possible," Waidelich told them. "We're buying our own stock to give us time to cut a deal. If we can't find a merger partner, we'll liquidate the company. I'm optimistic about a merger. I've already been approached by the head of a major U.S. company with a keen interest."

* * *

Geoff Boisi read the front-page *New York Times* article about Waidelich on the train from Port Washington to Manhattan the Monday after his talk with Friedman. That Cities was actively looking for bids was good news; Cities would be hard-pressed to turn down an offer from Oxy. That Cities had already been approached by the head of a "major company"—probably Allied— was worrisome; clearly the first company to bid had a big advantage; Goldman and Oxy had to move fast.

Boisi had already started putting together a proposal. On Sunday night, when they got the word from David Murdock that Hammer was interested in Cities, Boisi had pulled out a yellow legal pad and made out a check list of deal points. Boisi had called his oil and gas specialist at home to ask him to start updating the valuation study of Cities Service.

Now he called the arbitrage department and he talked to the oil analyst. He called Ken Brody in corporate finance. "Over the weekend, we talked to David Murdock about Occidental being a good fit for Cities Service. Oxy wants to look. We're putting a team together. This is going to be tough. We're going to have to be creative."

Ken Brody is independent. He's forty, balding and ever cheerful. Brody lives in an elegant apartment overlooking the East River; he zips about Long Island in a silver Porsche Targa and a red rollbar jeep; he plays squash at the Harvard Club several times a week. Brody plays Scrabble, backgammon and tennis. Brody is a big supporter of the Alvin Ailey Dance Theatre and a member of its board; he once rented New York's hottest night club for a night to celebrate the opening of modern art show at a friend's gallery. He's got a copy of *Who's Who* in his personal library: his secretary insisted he buy one the year he was listed.

Brody is the son of a laundry truck driver. He studied electrical engineering at the University of Maryland, but a summer working at Bell Labs convinced Brody that analyzing electrons wasn't for him. He didn't know what was. After he graduated in 1964, he started work on an M.D., but quit after six weeks and landed a job at the Chesapeake & Potomac Telephone Company in Washington, D.C. A year later, he was drafted and sent to Germany to manage a U.S. Army supply depot. When he got back to the States in 1968, Brody headed to Harvard Business School, and decided to become an investment banker. He got an offer from Goldman, Sachs' corporate finance department, and took the plunge. He quickly built a reputation as a crack thinker and a good people reader. Brody's corporate finance clients kept getting raided, and soon Brody was a pro at running defense. That made him the man on call if M&A needed extra hands.

From the start, Ken Brody and Geoff Boisi had been friends. They'd signed on the same year, made partner the same year, and worked together. They kept working together even after Boisi was running the merger department and Brody was focusing on financing high-tech companies.

When Geoff Boisi called to ask Brody to join the Occidental merger team, Brody agreed. "I figure the package has to total about $4 billion," said Boisi. Boisi's M&A staff had already done some preliminary computer runs.

It was clear that Oxy wouldn't pay with common stock. David Murdock owned 5 percent of Occidental; paying for Cities Service stock would dilute his influence, and it would also dilute earnings per share, and Hammer wouldn't like that. Oxy couldn't use bonds either; the company didn't have the cash flow to make interest payments.

"Oxy is going to have to sell assets to pay down the debt," said Boisi. "If our estimates come out wrong, Oxy will just have to sell oil and gas partnerships. We'll keep thinking. There has to be a way."

Boisi called the project team into the conference room. "We need to think about lockups," he said. A device that would discourage other bidders from topping Oxy.

The team talked.

Finally they settled on a lockup option to buy 13.75 million Cities shares at $50 in cash if the Oxy proposal fell through. If another bidder bought Cities, Oxy would profit.

"Who are the likely competing bidders?" asked Boisi.

The team put together a list.

Boisi handed the sheet to one of his assistants. "Run these through

124

the computer," he said. "We need to know what buying Oxy does to each company's cash flow and balance sheet and earnings."

"What's the best way to present an offer?" asked Boisi. "Do we want to bid at our first meeting with Waidelich?"

Yes. Bidding first was critical.

"Then what?" asked Boisi.

A bear hug—a high cash offer with a time fuse—and then a cash tender direct to the shareholders if it wasn't accepted. Making a tender offer set a deadline, and without a deadline, Cities could stall indefinitely and Occidental would just be a decoy, or stalking horse, for a bid by another company.

The meeting broke up.

Meanwhile, Boisi tried to find out what a merger combined with sinking oil prices would do to Oxy's stock price and to oil prices. Lower prices would cut Oxy cash flow, and it was clear that prices were headed lower.

Brody walked over to Boisi's office. They still had to settle the payment package.

"We need a security that Cities will be comfortable with," said Boisi.

"The Cities board is going to question Oxy's credit rating," said Brody.

"What does Cities know best?" asked Boisi. "Its own assets."

"Why don't we pay Cities with a Cities note?" said Brody. "We can tag a pool of assets to sell to pay the principal."

That made sense. Boisi had already planned to sell Cities assets to pay.

"What about a zero coupon bond?" suggested Brody. A bond that pays no interest but sells at a big discount to face value; Cities would make its money when Oxy paid off the bond at face value at maturity. No one had ever bought a company with zero coupon bonds—but that didn't matter if it worked.

Boisi nodded.

The head zero trader was there. Brody talked to him about the bond.

"Oxy can't afford to buy Cities just with zeroes," said Brody. "Oxy won't be left with enough equity. We'll have to pay for the rest with preferred stock. The Cities shareholders might not like that, but there isn't an alternative."

Brody and the traders settled on a package of bonds and preferred stock.

"What will that do to the credit rating?" asked Boisi.

Brody looked at the numbers.

So did the head of the Goldman credit department.

"Oxy debt is currently rated BBB + by Standard & Poor's," said Brody. "I'll bet that buying Cities with this package is going to push that down to B −."

B − was no good. B − securities were junk; B − companies had trouble raising cash.

"Let me have my people check that," said Brody. The Goldman team had just developed a computer program that mimicked the S&P process.

"Okay," said Boisi.

The run was done a couple of hours later.

"Triple B," said Brody. Investment quality, barely.

The package would work.

David Murdock flew in on Wednesday. He asked a lot of tough questions. "Looks good," he finally said. "Buying Cities Service is a way for Oxy to get oil and gas cheap."

Boisi called his father, vice chairman of Morgan Guaranty and a Cities director. "Goldman is representing a client that is interested in Cities," he said. "If that is a problem for you, I will excuse myself from the deal."

"It isn't a problem," said James Boisi.

Geoff Boisi called Waidelich. Oxy and Cities would meet for lunch on Friday.

Late Thursday afternoon, Boisi and Brody and the team headed to the Carlyle Hotel on Madison Avenue at Seventy-sixth Street to meet with Armand Hammer. Hammer had booked a big conference room for meetings; he was staying at his "hideaway" carriage house in Greenwich Village.

"Let's go over the numbers," said Boisi.

The bankers and executives talked.

"Buying Cities Service will make Occidental the eighth-largest American oil company," gloated Hammer. "Pretty soon, instead of Seven Sisters, there will be eight."

"We've got to settle the loose ends," said Boisi.

Everyone started to talk at once.

The president of Oxy stood up. He pointed to Boisi. "You stay," he said. He pointed to Brody. "And you. Everyone else leave."

The others started to leave.

They weren't going fast enough.

"Get out, get out," yelled the president.

Boisi and Brody and Hammer and Murdock talked about the concept of buying Cities and paying off the debt by selling assets.

The Goldman team needed to know whether Oxy would see Oxy assets too. Oxy would. The Goldman team wanted to make it crystal clear that buying Cities stretched Oxy to the limit.

"I understand," said the president. "If this works, we'll be heroes. If it doesn't, there will be no island small enough or far enough away for us to hide on."

By Friday morning, the offer was set. Oxy would pay $4 billion in cash, zero coupon bonds and preferred stock; Oxy would also get an option on a block of Cities Service stock; if Oxy got topped by another bidder, it would get expenses back from the profit on reselling the shares.

Boisi and Murdock and several of the takeover lawyers on the Oxy team drafted a letter to Waidelich explaining the offer. It was finished and cleared with Hammer at eleven Friday morning, just an hour before the lunch with Waidelich.

"We want this lunch to go smoothly," said Boisi. "We have to be firm. We don't want a misunderstanding. This is our best offer. We can't raise."

Everyone agreed.

"It's important that Oxy have just one spokesman," said Boisi.

"When the Doctor is in the room, Oxy has only one spokesman," said the president.

Chuck Waidelich and his team got to the Carlyle just after noon. Geoff Boisi introduced Armand Hammer. They shook hands.

Everyone sat down. Hammer sat in the center facing Waidelich; David Murdock was on Hammer's right.

Hammer started to talk about the weather. He drifted off.

Boisi didn't say anything. Hammer was the spokesman for Occidental.

Waidelich wondered what the Oxy-Goldman team was waiting for.

Hammer stood up and strode out of the room.

Waidelich looked at his investment banker. He looked at Boisi. This was certainly a strange way to start talks about a merger.

Everyone relaxed. The bankers and executives chatted.

Hammer came back in.

Everyone stiffened again.

Hammer looked around. "Let me tell you how I got started in the oil business," he said. He told the story of sinking fifty thousand dollars into Oxy as a tax shelter—and then building the company into a petroleum giant.

Waidelich shifted in his seat. He thought he'd come to talk about how the two companies fit together.

The waiters began to serve.

Hammer told another Oxy story.

Waidelich tried to make small talk.

Then someone knocked on the door. It was a Goldman vice president with a stack of papers. Boisi handed them to Hammer.

"Oxy wants to increase U.S. oil reserves," said Hammer. "We've been looking at Cities for a long time. We like the company. We like the company so much that we'd like to make a proposal to buy Cities Service." He passed the copies of the letter around the table.

Waidelich looked at his. It wasn't signed.

"We think that the highest compliment that one company can pay another is to offer to take significant dilution to buy it," said Hammer.

The man from First Boston choked. His fork clattered against his plate. He hadn't expected a bid. "We've got to go," he said. He stood up. "Come on." He tugged on Waidelich's sleeve.

Everyone stared at the banker.

Waidelich shook his arm loose. "We'll stay," he said.

The banker sat down. He picked up his fork.

Hammer tried to smooth things over. "Let's just talk this through," he said. He looked at his copy of the letter. "This is not a formal offer. It's just a proposal."

Murdock sat up in his chair. That wasn't what they'd agreed. He banged his palms on the table and leaned toward Waidelich. "This is a formal offer," he said.

Hammer glared. "David," he said. "It was agreed that I would speak for Occidental at this meeting."

The president of Oxy gulped his drink.

"We've put together a brochure of information about Cities Service," said the Cities chief financial officer. "I can get you a copy of that."

"No," said Boisi. "I think we have all the information we need at the moment." Oxy would have to sign a confidentiality agreement to get the book; after that, Oxy couldn't make a offer direct to the shareholders—and Boisi wanted to keep the options open.

The man from First Boston frowned.

"Let's go through the terms of your proposal," said Waidelich. They talked.

"This is less than $50 a share," said the man from First Boston. "That's not nearly enough."

"There may be a little price flexibility," said Hammer.

Murdock banged his fist on the table. "There is no flexibility," he said. "This is the price and not a penny more."

Hammer glared.

The Cities chief financial officer went out to call the Cities lawyer. "The lawyer said leave," he whispered to Waidelich when he came back in. "He said to make sure that we don't take a copy of the proposal with us."

Waidelich stood up. He left his letter next to his plate.

The Cities chief financial officer stood up.

The man from First Boston stood up.

"We'll be talking," said Waidelich.

They marched out the door.

Friday afternoon, Geoff Boisi got a call from the man at First Boston.

"I can't believe you're doing this," he said.

"Doing what?" asked Boisi. "All we want to do is make a proposal."

The man from First Boston mumbled something about a liquidation.

Boisi shook his head. "We ought to meet," said Boisi. "We need to talk. We want to compare views on what your assets are worth. Oxy is going to have to sell some assets to pay for Cities. Oxy assets and Cities assets."

"Let me send you a copy of our brochure," said the man from First Boston.

"No," said Boisi. "We need to meet."

The man from First Boston hesitated. "The Cities board is scheduled to consider the proposal on Monday," he said. "We can talk at my office on Sunday afternoon."

The meeting wasn't productive. The Cities chief financial officer, who joined the group, kept trying to give Boisi the Cities information book. The man from First Boston made it clear that the minimum price was $55 a share.

"We have to try to get this back on the right track," Boisi said later when he sat down with Joseph Flom, Oxy's takeover lawyer from Skadden, Arps, Slater, Meagher, & Flom. "We have to show some flexibility. They are obviously concerned that if they encourage us they are choking off other alternatives. They obviously want a higher price."

"Let's waive the lockup option," said Boisi. "Let's let them shop our bid." Show the terms of the Oxy offer to other companies that might be willing to top it.

Murdock agreed.

"Let's give it a try," said Hammer.

Boisi called the man from First Boston on Monday morning. "We want to respond to your concerns," he said. "Have Mr. Waidelich call the Doctor."

Waidelich called just before four.

"Occidental will drop the demand for a stock option," said Hammer. "We will let you shop our bid."

"I need that in writing," said Waidelich.

"You and I must have a face-to-face meeting," said Hammer.

"Maybe," said Waidelich. "But we can't do it now. It's after four. My board meeting starts at four-thirty. There isn't time."

"We need to talk," said Hammer. "Ask the board to recess the meeting. We'll talk tonight."

130

Waidelich paused. "Your offer expires at six. We don't have time to talk."

"True," said Hammer. "I'll change the deadline. It's midnight."

"I've got to get to the board meeting," said Waidelich.

"I'm waiting for your call," said Hammer.

The Armand Hammer lunch seemed to Chuck Waidelich like a scene straight out of a W. C. Fields movie—and however serious the offer was, the price was too low, about $47 a share. But no second bidder had presented himself, although Waidelich had been trying to find one. It wasn't easy. He kept saying that the Gulf announcement notwithstanding, antitrust wasn't a problem; Cities hadn't overestimated reserves.

"We've looked, but we haven't made a decision," said the chairman of Mobil.

"I'm looking," said the chairman of Texaco. "But I haven't made up my mind."

"We'll look," said the chairman of Sohio.

The chairman of Getty Oil was on vacation. Waidelich didn't even leave a message.

By Monday afternoon, a week and a half after Gulf dropped out, there were still no new bids. There was just the Oxy proposal.

Then Hammer called with the concessions. He asked for a meeting, but Waidelich made no promises. He set the receiver in the cradle and walked into the board room. "Let's talk about the Oxy proposal," he said.

The man from First Boston had brought in a team of assistants to do that.

One assistant talked about how risky Oxy's oil projects were.

Another explained that only 37 percent of Oxy's earnings came from operations. To buy Cities, they'd have to sell assets.

Another explained that the securities Oxy was offering were wrong for Cities shareholders—the individuals wouldn't like to pay taxes on the zeroes, and the institutions wouldn't like the low-quality preferred stock.

"Besides," said the man from First Boston, "the offer isn't enough. We figure that this package is worth less than $47 a share."

"What else can they put on the table?" asked James Boisi, Geoff's father, the vice chairman of Morgan Guaranty. As soon as Jim Boisi had heard that Goldman was representing Oxy on a bid for Cities Services, he had called Waidelich to offer to resign his board seat; Waidelich had said that wasn't necessary; Waidelich wanted Boisi's help considering the bid.

"More cash," said the man from First Boston.

"That just stretches the Oxy balance sheet even more," said Jim Boisi. "It means that Oxy will have to sell more assets to pay."

"Can't we make the deal tax-free?" asked a director. If Oxy paid for Cities as proposed, Cities shareholders would have to pay capital gains tax on their long-term profit.

"Not unless Oxy buys half of the company with stock," said the lawyer. "And they won't do that."

"If this proposal is turned down, does Oxy have the financial muscle and the staying power to succeed in a hostile offer?" asked a director.

"They told us they haven't excluded the possibility," said the man from First Boston.

"But it's unlikely," said one of the other bankers. "Ever since Mead, Hammer has been skittish about hostile deals."

Waidelich raised an eyebrow. A hostile bid seemed more than likely. That seemed like Hammer's style to him. "Why don't you step outside for a minute?" he asked the investment bankers. "Let's go through the alternatives," he said when the directors were alone. "Liquidation doesn't make sense. We've got a bid on the table. We're working on rounding up another bid but no one is ready."

"This offer really strains Oxy," said the chief financial officer. "I think we should keep looking for buyers."

"I don't know how long we can keep the Oxy offer on the table," said Waidelich.

"We shouldn't keep it on the table if Oxy isn't cooperative," said Jim Boisi.

The directors kept talking.

Finally they voted. It was unanimous. The Oxy offer was too low. Waidelich walked to his office. He had to call Armand Hammer.

Geoff Boisi, David Murdock and Armand Hammer had been waiting all afternoon for Chuck Waidelich to call. As soon as he'd got off the phone with Waidelich, Hammer had sent Waidelich a letter confirming the new deadline and the two concessions. That had been at four. It was after six, and they still hadn't heard what the board had decided. That was ominous.

"Let's talk about the options," said Boisi. "We should do everything possible to get negotiations started. If we can't, your only alternative may be an offer direct to the shareholders." If Oxy started a tender offer, it could buy Cities twenty days after its formal announcement. Cities would have just twenty days to cut a better deal.

Hammer nodded. They'd agreed the first night that if Cities didn't respond to the proposal, Oxy might have to tender for as much of Cities as it could afford.

"We should make one last try to go friendly," said Boisi. "Oxy can offer $52 a share if Cities agrees. Cities might not agree, but when the traders find out that Cities turned down a higher price, the pressure will be on."

Hammer nodded. He was still hoping to negotiate that night.

At eight o'clock, Waidelich called. Hammer stood with the receiver away from his ear. Boisi and Murdock leaned toward him to listen in. They couldn't hear very well.

"The meeting is over," said Waidelich. "The board has turned down the offer."

"What?" said Hammer. "You promised me that you were going to recess the meeting so we could talk."

Waidelich was silent. He hadn't promised anything.

"We've got to meet," said Hammer.

"Let's have breakfast tomorrow morning," said Waidelich.

"That's too late," said Hammer. "We have to meet tonight."

"We're tired over here," said Waidelich. "What about breakfast at the Helmsley Palace?"

"Unless your board has approved our deal by midnight, I don't see any point in the two of us meeting tomorrow," said Hammer.

"Let's talk about it at breakfast," said Waidelich.

Hammer slammed down the receiver. "I'm eighty-four years old and I'm not too tired to meet. How can he possibly be tired?"

"Do you think that anyone told the Cities board that we amended the offer?" asked Boisi.

"I don't know," said Brody.

133

"I'm flying back to Los Angeles first thing tomorrow morning," said Hammer. "There's no reason for me to stay here."

Later that morning, a messenger arrived with a letter for Hammer. But Hammer was in Los Angeles. Boisi opened it.

Dear Mr. Hammer:

This is in response to your August 16 letter, which was received after our Board of Directors had adjourned its meeting yesterday.

Prior to yesterday's board meeting, we had been given to understand by your financial advisers that a letter along the lines of your August 16 letter would likely be delivered prior to our board meeting, after your executive committee had formally approved it.... Nevertheless, the board was advised of the contents of the proposed letter and took them into consideration when reviewing your proposal.

I regret that you were unable to attend our scheduled meeting this morning. I can only repeat our readiness to discuss with you what basis might exist for a revision of your proposal.

Boisi shook his head. Waidelich seemed to be saying he wanted to do a deal—the problem was price. Maybe negotiations were about to begin.

Someone from Occidental called Boisi to read Hammer's response.

Dear Mr. Waidelich,

As I told you on the telephone last night and as I confirmed in a letter delivered to you last night, Occidental was willing to and did extend its proposal to midnight to permit your board to further consider the proposal. At that time, I responded to your request for a breakfast meeting and informed you that unless your board acted favorably on Occidental's proposal prior to its midnight expiration, there would be no need for any breakfast meeting. I also offered to come and see you last night before the expiration of our proposal, but you said you were too tired. I then awaited your response to my letter and since I did not receive a call from you made my arrangements to return to Los Angeles.

Your August 17th letter states that you received my letter after your board had adjourned its meeting yesterday. The fact is that I did not sign that letter earlier because you called me yesterday before your board meeting, requested a face-to-face meeting with me, promised that you would not adjourn your board meeting but instead would call me while the meeting was in recess so we could then meet in person to discuss Occidental's proposal. I agreed to all your requests on the understanding that you would not adjourn your board meeting. I then waited until 8 p.m. when you telephoned me and told me that your board of directors had adjourned its meeting and you could not see me because you were too tired.

Boisi called Joe Flom, Oxy's takeover lawyer. "Oxy can't send that letter," he said. "Oxy is trying to be friends not enemies."
"I'll talk to the Doctor," said Flom.
Hammer wouldn't listen. The letter went out that afternoon.

Dear Dr. Hammer:
While we have different understandings of what happened yesterday, Cities and I reiterate our desire to discuss revision of your proposal.

Cities wasn't sending very clear signals.
Boisi dialed the man at First Boston. He wouldn't clear up what Cities really meant. Boisi dialed Marty Lipton. Lipton would know what his client was trying to tell Oxy.

"Have we gotten off on the wrong foot?" asked Geoff Boisi over coffee and Danish at Marty Lipton's office Wednesday morning. Lipton, the takeover lawyer who was advising Waidelich, was Boisi's last hope: maybe he would tell Boisi what Cities wanted. No one else had given Boisi any clues. "We have to get the companies talking, otherwise we'll never get anywhere."
The man from First Boston sipped his coffee.
"We think we've gone over every payment alternative," continued Boisi. "But maybe we missed something. We want your input. We want to know what it will take to do this deal."

135

"How much more cash can you give us?" asked the man from First Boston.

"We might be able to raise our price by a dollar a share," said Boisi.

"That's not enough," said the man from First Boston.

Boisi got the impression that the price was $55 a share.

"We want the deal to be tax-free," said the Cities chief financial officer. "You have to pay half in stock."

"We can't do that," said Boisi. "I explained that before."

Everyone was silent for a minute.

"What do you need to do a deal?" asked Boisi. "What does the Cities board of directors want?" He looked at Lipton.

Lipton shrugged.

Boisi looked at the Cities chief financial officer. The finance man shrugged.

Boisi looked at the man from First Boston.

The man from First Boston shrugged.

Suddenly Boisi had the answer. The problem must be the Cities board: the directors must not agree. "Would it be helpful for the Cities board to hear from Goldman Sachs?" he asked.

"I think a meeting would be helpful," said Lipton.

Later that morning, Lipton called Boisi. "A committee of directors will see you at noon," he said. At the Cities Service office.

"Which directors?" asked Boisi.

"Peterson, McGillicudy, Bam, Michel," said Lipton. The chairman of Lehman Brothers, the chairman of Manufacturers Hanover Trust Company, the two largest shareholders. "Your father."

Boisi called Brody. They talked strategy for a few minutes. They flagged a cab uptown.

Brody looked at Boisi.

Clearly Geoff was nervous. Boisi had to tell the Cities board what Oxy had decided the day before: that if Cities didn't accept a friendly offer, Oxy would go direct to to the shareholders with a tender offer—and he had to confront his father professionally.

"I'll bet that this is the first time you have ever gone to a meeting and been sure that someone in the audience knew how to pronounce your last name properly," said Brody.

* * *

The directors were waiting for Geoff Boisi and Ken Brody at noon. Chuck Waidelich did the introductions.

Boisi looked at his father. He looked at Brody. "One of the pros to coming to a meeting like this," he said, "is that this is the first time that I've ever stood in front of a board and been sure that someone in the audience knew how to pronounce my last name properly," he said.

The directors laughed.

"Tell us what you have in mind," said Waidelich.

"We were brought into this a week ago," said Boisi. "There has been some significant miscommunication in the past couple of days. We can't seem to get a dialogue going." He looked around the room. "We have come to see whether there is any basis for a negotiated deal."

None of the directors spoke.

"After this board announced that it would welcome a bid, we spoke to a number of companies," said Boisi. "One of those companies was Occidental Petroleum. Oxy told us that it had been studying Cities for two years and that a merger made sense. We at Goldman thought that a merger made sense too. So we tried to put together a financial package that made sense." Boisi looked around the table again.

The directors stared stonily back.

"We attempted to construct it based on what we perceived the objectives of this board to be," said Brody. "Gulf offered you $63 a share in cash, so we included as much cash as we could afford. We made the securities as safe as possible. We included the zero coupon bonds to conserve Oxy's cash flow. This offer is so finely tuned that we can't change it much. Changing it would set a ripple through Oxy's financial structure."

"We recognize that you feel the business is worth substantially more than we have offered," said Boisi. "We tried to respond to that by giving you the right to shop the company. We thought that that was a helpful and conciliatory move. But somehow the fact that we were trying to be helpful and conciliatory was lost in the shuffle. Before Oxy's concessions were announced to the Cities board, Mr. Waidelich and Dr. Hammer talked about whether they should discuss the Oxy proposal further. Dr. Hammer's understanding was that the two agreed that they should. It came as a shock when Mr. Waidelich called at eight to say that the board had rejected the Oxy offer." Boisi looked at Waidelich. "It was not intended as an affront that Hammer didn't show up for breakfast yesterday. That was the result of a genuine misunderstanding." He paused. "We would like to establish a basis for negotiations. We have to tell you that the Occidental board met last night. It has terminated its original proposal. It has taken action that it is prepared to execute today."

Waidelich frowned.

"We stand ready to answer any questions that you have about our offer," said Boisi. He was hoping that the directors would talk about what they needed to do a deal.

"If you're so eager to do a deal, why haven't you looked at our brochure?" asked Jim Boisi.

"There are a couple of reasons," said Geoff Boisi. "First, as we told you, Occidental has been looking at Cities Service for two years and they feel they understand it. And we at Goldman Sachs asked questions of your chief financial officer and your investment bankers. We feel that we are not in terrible disagreement on values." Also, Boisi wanted to keep Oxy's options open; if he took the brochure, Oxy couldn't make an offer direct to shareholders.

"Why does a tax-paying shareholder want a zero bond?" asked Jim Boisi. Zeroes don't pay interest, but the IRS says that holders have to pay taxes on "imputed" interest that they don't receive."

"If a shareholder doesn't want the zeroes, he can sell them," said Brody. Oxy couldn't afford Cities without the zeroes; interest and dividend payments would be too high."

"That zero is a Cities note secured by Cities assets," said Geoff Boisi. "We put it in the package because we thought you'd rather have a Cities note backed by assets you know than an Oxy note."

The directors nodded. They didn't want an Oxy note.

"Can't you make the securities safer for Cities shareholders?" asked a director. "Can't you pay in stock so that the deal is tax-free?" asked another director who was also a large Cities shareholder.

Geoff Boisi and Brody explained that the offer as it stood was the best Occidental could do.

Then Jim Boisi spoke. "Are you saying that an examination of Cities Service shows that it is a fine company but you just can't afford to pay the ticket price?" he asked. "Isn't that rather like the guy who goes into a Rolls-Royce dealership and says 'I can't afford your car, but here's what I'm prepared to pay, and if you have any other suggestions, let's talk about it'?"

"A company is worth what someone will pay for it," said Brody.

"At the beginning of the summer this might not have been a good offer," said Geoff Boisi. "A lot has changed since then. Today what we are offering is quite respectable." He looked around the table. "Oxy is ready to negotiate," he said. He paused. "We're willing to look at anything. We think we've considered every option, but if you think we've missed something, let's talk about it. We want to work something out."

One of the directors said something about $55 a share.

"Oxy could look at that number until it is blue in the face," said Brody. "The money isn't there. The fact is that Oxy has gone as far as it can go. You have already heard the best price."

The room was silent for a minute.

"What would happen to the company after a merger?" asked Waidelich. "We're worried that the new company will be so weak financially that it won't be a viable competitor."

"We don't believe Oxy will be that weak," said Brody. "Buying Cities Service won't break Occidental. Buying Cities takes Oxy just to the edge of financial prudence."

"Oxy stock-watchers like the idea," said Geoff Boisi. "The shares are trading way up."

"Oxy doesn't have a good credit rating," said one of the directors.

"Oxy has oil fields in countries that are unstable," said Brody. "True. That makes the rating agencies skeptical. But, in fact, Oxy has a much stronger balance sheet than many other BBB+ companies—and a BBB+ rating isn't that bad to start with. This merger will make the asset base more stable and the balance sheet weaker. We figure the rating will drop to BBB."

"At breakfast this morning, you were talking about an additional dollar," said the man from First Boston. "Is that still on the table?"

"Yes," said Geoff Boisi. "One dollar. Just one."

Waidelich frowned.

The directors were silent.

"We need to talk," said Waidelich. "You two wait outside."

Boisi and Brody walked into the hallway.

"Let me bring you up to date on where we stand with other companies," said Waidelich. "Mobil has looked at our records: they're interested in the oil and gas fields; they've talked to Amerada Hess about a joint bid. Sohio is sending people in this afternoon. Texaco is due in on Friday."

"We're getting Arco to look," said one of the investment bankers.

"My guess is that we will have another offer or two," said Waidelich. "I don't think that Mobil or Texaco will let Occidental buy Cities Service for less than $50 a share."

The first thing Geoff Boisi did after the directors' meeting, was to call Armand Hammer. He was with David Murdock at Joe Flom's office. "We made our pitch," he said. "I think we made some headway. They want $55 a share. We need to show some flexibility now. I think we can go to $52. Let's try our best shot." The bear hug.

Hammer called Waidelich right away. "We want to do a friendly deal," said Hammer as soon as Waidelich got on the line. "We're willing to increase our cash offer to $52 a share."

"Fifty-two a share isn't enough," said Waidelich.

"If the Cities board does not accept this offer, we will make an offer direct to your shareholders," said Hammer. "At $50 a share."

"Fifty-two a share isn't enough," said Waidelich. "I can't recommend that to my board."

Hammer set the receiver in the cradle.

Boisi and Brody walked in from the Cities meeting.

"We're going to the shareholders," said Murdock. "The board has had its chance."

Hammer set up a telephone meeting with Occidental's directors; they okayed the offer.

Boisi looked at his watch. Four o'clock. The stock market had just closed.

Flom barked out the orders.

"File the papers," he told his Washington partner.

"Send this to Waidelich by messenger," he told his secretary.

"Call the *Times,*" he told the press assistant. "Read the news statement."

There were a hundred things to do.

Boisi and Brody and Murdock worked at the law office for hours.

"Let's see how the newspaper story looks," suggested Murdock just after two in the morning.

Boisi and Brody and Murdock took the elevator downstairs. They walked to the newsstand on the corner. Brody picked up the *New York Times.*

"Occidental: New Tack on Cities," read the headline. "Company Sets a Direct Bid to Shareholders."

As soon as he got off the phone with Armand Hammer on Wednesday afternoon, Charles Waidelich looked across the board room at Marty Lipton. "The Doctor just offered to pay $52 a share," he said. "I told him I couldn't recommend that to my board. He's going direct to the shareholders."

Waidelich's secretary buzzed. A package had arrived from Occidental by messenger. And an Oxy announcement had just crossed the wire:

Occidental Petroleum Corp. said its directors authorized a cash tender offer for 38.2 million shares of Cities Service Co. common stock, about 49% of the outstanding shares for $50 a share. Occidental said that after completion of the offer it intends "to seek to consummate a merger or a similar combination" between Cities Service and Occidental. Occidental said that it had not yet determined the form or amount of consideration to be offered to holders of Cities Service shares in any such transaction, but it expects that such consideration will "consist of securities of Occidental and/or Cities Service rather than cash."

"We can't attack this very hard," said Lipton. "We invited offers. The only thing that we can do is say that we think we can find a better package, and it is up to each shareholder to make up his own mind."

141

That made sense. Waidelich figured that most shareholders were going to sell fast. The arbs had bought their stock for $53 a share; it currently was trading at $37⅝.

"The only alternative now is to find a white knight," said Lipton. "Liquidation is out. There isn't enough time to cut a deal with a bidder or time to get shareholder approval even if we had a bidder."

Waidelich nodded.

"We don't have much time to find a bidder either," said Lipton. "Oxy will have a deal sewed up in ten days." Shareholders who sent their stock to Oxy during the first ten days got cash; shareholders who sent the stock later didn't; after the first ten days, no one would send his stock to a new bidder. "We've got to put out some feelers to Oxy. We've got to try to push up the price as high as we can."

Ten days was the following Saturday. Waidelich might not be able to flush out a bid in time. Negotiating might be the only option.

"This isn't their last offer," said Lipton. "They'll go to $52 a share. They may go higher."

"We've got to put out an announcement," said Lipton. "We want other bidders to know that the game isn't over." He handed Waidelich a draft press release.

Waidelich read:

Cities Service Co. chairman and chief executive Charles J. Waidelich stated today that he regrets that Occidental Petroleum saw fit to reject the repeated offers made by Cities Service since last Friday and again several times today to make information available to Occidental in connection with its offer to acquire Cities Service. The Occidental tender offer announced today is a unilateral offer and not the result of discussions or negotiations between Cities Service and Occidental. The offer will be considered by the Cities board at a meeting to be held in the very near future. Pending such meeting, Cities Service recommends that its shareholders reserve judgment with regard to the Occidental tender offer. Mr. Waidelich noted that the Occidental tender offer is substantially similar to, but not as specific as, the proposal Occidental made on

August 13 and which the Cities Service board determined to not meet the objective of maximizing values for the Cities Service shareholders. Mr. Waidelich further noted that discussions are continuing with a number of companies that have expressed an interest in acquiring Cities Service or major segments of its business.

Ever since Oxy had made its formal offer for Cities, Geoff Boisi hadn't had a moment of peace. Company presidents and investment bankers kept calling to ask about buying Cities—or Oxy—assets when Oxy started to raise cash to pay off debt.

Friday morning, Boisi called First Boston.

"The Cities board is going to meet," said the man. "We have some options." The man mumbled something about other bidders. "We can always liquidate the company."

Boisi hung up. It was clear that the man wasn't focusing on how to make an Oxy deal work—he was still trying to sell Cities in pieces. Boisi clearly wasn't going to get anywhere talking to the banker. He dialed Marty Lipton.

"The directors liked your presentation on Wednesday," said Lipton. "They have a lot of confidence in you."

That was good to hear.

"The board is worried about how Oxy is going to be managed after the merger," continued Lipton.

"Cities will be a separate Oxy subsidiary," said Boisi. "It will have its own board. It will have representation on the Oxy board."

"I'll get back to you," said Lipton.

That sounded good.

Later that morning, Lipton called back. "Waidelich will talk to the Doctor."

"There's been a lot of miscommunication," said Boisi. "We need to clear the air. I think that a meeting in a social setting might help. No bankers." Just executives.

It was set for Sunday afternoon at Joe Flom's duplex on East Seventy-ninth Street.

Armand Hammer strode into the apartment at two o'clock in the afternoon. He had a copy of his collection catalogue tucked under his arm; Flom and his wife were art collectors, and the book was a present for Claire.

Claire Flom was sitting on the couch.

"Look," said Hammer. He handed her the book.

She turned the pages.

Hammer sat down beside her. He told her the story of how he got each painting.

Waidelich arrived a few minutes later. Boisi and Flom walked into another room to wait.

"Let me tell you about Occidental," said Hammer when they were alone.

Waidelich nodded.

Hammer gave a quick company history. He talked about current operations. He talked about company goals. His eyes twinkled.

Waidelich told Hammer about Cities Service operations and goals. "You're going to have to borrow to buy Cities," said Waidelich. "How are you going to pay down that debt?"

"We'll sell assets," said Hammer.

"Which assets?" asked Waidelich.

"Assets," said Hammer. "Some assets of both companies."

Waidelich frowned.

"This merger is a masterstroke," said Hammer. "With your domestic assets and our international assets, we'll have a great company."

Waidelich stood up to go.

Boisi got a debriefing. Communication was finally working better.

"I met with the Doctor yesterday," said Chuck Waidelich at the Cities board meeting Monday afternoon. "We talked about our companies. I didn't learn anything new. But if we can't drum up another bidder, we're going to have to merge with Occidental."

"Is an Oxy merger going to work financially?" asked a director.

"Oxy is going to sell assets to make it work," said Waidelich. "Hammer wouldn't say what assets."

"We need guarantees for our shareholders," said a director.

"Can Oxy promise that the Cities zeroes will be paid down as soon as there is cash to pay anything?"

"We'll try," said Waidelich.

"We have serveral constituencies," said another. "The shareholders, the banks, the employees. We need to try to do the best for them all. We need a guarantee that headquarters will remain in Tulsa."

A secretary handed Waidelich a pink telephone message. He walked to the corner phone and picked up the receiver. It was the chairman of Mobil; he wouldn't be a white knight. Sohio had dropped out a couple of days before; only Texaco was left, and Waidelich figured that it was too late now for Texaco to win even with a high bid.

Just after eight, Monday night, Geoff Boisi's phone rang.

It was Marty Lipton, the Cities lawyer. "The board has rejected the Oxy offer," he said.

Boisi had expected that. Cities had said as much in the press release the week before.

"Let me read you the announcement," said Lipton:

Cities Service stated that at a meeting this afternoon to consider Occidental Petroleum's partial cash tender offer for approximately 49% of Cities Service common stock at $50 a share, the Cities Service board unanimously concluded that the Occidental offer is inadequate. However, the board also unanimously determined that in light of the unprecedented circumstances resulting from Gulf's abrogation of its merger agreement with Cities Service and the grave disadvantage that has been inflicted on Cities Service shareholders, it would be inappropriate for the board to "second guess" each shareholder's own evaluation of the Occidental offer. Accordingly, each shareholder is advised to make his or her own decision with respect to the offer. The board urges shareholders to obtain professional advice in making their decision.

That was a pretty weak rejection.

"We need to talk," said Lipton.

The negotiations had finally begun.

145

By six o'clock on Tuesday, it was clear that the key was cash. The Cities directors needed $55 a share. That was what they had paid Boone Pickens two months before.

"You know we can't afford $55 a share for half the stock," said Boisi. "Do you think $55 a share for less than 50 percent would be acceptable?"

"That could work," said Lipton. "I'll get back to you." Half an hour later, he told Boisi that Waidelich wanted to see Hammer.

"Okay," said Boisi. He knew that the Doctor wanted to see Waidelich.

"Tomorrow morning," said Lipton. "Ten o'clock in New York."

Early Wednesday morning, Boisi took a cab from Port Washington to Manhattan. "Fifty-five a share in cash is important," Boisi told Hammer at a pre-meeting conference. "The board is worried about more law suits. They paid Boone Pickens $55 a share. We can't pay that for all the stock. The best we can do is 45 percent. We're more flexible on securities, but not much more."

Hammer nodded.

"Let's look at the possibilities," said Boisi. He handed Hammer a matrix that the oil and gas vice president had prepared. Inside each square were the terms of a different package of securities that Oxy could use to buy Cities and the value of each one. Boisi explained the pros and cons of each choice. "That's as high as we can go," said Boisi. He pointed to one of the squares marked $52.

Hammer nodded. He tucked the page into his breast pocket.

At ten o'clock, Waidelich and Lipton arrived. The man from First Boston wasn't along. Waidelich had just found out that Texaco wasn't going to bid for Cities after all.

Hammer and Waidelich met alone in Hammer's lawyer's personal office.

"You're going to be vice chairman of Occidental," said Hammer.

"Let's settle the economics," said Waidelich. "We need better securities."

They negotiated.

At ten-thirty, Hammer signaled for Boisi.

Boisi walked into the office. Hammer was alone. Hammer and Boisi talked through the alternatives once more. They agreed that Oxy could afford $55 a share in cash for 45 percent of the stock—

and a package of securities worth $50 a share for the rest.

Hammer waved Waidelich into the office.

"What's the problem?" asked Boisi.

"We've got to have better securities," said Waidelich.

"Maybe we can do something," said Hammer.

Boisi looked at Hammer. Hammer was an ace negotiator. Boisi scribbled a note. "You've already gone higher than we talked about. This is absolutely our top number."

Hammer read the note. He looked at Boisi. He looked at Waidelich. He agreed to give Cities stockholders an extra 50¢ of preferred stock per share.

Finally Hammer and Waidelich shook hands.

Waidelich looked at Boisi.

"Oxy went higher than we've talked about," said Boisi. "That's okay, but Goldman Sachs would have been uncomfortable at anything higher."

"The Doctor and I just shook hands," said Chuck Waidelich at the Cities board meeting that afternoon. "He raised his offer to $55 a share in cash for 45 percent of the stock. He's offering $1.6 billion of preferred stock and $533 million of zero coupons for the rest. Goldman says the package is worth $52.59. We'll have two directors on the Oxy board. We'll stay in Tulsa."

Waidelich looked around the room. "Geoff Boisi told me that Hammer had gone past Goldman's top recommended price," said Waidelich. "This is Oxy's best offer."

Waidelich called for a vote.

It was unanimous: Cities would merge with Oxy.

Someone brought in a bottle of champagne. Waidelich popped the cork and poured the glasses.

The Cities directors and Hammer and Murdock and Boisi and Brody all headed to the "21" Club for dinner.

Between toasts, Waidelich looked across the dining room. Bill Agee and Mary Cunningham were sitting at the table in the back. That morning, Bendix had bid $1.6 billion for Martin Marietta.

Geoff Boisi unfolded the *New York Times* on the train from Port Washington Friday morning. He'd missed a lot of news during the three-week battle. He scanned the front page. There was the story: "Cities Service Agrees to Occidental's Bid in $4 Billion Merger."

The Federal Trade Commission gave Occidental and Cities Service the go-ahead to merge the next morning. But for Occidental—and Goldman Sachs—merging was only the beginning. Now the Goldman team had to sell some $2.5 billion of Cities and Oxy assets to pay off the purchase. That would be no small task. Hammer had promised to sell $1.8 billion of assets within a year.

Most Oxy watchers didn't think that Hammer and Goldman could do that, so the Goldman partner on the account—Boisi had handed Oxy over to an oil and gas specialist while he worked on another deal—decided to start with a blockbuster sale. The best prospect: the Cities gas pipeline. Northwest Energy had made an offer of $300 million, all in cash, during the final Cities board meeting. At the end of October, Goldman invited companies to bid in a sealed auction. The winner: Northwest Energy for $360 million plus a coal mine.

By the end of March, Goldman had sold the Cities refining and marketing operations to Southland—owner of 7-Eleven—for $1.1 billion, the copper mine to Newmont for $110 million, the Columbian Chemical Company to Consolidated Industries S.A. for $85 million and Canadian Cities Service to Oxy Canada to the public for $300 million.

In January 1983, five months after he made his promise, Hammer hand-delivered to Roger Anderson, chairman of the Continental Illinois National Bank & Trust Company, a check for the first $1 billion of his debt.

The Cities deal went smoothly, but life was rough for Occidental after that.

In January 1985, Oxy struck a deal to buy Diamond Shamrock, the nation's nineteenth-largest oil company, for $3.3 billion. Hours after Hammer and the chairman of Shamrock shook hands, the Diamond Shamrock board vetoed the deal. The rumor was that they didn't want to sell the company unless their chairman would have a role in running it—and clearly Hammer was going to kick the chairman out.

Charles Waidelich concluded early on that there wasn't a job for him at Occidental, so in November 1983, when the two companies had integrated into one, Waidelich handed the Doctor his resignation. A couple of months later he bought a house in Rancho Santa Fe north of San Diego. Waidelich is catching up on his reading—"books people gave me ten years ago"—looking for a small nonoil company to buy, and learning to play golf.

In April 1984, Oxy replaced Goldman Sachs with Drexel Burnham Lambert; by the end of the year, Drexel had raised almost $2 billion. Goldman hated to lose the business, of course, but, in fact, 1984 had been a blockbuster year. Equity leapt from $502 million to $585 million, and merger assignments kept rolling in. That year, the firm handled ninety-eight transactions, fifty-five valued at over $100 million.

Just after he finished the Cities-Oxy negotiations, Ken Brody was assigned to advise the U.S. Transportation Department on the sale of Conrail. In 1983, he was put in charge of setting up a new issues department. That was done by the end of 1984, and in January 1985, Brody was shifted to the real estate department to help supervise Goldman's skyrocketing growth. Soon he was orchestrating the biggest real estate deal ever: the sale of the sprawling Rockefeller Center in New York City to a group of private and public investors.

Geoff Boisi negotiated merger deal after merger deal. In the spring of 1983, Boisi helped Bank of America to buy Seafirst. He negotiated General Foods' purchase by Philip Morris in September 1985. In 1984, *Esquire* magazine named him "one of the best of a new generation" under forty years old, and in March 1985, *Institutional Investor* chose Boisi as one of twelve "ascending stars" in the investment-banking world. Six months after that, Boisi was promoted to cohead of Goldman's investment-banking services department. That puts him right in line for the top job at Wall Street's most profitable bank.

(4)

Citibank

"The Citi Never Sleeps"

"How are your countries?" asked Walter Wriston. He leaned against the red-and-white-striped sofa in Bill Rhodes' office.

"Progressing well enough that I'm hoping to get some of the vacation that I've missed during the past two years," said Rhodes. Rhodes' last real vacation had been in December 1981—and now it was already June 1983. "Mexico is on target. We're close to wrapping up that $1.5-billion Argentine loan. We've just about finalized Peru's restructuring. We've almost got a handshake on the package for Uruguay."

Wriston nodded. "Paul Volcker is worried about Brazil," he said. "He's heard the rumors that Brazil is going to freeze its interbank lines. We've got to get things back on track."

Rhodes raised his eyebrows. "That's going to be a tough job," he said. Rhodes took a Jamaican Macanudo cigar out of his jacket pocket and bit off the tip. "The banks are losing confidence in Brazil's economic team. The ministers keep talking about getting the economy back on track, but they haven't done much to make it happen." Rhodes lit his cigar. "The banks don't trust each other. They aren't organized. They don't have enough input. There's not enough teamwork."

Wriston nodded. He knew that. "We'd like to draw on your experience," he said. "Brazil needs the kind of package you put together for Mexico last fall. Brazil needs a bank committee."

Rhodes looked at Wriston. He looked at the photograph of the Mexican loan-signing ceremony on the wall in front of him. He looked at the red fire helmet his colleagues had given him "in recognition of your efforts around the world" on the credenza. He puffed on his cigar.

"Bill," said Wriston. He stared through the window at the traffic on Park Avenue. "I know you need Brazil like I need a hole in the head, but I'd like you to chair that committee."

Rhodes was silent for a minute.

"Brazil needs you," said Wriston.

"There's not a lot of time," said Rhodes. "Brazil got a thirty-day extension on a $400-million payment due yesterday, but Brazil isn't going to be able to pay up until the IMF [International Monetary Fund] and the banks release the next $635 million installment of our loan. I don't see that happening by July 1."

"We've got to get this fixed by the end of the year," said Wriston. "The press keeps saying that the world banking system might collapse if we don't have a package by then."

"Government money and moral support were the key to the Mexican deal," said Rhodes. He stood up and paced across the office to his desk. "The U.S. government and IMF officials seem to be willing to help out on Brazil too, but the banks that have been handling this haven't taken advantage of that. The banks have to have more consistent contact with the top people at the IMF and the Treasury and the Fed."

"I know," said Wriston.

Rhodes paced back to the yellow armchair in the corner. "Just keeping Brazil afloat while we work out a deal is going to be tough," he said. "Some of the banks are panicking. Brazil has lost $1.8 billion of interbank lines since the banks tried to rescue Brazil last December."

"I know," said Wriston. "If we don't get the rescue on track, Brazil will lose more."

"Well," said Rhodes. "We'd better get moving. This time the banks are going to be organized like an army. This time there's going to be communication. This time every bank is going to participate."

Wriston nodded. He stood up. "Do your best," he said. "The banks are counting on you."

Rhodes stood up too. "I'll try," he said.

In financial circles, Citi slickers are known for their arrogance. They look down their noses at other bankers. Not William Rhodes. Rhodes is easygoing. He's forty-seven, with thin black hair and wire-rimmed glasses. He talks like a homebody, smokes up to six cigars a day, and refuses to have a secretary buzzer on his telephone. He likes to quote FDR on crises ("The only thing we have to fear is fear itself") and Frederick the Great on decisions ("It's better to make a bad decision than no decision at all"). Rhodes visits his mother on Long Island whenever he has time, and drives to Hartford several times a month to take his eighteen-year-old daughter out to lunch. Rhodes relaxes on the dance floor—he's particularly fond of Latin American steps—and jogs around the reservoir in Central Park when he has time; he unplugs the wall phone at his apartment for peace and quiet at night. He likes fine wines, Jets games and Robert Ludlum; "Kennedy liked adventure too," he says. Jacques de Larosière, managing director of the International Monetary Fund, divides bankers into two groups: those who are allowed to smoke cigars in his office and those who aren't. There are only two bankers in that first group: Federal Reserve chairman Paul Volker and Bill Rhodes.

Rhodes grew up in New York City and majored in history at Brown University. He wrote his senior thesis on Russian-Polish relations, but when he graduated in 1957, he realized that there were no jobs in Russian studies. Citibank was hiring in Latin America, and Rhodes figured he was qualified for that: he spoke Spanish well—he'd spent two summers working on a South American cargo boat—and he was sure that anyone could bank. Citibank sent him to Maracaibo, Venezuela, as a junior lending officer. Unlike many *Yanqui* bankers, Rhodes mixed with the locals. He went to baseball games, bullfights and cocktail parties. Soon his network of contacts included businessmen, government officials, opposition leaders. These contacts got him elected president of the Venezuelan-American Chamber of Commerce; they also got him accounts. In 1975, when Venezuela changed the banking laws and many American banks sold out, Citi decided to stay. And Citi Venezuela flourished, thanks largely to Bill Rhodes.

By 1977, Rhodes was back in New York as one of three executives responsible for all of Latin America. Three years later, he was made a senior corporate officer. He had a seat on the Citibank policy committee; and that meant that Rhodes' name was on the line when things went wrong south of the border.

And so was Citibank's.

By the late seventies, Citibank was the biggest foreign bank in Latin America and the biggest bank in the world. It was also the most aggressive.

"The Citi Never Sleeps" goes the jingle, and Citibank doesn't. Citi was the first American bank to open a branch overseas, the first to offer personal loans to consumers, the first to court corporate customers with the negotiable certificate of deposit. Citi is creative. Banks are formally forbidden to sell insurance or underwrite stock, but Citi circumvented that regulation by setting up a "one-bank holding company" called Citicorp that is allowed to own half a dozen different kinds of money-handling companies, provided it owns just one bank. Citicorp boasts a finance company, a traveler's check company, a stockbrokerage company, an insurance company, two credit card companies and a British merchant bank. Citi pioneered automated teller technology; it bought sick thrifts so that it could cross state lines. Competitors sneered that Citi officers were so ambitious they all dressed just like Citi chairman Walter Wriston, so narrow-minded they'd never heard of Cyndi Lauper or Boy George. But whatever else they were, Citi officers were effective. Citi profits set new records almost every quarter. By 1983, Citi had become a Gibraltar of finance with a blue and white flag in ninety-five countries around the world.

National City Bank was founded in 1812. At first, the bank just made loans mostly to cotton, sugar, copper and coal merchants, but later it expanded into loans to any business. In the 1910s, corporate America began to go multinational; U.S. Steel, W. R. Grace and Standard Oil opened sales centers in Latin America. The chairman of Big Steel called Citi to ask the bank to migrate south; Steel needed a bank to finance foreign inventories, process wire transfers and cash paychecks. Citi was eager to oblige, but there was a hitch: nationally chartered U.S. banks were not allowed to set up offices overseas. Citi sent a lobbyist to Washington, and in 1913, Congress changed the law. Months later, Citi opened its first offshore branch in Buenos Aires. A year after that, Citi hung a shingle in São Paulo, and by 1929, Citi boasted an empire that stretched from London to Singapore, from Santiago to Shanghai.

For fifty years, the Latin American department made money mostly by making modest three-month trade loans secured by cargoes of coffee, rubber, beef and cotton. Then in 1959, a senior vice president named Walter Wriston was put in charge of the overseas division; Wriston was determined to make the division into a money machine. Citi would lend to Ford and Alcoa and Exxon to finance new plants in Venezuela; Citi would open consumer branches to collect savings deposits and make car loans in Argentina; Citi would even extend credits to the Mexican government to build roads, schools and airports.

Wriston's boss liked the idea of lending to Ford Venezuela. He liked the idea of lending to Argentine car buyers. He wasn't so sure about financing Mexican roads and airports. There was no question that the loans were profitable: Citi could charge the Mexican government construction company much more interest than it could charge a company like International Harvester. But they were also risky. Citi couldn't seize a Mexican road and sell it if the government construction company went broke.

"A country is different from a company," said Wriston. Countries have people and resources. Countries can't go bankrupt.

The boss decided to try.

Citibank lent to Mexico. Citibank lent to Argentina. Citibank lent to Venezuela and Chile and Uruguay and Ecuador and Peru.

Most of all, Citibank lent to Brazil. Brazil seemed to have more promise than the other countries, and Brazil had a better team of economic technocrats, technocrats like Antônio Delfim Netto, minister of finance.

Antônio Delfim Netto is an optimist. At fifty-five, he's a little over five feet tall and has weighed as much as 231 pounds. Delfim wears thick glasses, speaks English with a heavy accent, and has eaten as many as eleven dozen oysters at a single meal. Delfim has a knack for making contacts and currying favors and putting a convert at ease. He always wears a jacket and tie, even when everyone else is in shirtsleeves. Although Delfim Netto loves night-life—he's a clubaholic—he hates to waste time. He has begged off cocktail parties with excuses as flimsy as "I'm going to be in the Amazon this evening."

He's a native of São Paulo, the second-generation son of Italian immigrants. He worked his way through the University of São Paulo, wrote a Ph.D thesis on "Coffee in Brazil" and landed a job teaching economics at his alma mater. While there, he cultivated businessmen and courted officials, and when the post of secretary of finance for the state of São Paulo opened up in 1966, the reigning general appointed Antônio Delfim Netto to the job. Delfim had only just begun to slash the state's billion dollar debt and make sense of the administrative mess when he got another call. This time the general needed a national finance minister. Delfim Netto moved to Brasilia, the new capital.

Being finance minister was quite a job. In the 1960s, the country was just a textbook case of promise. Brazil had iron, gold, bauxite, manganese, copper, nickel, people and poverty. For years, the economy had been based on three cash crops: coffee, sugar and rubber. For years, inflation had raged at 100 percent. For years, politics had been so unstable that businessmen joked that the way to break the Russians was to send them to organize Brazil. Politics settled down when a military junta took control in 1964, but even then, prosperity didn't seem to be around the corner: GNP totaled just $26.8 billion, inflation was 24 percent, per capita income was $315.

To change Brazil's economy, Delfim Netto increased exports.

His logic was simple: selling steel and cars and shoes to the U.S., the U.K., France, Germany and Japan meant jobs in factories and mills in São Paulo and Rio, and it meant jobs in power plants and shipping companies and banks in every province. The Brazilian government would help companies line up the cash to build the plants and mills; they would subsidize production costs so that prices would be competitive; they would build roads and power

155

plants to get the goods to port. But Brazil had to borrow to do that.

In 1967, Delfim called Citibank.

"Brazil's projects make sense," said the officer in Rio. "Brazil has promise. We'll make loans." Citi made big loans, sometimes as big as $100 million. So did other banks.

The plants were built. Exports soared. The Brazilian economy grew 10 percent a year. Delfim Netto was a national hero. Brazil was on its way to becoming the world's number-two ship builder, number-seven steelmaker, number-eight car manufacturer, number-twelve paper miller—and the number one LDC—Less Developed Country—debtor. Borrowings grew from $2.9 billion in 1967, to $5.3 billion in 1970, to $12.6 billion in 1973.

In 1974, OPEC raised the price of oil from $3 per barrel to $12. Brazil's oil bill shot up. The money that had been tagged for building steel mills had to be used for buying crude.

Brazil had a choice: borrow more to build the mills or tighten the belt.

Delfim called Citibank.

"We want a syndicate," he said. If a lot of banks lent, Brazil wouldn't depend on a single institution.

Citi agreed. It had billions to lend: the OPEC sheiks had just deposited their new fortunes. The bank insisted on just one precaution: Citi would lend only at floating rates; when Libor—the London Interbank Offering Rate, the international equivalent of U.S. "prime"—hit 20 percent, Brazil's rate would go to twenty-two.

Brazil's debt shot up: $21.2 billion by 1975, $43.5 billion by 1978.

By then, things had begun to go awry.

When oil prices quadrupled in 1974, Brazil's biggest trading partners didn't borrow; they tightened the belt. The United States, the United Kingdom, France, Germany and Japan went into deep recession; they stopped ordering Brazilian shoes and steel and cars. Brazilian exports slipped. Cash income came mostly from sugar and coffee sales; but that wasn't enough. The central bank printed money to make ends meet.

Inflation doubled to 40 percent.

In 1979, Delfim was appointed minister of planning, supervisor of the ministers of finance and agriculture and the head of the Central Bank. Then, against the advice of most economists, he began to borrow.

More plants went up; the subsidies increased; Delfim pegged wages to rise as fast as, or faster than, inflation.

Things didn't work out as planned. Delfim's subsidies were so high that the United States, the United Kingdom, France, Germany and Japan accused Brazil of dumping—selling exports below cost— and barred Brazilian shipments. Private companies couldn't afford to increase wages, so they fired employees. Government companies couldn't fire workers, so the Central Bank printed more money to meet the payroll.

Unemployment soared.

So did inflation.

Everything was expensive except car alcohol, a gasoline substitute, so the unemployed drowned their woes in that. Delfim ordered the alcohol company to mix in kerosene. The poor kept drinking.

In 1980, commodity prices collapsed. Selling sugar wasn't profitable anymore.

OPEC doubled the price of oil. Brazil's oil bill doubled.

Inflation hit 100 percent. The unemployed started to riot.

Delfim was having trouble lining up loans to cover interest payments on the earlier loans. He knew that the banks didn't like Brazil's economic statistics, so he started to fudge the numbers. He'd already taken fast-rising beef prices out of the consumer price index; now he "froze" export prices—and looked the other way when steelmakers shipped "kilos" that weighed 850 grams. The official total debt stayed steady at $60 billion. Actual borrowings spiraled up to almost $100 billion.

By now, Citibank earned more in Brazil than in any country except the United States. Brazil was the number one borrower: loans totaled $4.4 billion, 80 percent of Citi equity. Citi's "local" cruzeiros-only bank was one of the top ten banks in Brazil; Citi owned a Brazilian brokerage, a finance company and a credit card outfit.

"I'm putting Brazil on an austerity program," Delfim told the

Citi officer in 1981. "No new projects. No new subsidies. Once exports jump again, we'll be fine. We'll make it through this rough patch as long as we can borrow $1.5 billion or so a month."

Citibank was convinced that Brazil could make it if the banks didn't get scared. Citi's publishing department produced a glossy booklet on Brazil. "Brazil's future can be summed up in a single word: *opportunity*," read Walter Wriston's introduction. Brazil will pay its debts.

In April 1982, following Argentina's attempt to wrest control of the Falkland Islands from Great Britain, the British banks froze Argentine assets. The Argentine economy started to teeter.

Citi's loans started to look shaky, but Wriston insisted that Citi had been right to lend. No one could have predicted this war.

Delfim began to have trouble lining up his $1.5 billion a month. He knew the Brazilian bank branches abroad had about $10 billion in borrowed cash. It was "interbank" money, cash that one bank puts on deposit at another for one night to ninety days. Delfim told the branches to transfer the money to their headquarters in Brazil. As long as the lending banks kept renewing the loans, no one would know where the money really was.

In mid-summer, oil prices collapsed.

Mexico had mortgaged its oil-in-the-ground for $60 billion. Now crude profits didn't cover interest payments. By August, Mexico was out of cash.

The Mexican finance minister called Citi. Bill Rhodes said he'd handle it. But he wasn't sure what to do. No big country had ever run out of cash before.

He was sure of one thing, though: Mexico had to keep paying interest. Otherwise the big banks would be reluctant to lend more. And Mexico had to figure out how to fix its economy. Fast. The banks couldn't tell Mexico how to do that without smacking of meddling *Yanqui* imperialism; but the International Monetary Fund could. The IMF is a multinational agency that collects quota "subscriptions" from member governments and makes loans to ease the way through short-term cash crunches.

The Mexicans made an appointment at the IMF. They named a bank committee to renegotiate the terms of the debt. But before the talks could get off the ground, Mexico did the unthinkable: it nationalized its banks.

"There won't be a problem in Brazil," the head of the Brazilian Central Bank told Rhodes at the beginning of September. "Brazil has some cash. We have a diverse economy. We didn't waste our money; we built cash-producing projects."

"You have to be careful," Rhodes warned him. "Short-term loans that you get today might not get rolled over tomorrow."

"Don't worry," said the head of the Central Bank.

But Rhodes was right. The next day, Argentina, $45 billion in hock, told its banks that it was all but out of cash to pay its interest. U.S. banks immediately went skittish on Latin America. They called their interbank lines.

"We will conserve cash by buying goods on barter," announced Delfim. "We will swap shoes and weapons for Nigerian oil; we will swap steel for Argentine wheat."

That didn't always work. Poland owed Brazil $1.5 billion.

"We'd like to pay," said the Polish finance minister. "But we don't have dollars. Do you want our state-of-the-art icebreaker instead?"

By the middle of October, Delfim had lost almost $3 billion of interbank lines. He tried to line up a jumbo loan in Europe.

"We've got to do something," Delfim told Carlos Geraldo Langoni, the head of Brazil's Central Bank. "We've got to get the Europeans on board."

Langoni didn't know how.

"Call Guy Huntrods," said Delfim. The top Latin-American officer at Lloyds Bank International.

At fifty-nine, Guy Huntrods is tall and balding with a bulbous nose and a fast-clipped British accent. He's a bit of a bulldog: outspoken, self-assured. He never hesitates to "call a spade a bloody shovel." Huntrods carries a black fabric-covered notebook in his briefcase—he's done that since his days in the British Navy—to jog his memory on everything from how he spent a day off to what the foreign finance minister said, and Huntrods is quick to read a quote if the man later changes his mind.

He grew up near England's Lake District. During the war, Huntrods was a seaman in the British Navy. In 1946, Lieutenant Huntrods got a job at the Bank of England as a junior officer. He learned Spanish, then spent a year traveling and making contacts in Latin America. In 1965, when Brazil asked the IMF to suggest a man to help it set up a central bank, Huntrods got the nod. Two years later, Huntrods became Britain's alternate executive director at the IMF. He helped to arrange the IMF loan and the austerity program when the United Kingdom ran out of cash in 1967. In 1975, he got an offer he couldn't refuse: a directorship at Lloyds International, the premier European bank in Latin America.

In mid-October, Huntrods' boss asked him to go to Brazil. "We've got a problem with the Central Bank," he said. "Will you go and sort it out?"

"Brazil needs a jumbo loan," said Langoni when he and Huntrods sat down. "The American banks say they'll lend. We need help from Europe. But the reaction I got when I visited was disappointing."

"I'm just speaking for Lloyds," said Huntrods. "But you must face the fact they you're not going to get help until you put together a stabilization program." Tighten the belt.

"We have a cash flow problem," said Langoni. "We need support."

Huntrods shook his head. "You have a cash flow problem because you let inflation get out of control. Inflation is a dirty word in Europe. Europe expects Brazil to swallow some tough medicine and to get a handle on inflation before they'll lend again. They don't want to throw good money after bad."

So much for the European jumbo.

A few days later, Delfim's finance minister flew to Geneva for an international trade meeting. Between sessions, the finance minister lined up a $1.23-billion "bridge" loan from the U.S. Treasury. President Reagan announced the agreement at a state dinner in Brasilia on December 1. Then he lifted his glass to toast "the people of Bolivia."

The State Department sorted out the toast problem, but the treasury bridge wasn't a permanent solution.

"We have to go to the banks for long-term help," Delfim told Langoni. "But this isn't the right time." Brazil's congressional elections were planned for the middle of November. Going for help now was bad politics. And scheduled for the following year was the presidential election, the first since 1964. Delfim planned to be a candidate. "But we have to be ready. Talk to the bankers. Talk to Citibank."

Langoni flew to New York. He told Wriston that he had a cash flow problem.

"We have faith in Brazil," said Wriston. "But the world financial system could deal with only so many crises like Mexico or Argentina at one time." That meant that the best rescue for Brazil was a "voluntary" loan. Brazil would go to market for an eight-year jumbo loan. "You'll have to talk to the IMF," said Wriston. "You'll have to devise a plan to get the economy back on track."

"We'll need a $600-million bridge loan to tide us through till we get the new cash," said Langoni.

Wriston said he'd take care of that. He'd call the syndicate departme it. No need to bring in Bill Rhodes. Brazil wasn't sick enough for a rescue.

Brazil held its elections. The opposition party scored big gains. Langoni called the IMF.

The IMF sent a negotiating team to Brasilia.

By the middle of December, Brazil had agreed to a plan.

"Brazil is hosting a meeting December 20 at the Plaza Hotel," Delfim telexed each of the eight hundred banks that had lent to Brazil.

Huntrods flew in from London.

Delfim Netto sat on the dais, but he didn't speak. Speaking didn't seem politic.

The finance minister took the podium. "Brazil will solve its problems," he said. "We will cut the federal deficit to 3.5 percent of GDP (Gross Domestic Product), slash inflation to 85 percent, and up the trade surplus to $6 billion."

Huntrods raised an eyebrow. That didn't seem likely any time soon. The deficit was now 5 percent of GDP; inflation was almost 100 percent; net exports were $780 million.

Jacques de Larosière, the managing director of the IMF, aka "the M.D.," stood up. He was sure that the economic plan would work. "Brazil needs $9.9 billion," he said. "If the banks raise $4.4 billion, I will recommend that the IMF lend $5.5 billion."

"We have chosen Citibank and Morgan Bank to handle the

loans," said the finance minister. Citi, Brazil's biggest lender; Morgan, the bank with the closest ties to the Brazilian government. "Chase Manhattan will oversee trade lines." The short-term loans secured by export cargoes. "Bankers Trust will oversee interbank lines." The overnight money that had dropped by $4 billion since June. "We have lined up a $1.2-billion bridge loan from the BIS to tide us through until we have your new cash." The Bank of International Settlements, the Basel-based union of central banks that sometimes makes emergency short-term loans to cash pinched countries.

The meeting was over.

Huntrods didn't think the Brazilian plan would work. The four separate bank committees didn't make sense. And no one seemed to have realized that banks would choose to pull interbank lines to pay for their contribution to the new $4.4 billion loan. He wished that just one of the four coordinators was a European. After all the British had lent $8 billion to Brazil; the French had lent $5.6 billion. And why were only the big banks putting up new cash?

But Huntrods knew that Lloyds had to participate. The M.D. was behind the rescue.

By the end of March, the banks had raised the $1.4 billion and the IMF approved the $5.5 billion. But the rescue seemed doomed to failure.

Morgan asked only the top 120 banks to contribute to the $4.4 billion. That made those big banks mad.

At the same time, the European and Arab and small American banks pulled their old interbank lines, and that made Brazil lose millions of dollars a day.

Then in February, Citi and Morgan distributed a list of interbank exposures; the numbers were supposed to show just which banks weren't doing their fair share.

The lists made the banks mad. Some of the figures were wrong.

One of the lists found its way into the *Wall Street Journal*. That made the banks madder. Lending totals were supposed to be secret.

On February 23, Walter Wriston and Paul Volcker met with the chairmen of Morgan and Chase. "We can't keep increasing our overnight lines," said Wriston. "Brazil is using the American bank money to pay off the European CDs."

"We're going to cut our interbank lines too," said the chairman of Chase.

The chairman of Morgan didn't say anything.

The next morning, Citi began to cut its overnight lines.

Citi kept cutting $10 million a day.

Just after the first cut, thousands of unemployed workers marched on the government palace in São Paulo, destroying $10 million worth of property along the way.

The first $400 million installment of the BIS bridge was coming due. Brazil was short of cash. Delfim suggested a rollover. Delfim had to use up reserves to pay.

Brazil's new $9.9 billion loans were made in parts. Brazil got $1.2 billion from the IMF and $3.8 billion from the banks on signing the loan; the next two payments were conditional on good behavior. The statistics for the first quarter came in at the end of April. Brazil had missed every target.

The IMF froze its remaining $3.2 billion.

The banks froze their $1.7 billion.

The rumors started. "Brazil is going to freeze its bank lines to pay," said a banker. "We're all caught. We're never going to get out."

Suddenly the world seemed to be coming apart. *Newsweek* ran a cover story headlined "The Dynamite Issue: Despite a Building Recovery and Rescue Efforts, the Third World Debt Bomb Threatens to Explode."

On Tuesday, May 31, Volcker called a meeting of bank chairmen in New York.

It was clear that the rescue wasn't working.

As soon as he got back to his office, Walter Wriston got a call from the chairman of Chemical Bank.

"We've got to start fresh," said the chairman of Chemical. "We've got to handle Brazil the way we handled Mexico. Another quick fix won't work."

"You may be right," said Wriston.

"Soon," said the chairman of Chemical. "The second installment of the BIS loan is due on July 1." The BIS had given Brazil a thirty-day extension. "Brazil can't pay that $400 million unless the IMF and the commercial banks give Brazil the cash. And we're not giving Brazil the cash until something gets worked out."

After the meeting, Wriston popped his head into Rhodes' office. "Got a minute, Bill?" he asked.

"Sure," said Rhodes.

Wriston asked Rhodes to take over the Brazilian committee.

Rhodes said sure to that too.

The next day, Bill Rhodes' phone rang. It was the Brazilian finance minister. "I'm taking charge of liaison with the commercial banks," said the minister. Delfim Netto had decided that the finance minister and the head of the Central Bank should handle all debt questions; Delfim was making himself scarce until the crisis blew over. "We've got to talk about the new negotiations. There's going to be a new committee to represent the banks. We're thinking of a big committee, say twenty-four banks."

"Twenty-four is too big," said Rhodes. "Twenty-four banks can't negotiate anything. It can't be more than fourteen."

"Everyone has to have a voice," said the finance minister.

"Everyone will," said Rhodes. "The seats will be divided up based on exposure and geography. The Americans lent less than half the money. They will get just half the seats."

"I want two deputy chairmen," said the finance minister. "One American and one non-American. The American deputy will be Morgan Bank." Morgan was still the bank with the closest ties to the Brazilian government. "I haven't chosen the non-American."

"Lloyds," said Rhodes. "We need Guy Huntrods." Rhodes had worked closely with Huntrods on Argentina. Besides, Huntrods knew Brazilian finance like the palm of his hand.

Rhodes and the finance minister chose six non-American banks for the committee.

"Clearly the American banks with the biggest exposures have to be on the committee," said Rhodes. The U.S. money-center banks had lent $19 billion.

"Citi, Morgan, Chase, and the Bank of America," said the finance minister. Citi and Morgan, old coordinators. Chase and Bank of America, the two biggest lenders after Citibank.

"What about Manufacturers Hanover and Chemical?" asked

Rhodes. "They have big exposures." Two-point-one billion dollars and $1.3 billion respectively. "Manufacturers has good contacts with small banks around the country. Chemical supervised inter-bank lines from Mexico."

"Maybe," said the finance minister.

"They have to have seats," said Rhodes. "So does Bankers Trust. It played a key role the first time around."

"We'll see," said the finance minister.

"The banks aren't going to give you another penny until you strike a new agreement with the IMF," said Rhodes. "The $2 billion left over from the first loan is frozen until then; so are talks on a new loan."

Rhodes set down the receiver.

The phone rang.

It was Leighton Coleman, the top country workout man at Morgan Guaranty. "I'm representing Morgan on the new committee," he said. "Let's talk."

Leighton Coleman is punctilious. At fifty-two, he has steel gray hair and a round red face. Coleman spends weekends with his kids—eighteen and twenty-one—in Stony Brook, Long Island. He plays tennis badly, reads spy adventure stories, and unwinds with a vodka and Perrier; he chain-smokes Camels. Whenever negotiations get stuck, Coleman throws up his hands and says, "You won't get perfect justice until you meet the Great Rescheduler in the Sky."

Coleman grew up in New York and majored in diplomatic history at Yale. Armed with an M.B.A. from Columbia, Coleman landed a job at Morgan as a credit trainee. Six months later, he was drafted. After two years at Fort Dix, Coleman was back at the bank, first in the government bonds department, then in general banking working on loans for clients like Singer, CBS and RCA. In 1970, Coleman was sent to the Paris office, but a year later headed back to New York, with a brief stopover in Morgan's London headquarters. He stayed on in London to handle big "off-shore" loans, loans to governments and multinational companies booked through a branch outside the States and hence not subject to U.S. government restrictions. In 1977, Coleman moved his department to Morgan headquarters in New York. Two years later, Coleman was rotated to East Asia Pacific.

But in March 1981, Poland went bankrupt. Coleman, with his Eurosyndication expertise, was sent to Zurich to negotiate. It seemed clear to the Morgan brass that Poland was only the beginning. Coleman was detached to handle cash-squeezed countries all across the globe, including Mexico and Argentina.

But Coleman didn't deal with Brazil: through the winter of 1983, Morgan believed that Brazil didn't need a rescue.

Then the Brazilian rescue collapsed.

Brazil was out of cash.

The chairman of Morgan called Coleman. "You're a deputy chairman of the new rescue team," he said. "The other deputy chairman is Guy Huntrods. Call Bill Rhodes."

Coleman knew Rhodes: they had worked together on Argentina and Mexico. He set up a meeting.

Later that week, when Coleman arrived at Citibank, Huntrods was already waiting.

"We have to do this right," said Rhodes. "Otherwise it will be like *A Bridge Too Far*."

Coleman smiled.

"The three of us are going to work as a team," said Rhodes. We will do everything together. We will be equals."

"That's good," said Huntrods.

"We've got to approach this deal carefully," said Rhodes. "The banks are already panicking. The newspapers say that the world is falling apart. We have to give off an air of tranquility. We have to have an organized plan. If we appear to be running around haphazardly, it will be like putting gasoline on a fire."

"It's clear that there will be a rescheduling of payments due in 1983 and 1984," said Coleman. Principal payments, not interest payments. "It's clear that there will be a new loan. It's clear that the IMF can't lend more; it's already lent Brazil the maximum."

"We're in a holding pattern until Brazil strikes a new agreement with the IMF," said Huntrods. "We've got to maintain the trade lines." The $10 billion that kept Brazilian iron barges and coffee boats cruising around the world and got Brazil the dollars it needed to pay interest. "We've got to keep the interbank lines in place."

The $5.7 billion of overnight money still on loan. "That isn't going to be easy."

"Last time, the banks complained that they weren't getting enough information," said Rhodes. "This time, communication will be a priority. Last time, the banks complained that they were starved for economic data. This time, there will be a subcommittee to get the correct numbers. Last time, the banks felt that the deal was being crammed down their throats. This time, everyone will participate."

"Last time, the banks didn't work very effectively with the IMF and the Treasury and the Fed," said Huntrods. "This time, we will get government support. We will get export credits." Government loans to finance trade. "This time, we will get government support on the new money drive. Brazil is a key country in the international economy. Helping Brazil helps Europe and America."

"The U.S. government helped Brazil last fall," said Coleman. "But the mood isn't good now. Look what's happened to the IMF bill," he said.

The IMF committed most of money to loans to Mexico, Argentina and Brazil. The agency had asked all member countries to increase their subscriptions by 45.5 percent and had asked the ten biggest industrial countries to increase credit lines as well; the requested U.S. increase totaled $8.4 billion, and the authorization bill had been blocked in the House for months. Putting cash on deposit at the IMF so that the IMF could lend to bankrupt countries didn't cost the United States anything—the United States even got interest from the IMF—but it looked to the lawmakers like a bank bailout.

"What are we going to do about the BIS?" asked Huntrods. The BIS had just deferred the $400-million payment for an extra fifteen days.

"Like it or not, the BIS will have to roll over," said Rhodes. "But it won't be for long. We should have an agreement by the end of the summer."

Wednesday afternoon, June 15, Bill Rhodes caught a cab up Park Avenue to the Carlyle at Madison and Seventy-sixth. The bankers who had agreed to serve on the international rescue committee were waiting for him. He banged his fist on the table for attention. "This negotiation is going to be different from the last one," he said. "That was Phase I. This is Phase II." Rhodes looked around the table. Many of these bankers had already served on the Mexican and Argentine committees. He nodded at the men representing the Bank of Tokyo and Deutsche Bank and Crédit Lyonnais, the Bank of Montreal and the Union Bank of Switzerland. The only new face was the man from Arab Banking Corporation.

"We've got to do something fast," said Coleman. "Brazil can't make interest payments—its loans from the IMF and from us have been frozen since May. We've got to have a deal by the end of the third quarter." September 30. "Otherwise the loans will go bad. And the banks will be in big trouble." Bank accounting laws are complicated. If a borrower pays any interest within ninety days, the bank will credit the account as if it had been paid in full. If a borrower misses an interest payment altogether, then the bank not only credits "no payment," but also subtracts "payments" that were previously credited but not actually paid. The problem was most serious for Citi: if all its Brazilian loans went bad, the bank would lose twenty percent of its after-tax income.

"The first thing Brazil needs is a new agreement with the IMF," said Rhodes. He took a cigar out of his jacket pocket, bit off the tip and lit it. "Once Brazil and the IMF agree on a new set of economic targets the IMF can release the next $400 million of its loan and we can release the next $635 million of our loan and Brazil can pay our interest." Brazil could also pay the $400 million to the BIS and the $600-million commercial-bank bridge and the $1.23-billion treasury bridge. "Then we can talk about another loan. Brazil is going to need more cash this year." Rhodes puffed on his cigar.

"Phase II will have two operating principles," said Huntrods. "First, all banks with loans to Brazil will participate equally. Second, international agencies and governments will participate. Phase II is not going to be a purely commercial bank rescue. There's going to be a sharing of burdens."

Rhodes took another puff on his cigar. He looked around the table. "Each of you will need to talk to your own government." He looked at Coleman and Huntrods. "The chairmen will go to

168

Washington every week until the cash comes through. We're going to talk to everyone that has money or influence." He ticked off a list of government and development agencies.

"This is basically an organizing meeting," said Rhodes. "From here on, I want to schedule a meeting at least every other week. We'll use 33A." Conference room 33A at Citicorp Center, the same conference room Rhodes had used for the Mexican and Argentine and Peruvian and Uruguayan negotiations. "We'll start at nine-thirty and go until we're done."

Rhodes paused and scanned the room. "We've got to have a division of labor," he said. "I want to send a team of economists to Brazil. The banks don't trust the Brazilian numbers. I need a volunteer to chair the economic subcommittee."

The man from the Bank of Montreal raised his hand. He had been a member of the economics team for Mexico too. Rhodes called him a "stand-up economist" because he liked to crack jokes.

Good. A non-American bank. Rhodes made a note. He looked at the man from Bankers Trust. "We need a committee to monitor interbank lines. We have to stabilize cash."

He looked at the man from Chase Manhattan. "And a committee to monitor trade lines."

"We'll have a coordinating committee of fifty banks to handle communications with everyone who lent," said Rhodes. "One last thing. These meetings have to be strictly confidential. Don't talk to the press. There were too many rumors last time. There were a lot of misunderstandings. Let's not let that happen again."

Two weeks after that first committee meeting, things didn't look promising. Guy Huntrods, Bill Rhodes and Leighton Coleman had gone to Washington to pay their first calls on the IMF, the World Bank, the Inter-America Development Bank (IDB), the Treasury, the Fed, and the State Department. Even the most sympathetic had made no promises; some of the officials had been downright hostile.

Progress with the bankers' committee meetings weren't much better. Clearly it would take a lot of meetings to reach a consensus.

But at least Brazil seemed to be moving.

The IMF had sent a negotiating team to Brazil on June 10, and a week later, President João Baptista Figueiredo had introduced a tough austerity plan. He hiked petroleum prices 45 percent and accelerated the slashing of $5 billion of government subsidies to coffee, sugar and other products. It looked like Brazil would have a new deal by the end of August or early September.

Two weeks later, Figueiredo announced that he would cut government spending by $1.2 billion. Income taxes would go up; there would be new taxes on stock market transactions.

"Interbank lines are stable," the man from Bankers Trust had said at the subcommittee breakfast eight o'clock Tuesday morning in July.

Huntrods sipped his coffee. So far so good.

Then suddenly things weren't so good.

In Brazil, the new government austerity hit hard. Prices were skyrocketing. Layoffs were increasing. In June workers in Rio and São Paulo walked off the job in protest. There were pickets. There was looting. Millions of home buyers launched a "strike" on government housing loan payments which now rose faster than wages.

"The negotiations with Brazil are stalled," Jacques de Larosière, the IMF managing director, told Huntrods and Rhodes and Coleman at their June 21 meeting. "Brazil has to stop indexing wages. That's the only way to break the inflation spiral. A wage bill is the key to a new package." And Brazil wouldn't budge.

"Why don't we forget about making a new loan to Brazil," said the man from Deutsche Bank at the committee meeting on June 28. "Instead we'll capitalize interest." The banks would simply add the interest that Brazil owed, but didn't pay, to the total principal on the books. Some of the German banks were convinced that they'd never get another penny out of Brazil; they didn't see the point in giving Brazil money they could otherwise lend to other borrowers, borrowers that paid them back.

"That won't work," said Rhodes. "We need cash."

"Capitalizing interest might be a good idea," said the man from the Bank of Tokyo. "Capitalizing interest is equitable. No one has to volunteer. No one can cheat. Equity is very important." Because capitalizing interest was entirely on paper, the banks didn't have a choice as to whether they would "contribute" or not.

The bankers argued.

"Let's break for lunch," said Rhodes.

The bankers walked into the small conference room down the hall. There were platters of sandwiches, Cokes and napkins, on the table. The same catered sandwiches that they'd eaten through the Mexican and Argentine talks: chicken on pita bread, steak on French, turkey and tomato on pumpernickel. The sandwiches were good, but it was time for some variety.

"I think we should consider capitalizing interest," said the man from Deutsche Bank when the bankers sat down at the negotiating table again after lunch. "Capitalizing interest makes sense."

Rhodes puffed on his cigar. "The U.S. bank regulators won't approve," he said. "Paul Volcker won't like the idea."

"Rhodes always lets you know who he's talked to," whispered a banker to the man next to him. He raised an eyebrow.

"It gets on your nerves after a while," said the man. "But at least you know where you are."

Bill Rhodes spent the Fourth of July weekend in Toronto catching up on his reading and rest. He was back in the office on Tuesday, July 5.

By then, Brazil seemed to be sinking fast. June inflation came in at a record 12.3 percent—an annual 302 percent—and unemployment soared to more than 20 percent. College-educated Brazilians were selling bananas on street corners. The industrial work force in São Paulo dropped to 1.6 million, the level it had been in 1973. There were pickets at dozens of government offices. One day fifty thousand protesters marched in Rio, shouting "Down with the IMF" and "Moratorium Now." Rumors swirled that Delfim was about to be fired, that Brazil's whole economic team was about to be fired. The only good news was that the trade surplus surged to $829 million, more than the surplus for all of 1982.

The world was losing faith in Brazil. Royal Dutch/Shell demanded payment in advance for oil shipments. American Airlines could not get dollars for its tickets, so it canceled all flights to Brazil. On July 7, New York traders heard that Brazil was going to default. Sell orders flooded the New York Stock Exchange. The Dow-Jones Industrial Average plunged 11 points in half an hour; gold soared $17.50 an ounce.

"We're deadlocked," said the head of the Brazilian Central Bank when Rhodes called the next morning. "The IMF is asking for too much. Brazil needs to tighten the belt, but not this fast. Brazil can't meet the tough targets that the IMF wants."

"There's no progress," the M.D. told Rhodes on the phone Friday. "And we're running out of time. Figueiredo flies to Ohio next week." President Figueiredo was scheduled for medical tests at the Cleveland Clinic in Ohio on July 13. It wasn't clear how long Figueiredo would be in the States—that depended partly on whether he had to have an operation—and the vice president would be chief administrator while Figueiredo was gone. The word in Brazil was that no major decisions would be made until the president returned. The vice president and Delfim Netto were bitter political enemies; Delfim found the vice president so irritating that he left Brazil every time the vice president took charge.

Rhodes thought. Brazil was $2.3 billion behind in interest payments; the average payment was forty-three days late. Currency reserves were almost gone; so was the gold stockpile. Rhodes dialed the finance minister.

"We will pay," said the man. "Don't worry. Things are going fine."

There was only one way that Brazil would pay: by making a deal with the IMF. Then the IMF would pay the next installment of its $5.5-billion loan; the banks would pay the next piece of their $4.4-billion loan.

The undersecretary of the Treasury called. "We told Brazil that we might extend a new $600-million bridge once they have a deal with the IMF," he said.

The president of the BIS called. "Our loan payment comes due July 15," he said. "We have already deferred our $400-million payment forty-five days. We cannot defer again."

The pressure was on.

A storm had broken over southern Brazil on July 6. By Monday the tenth, three provinces were flooded with twenty-six inches of water and the people had no food or water. One million tons of grain were destroyed, herds of cattle were drowned, a hundred people were killed. The preliminary estimate of damages: $1.5 billion.

Then late in the afternoon, the head of the Central Bank called Bill Rhodes. "Figueiredo is going to make a television speech tonight," said Langoni. "It might be important."

Rhodes couldn't tune in, but the Citibank man in Rio did.

Figueiredo stood on the platform flanked by his cabinet. "The moment is critical," he said. "The economy is sick." He announced that wage increases would be limited to 80 percent of the inflation rate.

Brazil had finally buckled. Now there could be an IMF agreement—and a bank rescue.

Figueiredo flew to Cleveland for tests. Langoni flew to New York for bank meetings. The head of the BIS announced that although the BIS would not formally extend its loan, it would wait for payment until the IMF released the cash.

Rhodes heaved a sigh of relief.

The M.D. called Monday to say that there was a tentative agreement, but there was also a snag. The IMF couldn't release the loan until the wage limit that Figueiredo had announced became law, but the bill wouldn't be introduced until the Brazilian Congress went back into session on August 1. Moreover, Figueiredo's party didn't have the votes to pass the bill—so the law would stay on the books only if the bill wasn't defeated within sixty days.

There might not be any money for Brazil until early October.

"We banks are going to have to hang tight," said Rhodes at the bank meeting Wednesday, July 21.

The man from the Arab Banking Corporation cleared his throat. "I have a message from the home office," he said. "Brazil is way behind on its payments. We need to have our money on time."

That was like the Arabs. They didn't answer telexes—and then demanded their cash.

"You've got to be patient," said Huntrods. "Brazil doesn't have money."

"We need to be paid," said the man from the Arab Banking Corporation.

"The economics subcommittee has been to Brazil," said the man from the Bank of Montreal. "We've looked at the numbers. We've made some estimates." He looked at a page of computations. "Brazil will need $3.5 billion this year and another $5.8 billion next year."

The bankers squirmed.

Rhodes tapped his fist on the table. "The head of the Brazilian Central Bank is here to make a presentation," he said. Rhodes and Coleman and Huntrods had talked to Langoni just before they walked into the bank meeting, but he'd refused to tell them what he was planning to propose.

"We've got a deal with the IMF," said Langoni. "We're waiting for approval from the M.D. We're expecting that next week. But even when we have a handshake, we won't be able to begin paying back the interest. We can't touch the frozen cash until the wage law is set. We are going to need an advance."

"I saw Delfim Netto in New York on Sunday," the M.D. told Rhodes and Coleman and Huntrods when they met in Washington on Thursday, July 28. "We talked through the program. We've got a basic agreement on wages. We've got a basic agreement on spending targets. We've set more targets this time." A target for the government deficit. A target for the budgets of the government companies. "But before we can finalize an agreement, we need an early warning system. We want the data in three weeks, not two months. We want monthly reporting. We're sending a second negotiating team to Brazil."

Meanwhile, Brazilian opposition politicians were talking a debt moratorium. There were rumors that Brazil would nationalize the banks. There were more strikes and more protests. The head of the Gallup polling organization reported that Delfim was "the most unpopular man in the country. People hate him." The economy was teetering. Inflation for July came in at a record 13.3 percent. Brazil was so short of cash that all dollar earnings had to be handed over to the Central Bank to pay the oil bill.

Then someone leaked to the press. A London financial newsletter quoted a banker as telling the committee he wouldn't lend another penny to a "rat hole" like Brazil. The banker hadn't actually used those words, but the thought was right.

Rhodes looked around the room at the August 4 meeting. "I

thought I made it clear that you had to be careful about leaks," he said. "A leak could sabotage an agreement."

Guy Huntrod was very worried. On August 9, the Brazilian press reported that the government party was splintering. The opposition faction—opposed to Delfim and supporting the vice president—was gaining strength. According to the papers, that meant that the wage law wouldn't pass. The whole rescue package might collapse.

The clock was ticking. Another $400-million BIS payment came due on September 1. The American banks had to close their third-quarter books on September 30. Unless Brazil reached an agreement with the IMF there would be no money to pay.

"We'll have to go to Brazil to talk to Delfim Netto," said Rhodes. "We've got to establish a direct dialogue. That's the only way to find out what is really going on." Rhodes switched on the speakerphone. He dialed the finance minister.

"We'd like to come to Brazil," said Coleman. "We need to talk to you and Delfim."

"You can come," said the finance minister. "But your visit has to be secret. We don't want anyone to know that you're here." The Brazilians were paranoid about the press. "A story about a bank visit to Brazil is going to make people think that the negotiations have collapsed. We might lose all our interbank money."

"I guess we can think of a cover," said Rhodes. He didn't quite understand the need for secrecy.

"What are you going to do if someone finds out that we're in Brazil?" asked Huntrods.

"We'll say you aren't here," said the finance minister.

"You can't outright lie," said Huntrods.

"We'll say you aren't here," repeated the finance minister.

Rhodes broke in. "If we schedule the meeting the day after we sign the Argentine loan package and hold the meeting at someone's house, the press probably won't find out," he said. Rhodes had just worked out a rescue for bankrupt Argentina.

"We'll meet at my house," said the finance minister.

Wednesday morning, August 16, Rhodes signed the loan papers

at the Argentine consulate on West Fifty-sixth Street.

The room was mobbed with reporters.

Huntrods mingled with the crowd. He tried to disguise his accent. He didn't want to talk to the man from the BBC.

Coleman stood in front of the table and watched.

After the ceremony, Rhodes and Coleman and Huntrods slipped out the door and headed for Teterboro Airport, the New Jersey strip for private planes. The Citi plane was in the hangar for repairs, so the bankers boarded a time share. The engine malfunctioned en route and they had to stop in Barbados for five hours for repairs. It was four in the morning when they finally touched down at Brasilia International Airport.

A government car was waiting.

"You've got to come to a prompt agreement with the IMF," Rhodes told Delfim later that morning. "The past-due interest is backing up almost ninety days. We can't keep the banks on board much longer."

"You've got to speak with one voice," said Coleman. "The three of you can't have separate policies."

"There is a smell of defeat around the streets of Brasilia that reminds me of France before Dunkirk," said Huntrods. He looked at Delfim. "We can't have this defeatism."

"That's right," said Rhodes. "You've got to have the spirit that won the Battle of Normandy."

Leighton Coleman frowned at the newspaper. On Sunday, August 22, the *Washington Post* had labeled Rhodes a "superman" and the Brazilian rescue a "Mission Impossible." The regional banks had told the *Post* that they weren't going to make any new loans to Brazil. Ever.

Still, other things were going well.

The Export-Import Bank had announced that it was willing to loan Brazil $1.5 billion to help it buy U.S. imports. That was the largest trade package that the bank had ever offered.

Delfim had made a pact with the M.D. in Paris. Brazil would cut inflation to 60 percent in 1984, down from 150 percent in the last year. Brazil would balance the government budget, down from a $15-billion deficit in 1982. Brazil would increase the trade surplus from $780 million in 1982 to $6 billion in 1983 to $9 billion in 1984. Brazil would report to the IMF once a month; its lag time for computing the numbers would be cut to three weeks.

Right now, Coleman's biggest worry was time: the quarter ended September 30.

"Langoni is here with a proposal," said Rhodes at the bank meeting August 26. Rhodes didn't know what the proposal was; as usual, Langoni had been evasive when Rhodes and Huntrods and Coleman had tried to find out.

"He certainly looks perky," said a banker to the man next to him.

"He always does," said the man. It annoyed the bankers that Langoni didn't seem to work very hard; he also gave the impression that he was contemptuous of commercial bankers.

"Brazil needs $8.4 billion in new cash for 1983 and 1984," said Langoni.

Rhodes thought he was being optimistic. He would have estimated $1 billion more. "I've just been to Washington," continued Langoni. "There isn't going to be any additional money from the World Bank or the IDB."

Coleman raised an eyebrow. That wasn't true. He had been to Washington with Rhodes and Huntrods several times during the summer, and he was certain that there would be government money.

"You commercial bankers cannot possibly raise another $8.4 billion in cash for Brazil," said Langoni.

True.

"I don't think you bankers can even raise five," he said.

Maybe not.

"However, there is a way around this problem," he said.

Rhodes stared.

Coleman stared.

Huntrods stared.

The bankers around the table stared.

There was?

"It just so happens that Brazil owes the banks $8.4 billion in cash between now and the end of the year," said Langoni. "We can capitalize the interest. You won't have to put up any cash."

177

The bankers were silent.

"It's just an idea," said Langoni. "It's not a hard and fast position, it's an idea."

Rhodes signaled to Langoni to leave the room.

The bankers all started to talk at once.

"We can't capitalize interest," said one of the Americans. "We've been through this before."

"Capitalizing interest doesn't make sense," said Huntrods. "Capitalizing interest won't solve Brazil's problems. It may be an easy way out; it may be an equitable way out, but it isn't a good way out. Brazil has to get its economic house in order. Capitalizing interest just pushes the problems into the future." He looked at Rhodes. "If Brazil has to pay interest every quarter, it has to earn cash every quarter. Paying cash interest forces Brazil to be disciplined. And we all know that Brazil isn't very disciplined on its own."

"Once we let Brazil capitalize one interest payment, we'll never get cash interest again," said Coleman.

Rhodes puffed on his cigar.

The bankers argued.

"Let's go around the table," said Rhodes late in the afternoon; he avoided calling for "votes"; that sounded adversarial.

The bankers agreed: they would not let Brazil capitalize interest; instead, they would raise the $4 billion or so in cash. Brazil needed to pay interest the way they had for Mexico and Argentina, by assessing each bank a percentage of what it already had on loan.

Bill Rhodes sat in the big armchair in his apartment. It had been a rough week. Brazil's negotiations were going slowly. The BIS was rumbling about the $400-million payment. Just that day, *Veja*, the Brazilian newsweekly, hit the newsstands; "They Want Delfim's Head (And Why Fugueiredo Won't Give It to Them)" blared the headline across a photograph of Delfim without a head.

It was time to take a night off. Rhodes picked up his copy of William Manchester's *The Last Lion* and opened to the place mark.

The telephone rang.

It was the Brazilian finance minister. "Langoni is out," he said.

Rhodes didn't say anything. At the meeting in Brasilia just two weeks ago, Delfim had insisted that the team would stay together.

"We think we've decided on Celso Pastore," said the finance minister.

Afonso Celso Pastore was an economics professor at the University of São Paulo and a former secretary of finance for the state of São Paulo. Pastore was a protégé of Delfim Netto, but he had a reputation for independence. "The bankers respect Celso," said Rhodes. "He's a good man."

"Don't say a word about this," said the finance minister. "We don't want word to leak before our announcement."

Rhodes didn't say a word about the call when he met with Coleman, Huntrods and the M.D. on August 31; he had promised.

"We are close to an agreement," said the M.D. "It's time to talk about the new cash." He paused. "Brazil needs $9.3 billion. The IMF cannot put up more cash. We have already lent the maximum. There is only one other source of money: the commercial banks. You must raise $9.3 billion."

"There is no way the banks can put together $9.3 billion," said Coleman.

"We can't raise close to that," said Huntrods.

The M.D. fell back in his chair. Raising the money had to be possible. Brazil needed $9.3 billion.

"You haven't said anything about government money," said Huntrods. "Couldn't the governments put up export credits?"

"That's right," said Rhodes. "The goverments lined up $2 billion for Mexico."

The M.D. didn't look convinced.

"Where there's a will, there's a way," said Coleman.

"We've got to iron out the details of the new lending agreement," said Rhodes at the meeting on Thursday, September 1. "We're talking about a lot of money. Our part will be at least $4 billion. We've agreed that each bank will put up a percentage of his exposure at some base date. That seems to be the most equitable arrangement. We've got to choose the date. It seems to me that there are three alternatives." Rhodes and Coleman and Huntrods had talked this through on the long plane ride to Brasilia two weeks ago: June 30, 1983, the end of the most recent full quarter;

December 30, 1982, the quarter end closest to the meeting at the Plaza, Brazil's first formal call for help; June 30, 1982, the quarter end closest to when the banks began to pull their interbank lines.

The man from the Bank of Tokyo coughed. "We have prepared a memorandum on this question," he said. He passed out copies of a five-page paper.

Rhodes read. The English was convoluted, but the ideas were clear: there was only one equitable date, June 30, 1982. Until then, the banks had believed in Brazil. After that, the banks had begun to pull their lines. No bank should be allowed to benefit because it had pulled its lines after Brazil began to slide.

Rhodes was poker-faced. The Japanese were among the few banks that had increased their lines after June 1982; almost everyone else had cut back. Setting the base date back meant that the Japanese had to contribute less to the new loan.

"That doesn't make sense," said a banker. "The banks that were smart enough to see trouble coming shouldn't be penalized now. December 1982 is the date."

"I'm with the Japanese," said another banker. "June 1982 is the first date to use."

Huntrods tapped on the table for attention. "The base date cannot be set before the day that Brazil formally asked for help," he said. "There must be a logic to the date we choose. The Plaza date—December 30, 1982—is the date that the Brazilians asked for help. Choosing an earlier date means punishing the banks for good banking."

The room was silent for a moment.

Then the bankers began to argue again.

"We need complete justice," said the man from the Bank of Tokyo.

"Complete justice," snapped Huntrods. "As Leighton Coleman would say, such is possible only on the day that you meet the Great Rescheduler in the Sky."

The bankers kept arguing.

Finally Huntrods looked at Rhodes. "The dogs bark," he said, "the caravan moves on."

The meeting broke up.

Rhodes went home feeling frustrated. Brazil hadn't signed an agreement with the IMF. The banks couldn't cut a deal. Something had to give.

First thing next morning, the Brazilian finance minister called. "It's official," he said.

The head of the Central Bank had resigned. And Pastore had been named to succeed him.

Bill Rhodes boarded Delta Flight #93 for Nassau. He was going to spend Labor Day weekend on the beach in the Bahamas enjoying himself. He needed a break; he'd been working past nine most nights and many weekends. Four days of sunshine would make a big difference; he'd finally "recharge the battery."

By the time Rhodes got back, things had started to move.

The BIS announced that it would let Brazil postpone the $400 million due September 1 until Brazil got its cash from the IMF and the banks.

The M.D. called to say that Brazil had finally put together the details of the IMF agreement. The new head of the Central Bank had just left Washington for a meeting of the Brazilian National Monetary Council in Brasilia. After the council gave its approval, the man would fly to Washington again to put his name on the Letter of Intent, the formal agreement in principle with the IMF.

Wednesday, September 14, Rhodes and Coleman and Huntrods caught a New York Air shuttle to Washington to see the M.D.

"I saw Pastore and Ernane Galvêas on Monday," said the M.D. Galvêas was the finance minister. "The IMF board tentatively endorsed the Brazilian agreement this morning. The board will give its final approval after the wage law passes." He looked at Rhodes. "Brazil still needs $9.3 billion." The same total that the M.D. had asked for the last time Rhodes and Coleman and Huntrods had been in Washington. "I've talked to the World Bank and the IDB. They can put up some cash. I had lunch with the G-10 finance ministers." The Group of Ten (G-10), the policy-coordinating union of the ten biggest Western economies. "They have agreed to increase export credits by $2.5 billion." He looked at Rhodes. He looked at Coleman. He looked at Huntrods. "That means that the commercial banks must contribute $6.8 billion.

The IMF board won't give the final approval unless a critical mass of that commercial bank money has been committed." If Brazil collapsed because the commercial bank money didn't come through, the money that the IMF lent would be wasted.

Rhodes took a cigar out of the pocket of his jacket, bit off the tip and lit it. "I don't think that the commercial banks can put together $6.8 billion," he said. "We might be able to do $5 billion."

"Brazil needs $6.8 billion," said the M.D. "I have tried every other financial institution. That money must come from the commercial banks." He paused. "And it must be lined up in time for the board meeting. Without the commercial bank money, there will be no IMF agreement."

And without the IMF agreement, there would be no commercial bank money.

Coleman shifted in his seat. The M.D. hadn't said how much a "critical mass" of money was, but Coleman figured it was 90 percent: that had been the M.D.'s definition of the critical mass of Mexican money. "You haven't given us a lot of time," he said. "We've only got about a month before your next board meeting."

"Look," said Rhodes. "The banks have already lent Brazil $4.4 billion this year. You're asking us to bring the total to more than eleven."

"It will be $6.8 billion," said the M.D.

The bankers argued.

The M.D. repeated that there was no choice. Everyone else had contributed.

Finally, Rhodes stood up. There was no point in arguing more tonight. The M.D. would have to talk to the commercial bank chairmen themselves.

The M.D. nodded.

Rhodes looked at his watch. It was almost eleven.

"We talked to the M.D. last night," said Rhodes at the committee meeting the next afternoon. "He is going to settle the question of how big the bank loan to Brazil will be with each of your chairmen separately. We've got to agree on a bargaining position. The M.D. wants an additional $6.8 billion."

The bankers stared. Then they started saying it couldn't be done.

"Look." The man from the Bank of Montreal tapped his fist

on the table. "I've put together a presentation on how much cash the banks can lend," he said. He passed out a three-page position paper. "This deal has to be equitable. It has to be equitable not only among the banks, but also among the other lending institutions. If half the money has to come from the commercial banks, then the rest has to come from governments and agencies. Let's look at the numbers. The IMF's $9.3 billion includes adding $2 billion to reserves. Brazil doesn't have any reserves right now, but this isn't the time to add. If we forget about reserves, we're talking about a $7-billion package. The banks should put up $3.5 billion, the other institutions $3.5 billion." He paused. "The IMF is being greedy when it asks us to put up $6.8 billion. The IMF isn't putting up a penny. The IMF is taking advantage of the banks."

The woman from Manufacturers Hanover smiled. The man from the Bank of Montreal had made the same argument about the loan to Mexico.

"We can't tell the IMF to give more money to Brazil," muttered Huntrods. The IMF had already given Brazil as much as it was allowed to give.

"We aren't getting very far," said Rhodes a couple of hours later. "Let's move on."

The bankers nodded.

"The Brazilians want concessions," said Rhodes. "Leighton and Guy and I talked to Pastore." The new head of the Central Bank. "He says that Brazil has enough cash only for necessities like coal and oil. He says that Brazil can't afford much more interest and he's worried that inflation is going to rise."

"Every percentage point increase in interest rates costs Brazil $800 million," said Coleman.

Rhodes looked around the table. "Pastore wants five years of grace," he said. Five years before the country had to pay back any principal on the new loan. Brazil would start paying interest immediately.

"Mexico only got four years of grace," said a banker. "Brazil had only two and a half years on the $4.4-billion Phase I loan."

"Let's give Brazil five years," said another. "That's a realistic concession."

183

The bankers talked.

Rhodes went around the table.

Five years of grace.

"Let's cut the interest rate an eighth of a percentage point," suggested Coleman. Rhodes and Huntrods and Coleman had agreed that it was psychologically important to give Brazil concessions. Brazil seemed to be making a real effort to get the economy back on track. "Cutting the interest rate an eighth of a point costs us just $7 million a year."

"Why do we want to do that?" asked a second. "Usually we cut the interest rate to reward good performance. Brazil hasn't performed well."

"Brazil has signed a new letter of intent," said Huntrods. "That's progress."

The bankers talked.

Rhodes went around the table.

The banks would cut the interest rate.

"Why don't we cut the rescheduling fee too," said Huntrods. Banks usually charged a troubled borrower 1.5 percent of his principal outstanding to put together a new schedule of payment dates; for Brazil that would run $75 million up front. Rhodes and Coleman and Huntrods had talked this through too. "Let's charge just 1 percent—$50 million."

"We could let Brazil pay the fee in installments," suggested Coleman.

The bankers agreed to the cut and the installments.

"We still haven't settled the base date," said Huntrods. "I think we ought to choose December 1982."

The bankers argued for hours.

Rhodes went around the table. December 1982.

"We have to agree on a bargaining stance," said Bill Rhodes at the meeting September 22. "The M.D. wants $6.8 billion."

"Six billion is about as high as we can go," said Coleman. "We can go a little higher, but not much." He paused. "Six billion is 10 percent of our exposure. The $5 billion we gave Mexico was only 7 percent."

The bankers argued all day.

"We don't seem to be able to agree on a number," said Rhodes at nine that night. "Why don't we choose a range. How's $5 billion to $6 billion?"

The bankers argued.

"Let's go around the table," said Rhodes at eleven.

A range it would be: $5 billion to $6 billion.

First thing next morning, Rhodes took the elevator to Wriston's fifteenth-floor office.

"The M.D. wants the commercial banks to give Brazil $6.8 billion," Rhodes told him. "We think $6 billion is the maximum. We think that $5 billion is more realistic. You bank chairmen will have to thrash it out in Washington."

Wriston looked at Rhodes. "We'll work something out."

Walter Wriston took the podium in the IMF boardroom. The chairmen of the world's leading banks were there.

"Let's get this settled," he said. "The World Bank and the IDB have offered to pitch in. We only have to put together $6.5 billion."

The bankers argued.

"It has to be $6.5 billion," said the chairman of Manufacturers Hanover. When the meeting had started, the man had been adamant that $6 billion was too much, but now he realized that the banks didn't have a choice.

Another chairman agreed.

And another.

Finally, just before six-thirty, the bankers had a handshake.

Wriston called the M.D. into the room. "We've got a deal," he said. "We will raise $6.5 billion. The World Bank and the IDB have agreed to lend an extra $300 million." Rhodes had lined up those commitments earlier in the afternoon.

Rhodes and Coleman and Huntrods flew back to New York at the end of the week to iron out the last wrinkles.

By then, it was September 30. Brazil hadn't paid any interest since late July. Arrears were up to $2.84 billion. Bank earnings would be down for the quarter, and down for the year.

Thursday, October 6, the representatives of fifty big banks flew to Washington for a meeting at the IMF.

Rhodes was edgy. The smaller advisory committee had agreed

185

to the rescue, but none of the other banks had heard the details. If the banks at this meeting didn't like the package, Brazil was in deep trouble—and so was Citibank.

Just before the session started, Coleman told Rhodes that he'd read in London's *Financial Times* that Carlos Geraldo Langoni, the old head of the Brazilian Central Bank, had publicly denounced the IMF plan for Brazil as too tough.

Rhodes frowned. The banks were already worried about Brazil. The didn't need Langoni to stir them up. There wasn't much he could do. Rhodes walked into the auditorium and called the meeting to order. He outlined the terms of the financing package. "We're talking about a $6.5-billion loan from the commercial banks," he said. Due in nine years with five years of grace at an interest rate 2 percent over Libor.

"That sounds possible," said one banker after the next.

Maybe this rescue would really work.

Wednesday, October 12, Rhodes and Coleman and Huntrods were off on a week-long trip around the world to try to convince the banks to lend to Brazil.

The meetings seemed to go well.

Seven days later, Huntrods and Coleman were on their way to the Zurich airport after the final meeting with bankers. "I don't like the news out of Brazil," said Huntrods. There had just been a wave of riots and supermarket lootings. The police had attacked crowds with tear gas and clubs; men, women, even children, had been injured.

"Politics are out of control," said Coleman. Left wing intellectuals were calling for a complete break with the IMF and a twenty-five-year moratorium on debt payments. Middle-of-the-road politicians were against the IMF plan. The vote on the wage law was coming any day now.

"Pastore says the wage law is solid," said Huntrods.

"He had better be right," said Coleman. "If that bill is defeated, the IMF program will collapse. The bank loan will collapse. Brazil will collapse."

Huntrods headed to the Swissair gate for his flight.

Coleman walked to the TWA gate. He had time to kill before his flight left for New York. He strolled over to the Reuters machine

186

to see what was going on in the world. The ticker was clicking. Coleman looked down.

Brasilia, Oct 20. The Brazilian government issued a decree setting wage rise levels for the next five years, restricting rent and mortgage levels, raising certain taxes on investment income and increasing income tax for high wage earners, a presidential palace spokesman said. The measure, Decree Law 2064, replaces Decree 2045, which parliament rejected last night. The Decree becomes law on its publication today and parliament has three months to approve or reject it.

"Holy Christ," said Coleman. The wage law had been defeated. There would be no IMF package. There would be no bank package. The international banking system would come tumbling down. He had to do something. Coleman ran to the telephone. He called Rhodes at the International Hotel. He had stayed on to meet with the Argentine rescue committee at Crédit Suisse bank.

Rhodes wasn't in his room.

Coleman called Huntrods at his office at Lloyds' headquarters in London.

Huntrods was still in the air, on a flight from Zurich to London.

Coleman called Brazil.

He couldn't get through.

Coleman called Crédit Suisse and left a message for Rhodes.

TWA flight #801 to New York was boarding.

There was nothing more that Coleman could do. He walked through the gate onto the plane. He buckled up. As soon as he got to New York, he would call Brazil, he'd call the IMF, he'd call Huntrods, he'd call Rhodes.

While Coleman was making his credit card calls at the airport, a Crédit Suisse secretary walked into Rhodes' committee meeting with a note. Pastore of the Brazilian Central Bank was on the line.

Rhodes walked out to the telephone.

"I just landed in Brasilia," Pastore said when Rhodes picked up. "The wage law was defeated last night. The opposition said it wasn't equitable. We've put together a new wage law. Workers at the bottom of the scale will be allowed to get bigger raises than workers at the top. This time, the law will pass."

187

Rhodes hung up. The rescue would be in limbo until the law got through. Rhodes walked back into the Argentine meeting. There was nothing more he could do about Brazil.

Except line up the money. The M.D.'s deadline for "critical mass" was November 18.

Rhodes and Coleman and Huntrods began that as soon as Rhodes was back from Zurich.

The pledges were already coming in.

The first: $220,000 from a small bank in Scandinavia, 11 percent of its exposure, just shy of the price of a Rolls-Royce.

Rhodes sat in his red leather swivel chair and called holdout banks.

Coleman and Huntrods came up to Citibank and sat in the conference room next to Rhodes' office and called.

"A lot of banks are on board," said Rhodes at the beginning of November. "But there are holdouts. We've got to increase pressure." Coax, cajole, needle. "Every bank has to do its share."

Rhodes kept calling. Coleman commandeered the office next door to Rhodes and called. Huntrods borrowed a secretary's phone to call.

"We're over $3 billion," said Rhodes on Wednesday, November 9. "The telexes are coming in fast and furious."

"Our deadline is coming up," said Coleman. "The IMF board meeting is November 22. We've got to have critical mass by then. We've got to have $6 billion by a week from Friday."

The bankers kept calling.

Friday morning, Coleman added up the total. "We're at $4 billion," he said. "And the telex machines are overloaded."

The bankers kept calling.

"We're up to $4.5 billion," said Rhodes at the end of the day. "We're still getting more telexes."

The bankers called all weekend long.

By Monday night, November 14, the total was $5 billion. And rising.

The bankers kept calling.

"We're slightly over $5.5 billion," said Rhodes on November 17, the night before the deadline. "That's 85 percent."

The bankers kept calling.

188

At ten-thirty the night of the eighteenth—the last night—the bankers sat down for dinner. They were just short of $6 billion.

An assistant walked in with a telex. A Spanish bank had just committed $10 million. They were over the top.

"Gentlemen," said Huntrods. "A miracle has just occurred."

The Brazilian wage law had passed on November 8. On November 22, the IMF board of directors approved the new Brazilian economic package.

By mid-December, the IMF had released the next $400-million installment of its loan and the banks had released the remaining $1.8 billion of their Phase I loan. Brazil used the money to repay the BIS loan and to pay bank interest through October 4.

Rhodes and Coleman and Huntrods made a marathon of phone calls to line up the last $500 million of commitments. The head of the Brazilian Central Bank flew to New York to call.

"We need you here," Rhodes told him. "We have to get this done."

The money trickled in.

Rhodes scheduled a loan signing.

The money was still coming.

He rescheduled the signing.

The money kept trickling in.

At the end of January, Rhodes had the commitments. He signed the loan at the Pierre Hotel on Fifth Avenue.

After the head of the Brazilian Central Bank and the finance minister and Delfim Netto had all signed the loan, Rhodes walked to the pay telephone to call Walter Wriston. "We just signed," he said. "We just completed Mission Impossible."

Brazil got the first $3 billion of Phase II money at the end of March. And by then, the economic medicine seemed to be working. Government spending was down and the export surplus had risen briskly. By the end of 1984, Brazil was on target on government spending—down $7 billion from 1983—and above target for exports—$13 billion, more than double the 1983 total. In August,

189

the new head of the Central Bank flew to New York to begin negotiations on a new rescheduling. He wanted an interest rate just one and an eighth percentage points over prime. That was a big concession, but Brazil had done so well that the banks agreed. As oil prices fell below $15 a barrel in the spring of 1986, Brazil's future again looked bright.

Walter Wriston retired as chairman of Citicorp in August 1984. His successor, John Reed, was the brains behind Citi's consumer victories, but Reed quickly made it clear that Latin America was still key to Citi's future. He named the executive vice president for Latin America to be vice chairman of Citibank, and he promoted Rhodes to chairman of the newly organized restructuring committee.

The new post meant more work for Rhodes. Now he was in charge of Poland, Yugoslavia, Zaire and the Philippines as well as Mexico and Argentina and Brazil. But at least Rhodes had gotten a two-week vacation after signing Brazil. For his fiftieth birthday in August 1985, the bankers on his three Latin American committees gave Rhodes a present: a small wooden gavel with his initials mounted in gold on the head. Rhodes doesn't have to wear down his knuckles getting the bankers' attention any more.

(5)

Continental Illinois National Bank & Trust Company

"We'll Find a Way"

"Harold," said Fred Florjancic. His deep, gruff voice rumbled over the clatter of the restaurant. "You know you've got to give us the money."

Harold Dietz scowled. "I don't have to give you anything," he said.

Florjancic sighed. He sipped his Scotch and soda. Before he had started work on this deal, he had liked The Palm steakhouse with its big booths and brass railings, but after negotiating over dinner every night for five weeks, Florjancic hated restaurants, period. "Harold," he said. "You're not being reasonable."

"I am being reasonable," said Dietz. "I don't have to give you anything." Dietz tipped his chair back, tucked his thumbs in his vest pockets and glared across the table at Florjancic.

Florjancic pulled the gold Cross pen from the breast pocket. He looked at Dietz.

Dietz didn't say anything.

"Harold," said Florjancic. "We're all in this together." Florjancic had said that before, to Dietz and to the others. "We've got to compromise if we want to keep International Harvester alive."

"Giving you that money won't help Harvester," said Dietz. "It just helps you." Dietz sipped his drink.

"Harold," said Florjancic. "I know you've got a different per-

191

spective on this. The finance company loans are better than the parent company's. But we both lose big if Harvester tanks, and we got six days." The drop-dead date was October 14. "You have to give us that $100 million. If we banks that have lent to Harvester in the past don't get that $100-million payment, we won't sign a new agreement, and then Harvester will be forced to file bankruptcy."

Dietz didn't say anything; he just glared.

"Harold, Harvester owes us $1.4 billion," said Florjancic. "Harvester owes you $2.6 billion. It doesn't make sense to throw away $2.6 billion just to keep us from getting $100 million. Harvester is worth more alive than dead."

"If you want us to pay you $100 million, then we need some concessions," said Dietz.

Florjancic played with his pen. "What's your number-one issue?" he asked.

"You know it's rebates," said Dietz. "Financing the rebates that the company is giving costs Irving Trust money."

"You've got to finance rebates," said Florjancic. "Harvester can't afford to. Financing rebates would cost the company $150 million over the next three months."

"I'll walk out if I don't get some concessions," said Dietz.

Florjancic shook his head. "Let's talk about rebates," he said.

They talked. Florjancic pulled a legal pad out of his battered briefcase and jotted down some notes. The waiter cleared the dinner plates and brought coffee. The bankers kept talking. The other tables emptied one by one. The bankers kept talking. But by midnight, they had an agreement: the company would change the way it paid rebates; Dietz would pay the $100 million.

International Harvester would live.

In the banking world, Continental officers are known for their down-home charm, and Fred Florjancic (Floor-*jan*-sick) has plenty of that. At thirty-six, he's blond, blue-eyed, and built like a baseball player. He lives what he calls a "typical suburban life: a wife, two kids, a station wagon and a dog." He plays golf on Saturday morning, vacations with his wife in Acapulco or the Caribbean for a week every winter, and takes his two kids skiing in the Rockies for two weeks in February or March. He has bacon and eggs for breakfast and prefers apple pie to blancmange. Florjancic is clean-cut; he avoids night clubs, New York and nicotine.

Frederick Florjancic grew up in a small town in Pennsylvania and went to college at Indiana University. His freshman year, he studied economics and played baseball. After that he got serious; he dropped sports and switched to accounting; he seemed to have a knack for numbers, and when he finished his M.B.A. at Indiana in 1970, Florjancic got job offers from a dozen companies, including Ford, Westinghouse, Monsanto, Citibank and Continental Illinois. Florjancic couldn't decide what industry he wanted to work for, so he decided to work for one of the banks instead; he figured that at a bank he'd see the inside of lots of different kinds of companies and then he'd be able to decide what he really wanted to spend his life doing. There were just two banks to choose from, and since Florjancic didn't want to live in New York City, he headed for the Continental Bank in Chicago.

Florjancic thought he had just picked a city, but in fact he'd picked a style of business. While most banks advertised safety, Continental boasted "We'll find a way." Continental's chairman, Roger Anderson, wasn't like other bankers: he was a gambling man. In just ten years, Anderson would transform the bank from the scaredy-cat of the lending world to the consummate financial crap-shooter.

The Continental Bank had bet big on land and stock during the roaring twenties; when the market crashed, the bank faltered— and it survived the Great Depression only with the help of a $50-million loan from the federal government. After the bailout, Continental was so scared of making bad loans that it shied away from making any loans at all; the bank put its money in government bonds instead. Gradually the bank began to make loans again, but only to the strongest midwestern behemoths: Standard Oil of Indiana, Swift & Company, the Illinois Central Railroad, and International Harvester. Anderson was named chairman in 1973, and he quickly began to bring the bank into modern times. He installed an escalator between the two neoclassical banking floors; he bought a robot to carry mail down the mahogany paneled corridors. He told the corporate lending officers that the time had come for Continental to start making more risky loans. Fast.

Illinois banks aren't allowed to have branches. Continental could grow only by booking big loans to big companies from its headquarters in Chicago. The Continental booked. It lent to industrial giants: Baldwin-United, the Wickes Companies, AM International; it lent to real estate baronies: American Invsco, the largest condominium developer in the world; it lent to oil and gas independents: NuCorp Energy, Good Hope Refineries and a host of wildcatters. Continental was innovative and aggressive. When interest rates shot up, Continental introduced a floating rate loan with a preset cap. When real estate prices collapsed, Continental swapped bad loans for prime land that it later sold at a profit. Continental always offered the lowest rates when it bid for loans; it always insisted on bigger hog shares when it joined syndications. When the borrowing applications didn't come in fast enough, Continental bought loans from other lenders, mostly small institutions like the Penn Square Bank of Oklahoma City.

By 1980, Continental was the sixth-largest commercial bank in America; Continental was *the* corporate bank; it had loaned $11.1 billion to American companies, a much higher percentage of total loans than at any other major bank. Being the corporate bank was highly profitable: Continental's return on assets was the fourth-highest in America. Being the corporate bank also had its risks: there's no such thing as a small corporate bankrupt.

When Florjancic took the Continental job, the bank was still on the up and up. Florjancic didn't much care: he only planned to stay at the bank for three years before moving into industry. It didn't work out that way. Florjancic climbed up the ladder in Continental's Chicago corporate division. Then he got transferred to a newly formed division that handled companies with factories and sales units around the world. In 1982, Florjancic was made division manager of Multinational West, responsible for $1 billion in loans to sixty companies with headquarters from the western half of Chicago to the Pacific Ocean. Among them: Litton Industries, Hallmark Cards and International Harvester.

Continental and Harvester had always been close. Continental had been banking for Harvester since the late 1800s when Continental was called the Chicago Merchants Bank and Harvester was McCormick Harvester. For years, Continental had had a director—most recently Roger Anderson, chairman—on the Harvester board and Harvester had had a director—most recently Keith Potter, chief financial officer—on the Continental board. In 1975, Continental commissioned Wedgwood to design a Chicago bowl for the bank to present to key customers. Two years later, Fred Florjancic presented one of the first bowls to International Harvester in commemoration of the seventy-fifth anniversary of the relationship.

That wasn't the only thing that Florjancic did for Harvester. He put together syndicated loans, lines of credit and receivables purchase agreements; he helped Harvester manage currency transactions and hedge interest rates. By 1981, Harvester borrowings had ballooned to more than $2 billion—including $200 million from Continental, the bank that coordinated loans and led almost all syndicates; $200 million from Morgan Guaranty; $300 million from Bank of America; $800,000 from a Chicago bank so small it didn't have a telex machine—but Florjancic wasn't worried. After all, Continental made its money collecting interest on corporate loans. Then in February 1981, Archie McCardell, the chairman of International Harvester, called. "I need to see you," he told Florjancic. "Now."

For years, International Harvester had been one of America's proudest corporations, known around the world for the red color it painted all its tractors and other farm machines. By 1979, Harvester was the twenty-seventh largest company in America, the world's largest manufacturer of heavy trucks and the number-two maker of agricultural equipment. Harvester was one of the thirty companies whose stock price is used to figure out the Dow Jones Industrial Average, the key indicator of stock market performance. It was a keystone of the midwestern economy, providing jobs for almost a hundred thousand workers and orders for hundreds of small parts makers. Now, McCardell told Florjancic, it was close to being the world's biggest bankrupt.

The company got its start back in 1831 when a Virginia farmer named Cyrus McCormick invented a mechanical reaper, a huge iron contraption for mowing grain. The machine was so efficient that with it a farmer could do in a morning what it took six men to do with conventional scythes. Efficient though it was, the reaper didn't sell—farmers refused to risk their livelihood on a newfangled machine—so to move product, McCormick had to invent modern marketing. McCormick advertised the reaper in the Lexington (Virginia) *Union,* and, when that brought in buyers, in dozens of papers across the country; he set up his own sales force, the first company sales force in the world; he gave his customers the first written guarantees of quality; and he offered the first farm installment plan: one third down, one third after each of the next two harvests. Sales boomed, and soon the company—renamed International Harvester in 1902—had sales offices around the world and a product line that included plows, corn shellers, manure spreaders, the agile Farmall internal combustion tractor, the Auto Buggy, the Auto Wagon and a full line of construction equipment. Soon there was a finance subsidiary, International Harvester Credit Company (IHCC), that borrowed money from the big banks to relend to farmers, builders and truckers who wanted to buy tractors, haulers and trucks. Harvester was the biggest farm implements maker in the world, so beloved by farmers that some painted the roofs of their barns International Harvester red.

Harvester began to get complacent. It tried to remain number one simply by offering more products through more dealerships on easier payment terms. Soon there were so many truck and tractor models that each one was all but custom-made, the dealer network was so overextended that there seemed to be a Harvester showroom on every corner, and costs exploded out of control. Harvester added layer upon layer of management; product research languished; the factories became obsolete. Purchasing was so disorganized that expensive parts were left stacked in the factories gathering dust. Union wages and work rules were disastrously overgenerous: Harvester gave away the right to require union members to work overtime on weekends, and Harvester agreed to let any UAW member have a job transfer whenever he wanted one; one employee got nine transfers in just eight months. By 1979, Harvester had borrowed more than $2 billion.

In 1977, Harvester hired Archie McCardell, president of Xerox, to fix the problems. McCardell smoked cigars; he rolled up his shirt sleeves and took off his shoes to work. He was a financial wizard, but he didn't know anything about making tractors or haulers or trucks.

McCardell's answer to Harvester's problems was to increase capital spending. He said that Harvester needed $500 million worth of new factories and an $80-million technology center. At first, the McCardell solution worked. Sales spurted 25 percent in 1979 to $8.4 billion; profits hit a record $370 million, and McCardell bet that earnings would double to $700 million by 1984. "I'm a bit of an optimist," he told a Chicago business magazine in 1979. "You know, if we had a six-month strike or if the economy ended up being a third of what it is right now, I suspect we'd have a bit of a problem. History tells us that that's not going to happen."

History was wrong.

In the fall of 1979, the union struck. Six months and $479 million later, Harvester surrendered. To earn back its losses, McCardell bet on a big spring selling season—and he borrowed big to buy the steel and bolts and tires. By then, the country had fallen into the worst recession since the 1930s; pinched farmers couldn't afford new sixty-thousand-dollar tractors or hundred-thousand-dollar combines. Interest rates doubled; so did monthly payments on Harvester's massive debt. The losses piled up: $96 million in the last quarter of 1980; another $79 million in the first three months of 1981.

McCardell tried to solve the problem by trimming costs. He slashed the dividend Harvester paid to stockholders and then eliminated it altogether. He cut executive paychecks 20 percent. He pared the capital spending budget by $150 million and canceled the new technology center.

That wasn't enough.

Harvester was so sprawling and mismanaged that it could no longer make money. To get profitable, Harvester had to close factories and sell whole divisions. That would take time, and Harvester didn't have time. Harvester was almost out of cash to meet its payroll. There was only one answer: a moratorium from the bankers. There were two ways to get that. Harvester could file for protection from its creditors under Chapter 11 of the federal bankruptcy laws and let a bankruptcy judge supervise the "restructuring" of operations and the repaying of the debt. Or Harvester could beg the banks to let the company go bankrupt out of court.

As McCardell saw it, the choice was clear: going bankrupt meant closing Harvester down for good. Farmers and builders and truckers weren't going to buy machines from a "bankrupt" company that might not be around in ten years to provide sales and service.

In the middle of February 1981, McCardell invited Florjancic to come up to his office. "We have to restructure the company," McCardell said. "We've decided to stop paying principal until you banks renegotiate our debt."

"Harvester is bust," Fred Florjancic said at the emergency meeting of Harvester's lenders in early March. "McCardell won't pay principal until we work out a new payment schedule. We have to decide whether we want to negotiate or force Harvester in the tank."

The bankers were angry; they wanted their money.

"We've got to stay calm until we figure out the best thing to do," said Florjancic. If any three banks sued Harvester for nonpayment, Harvester would be declared bankrupt. "It's a question of which way we get the most money back. Harvester can't survive if it declares bankruptcy," said Florjancic. "Harvester's plants are so old that they aren't worth much. But an out-of-court bankruptcy isn't going to be easy; it takes a lot of time and effort to get all the banks to agree."

"There have only been two out-of-court settlements," said a banker. Chrysler and Lockheed. "Both times with help from the federal government. We're not going to be able to get government help."

Florjancic knew that; President Reagan didn't believe in bailouts. "I think Harvester can make it without a bailout," said Florjancic. "Harvester has a first-rate product and a first-rate service reputation. It seems to me that the problem is financial mismanagement coupled with the worst farm economy since the Depression."

Some of the bankers looked skeptical.

"We'll get more money if we negotiate," said Florjancic. "We don't have much choice."

The bankers talked.

Florjancic took a vote. The bankers agreed to try an out-of-court arrangement.

Then they began to negotiate with each other. There were 220 banks and all 220 weren't equal. Some of the banks—like Continental—had lent straight to Harvester; their collateral was Harvester's antiquated factories and worn-out machine tools. Some of the banks—like Irving Trust Company—had lent to the International Harvester Credit Company (IHCC); their collateral was the sparkling new trucks and road rollers and tractors on the dealer lots. Since all of the banks couldn't negotiate at once, McCardell named a committee, chaired by Florjancic, to do the job.

The interbank talks weren't easy: by the end of the second week, the bankers began their bargaining at eight-thirty in the morning and rarely broke before nine at night. Florjancic got to the Naperville train station before five each morning to catch the "milk train" to work in the morning, and boarded the last train out at twelve-thirty for the fifty-minute ride home; after a month, his wife Barbara told him to get a hotel room in town—Florjancic chose the Whitehall—so he could get a little sleep. By July, the bankers finally shook hands: Harvester and IHCC were separate companies, and the hundreds of small loans were consolidated into two big loans due December 15, 1983. Henceforth, there would be tight bank supervision over cash: Harvester had to maintain net worth above a bank-set minimum and it had to fork over to the banks half of what it got each time it sold a subsidiary.

Meanwhile, McCardell had begun to cut the fat from the company. He slashed inventories by $500 million; he closed factories; he cut salaries; he ordered the office manager to stop renting potted plants. McCardell broke the lease on five and a half of the company's thirteen headquarters floors and grounded the company plane. He fired the International Harvester limousine drivers, sold the company cars, and he told the communications department that this year's annual report would have no shiny pages.

While the banks were still negotiating with each other, McCardell marched into a bankers meeting. "I've sold the turbo machinery division to Caterpillar for $505 million," he announced.

199

"That means we get $250 million," said Florjancic. "Where's the money?"

"No," said McCardell. "The cash is in a special account." That the banks couldn't freeze. "We need it to run the company."

Harvester lost $319 million between August and November, and another $299 million in the three months after that.

"I figure we'll lose $450 million in 1982," McCardell told the bankers at the beginning of the year. "We'll be breaking even in the fourth quarter."

Harvester lost $498 million in the first six months of the year. The board fired McCardell.

Harvester lost another $130 million in the third quarter, $1.01 billion in the fourth.

Just after that fourth-quarter announcement, Florjancic got a call from Jim Cotting, Harvester's new chief financial officer. "We've got a negative net worth," said Cotting. Harvester had more debt than assets.

Florjancic braced himself.

"Harvester has to have less debt and more cash," said Cotting. "We're going to swap some of that debt for a new asset: Harvester stock." Brand-new stock that Harvester would print just for the banks.

Florjancic was shocked. "You can't do that," he said. Swapping debt for equity meant swapping status. Stockholders don't get paid anything if a company goes bankrupt. Lenders do. Swapping debt for stock was throwing money away.

Cotting was firm: it was new stock or nothing at all.

While Florjancic talked to the banks, Harvester rounded up concessions. The United Auto Workers agreed to $200 million in temporary wage cuts; there wouldn't be a strike. Harvester suppliers agreed to $83 million in temporary price cuts; they weren't going to suddenly demand payments. Dealers took their $47 million in 1982 volume discounts in Harvester stock; they weren't going to stop giving Harvester floor space.

In February 1983, the banks swapped $350 million—$200 million of principal and $150 million of interest—for 17 percent of Harvester's stock. It was the second-largest debt-for-stock swap ever.

The ordeal wasn't over. The bank had decided in July that the remaining $1.4-billion debt would come due on December 15, 1983. Clearly Harvester couldn't pay. There would be another round of negotiations in the fall. So just after the stock-for-debt swap, Fred Florjancic called Jim Cotting. "Let's have lunch," he said. "I want to know where you're headed this time around."

"Nothing's firm," said Cotting.

"Let's talk," said Florjancic. "Next week. At Morton's."

James C. Cotting is methodical. At fifty, he's a big, bulky man with stiff brown hair and watery blue eyes. He wears a rumpled brown suit and tasseled loafers; there's a ball-point pen in his shirt pocket and a yellow slide rule in the canister next to the telephone. Cotting gets to work at seven every morning and works until he's done, often nine at night; he always goes home—he lives in Barrington, an hour and a half by train from downtown Chicago—and he never takes a briefcase full of papers. He seems to do just fine on only four hours of sleep. He likes the outdoors. During the winter he skis cross-country. Whenever the weather permits, he's on the golf course; he says he's not a good player—he doesn't hit the ball far enough—but even in the heat of the debt negotiations, he got in two golf games each weekend; one on Saturday afternoon with his three teenage kids and another on Sunday afternoon with his wife.

Cotting grew up in Ohio and went to Ohio State. He worked his way up the financial ladder at International Paper Company until he was its controller. In 1978, Archie McCardell offered Cotting the job as Harvester's chief financial officer, and Cotting didn't hesitate. It was a big step up in responsibility, and he'd heard that Harvester had cost-control problems. Cotting thought that he'd enjoy the challenge of straightening out the company's finances. He never dreamed what that would mean.

The family drove out to Chicago from New Jersey. Cotting toured all the Harvester factories. He started to put together a new strategic study of what products Harvester should make. But before Cotting finished his study, the UAW walked out on strike.

A year after that International Harvester was de facto bankrupt

201

and Cotting was helping McCardell slash costs and handling negotiations with the bankers. During 1981 and 1982, Cotting kept a packed suitcase in his office. He wanted to be able to visit a banker anywhere in the country on five-minutes notice and know that he'd have clean underwear the next day. In the fall of 1982, he'd taken the suitcase home, but he still kept in close touch with the bankers, particularly with Fred Florjancic. He tried to see Florjancic once a week—even if it was only to share a cab to the train station.

Cotting had just started to think about the next Harvester restructuring when Fred Florjancic called to invite him to lunch at Morton's. Cotting was happy to talk.

"What kind of numbers are you pushing around?" asked Fred Florjancic when he and Jim Cotting sat down for lunch. "Is this going to be another one-year loan package?"

"I haven't put together the details," said Cotting, "but it's clear to me that this deal has to be long-term. I'd like twenty years. I think I'll ask the parent-company banks to swap half our debt for stock."

"I don't think that the banks are ready to give you more than a year," said Florjancic. "I don't think they think Harvester is out of the woods yet."

"We've got to have longer than a year," said Cotting. "We can't keep negotiating our debt every twelve months. We need time to run the company." Negotiations with the banks were a full-time job: Cotting and everyone else on the financial staff often spent eighteen hours a day, six days a week putting together studies and cranking numbers.

"You lost $111 million last quarter," said Florjancic.

"We lost $1.01 billion the quarter before that," said Cotting. "The company has changed a lot since this started. We've sold plants. We've closed plants. We've fired workers. The company is finally ready to go."

"Some of the bankers think Harvester will run out of cash completely in six months," said Florjancic. "That stock will be worthless if Harvester tanks."

Cotting shook his head. "All you bankers ever talk about is money. There's more to International Harvester than money; there are people." Jim Cotting cared about people and he'd already had to slash Harvester's payroll by fifty-five thousand to stay alive. "We've still got forty-three thousand employees. You've got to give us a chance."

Florjancic raised his eyebrows.

Cotting knew he had to accept what the bankers offered or else declare formal bankruptcy. He was ready for formal bankruptcy. The papers were already drafted and stacked in the credenza in his office. All that Cotting had to do was sign.

"I don't think that the parent-company banks are going to accept more stock," said Florjancic. "They just let you pay $350 million of debt with stock."

"We've got to get interest payments down," said Cotting. "Right now we're paying $140 million a year. If you swap $700 million of debt for stock, then we will have just $700 million of debt and $70 million of interest. I think we can handle that. We could have a couple of bad quarters and still have a positive net worth." Cotting figured that the Harvester could handle up to $100 million of interest a year.

Florjancic played with his spoon.

"I've been looking at the Chrysler numbers," said Cotting. "Chrysler's banks swapped $1.1 billion of debt for stock."

"Chrysler got help from the federal government," said Florjancic. Loan guarantees to convince investors to buy $1.2 billion of new Chrysler securities. Even then, the Chrysler lenders hadn't been happy about the swap. When one banker was asked how he wanted his stock delivered, he had quipped that his should be sent prepasted and rolled so that he could put it right on the wall.

"If this company is going to stay out of bankruptcy court, the banks have to swap," said Cotting.

"If we make concessions, we're going to need some cash up front," said Florjancic. "The more the better."

"We'll pay some cash," said Cotting.

"Harvester doesn't have any cash," said Florjancic. There was just $100 million in the company account.

"International Harvester Credit Company has cash," said Cotting. Truck and tractor sales were so low that $500 million of the money that Harvester had borrowed to relend to farmers was just sitting in the bank. "IHCC is going to pay the parent a $100 million 'dividend' and the parent company is going to pay that money to the banks."

Florjancic raised his eyebrows. The banks had agreed in July that IHCC and Harvester were separate companies. "The IHCC banks aren't going to like that," he said. Especially not Harold Dietz, the redheaded banker from Irving Trust. "I don't think any of the banks are going to like this plan."

A couple of days after the lunch with Cotting, Fred Florjancic got a call from Carter Evans, one of the New York bankers on the negotiating committee. "I just had lunch with Taylor Wagenseil," said Evans. "Taylor's been hearing rumors about Cotting's new ideas. He doesn't like what he hears."

Florjancic sighed. Taylor Wagenseil of Citibank wouldn't like that plan.

"We've got to have a meeting," said Evans.

"Okay," said Florjancic.

"Next week," said Evans. "At my office."

"I'll be there," said Florjancic.

Taylor Wagenseil's a maverick. He is thirty-six, tall and ruggedly handsome, with brown hair and brown eyes; he's either charming or ruthless, depending on what he needs. Wagenseil wears dark, conservative suits and shiny shoes; he throws his jacket over the edge of his Citibank cubicle and rolls up his shirt sleeves to work. He's hard-working, witty and brash. Wagenseil was the only banker who would dare ask for a private meeting with Donald D. Lennox, the man who'd replaced Archie McCardell as Harvester chairman. Florjancic jokes that Wagenseil wanted a chair in Harvester's executive suite, just behind Don Lennox's.

Wagenseil's a Navy brat and majored in philosophy at Dartmouth. After four years in the Navy himself—he won a bronze star as commanding officer of a river gunboat operation in Viet Nam—and five years on Boston Mayor Kevin White's staff, Wagenseil decided his calling was commerce. When he graduated from the Harvard business school in 1979, he headed straight to Citibank. Wagenseil's first job was an assistant in the world corporation group, and one of his first clients was International Harvester. When Harvester hit the skids, the Harvester account was transferred to "Institutional Recovery Management," Citi's deadbeat division. Wagenseil went with it, and he showed up at Florjancic's first meeting in Chicago to press Citi's case.

Citibank had lent just $45 million of Harvester's $4 billion debt—in the early seventies, Citi had had a much larger exposure, but it had forced Harvester to pay off the loans by raising interest rates, much to the annoyance of other banks—but that didn't mean that Wagenseil could soften the bank's hard line. Citi was worried about the farm equipment industry in general: in addition to the loans to Harvester, Citi had also lent $40 million to Massey-Ferguson, a near-bankrupt Harvester competitor based in Toronto. Now, at the end of February, after picking up the rumor about Cotting, Wagenseil was eager indeed to talk to Florjancic.

"I hear that Jim Cotting wants twenty years and a $700-million swap," said Wagenseil when he and a small group of key Harvester bankers caucused in New York. "That's impossible. We ought to be looking at six months and $250 million."

Florjancic had said the same thing to Cotting, but he didn't tell Wagenseil; this wasn't the time to dig trenches for a bargaining position. "Jim's just throwing some numbers around," he said. "Let's wait until Cotting's put together a formal proposal."

"I'm not convinced that this company is going to survive," said Wagenseil. "And I'm not going to negotiate until I am."

The bankers talked. They agreed that they didn't like Cotting's new plan, but they did like a lot of things about the company.

They liked Jim Cotting. They hadn't at first—they knew that they would spend a lot of time arguing with him—but Cotting was so upright that they had quickly changed their minds.

They also liked Don Lennox, the new chairman. Lennox had told the bankers at his first meeting with them that the company had big problems, and he didn't know what the answers were. Lennox had made tough decisions: he'd sold the construction division to Dresser Industries; he sold the truck axle and transmission business to the Dana Corporation; he'd even closed Harvester's

205

plant in Ft. Wayne, Indiana, Harvester's first "modern" truck plant, built in 1922.

"Harvester isn't the same company that got into trouble back in 1981," said Florjancic. "Cotting tells me that manufacturing space is down by a third. He's cut the white-collar work force in half and blue-collar by two thirds. Administrative overhead is down 40 percent; inventories are down 38 percent."

"Yes, but the economy is in terrible shape," said Wagenseil. "Tractor sales were way down last year and they are going to be down again this year. It doesn't matter how many problems Harvester has solved if farmers won't buy tractors from any maker." He paused. "I'm not going to negotiate until I'm convinced that Harvester is going to survive."

The bankers were silent for a minute.

"I think we ought to hire consultants," said Carter Evans. "The consultants will help us figure out whether Harvester is going to survive. Then we can talk numbers."

"Okay," said Florjancic. "I'll call Cotting."

"The bankers don't like your restructuring plans," Florjancic told Cotting the next day. "They are worried that Harvester is going to collapse. They want to come out to Chicago to talk to you." He paused. "Look Jim," he said. "I think it would be a good idea if the bankers took a look at the Harvester plants. That way they won't do a 'paint by numbers' restructuring."

"A tour?" said Cotting. A tour would keep the bankers busy while he worked up a formal proposal. Besides, Cotting figured that the best way to convince a doubting banker that Harvester wasn't making tractors the way they did in the Dark Ages was to let him see the plants for himself. "We can arrange that."

The bankers flew to Chicago on March 31. They ate a beef stroganoff dinner in Harvester's boardroom with Jim Cotting and Don Lennox.

"We like what you've done to the company, at least on paper," said Florjancic. "Our biggest worry is the economy. We want to hire consultants to take a look at the company."

"Consultants are okay—but we'll hire them," said Cotting. "We know the company best and we know which consultants to hire."

Florjancic didn't like the sound of that. In 1981, McCardell had

206

hired Booz Allen, the big consulting firm, to help the bankers, and Booz Allen had just confirmed McCardell's rosy projections. That wasn't going to happen again. "We will hire the consultants," said Florjancic. "They will work for us."

Lennox shook his head. "We will hire the consultants and tell them to work closely with you. We'll arrange a series of plant tours to show you what we've done. We want you to believe in International Harvester."

The meeting broke up.

Jim Cotting called Florjancic a couple of days later. "I've chosen the consultants," he said. One of the firms he'd picked specialized in the truck business, the other in agricultural equipment. "I've put together a tour schedule." The bankers would visit the big truck plant in Springfield, Ohio; the Farmall tractor plant in Rock Island, Illinois; the crawler tractor plant in Melrose Park; the combine plant in East Moline; the engineering center in Ft. Wayne; the truck engine plant in Indianapolis, and the stamping plant in Shadyside, Ohio.

"Great," said Florjancic. "I'll pass this on to the others." Florjancic had just begun to make those calls when his phone rang. It was Harold Dietz from Irving Trust. Irving wasn't a big bank, so Dietz hadn't been invited to the meeting in New York or the beef stroganoff dinner at International Harvester.

"What's been going on?" he asked. "What kind of meeting was there while I was on vacation?"

Harold Dietz is energetic. At forty-two, he's a small man with a round, freckled face, red hair, fiery blue eyes—and a big temper. He works in his shirt sleeves, and carefully hangs his coat on the hanger on the back of his door. An expert in figuring out how a company can get out from under its debt, Dietz collects models of his clients' products—Allis-Chalmers combines, Braniff airplanes, International Harvester trucks. He tips his chair back when he talks and braces his foot against the bottom drawer of his massive wooden desk. Dietz always argues for whatever solution gives him the most cash back on his loan. During the Harvester negotiations, Dietz talked as if his life depended on getting the dollars back from IHCC; he made it sound like it was morally wrong for parent-company lenders ever to get money at all until finance-company lenders were paid off. In other negotiations when Dietz had lent to the parent company, he argued just as adamantly parent-company lenders should be paid first.

Dietz grew up on Long Island and got his B.A. at Baldwin-Wallace College in Berea, Ohio. When he graduated from the Columbia business school in 1965, he landed a job at Irving Trust Company. Dietz spent nine years working up the ladder in the corporate-lending division. Then in 1975, he was sent to Hong Kong to manage Irving's Wing Hang Bank affiliate. Dietz was back in New York two years later running the Asia district. In 1981, he was transferred to Loan Administration. One of his new clients: International Harvester.

Irving had lent $90 million to IHCC and nothing to the International Harvester parent. It seemed clear to Dietz that if Harvester went bankrupt IHCC would go bankrupt too: it would have no more products to finance. But unlike the Harvester bankers, Dietz thought that even if that happened, he'd get most of his money back; his loans were secured by brand-new trucks and tractors, not obsolete factories and worn-out tools. That meant that Dietz wanted to go soft on Harvester to guarantee that the company would survive, and hard on IHCC to guarantee that he'd get his cash.

Irving hadn't had a seat on the original bankers' committee, but he demanded one early on and Florjancic had agreed. At his first meeting, Dietz had been outspoken for the rights of the credit-company-only lenders, and after that, Dietz was regarded as the leader of the small band of IHCC-only bankers. Whenever he thought they were being short-changed, Dietz threatened that he and his cohorts would walk out of the negotiations en masse.

At the end of March 1983, Dietz got a call from a junior officer at Irving Trust. "I just found out that the other bankers working on International Harvester are having a meeting without you," said the junior.

"What?" asked Dietz.

"Meeting without you," repeated the officer.

"We'll see," said Dietz.

"Don't worry," said Florjancic when Dietz called him. "Those weren't negotiating sessions. They were just informal chats."

"Why are the reps from the big banks having informal chats with Cotting?" asked Dietz. "If there are any more informal chats, I want to be there."

Florjancic shook his head. The bankers were so suspicious of each other. "Sure, Harold," he said. It wasn't worth arguing. "We're going to start a series of plant tours next month. I hope you can make it."

"Don't worry," said Dietz. "I'll be there. I'll be at every one."

Fred Florjancic had been right about the plant tours: the travel gave the bankers a much needed chance to let off steam. Instead of grousing about how unrealistic Jim Cotting was, they griped about the crowded, unair-conditioned buses and the soggy takeout food. Instead of moping in Chicago restaurants, they spent their free time playing golf and testing out the Mini Grand Prix race track. Instead of yawning through another Cotting slide show, they drag-raced inventory around the truck plant parking lot.

The tours themselves were eye-popping. Many of the bankers had never seen a truck or tractor plant before—they had imagined dingy, ill-lit sweat shops stacked with rusty parts and manned by hostile unionists. But the factories looked logical; there were no stacks of extra inventory, no rows of tractors missing steering wheels. At the truck plant, shiny robots welded the cabs. The line workers wore two buttons in their caps; one said "UAW"; the other, "IH: We're Not Giving Up, We're Going On."

After the tour of the truck plant, the bankers filed into a conference room for a talk on cost cutting.

"We've been working on cheaper ways to design and manufacture the same parts," explained an engineer. "We've produced cheaper bolts, cheaper pins. Our proudest achievement is the countershaft. We figured out how to save eighty dollars per tractor. Let me explain..."

Harvester's treasurer interrupted. "Forget it," he said. "These are bankers. They don't want technicalities about a countershaft."

One of the bankers stood up. "Go on," he said. He looked at the treasurer. "When you're talking about the shaft, we understand."

Next, the bankers piled on a bus for their visit with a Harvester "red" farmer. The day they went, it was pouring rain, and the bankers got mud on their three-piece suits, except for Florjancic, who was wearing blue jeans.

"I like my tractor," said the farmer. "I like my dealer." He paused. "Ten years ago, there wasn't a red combine in this county," he said. "Now they're the most popular ones on the fields. That's testimonial to the quality of the product."

More important, it was proof that Harvester had a reputation that would sell. But would farmers buy? The dealer down the road said yes. "The farmers like Harvester," he said. "They buy red."

"Yeah?" said Dietz. He'd counted twelve Harvester combines lined up on the lot in the front of the store and a dozen Harvester tractors out in back. "How many years inventory is this?" he asked.

"I'll sell all those machines this season," said the dealer.

"Sure," said Dietz. "Sure." Dietz was so sure the dealer was wrong that he checked his totals in the 1982 dealership's sales log. Dietz was wrong. The dealer could sell them: he'd sold more last year.

After three months on the road, the bankers sat down with the consultants to talk about Harvester's future. The truck expert suggested consolidating plants. Harvester had already done that. The consultant passed out a table of projected truck sales. The bankers studied the numbers; the truck division would begin to break even in July.

"We don't know how to turn tractor sales," said the farm machinery consultant. "The problem is the economy, not the company. Harvester has already done everything that a farm machinery maker can do."

By June, the bankers began asking Florjancic when the negotiations with Harvester would start.

At first, Florjancic just laughed: no one was as suspicious as a bored banker. Then in mid-July, he got a call from John Payne, the workout man from Morgan Guaranty. "We've got to get the talks moving," said Payne. "These tours are taking too long."

"I'll talk to Cotting," said Florjancic. Calls from John Payne were not a laughing matter.

* * *

John Payne plays his cards close to his chest. At forty-one, Payne is short and stocky, with a friendly smile and twinkling blue eyes. He's precise; he never answers a question with two words if one will do; he can always recite a detailed list of reasons why what he wants makes sense. He's mastered the lightning switch from banking buddy to hard-nosed negotiator. Payne sticks by an idea until someone proves to him that it won't work; he raises an eyebrow and wrinkles his brow when he's skeptical. He's widely regarded as one of the best workout men in the business: quick to grasp how a complicated company really works, peerless at posturing until he gets what he wants. "Nobody negotiates like John Payne," says Fred Florjancic. "He walks to the precipice and waves."

Payne grew up on a farm in Shelburne, Massachusetts—his father used Harvester equipment—and majored in math at St. Lawrence University. He spent a college summer working for Morgan and signed on full-time when he graduated in 1965. Payne worked as a credit analyst while he went to night school at New York University. When he received his M.B.A. in 1968, he took a two-year leave of absence to teach farming in the Peace Corps in India. After three years handling Morgan's corporate business in the southern states and a stint as head of merchant banking in Nigeria, Payne was promoted to vice president in operations. In 1980, he was transferred to "special"—aka bad—loans. Payne has been in charge of corporate workouts since 1982.

Morgan Guaranty had lent $200 million to Harvester, mostly to IHCC, the finance subsidiary, and when the bankers reorganized the original eight-bank negotiating team into a larger steering committee, John Payne was picked to head the credit-company subcommittee. Payne's first worry was that a bankruptcy court might consolidate IHCC with International Harvester. He commissioned a study, and it turned out that that consolidation wasn't likely: IHCC had already moved out of the Harvester Building into the suburbs; it had hired its own legal counsel and its own accounting firm; it had even set up its own computer system.

During the spring of 1983, just before the plant tours, Payne

211

began to toy with the idea of holding a debt renegotiation for the credit company separately from the parent company. In the past, the bankers had negotiated together, even though they were making different agreements. Holding separate talks would eliminate the hard feelings between the two groups of bankers at the table. In mid-July, Payne told Fred Florjancic his idea.

Florjancic was stunned. "You can't do that," he said. "It doesn't make sense. You could negotiate a deal that meant simply liquidating the credit company. You'd get your cash, but you'd kill Harvester."

"We need to start negotiating," said Payne.

"I'll call Cotting," said Florjancic. "We'll get started. But there's going to be just one set of negotiations."

"The bankers are getting antsy," Florjancic told Cotting the next morning. "They think you're stalling. We need to have a preliminary meeting. Can you give us a preview of what you're going to ask for?" The bankers would use Cotting's proposal as a starting point for their intermural talks.

"Sure," said Cotting. "I've got everything ready except the final tables. I'll bring down what I have."

Cotting came to see the bankers several days later. He passed out a preliminary draft of his proposal. "I want the banks to swap $600 million of debt for stock," he said. "I want a seven-year deal."

"Bullshit," said one of the bankers.

Cotting stood up to leave. "We put together a package and all you do is throw stones at it," he complained. "We're holding this meeting to get your input, not to be harassed."

"Jim wasn't listening at that meeting in March," said one of the bankers after Cotting left. "We told him that we wouldn't swap that much debt; we told him we wouldn't go long-term."

Dietz glared. He was still mad that he hadn't been invited to the March meetings.

Florjancic didn't want the session to deteriorate into a squabble. "Let's talk about what we can do," he said. He started to poll around the table for suggestions.

"We can't start to negotiate yet," said Wagenseil. "I'm not convinced that Harvester is going to survive. There are too many tractor makers." International Harvester. Massey-Ferguson. J. J. Case. "Someone will have to close down."

Wagenseil got up to leave.

Florjancic shook his head. "Taylor," he said. "Sit down." Cotting had talked about the possibility of closing down the farm machinery division at one of the meetings that Wagenseil had missed. "Of course Harvester has looked at the idea of closing the agricultural machinery division. If you don't believe me, ask Don Lennox."

Wagenseil sat down again. As soon as the meeting was over, he called Don Lennox for an appointment.

A week later, Wagenseil sat down with Lennox and Cotting in Lennox's office.

"Closing the agricultural division would be too expensive," said Lennox. Harvester would have to pay employee severance, equipment-moving fees, real estate commissions. "We've talked to say a dozen companies. None of the offers were right."

"Who have you talked to?" asked Wagenseil.

"I can't tell you," said Lennox. "We promised the companies that we wouldn't reveal their names, not even to our bankers."

"What were the terms?" asked Wagenseil.

Lennox hesitated.

"We talked to ten companies," said Cotting. "We had serious negotiations with three." Cotting ran through the proposed terms.

Wagenseil frowned. "These offers are too low," he said.

"That's what we think," said Cotting.

"If anything else comes up, we want to know about it," said Wagenseil.

"We'll call," said Cotting.

Wagenseil nodded. He'd made his point. Later that afternoon, Wagenseil called Florjancic. "Citibank is ready to negotiate," he said.

Good. Florjancic wouldn't have to spend a lot of time bringing Wagenseil up to date on what the bankers had discussed during Wagenseil's boycott.

"When are we going to start?" asked Wagenseil. "It's already July. Harvester is stalling."

"The official proposal is in the mail," said Florjancic. Cotting

213

had told him that the "blue book"—the cardboard binder was blue this year—was finally ready.

"I can hardly wait to get started," said Wagenseil.

"Neither can I," said Florjancic.

Fred Florjancic got to the first negotiating meeting a few minutes early. John Payne came in and sat beside him at the head of the table; the Harvester parent lenders sat along one side, the IHCC lenders on the other. Florjancic pulled a stack of Xeroxed agendas out of his battered briefcase and passed them around. Then he made a couple of announcements. "We're going to meet four days a week," he said. "Mondays off to catch up on your non-Harvester work. We start at eight-thirty and break when we're finished. The deadline for the negotiations is October 14. Harvester's $4 billion of debt all comes due on December 15, so we've got to have a signed agreement by then. It's going to take us four weeks to get 220 banks to approve a deal, another three or four weeks for the lawyers to draft the papers, and we lose a week for Thanksgiving."

He paused. "Same negotiating procedure as last time. We negotiate until we get an agreement, then we present it to Cotting. He can suggest small changes, but that's it. We have enough trouble working out a bank agreement without negotiating with Cotting too." In fact, the banks did "negotiate" with Cotting too; when they had an agreement among themselves, they sent Cotting a term sheet to feed into his computer; Cotting came back to say that that forced the company to file—and the banks made concessions until Harvester had breathing room.

"I'll put together the agenda for each day's talks," continued Florjancic, "but anyone can bring up anything he wants to during the discussion, and we'll talk about it. We'll keep talking about a point until there's just one holdout." The "Repko cram-down," named after Bill Repko of Manufacturers Hanover. Florjancic had insisted on the cram-down on the grounds that if a banker decided to filibuster, Florjancic could never get a deal done.

"First we've got to talk about what we're trying to accomplish here," said Florjancic. "We need to send a signal to the market that Harvester is going to survive. And we need to work out terms that Cotting can meet. The best way to tell the world that we believe in International Harvester is to give the company a long time to get back on its feet before the next negotiation, to accept a lot of stock in payment for debt and to forgo a cash payment for more debt."

The others agreed.

"Time for the nitty-gritty," said Florjancic. "First we've got to work out the terms of the parent-company debt." He looked at Payne.

Payne nodded that that made sense.

"Let's start with how many years we want to wait before the next talks," said Florjancic.

"Cotting's proposal says that IHCC is going to pay a $100-million 'dividend' to the parent company for it to pay off its lenders," said Dietz. "We've got to talk about that dividend before we settle anything else."

"We'll get to that, Harold," said Florjancic. "First we have to settle Harvester."

"The parent-company lenders don't need more cash than the parent company can afford," said Dietz.

"We'll talk about that later," said Florjancic. "Let's talk about how many years we are willing to give Cotting to work things out. He wants seven years on part of the debt."

"If you strip off the Harvester name and just look at the numbers," said Wagenseil, "this is a six-month deal. This company just isn't ready for a longer-term restructuring." Wagenseil never thought that a company was ready for a longer-term restructuring.

"Six months isn't long enough," said Dietz. "If we don't show strong support, the suppliers and dealers and customers will abandon Harvester. It has to be at least a five-year deal."

"Dietz is right," seconded a banker who had lent to IHCC. "It's got to be long-term."

"Three years is long-term for this company," said another banker who had lent to the parent company.

"This is a six-month deal," said Wagenseil.

"Six months doesn't meet the red-face test," sputtered Dietz. Dietz often talked about the red-face test: he said that he had to

215

be able to explain the Harvester deal to his boss without blushing that he'd been too greedy.

"Let's move on," said Florjancic. He polled around the table. "How much debt are we going to swap for stock? Cotting wants $600 million."

"What about $500 million?" said one of the bankers. "Cotting asked for $600 million, so he can't possibly need more than $500."

"I think that we ought to let him have $1 billion," said Dietz.

"You've got to be kidding, Harold," said Florjancic. "Cotting only asked for $600 million."

"I'm not kidding," said Dietz. "Cotting didn't ask for enough." Harvester needed time and money to get back on its feet—and Dietz knew that IHCC couldn't survive without Harvester.

"Sit down, Harold, let's be serious," said Wagenseil. "This isn't your money we're talking about. This is parent-company money."

"I am being serious," said Dietz. "Every $100 million that you swap saves Harvester $10-to-$11 million in interest payments. Besides, the swap is tied to the $100-million dividend. If you guys want us to give you $100 million in cash, there had better be plenty of water under the bridge."

"The dividend is a separate issue," said Wagenseil.

"We'll talk about the dividend later," said Florjancic. He looked at one of the bankers. "How much debt do you think we should swap?"

The banker started to answer.

Dietz interrupted. "It has to be a billion."

Wagenseil looked at Dietz. "This isn't your money," he said.

"If we're going to pay you a $100-million dividend, you've got to give the company a chance," said Dietz. "Your cash is coming out of IHCC lenders' pockets."

"One issue at a time," said Florjancic. "We're working on the debt for stock swap."

"This has got to be a short-term deal," said Wagenseil. He had given up on six months. "We can't give Cotting longer than a year."

"What about three?" suggested a banker.

"One," said Wagenseil.

"Harvester needs more time, Taylor," said Florjancic. "We have

216

to tell the world that we believe in the company."

"Let's break," said a banker.

Florjancic walked out to the newsstand in the lobby to buy a sandwich. Two of Wagenseil's buddies were there. "Do me a favor," Florjancic said to them. "Check Taylor's pulse on the term." Florjancic couldn't tell whether Wagenseil was posturing or serious. "I don't want him walking out on the talks."

"Sure," said one.

"We'll talk tonight," said the other.

Florjancic walked back into the negotiating room. He called the meeting to order.

The bankers argued all afternoon and evening.

By Friday morning, Florjancic had started to worry that Wagenseil wouldn't give. Then, during a break, Wagenseil's buddies cornered Florjancic. "Taylor's softening," he said. "He'll settle for two years."

"He might do three," said the other. "He's worried that the deal isn't fair—the IHCC banks are getting more cash."

"Thanks," said Florjancic. Florjancic too was worried that the deal wasn't fair.

"I think three years is the right term," said a banker after another hour.

"So do I," said one of Wagenseil's buddies.

Wagenseil frowned. "Maybe Citibank can live with two years," he said. Two was better than three.

The bankers bargained.

Late in the afternoon, Florjancic called for a vote.

Wagenseil voted for two years.

Everyone else voted for three.

Three it would be.

Florjancic caught Wagenseil's eye. They had to talk.

After the meeting, the two headed for the Ritz-Carlton Hotel bar.

Florjancic ordered a Scotch and water.

Wagenseil ordered a dark rum and Coke.

"I'm willing to bargain," said Wagenseil, "but I don't think you're being realistic about how healthy Harvester is."

Florjancic sipped his drink.

"Cotting's blue book proposal isn't fair," said Wagenseil. "He offered to pay the IHCC banks 8.5 percent of their debt up front; he offered to pay us just 8 percent."

"This deal is going to be equitable," said Florjancic. "Everyone is going to get paid the same. We'll settle that first thing tomorrow morning."

"Jim Cotting proposed $100 million for parent-company lenders," said Fred Florjancic at the next meeting. "That won't even things up, the parent-company lenders have to get $120 million. One hundred million will come from the dividend." He looked at Hal Dietz. "The extra $20 million will come from Harvester's bank account."

"That's ridiculous," said Dietz. "The IHCC lenders aren't going to give the Harvester lenders any money."

Florjancic didn't want to argue. He'd have to have dinner with Dietz. He changed the subject. "Let's talk about how much debt we're going to let the company pay off with stock," said Florjancic. He polled around the table. "We were thinking about $300 million last week," he said.

"One billion is the number," said Dietz.

"We can't go higher than $200 million," said Wagenseil.

The bankers talked all morning.

By midafternoon, everyone but Citi was deadlocked between $400 million and $500 million. Citi was stuck at $250 million.

"Why don't we let Harvester pay off $400 million of debt with stock and offer to take another $100 million of stock if we can sell $100 million of Harvester stock to the public for some minimum cash price," said one of the bankers who'd had to swap part of his Chrysler debt for stock the year before. "We just sold 26 million shares of Chrysler for $400 million. I'm willing to own some Harvester stock if I know it's worth something."

"What if no one will buy it?" asked Payne. "What signal does that send to Harvester's dealers and suppliers and employees? What does that say to Harvester customers?"

"I'm pretty sure that the stock will sell," said Florjancic. He'd talked to the investment bankers that the lenders had hired to advise them on securities swaps.

218

"Four hundred million is too much," said Wagenseil. "But maybe we could figure out a way to make how much debt we give up contingent on whether or not the stock sells—and at what price."

That was too complicated for most of the bankers.

"Let's move on," said Florjancic.

Dietz picked up his blue book. "The company hasn't even addressed the most important issue: rebates. We've got to do something about that." All the big truck and tractor manufacturers were now offering rebates to try to spur sales. Dietz was all for improving sales; the problem was the mechanics. As soon as a new tractor came off the end of the Harvester assembly line, IHCC "bought" it at sticker price with cash borrowed from the IHCC banks. IHCC "sold" the tractor to a farmer and paid back the banks. The catch: the farmer who bought the tractor paid the sticker price minus the rebate—and Harvester paid the rebate; if Harvester went bankrupt, IHCC would never collect rebates for tractors on the dealer lots. "Rebates erode our credit. Harvester has got to finance its own rebates."

"Harold, the company can't afford to finance rebates," said one of the lenders. "And it has to have rebates. Everyone else pays rebates. Harvester has to compete."

"This could cost us $150 million," said Dietz. "Or at least I think it's $150 million. I can't get Cotting to give me a number. I keep asking."

"I don't think Harvester can afford to pay the rebates," said Florjancic, "but I can ask Cotting again for a number."

"I've got some other questions," said Dietz. He pulled out a list. He read off a dozen items. He passed the sheet around the table.

"I'll ask these too," said Florjancic.

After the meeting, Fred Florjancic took the elevator to the twenty-fourth floor of the Harvester Building. Jim Cotting's office was the first on the right. Many of the other offices were empty. One of the bankers joked that you could throw a bowling ball down the executive hallway blindfolded and not worry about hitting anyone. Cotting's secretary nodded that Cotting was waiting. Florjancic walked in and sat down on the orange couch in front of the window. "Bad news," he said. "The banks aren't enamored

219

with Harvester stock. They aren't going to swap more than $400 million."

"That's not enough," said Cotting. He shuffled the papers on his desk and then walked over to the orange chair across from Florjancic. "It's nowhere near enough. I can give you numbers."

"Jim," said Florjancic. "You can come into the negotiating room and bang your fists on the table and we aren't going to swap more than $400 million."

Cotting grumbled.

"And it's going to be three years," said Florjancic. "As we see it, Harvester is too risky to leave for longer than that."

"We need more time," said Cotting. "Why don't you at least give us three and a quarter years. That means we'll be negotiating in January instead of September. January is better for our planning schedule."

Florjancic thought for a minute. "I think we can do that," he said. "January is better for our schedules too. I've spent three summers in that conference room. I don't want to ruin another summer."

"Sometimes you're reasonable," said Cotting.

"We've got a lot of questions," said Florjancic. He handed Cotting Dietz' list.

Cotting frowned.

"I understand that Harold Dietz asked you some of these questions quite a while ago," said Florjancic.

Cotting threw up his hands. "I know, I know. I owe you some numbers. I'll get you answers. Later."

Florjancic shook his head.

"Let's play a game of golf when this is through," said Cotting.

"Okay," said Florjancic.

"It's already September 27," Fred Florjancic told the bankers at the end of the week. "Our deadline is October 14, two and a half weeks away. We should have had a rough proposal ready a week ago so that Cotting could run it through the computer. Right now, we don't know that what we're talking about makes sense—it could be so stiff it chokes the company." Florjancic paused. He had thought about limiting debate time, but he'd decided against it: some banker might get mad and walk out on the talks and then sue for payment; that could precipitate a Harvester bankruptcy. "If we don't hurry up, we aren't going to finish these negotiations in time—and that means that Harvester might have to file." He looked around the table. "Let's talk about the $100-million dividend."

"IHCC lenders are willing to talk about a dividend only if there's an agreement that there will be no future dividends," said John Payne, the chairman of the IHCC subcommittee. Payne hadn't said much until now; the bankers had been talking about Harvester debt, not IHCC debt. "Before we settle that, we IHCC lenders would like to discuss how much IHCC is going to pay us. We've made some projections. Cotting offered $212 million, but we think IHCC needs $525 million over three and a quarter years. Seventy-five million every six months."

"If IHCC pays you $525 million, there won't be cash left for the IHCC to finance buyers when Harvester sales pick up," said Florjancic. That would stifle the whole recovery plan.

The bankers argued about just how much IHCC could afford.

"You can't take $525 million," said Florjancic. "IHCC has to have a cash cushion."

The room started to get hot. The air conditioning in the building had gone off at five o'clock.

The bankers started to yell at each other.

The room got hotter and hotter.

Finally David Schulte, a consultant that Florjancic had hired to answer questions about the stock, raised his hand. "Excuse me, Mr. Chairman," he said. "I'd like to say something, although it's not my bailiwick. You guys are in outer space. Would you like a message from planet earth: finance companies don't pay their debt."

The bankers were silent for a minute.

"Well, this finance company is going to pay," said an IHCC lender. "There are other places to borrow money. IHCC can sell some bonds to the public."

Florjancic raised his eyebrows. A company that couldn't get money from its banks, couldn't get much money anywhere else.

Bang. Schulte slapped his palm against the table. He flipped

221

open the other hand up as if he were holding a walkie-talkie. "Scotty," he said. "Beam me back on board. There's no intelligent life here."

"I've got a draft proposal," said Fred Florjancic at the meeting two days later. Florjancic had been so frustrated at the deadlock the night before that after the meeting, he'd taken a cab to his office and dictated the memo. "This will help us get off dead center."

It did.

The bankers agreed to a $400-million swap. They agreed that if they could sell $100 million of stock for at least $7 a share, then they would swap another $100 million worth of debt.

"We've made enough decisions to talk to Cotting," said Florjancic. "It's time to get some feedback."

Late in the afternoon, Florjancic called Cotting. "We've got a proposal," he said. "We want you to come down and hear it first thing tomorrow morning."

"It's about time," said Cotting. Tomorrow was Friday, September 30.

The next morning, Jim Cotting stood at the end of the table facing Florjancic. He set his dictating machine in front of him and snapped the record button on.

Fred Florjancic read the term list. "The new pact will run out in three and a quarter years. We will swap $400 million of debt for stock; we will swap an additional $100 million of debt if we are able to sell $100 million worth of stock to the public for at least $7 a share." Florjancic looked at Wagenseil. He looked at Cotting.

Cotting made some notes on his pad.

"Harvester will pay parent-company banks $120 million cash up front. IHCC will pay its bankers $212 million up front plus $525 million over the next three and a quarter years."

Cotting frowned. He snapped off his machine.

"Any questions?" asked Florjancic.

222

"No," said Cotting. He paused. "I'll have to run the numbers through my computer." Cotting caught Florjancic's eye: he wanted to talk.

Florjancic adjourned the meeting after Cotting left. The bankers would hear Cotting's counterproposal on Tuesday.

After the meeting, Florjancic met Roger Anderson, chairman of Continental, in the executive dining hall. James Ketelson, chairman of Tenneco, the Houston conglomerate, was also there.

"We made a proposal to buy the Harvester agricultural equipment division last week," said Ketelson. "Harvester turned us down. I want to be sure that you knew the terms."

Florjancic nodded. Continental couldn't force Harvester to accept a deal with Tenneco, and he was a little surprised that Ketelson seemed to think it could.

Ketelson listed the terms.

Florjancic made notes.

Anderson listened.

"I've got to run to another meeting," said Ketelson when the three had finished lunch. "I'll give you a call."

Jim Cotting called Fred Florjancic at home first thing Saturday morning. "I'm in my office working on this," said Cotting. "You've made some progress. Isn't there a way to make it longer than three years? We need a longer-term deal."

"I know how you feel," said Florjancic. He didn't mention the lunch with Ketelson; he didn't think the Tenneco offer made sense. "I sympathize; I've been pleading your case at the bankers' meeting. But I lost and I don't think that I can open the issue again."

"We have to have more time to run the company," said Cotting. "We can't spend all our time worrying about how to pay off the banks."

"Jim," said Florjancic, "this is our best offer."

"This proposal doesn't show much support for the company," said Cotting. "I thought you said that the bankers believed in International Harvester."

"We do," said Florjancic. "The bankers think that they are showing support. This is our best offer."

Cotting called again a couple of hours later. By now, he had run the numbers through the computer. "Your proposal has got a lot of problems," said Cotting. "We can't afford to pay the parent-company banks $120 million in cash; $100 million is our best offer. We need a $600-million swap; $400 million isn't enough. We can't afford to pay IHCC lenders $525 million over the next three years. We don't have that much cash."

"We've gone over our projections," said Florjancic. "We think this will work."

"Well," said Cotting, "we might be able to make it if you let us pay $530 million of debt with stock. We might be able to handle a couple of hundred million in cash to the IHCC lenders over the next three years."

"What about rebates?" asked Florjancic. "You know Dietz is going to ask about that."

"We're working on it," said Cotting.

Florjancic drove his son to a soccer game.

Cotting called again that evening. He'd done some new computer runs; he had some suggestions. "Look," he said. "If you'll swap $500 million and go back to my $100-million cash payment, we'll be okay. I've got the computer print-out right here."

"The bankers are never going to agree to that," said Florjancic. "They think they've given you too much already."

"These payments are going to strangle us," said Cotting. "You bankers have got to settle for less."

"The banks are pretty firm," said Florjancic.

"You know," said Cotting. "Negotiating with you is like having glue on your hands; you just shake and shake and it's still there."

"I've run the proposal through my computer," said Jim Cotting at the bankers meeting Tuesday morning. "It's pretty disastrous. I want to make some suggestions. You've got to swap at least $500 million of debt for stock. You've got to scale back the cash to IHCC: we can't afford more than $300 million over the next three years."

Cotting looked at Fred Florjancic. He looked around the table. A banker shuffled his feet on the dull blue carpet.

"Thanks, Jim," said Florjancic. "We'll talk about it and get back to you."

Cotting headed back to his office to wait for the next call.

"It sounds like Cotting is getting used to our proposal," said Florjancic. "Let's move on. We've agreed to swap $400 million of debt. We have to decide how many shares of stock we want in exchange." What percentage of the company.

"We need 75 percent," said Wagenseil.

Florjancic shook his head. Even in a formal bankruptcy, the banks rarely get more than 80 percent of the stock and out of court, they got less; 25 percent of Lockheed, 48 percent of Chrysler. "Seventy-five sounds high," said Florjancic. "Don't you think that 50 percent is more appropriate? We might be able to sell some of that stock for cash soon. We can't possibly sell 75 percent of the company anytime in this decade. We don't really want Harvester stock; we want cash."

"If Harvester goes bankrupt our stock won't be worth anything," said Wagenseil. "We will have thrown away $400 million of valuable debt. We need to have a lot of stock to compensate for that risk."

Florjancic smiled; usually Wagenseil didn't call debt "valuable."

"Taylor," said one of the bankers. "When you own much more than 50 percent of a company, the problems are yours, not the company's."

By midnight, everyone except Wagenseil was settling on 50 percent.

Florjancic couldn't talk Wagenseil lower. He didn't want to use the cram-down rule unless he had to.

"We've got to finish," said Florjancic the next morning. "We have just six days left to cut a deal. Or else Harvester might have to file for bankruptcy."

"Let's talk about the dividend," said Dietz.

"We've got to settle the stock first," said Wagenseil.

"The dividend is important," said Payne.

They weren't making progress on the stock. "Okay," said Florjancic. "Let's talk about the dividend."

They talked.

"We credit-company lenders can't consider okaying this 'dividend' unless Harvester agrees that it will get no more dividends and it will finance rebates," said Payne.

225

"Harvester can't afford to finance rebates," said Florjancic. "We've talked about that."

"We need concessions," said Dietz.

The bankers kept talking.

"We've got to make decisions," growled Florjancic. He threw his gold Cross pen at his yellow legal pad.

The bankers kept talking.

"We've got to have 75 percent of Harvester's stock," said Wagenseil.

"We've got to settle the rebate question first," said Dietz. "We've got to talk about the dividend."

"We're not making any progress," said Florjancic. "Let's move on."

"We've got to settle this," said Dietz.

"How about dinner tonight, Harold?" said Florjancic.

Dietz nodded.

"The Palm steakhouse," said Florjancic. "Eight o'clock." He looked around the table. "Let's talk about stock," he said.

Late that afternoon, Wagenseil gave in—he was the lone holdout—and the bankers agreed that they would demand just 50 percent of Harvester's stock. They still had to agree on rebates; they still had to agree on how much cash IHCC would pay the banks over the next three years.

"We're not getting enough done," said Florjancic. "We're going to have to meet on Columbus Day." Columbus Day was October 10, the following Monday.

The bankers kept talking.

At the end of the day, Florjancic was angry that they still hadn't made much progress. He threw his gold Cross pen at his legal pad in disgust. The angle was just right. The pen hit like an arrow. Florjancic left it standing.

"We've got to settle rebates," said Fred Florjancic next morning. The dinner with Dietz at the Palm had made it clear that the bankers would have to solve the rebate problem to win Dietz' yes vote on the dividend. Florjancic polled around the table. "What do you think the answer is?" he asked each banker.

"Harvester has to finance its own rebates," said one IHCC banker after the next.

"Harvester can't afford that," said each of the Harvester bankers. "Harvester doesn't have enough cash right now."

"The only way we'll pay that $100-million dividend is if you give us some concessions," said Dietz. He looked around the table. Most of the parent-company lenders weren't paying attention; one scribbled a note to Florjancic and handed it to the banker next to him. The banker passed the note on.

Dietz peered over the top of the sheet. "Let's kick this upstairs and let the company shoot it down," read the note. Dietz didn't say anything, but he was mad. The other bankers weren't listening to him. If he didn't start getting some answers, he was going to walk out.

"You had better come down here and talk about rebates," Florjancic told Cotting on Wednesday morning. "We're deadlocked."

Cotting made a presentation that afternoon. He had some estimates on what the rebates totaled. He read the numbers. "I don't quite understand why this issue is so important," he said.

Dietz shook his head. Of course Cotting understood. Dietz would have to caucus with the credit-company lenders to decide what to do next.

After the meeting, Dietz and the other IHCC bankers met for a drink at the Ritz-Carlton bar. John Payne was there talking to a parent-company lender.

"Look what I found," said one of the bankers. He threw a memo on the table. "One of Cotting's people left this behind." The rebate numbers on the memo contradicted what Cotting had just read them. The memo explained how Harvester could fund rebates without using credit-company money. "Cotting's stonewalling."

Dietz looked at the memo. Indeed, it was clear that Cotting understood. "Maybe we should boycott the talks," he said.

"We're not getting much out of being there," said another banker.

"I'll talk to Fred," said Dietz.

Florjancic was sitting at the other end of the bar.

"IHCC lenders are being stonewalled," Dietz told Florjancic. "You aren't listening. The company isn't listening."

"We're listening," said Florjancic.

"I saw that note that one of the bankers passed you about kicking my proposal upstairs," said Dietz. "I saw that memo that Cotting put together on rebates."

"What do you want me to do, Harold?" said Florjancic. "Do you want me to get Cotting to come down to talk to us again?"

Dietz walked back to the other side of the bar.

Clearly Dietz was worked up about rebates. Florjancic wasn't sure that all IHCC lenders felt that way. Payne would know.

"What do you think it would take to get Harold to accept some level of rebate financing?" Payne was also in the bar.

"The only way that the IHCC lenders are going to support the $100-million dividend is if Cotting figures out a way to cut back our financing of rebates and promises to pay no further dividends."

After dinner, Florjancic went back to Harvester headquarters. Cotting was still in his office.

"Jim," he said. "Payne says he thinks that the IHCC lenders will agree to $100 million only if the parent company finances rebates and signs a covenant saying that there will be no more dividends. Dietz is threatening to walk out."

"We can't afford to finance the rebates," said Cotting.

Florjancic looked at Cotting. Cotting seemed to think that the IHCC lenders would change their minds. "You don't understand how mad the IHCC lenders are," said Florjancic. "This is a big issue." He paused. "Why don't you invite IHCC lenders to breakfast? They can tell you how important this is."

"It's Wednesday night," said Cotting. Too late to call a breakfast meeting for Thursday. "Let's meet Friday morning." Friday was October 14, the day the bankers were supposed to have made their deal. "I'll get a table at the Hyatt Regency."

"I don't like the way this package is shaping up," said Hal Dietz at breakfast two days later. "It isn't balanced. We're making more concessions than the parent-company lenders even though we have a stronger bargaining position. If Harvester goes bankrupt, IHCC lenders are going to get back ninety cents for every dollar they lent; parent-company lenders are going to get fifteen cents. We're getting short-changed."

Florjancic raised his eyebrows. Dietz was exaggerating. IHCC lenders would get more like eighty cents on the dollar; parent-company lenders would get twenty.

"IHCC lenders are willing to be flexible," said Payne. "It's clear that as Harvest shrinks, IHCC will shrink too. We think that the money should come to us. We think you can afford $525 million. If you need more money later, we'll increase our lines."

"No," said Cotting. "We can't afford $525 million. We've already pared forecasts to the bone. If we pay you, we'll miss our sales targets. We'll look at some alternatives."

Dietz was skeptical. Cotting had been saying he'd look at alternatives for weeks. "This is a bottom-line issue for us," said Dietz. "We're not prepared to move forward without adequate credit-quality protection"—no rebates—"and adequate amortization"—$525 million. "We're going to walk out if we don't get some concessions. This package isn't fair."

"The package is fair," said Cotting. "I'm trying to be responsive to IHCC problems."

"That's not true," said Dietz. "The company isn't trying to understand our problems. I saw that internal memo on rebates. The one that explains how you can fund rebates without the credit company."

"I don't know what you're talking about," said Cotting.

Dietz glared.

"We saw the memo," snapped Walter Koch, a regional IHCC banker.

Cotting looked around the table. He realized that he'd underestimated how mad the IHCC bankers were. "Let's go over each of the IHCC problems again," said Cotting. "That will help me come up with some answers."

Payne pulled out a sheet of paper; he'd made a list of deal points; he ticked them off one by one. Dividend. Rebates. Credit quality. Tax sharing.

Cotting scribbled.

"We're trying to scale back rebates," Jim Cotting told the bankers on Monday morning. "From now on, the banks aren't going to finance the rebates. Harvester will pay up front. You won't lose a penny of rebate money if we go bankrupt." Cotting looked at Florjancic.

Florjancic looked at Payne.

Payne looked at Dietz.

Dietz nodded.

Payne nodded.

"We'll sign a covenant saying that there will be no more payments from IHCC to Harvester," said Cotting.

The air in the room seemed to lighten.

The bankers asked a few questions.

Cotting went up to his office to wait.

All afternoon the bankers argued about the IHCC payment to the banks. John Payne held out for $500 million.

Florjancic tried to get a compromise on Tuesday.

Payne wouldn't give.

Florjancic took Payne out for a drink at the Ritz-Carlton bar on Tuesday night. "Can you settle for just $300 million?" asked Florjancic.

"We need $500 million," said Payne.

"I don't think that the company can give that much," said Florjancic. "You've got to be flexible."

"We might be able to settle for $450 million if the first couple of payments are bigger than the last ones," said Payne.

"You might have to settle for less than that," said Florjancic. "If we can't get this worked out tomorrow, International Harvester might collapse."

Payne didn't seem worried. "We'll strike a deal," he said.

The bankers didn't strike a deal Wednesday morning. Payne wouldn't accept anything less than $450 million.

At noon Florjancic called his secretary from the phone booth in the lobby of the Harvester Building. He dictated a telex. "I'll call when I'm ready to send that," said Florjancic. When he got back upstairs he asked Cotting for a computer analysis of a $450-million grant.

Two hours later Cotting came down to the conference room. "Four fifty will strangle us," he said. "We can only afford $300 million. We're willing to make the first two or three payments larger than the later ones."

"Three hundred million isn't enough," said Payne after Cotting had left. "I already told Cotting that. We've got to have more."

"How much more?" asked Florjancic.

"Four twenty-five might do it," said Payne.

Cotting came downstairs. He shook his head at the new proposal.

"Look," said Florjancic after Cotting had left. "I've dictated a telex canceling the bankers' meeting Friday. My secretary will send it to all 220 Harvester bankers as soon as I call. That telex will tank the company."

"We'll get things worked out," said one of the bankers. "Don't send the telex out yet."

"I can't wait much past five," said Florjancic. "If we have an agreement then, I've got to put together a presentation for the bankers meeting. I've got to make some charts. That takes time."

Florjancic went upstairs to talk to Cotting. "The IHCC lenders aren't going to bend much on this," he said.

"You know I can't pay what they want," said Cotting. He looked depressed. "I've had enough of this posturing. I'm only coming down once more."

"You ought to tell us that," said Florjancic. "Maybe that will put some pressure on the holdouts."

Cotting was skeptical. "I can try," he said.

"I just threatened to send out telexes canceling the meeting on Friday," said Florjancic. "You ought to say the same thing."

"I can try," said Cotting. "I don't think it will help."

Florjancic went downstairs.

"There's a possibility of a little flexibility," said Payne when Florjancic came in. He'd been talking with the IHCC subcommittee.

Cotting walked into the conference room. "This is the last time I'm coming down here," he said. "I can't keep running your numbers through the computer. If you can't agree to our $300 million, I'm going to have to cancel the bankers' meeting on Friday: there won't be anything to talk about." Cotting paused. "That might be the end."

One of the bankers turned to Florjancic. "What now?" he asked.

"I don't know," said Florjancic.

"I've run the numbers," said Cotting. "According to our forecasts, we can't pay more than $300 million." He went back up-stairs.

One of the bankers stood up. He looked at Payne. "We've got to compromise," he said. "We've got to put together a deal. Harvester is a Fortune 100 company. Harvester has 43,000 employees. Harvester owes us $4 billion. Harvester can't be allowed to collapse."

"Maybe we can do something," said Payne. He called another IHCC caucus. "We want to talk about guarantees on collateral," he said when he came back.

Florjancic called Cotting down.

He explained the problem.

Cotting shook his head. He went back upstairs. He called down half an hour later. He was coming down one last time.

"We redid our forecast," said Cotting. "If we really stretch, we could do $380 million, $58 million every six months. We can guarantee credit quality."

Florjancic looked at Payne.

Payne nodded. "Three hundred and eighty million is okay," he said. "We need more up front. We need $160 the first year, $122 the second and $100 the third." That made $382 million.

Cotting listened with his head bowed. When Payne finished, Cotting looked up. He glanced around the table. He turned to Florjancic. "Fred," he said. "I think we've got a deal."

Fred Florjancic had scheduled a committee meeting for eleven o'clock on Thursday morning. He didn't make it. He was hung over. So were the other bankers. So was Jim Cotting.

On Friday, Florjancic chaired the meeting of the 220 Harvester bankers. He ran through the terms. "International Harvester will pay parent-company lenders $120 million in cash on signing and $382 million in cash over the next three years. Parent-company lenders will swap $400 million of debt for 50 percent of Harvester's stock. IHCC will pay Harvester a $100 million 'dividend'; there will be no future payments from IHCC. Rebates will be paid up front—and they will be phased out over the next three years if that's possible given the market."

Florjancic flew to New York on Monday morning. He spent three weeks arguing with the lawyers about the drafting nuances. Then he flew to Europe to talk to foreign bankers. Florjancic was back in Chicago at the end of October. Now he had to make sure that every U.S. bank signed the deal.

By the beginning of December, there were just two holdouts: Lane Bank Group in Chicago and Trust Company Bank in Atlanta. Lane was a parent-company lender; Florjancic had to win that vote. John Payne doesn't usually lobby, but he agreed to go to Atlanta to explain why Trust Company should sign on.

Florjancic called Lane. The bank wouldn't budge. He went to visit. Still the bank wouldn't budge. On December 14, one day before Harvester's entire $4 billion of debt came due, Florjancic headed to Lane headquarters for the third time in three days. Lane finally agreed to sign the deal.

When Florjancic got back to his office, John Payne called from Atlanta. "No luck," said Payne. "I explained the deal over and over. They understand, but they won't budge."

Someone from Trust Company called Fred Florjancic late in the afternoon. By then, Senator Charles Percy of Illinois and Representative Dan Rostenkowski of Chicago had both sent telegrams to the governor of Georgia explaining that International Harvester was a keystone in the national economy; copies of the telegrams had been sent to Trust Company as well. "We've changed our minds," said the man. "We're on board."

Florjancic put down the receiver.

It was time to think about playing that golf game with Jim Cotting.

In February, International Harvester threw a party at the Drake Hotel for the bankers and their wives to celebrate the end of the negotiations. There was a buffet and a jazz band and every banker took a turn on the dance floor. For many of the bankers, it was a party to celebrate old times. They had moved on to other things. Wagenseil was taking care of two new bankrupt companies, Cooper Manufacturing and Storage Technology. Dietz was restructuring Mattel. John Payne had been promoted to chief credit officer in

233

Morgan's Treasury Division. There is still a monthly bankers' meeting to review Harvester finances, but a couple of bankers have asked Cotting to make the sessions quarterly; Harvester is doing so well that they think that monthly meetings aren't necessary.

In the spring of 1984, the bankers sold $100 million worth of Harvester stock to the public for $8 a share and agreed to swap an additional $100 million worth of debt for stock. In October, Jim Ketelson, chairman of Tenneco, called Don Lennox with an offer for the Harvester agricultural machinery division. He'd made an offer before, but Lennox had thought it was too low. This time, the $430-million price was right. The bill of sale was signed in late November. That let Harvester concentrate on its profitable truck division. Cotting hopes that Harvester will win back its A credit rating, and someday, he'd like to build Archie McCardell's technology center.

That's a long way off, of course, and for the present, Jim Cotting is happy just to know that the world and the bankers believe that Harvester is going to survive. He says that the second-best thing that happened since the negotiations ended was seeing the story on Harvester's second-quarter loss on page 43 of the *Wall Street Journal* instead of page 1. The best thing? In May 1984, five bankers stopped at Cotting's office to ask if they could arrange any new loans for International Harvester.

One after another, Continental's big corporate clients—AM International, Wickes, NuCorp, and GHR—went belly up. Mexico, Brazil and Argentina slid into informal default. Then the Penn Square Bank of Oklahoma City went bust, leaving Continental holding more than $1 billion in bad bought loans. By the end of the first quarter of 1984, the bad-loan portfolio had swollen to $2.3 billion. When Chairman Roger Anderson was ousted in March 1984, the big depositors began to pull their CDs, and in May, Continental had to borrow $4.5 billion from a consortium of big American banks. The Federal Reserve Bank of Chicago put up $5 billion and the FDIC tried to stop the runs by guaranteeing deposits. That was not enough. In July, the federal government bailed the bank out for the second time in half a century.

* * *

As soon as the last Harvester debt papers were signed, Fred Florjancic took his wife to Acapulco for a week. He had hardly seen her since August and he thought he owed her a trip. Early in 1984, Florjancic was made head of Continental's National Southwest division, handling U.S. manufacturing companies based in the plains states like McDonnell Douglas, Trailways, LTV. Soon after, he started to get job offers from other banks and big companies. At first, he brushed those aside, but as Continental's bad-loan total ballooned, Florjancic began returning calls. In the spring, he accepted the post of treasurer of McGraw-Edison, an electronics manufacturer based in Rolling Meadows, Illinois. When he took his first job at Continental, he told himself he'd only stay three years before he went to work for an industrial company; he was just twelve years late.

(6)

L. F. Rothschild,
Unterberg, Towbin

"Where to Find Fast-Growing
Companies—and What to Do with
Them"

"We want you to have a broad role in research and banking at the firm," said Tommy Unterberg. He looked across the dining room rable at Ben Rosen.

Jim Furneaux unfolded his white linen napkin. He looked at the green L. F. Rothschild logo in the corner; then he looked at Rosen. "You're the most respected technology analyst in the world," he said. "We're the premier technology underwriter. We think there's a place for you at L. F. Rothschild."

"Maybe," said Rosen. He sipped his water. "But I'm not sure that working for L. F. Rothschild is what I want to do. I've been an analyst for fifteen years." He had started following semiconductor companies in 1965; it was January 1980. "I've been at Morgan Stanley for five years."

"We don't want you just as an analyst," said Unterberg. "We want your advice on investment banking. We want you to be a partner without portfolio."

Rosen looked at Unterberg.

"This is important for us," said Furneaux.

The door of the dining room opened. A waiter in a black jacket walked in with a round silver serving platter. He set a plate in front of each investment banker.

"I appreciate your offer," said Rosen. "But right now, I think I want to be on my own. I've had enough of working for someone else."

Furneaux looked at Unterberg.

"I'm going to leave Morgan Stanley and just write my electronics newsletter while I figure out exactly what I want to do," said Rosen. "I've got some options."

They talked. "Okay," said Unterberg after half an hour. "But we'd like to have you as a resource."

"I can do some consulting for you," he said.

"Great," said Furneaux.

"What about the conferences?" asked Unterberg. Rosen Research, a biannual Semiconductor Forum and an annual Personal Computer Forum. "Maybe we could be a cosponsor."

Unterberg and Furneaux talked through how the conferences might work.

"We want you to keep thinking about joining Rothschild," said Furneaux.

Rosen nodded.

They gossiped about technology companies.

The door opened. The Rothschild waiter walked in. He cleared the plates and glasses from the table. "Coffee?" he asked.

Unterberg nodded yes.

Rosen crumpled his napkin. "I'm thinking of going into venture capital some day," he said. "Would you be willing to raise some money for me?"

The waiter set a platter of cookies and a silver coffeepot on the table. He poured three cups.

"We don't raise money for venture capitalists," said Furneaux. He reached for the silver sugar bowl. "We never have before."

"Venture capital is something I'd like to try," said Rosen.

Furneaux stirred his coffee. He looked at Unterberg. Rosen wasn't really going to try venture capital. He'd write his newsletter for a couple of months and then sign on as a Rothschild partner.

Unterberg nodded. If promising to raise venture money would seal the handshake, he could promise. He looked at Rosen. "Just give us the word." He paused. "Rothschild might want to set up a venture fund of our own," he said. He looked at Rosen. "We could swap ideas."

Rosen laughed. "You've got a deal," he said.

* * *

Thomas I. Unterberg looks surly. He is fifty-two, slight, with silver hair and blue eyes and an expressive face. He's so shy that some clients think he's unfriendly, and some investment bankers have written him off as downright rude. Unterberg gets up at six every morning, runs twenty-eight blocks to his health club for a forty-five-minute workout and runs back; he's behind his desk by half past eight. Unterberg is hands-on. He paces the trading floor with his shoulders slumped, his shirt sleeves rolled up to his elbows and a pencil tucked behind his ear. Unterberg doesn't put on airs. He still lives in the two-bedroom apartment he and his wife bought twenty years ago; he shares an office with his partner Bobby Towbin and Towbin's teddy bear. Every afternoon, he gripes that he knows exactly what kind of takeout food the traders ordered for lunch: he can smell it. He's conscientious. When the firm got asked to do some corporate finance work for David's Cookies, Tommy Unterberg polled all his friends to find out whether they liked David's or Mrs. Field's; Unterberg himself likes Mrs. Field's—and he wanted to be sure that David's was a winner.

Unterberg grew up in New York and majored in nuclear chemistry at Princeton. After a two-year stint in the Army, Corporal Unterberg headed to the Wharton Business School. When he graduated in 1956, Unterberg signed on at C.E. Unterberg, Towbin, his father's trading firm, as a junior associate.

Clarence Unterberg founded C. E. Unterberg & Company, an "over the counter" bank stock trading company, in 1931. Unterberg couldn't run a brokerage by himself, so he hired a young business school graduate named Belmont Towbin as messenger, bookkeeper and boy Friday for a bargain basement salary of eleven dollars a week. Unterberg taught Towbin to trade, assigned him to handle nonbank stocks and watched the firm grow. Towbin's big break came during the Second World War when he got assigned to the Navy's Bureau of Aeronautics. While Towbin learned about technology, he made a key contact: one of his division mates was a lieutenant named Laurance Rockefeller, a son of John D. Rockefeller, Jr., of Standard Oil and one of the founders of Venrock, the family venture capital company and one of the largest venture capital outfits in the world.

238

After the war, Towbin went back to the trading desk. Then Rockefeller called. Could Towbin underwrite $300,000 worth of stock for a young company called Marquardt Aircraft? C. E. Unterberg & Company was a trader, not an underwriter, but Towbin agreed to take the assignment and promised Rockefeller that he'd do a "Tiffany" job. Towbin did—and cleared $25,000 doing it. Soon C. E. Unterberg & Company was selling half a dozen stock issues a year, mostly for fledgling technology companies like High Voltage Engineering, Thermoelectron, Geophysics Corporation, and Gerber Scientific.

By 1959, both Tommy and Belmont's brother Bobby had joined the firm, bringing the payroll to five. C. E. Unterberg, Towbin stayed small, for years the only investment bank to specialize in underwriting technology. Unterberg, Towbin had always been a pioneer. It was the first investment bank to stake its name on high technology, the first to send corporate clients on money-raising road shows, the first to open a marketing department to figure out how to sell risky investments as aggressively as Colgate-Palmolive sells shampoo. Unterberg, Towbin's first marketing conference in 1975 featured beer and peanuts at Max's Kansas City bar on Park Avenue South and Fifteenth Street in Manhattan, hosting the presidents of "Five Under Five," five companies whose stock sold for less than five dollars a share.

In 1975, Unterberg, Towbin merged with the L. F. Rothschild & Company brokerage. The firm soon began hosting six hundred events a year, from cocktails aboard the USS *Intrepid*, to the four-day Technology Investment Forum in Palm Springs. L. F. Rothschild, Unterberg, Towbin has a special touch: dinners for investors feature five-star cooking and a glittering array of door prizes. Good food makes for good stock orders—and door prize tickets are the most unobtrusive way of taking roll. The food may have changed, but the young company's focus didn't. Rothschild was the leading technology underwriter in America, the biggest of the industry's "Four Horsemen." "We know where to find fast-growing companies," says Unterberg. "and what to do with them when we find them."

In 1971, six years before Rothschild had come into the picture, Tommy Unterberg got a call that would change the course of Unterberg, Towbin forever. It was from a venture capitalist named

239

Arthur Rock. "I need your help," said Rock. "I've got a hot company called Intel. It makes an 'integrated circuit.' Can you raise $8 million for a factory?"

"Let me think," said Unterberg. Eight million was a lot of money to raise for an investment bank that had just $3 million in capital and one salesman. He asked his sales partner what he thought about the idea that Saturday while they were playing golf.

"What's an integrated circuit?" asked the sales partner.

"I'm not quite sure," said Unterberg. "I think integrated circuits are used to make electronic calculators."

The sales partner shrugged. "Why not?" he said. "There's a big market for calculators. Let's go ahead with it."

What Unterberg and his partner hadn't realized was that integrated circuits were not only used to make the brains of calculators, but they were also used to make the brains of computers. Investors snapped up the shares. The market for computer brains was gargantuan.

And getting bigger. In 1974, Intel unveiled the 8080 "microprocessor," a whole computer brain etched on a silicon chip that was small enough to be swallowed. Suddenly, using a computer didn't have to mean plugging into central processing. Using a computer could mean owning a personal machine.

Altair Electronics brought out the first do-it-yourself personal computer kit. Sales were slow; assembling a computer was complicated. In the summer of 1976, a company called Apple unveiled the first preassembled personal computer. It sold like wildfire. By 1981, Apple Computer was on Fortune's list of the five hundred largest companies in the country, and there was a personal computer industry.

There were half a dozen different models: office machines like the Tandy and the Osborne; smaller and cheaper home models like the Atari and the Commodore Vic. There were programs to compute scientific equations, analyze budgets, play Asteroids, teach children to spell. There were attachments to draw graphs, type letters, take information over the telephone. Electronics stores began to offer computers. So did computer boutiques like ComputerLand and Entré computer centers.

A new industry meant new business for Tommy Unterberg.

240

The money-raising assignments poured in:

Thirty-two million dollars for Tandem Computers.

Fifty-four million for Convergent Technologies.

Sixty-nine million for Altos Computer Systems.

Unterberg rounded up the dollars from banks, insurance companies and pension funds. These sophisticated investors didn't mind putting money on companies they'd never heard of; and they didn't mind owning a stock that didn't pay a dividend, and wouldn't pay one for years.

Soon there were dozens of companies in the market. Luckily for Tommy Unterberg, everyone made a personal computer except the king of computer manufacturers: IBM.

Unterberg knew that the small companies he underwrote would have problems competing with IBM. No company ever had. In the 1950s, IBM had steam-rolled past General Electric, RCA, Sperry Rand, Control Data and Honeywell to grab 80 percent of the mainframe market, just as IBM had later stamped out competitors in computer leasing.

Unterberg figured that Big Blue was just around the corner. IBM was too smart to miss a market.

Time proved Unterberg right.

In August 1981, IBM unveiled its own personal computer, the "PC," at a gala affair at New York's Waldorf-Astoria Hotel.

"This is the computer for all seasons," said the IBM host. "The PC can do accounting, word processing, and systems analysis. The PC has a specially designed screen that displays typewriter-style letters complete with serifs." The Apple screen didn't; the Apple screen was very hard to read. "The PC can draw maps in sixteen different colors. The PC can whistle Beethoven's Fifth. The PC can store over 250 typewritten pages of information."

The lights dimmed for a demonstration.

"The price starts at $1,565," said the host when the show was over. "The most sophisticated version goes for about $6,000. We will sell the machines at ComputerLand and Sears—and we will send a copy of the programming specs to anyone who asks. We will pay royalties to engineers who write software for us to market."

"IBM isn't selling this computer the way it sells its other machines," Unterberg told the sales partner after the meeting. "IBM isn't depending on its own salesmen. IBM isn't protecting all its secrets. The new strategy is smart. IBM doesn't know how to sell to consumers. Sears and ComputerLand do. IBM can't write enough programs to boast that the PC can do something for everyone; ten thousand software engineers can. Soon IBM will rule the personal computer world."

The sales partner thought so too.

And so did almost everyone else.

"In five years the PC will be the best-selling personal computer in America," said one computer industry expert. "Consumers trust IBM."

"The IBM PC will change this industry," said a second. "Personal computers won't be just for nerds. They'll be for businessmen and bureaucrats. Soon there will be a personal computer in every den."

"Throw out everything I've ever sent you about personal computers," said a third. "Those studies are irrelevant. Soon we'll be talking about the two periods in the personal computer industry: before IBM, and after."

Tommy Unterberg got more new business. Companies that planned to make products for the PC needed money, and Unterberg raised it. But Unterberg also knew that there would be a change in the personal computer industry. Although some companies kept making computers just the way they always had, others began to try to mimic the IBM. If a company could make a computer that used all the programs designed for the IBM, it would be a success too.

In October 1981, Unterberg got a call from Jim Furneaux, one of his partners.

"Ben Rosen wants to be a venture capitalist," said Furneaux. "He's asked us to raise $25 million."

"Let's talk," said Unterberg.

James Furneaux is feisty. At forty, he has reddish brown hair and blue eyes. Furneaux knows the computer business like the palm of his hand; he's got a network of contacts in the supplier and dealer system; if he has a question, he heads to his favorite computer store and pumps the manager. He usually gets the story right. Furneaux is always on the move. Partners are lucky to catch a few minutes with him in a taxicab for consultations. The pace doesn't get him down. When he needs a break, he climbs aboard his twenty-six-foot speedboat for a day on the Atlantic, and although there is a telephone on board, he hasn't given the number to his partners, or his clients.

Furneaux grew up in Lawrence, Massachusetts, and majored in economics at Northeastern University. He spent five years in the Air Force; in 1972, Captain Furneaux, twenty-eight, with a wife and two young children, decided it was time to "repot." He spent two years at the Dartmouth business school and landed a job as a technology analyst at the Keystone mutual fund company in Boston. He quickly became the Keystone expert on telecommunications, electronics and semiconductors. By 1975, Furneaux was the lead technology analyst for all the Keystone funds. A year and a half later, Tommy Unterberg called and asked him to join Unterberg, Towbin. In October 1976, he made the leap. At first Furneaux worked on both research and banking, but by 1978, he dropped the report writing to focus on clients. In January 1981, he was made a partner. He was thirty-seven years old.

In January 1980, Furneaux had lunch with his friend Benjamin Rosen, the top technology stock watcher at Morgan Stanley. Furneaux had known Rosen since his days at Keystone. Apple Computer had gone public less than a month before, and Rosen was annoyed that Morgan Stanley hadn't given him a bonus for snagging a key technology client out of the hands of L. F. Rothschild. "I'm thinking of leaving Morgan," Rosen told Furneaux. "I'm going to work full-time on my electronics newsletter." For nine years, Rosen had published a newsletter—sometimes referred to as the industry bible—in his free time. He made over $1 million a year from subscriptions. He could support himself on that.

Furneaux frowned. "Don't do that," he said. "If you're going to leave Morgan Stanley, you ought to think about working for us."

Rosen was noncommittal.

"Let me set up a lunch with Tommy Unterberg," said Furneaux. The three sat down a couple of weeks later.

Rosen wasn't ready to join Rothschild, but he agreed to sign on as a consultant.

Rosen spent the next year and a half writing the *Rosen Electronics Newsletter* and looking at job alternatives. In October 1981, he called Jim Furneaux.

"L. J. and I are just about ready to do a deal," he said. L. J. Sevin, founder of Mostek, a semiconductor pioneer.

Furneaux nodded. He knew L. J. Furneaux's Keystone fund had owned a lot of Mostek stock.

"Remember you promised you'd raise some money for me?" asked Rosen. "L. J. and I have decided to start a venture capital company."

"How much do you need?" asked Furneaux.

"Twenty-five million," said Rosen.

Furneaux called Unterberg.

L. F. Rothschild quickly put together the dollars.

Rosen began to look for technology companies for the Sevin Rosen Fund to back. He invested in Osborne, Lotus Development and Quarterdeck Office Systems.

About the time that Rosen decided to become a high-tech company sponsor, Tommy Unterberg decided to start a venture fund of his own. He figured that since he was already in the business of financing young companies, it made sense to branch into financing start-ups too.

Rosen and Unterberg shared ideas.

Unterberg put $250,008 into Apollo Computer, $320,012 into Convergent Technologies, and $150,000 into Software Publishing.

In January 1982, Ben Rosen called Tommy Unterberg. "I just met a great team of engineers from Texas Instruments," he said. "They are going to start a company, and I think I'm going to back them. So is Kleiner, Perkins." Kleiner, Perkins, Caufield & Byers was one of the oldest and most prestigious venture capital companies in America.

"We'll invest," said Unterberg.

Unterberg put up $250,000 on Rosen's recommendation. In order to keep an eye on his investment, he assigned Jim Furneaux to the account.

Furneaux flew out to Palo Alto for the West Coast Computer

Faire. He stopped in at a cocktail party in honor of Rosen and Sevin at Rickeys Hyatt House in San Jose a couple of weeks later.

Two of the three engineers from Texas Instruments were there. Furneaux chatted with Rod Canion and his partner.

"Ben's right," Furneaux told Unterberg when he got back from Dallas. "Those guys are good. That company is going to be a winner."

Rod Canion is hard-working. At thirty-seven, he has reddish brown hair and watery brown eyes. He's plodding. He's conservative. Unlike most computer executives, he goes to the office in a suit, tie and white shirt, and drives a '77 Chevrolet. Canion's not an adventurer. He gets to work at six-thirty every morning and rarely leaves before six at night. When he gets mad, he never yells, never swears; friends know he's hot under the collar because his ears turn red. He's a family man. Canion spends his weekends watching his kids at their soccer games and swimming meets; he sometimes takes an afternoon off to hear his son play the trumpet in the junior high school band. Canion goes to cocktail parties only when he has to. His idea of good fun is the picnic he threw at Cypresswood Park near his house for his friends just after he founded his company. There was lots of watermelon and a barbecue and a volleyball game. Canion enjoyed himself so much that he's made the picnic annual.

He's a native of Houston. Canion majored in engineering at the University of Houston and started to work on his Ph.D. He quit that after two years. Canion was stuck on his thesis, his wife had just had a baby, and a family couldn't live on a researcher's salary. In those days, up-and-coming Texas engineers all worked for one company, so in 1968, Canion got a job at Texas Instruments. Canion began designing electronics, then moved up to designing products with microprocessors in them, then managed a terminal design group, and then headed a team to develop the Winchester disk, a high-power memory device for a personal computer.

At first, Canion loved Texas Instruments. In those days, Texas Instruments was still so young there was no bureaucracy, no red tape. There was spirit, and there was plenty of energy. By the time

245

Canion was put in charge of Winchester disks, though, Texas Instruments had grown big and successful and bureaucratic. Canion thought he was treated as a pawn, not a person: he was transferred from Houston to Austin to Houston; he was transferred out of disks just when the department got successful; he was constantly mired in red tape. He spent more time convincing Texas Instruments to let him be an engineer than he did engineering.

"You're not happy at Texas Instruments," said Canion's wife. "Why don't you start your own company? If you are going to work as hard as you're working, you ought to be working for yourself."

Canion shook his head. He was an engineer. He didn't know anything about starting a company.

But he had met people who did.

Canion talked to them. He started to feel optimistic.

Then Canion bumped into a friend who designed electronic systems. They sat down for a cup of coffee.

"I want to start my own company," said the friend. "Here at Texas Instruments, I'm mired in red tape."

Later Canion talked to a friend who specialized in computer marketing. He wanted to start his own company too. That did it. The three friends would start one company.

"We have to resign," said Canion at the end of October. As long as they worked for Texas Instruments, all their ideas belonged to TI—and TI is aggressive about suing ex-employees for idea-snatching.

"My wife is going to have a baby next month," said the marketing man. "If the baby is healthy, I'll resign. If the baby is sick, I have to stay. A man with a sick baby needs a steady job."

"We'll wait," said Canion. It would only be a couple of weeks.

In the middle of November, an old friend who was the president of a computer research firm told Canion he knew of a new venture capital partnership.

Canion called Ben Rosen in New York.

Rosen told him to see L. J. Sevin, his partner in Dallas.

Canion flew to Dallas. He explained that he wanted to make a PC attachment that would read information stored on a hard disk in the computer. He'd use Texas Instruments parts.

Sevin didn't like the idea. Too many companies made disk readers. But he did like Canion. He made it clear that there was money if Canion thought of a better product.

Then the marketing man's baby came. It was sick.

Canion resigned.

The design man resigned.

The marketing man stayed on.

Canion sat in the den thinking about products. He looked at computer brochure after computer brochure. He called the design engineer. They made a list of possibilities: a two-way radio pager for executives, a disk drive, even a restaurant.

Nothing seemed right.

Then, in the middle of January, five months after IBM unveiled the PC, Canion had an idea: a fully functional portable personal computer. One that worked just like the IBM.

The design man was skeptical. "We can't compete with IBM," he said. "No one has ever competed with IBM and won."

"We won't compete," said Canion. "We'll be complementary. The PC is going to become the standard computer. We're going to be the first non-IBM machine to meet the specs."

"It won't be easy," said the design man. IBM had published the PC specs—but it had also copyrighted them. Canion's company would have to "backwards engineer" the machine. "Even if we can make a machine that works just like the IBM, it might not sell. I'm not sure that anyone wants a portable computer."

"Look," said Canion. "The only portable now on the market is the Osborne and those are selling like hotcakes. But the Osborne is limited. It has a five-inch screen and it weighs twenty-four pounds. It doesn't have enough memory to handle a big document. It can't do complicated spread sheets. A businessman can't use that to write reports on the road."

"Maybe you're right," said the design man.

They would try.

"We need a drawing," said the design engineer. They had to have something to show Rosen.

Canion called an industrial draftsman. The two engineers met the man at ComputerLand to look at PCs. Then they went to the House of Pies in west Houston for coffee. Canion sketched the

247

computer on his place mat. The industrial draftsman watched. At the end of the week, the drawing was ready. It looked just fine.

When Canion explained the idea to Rosen, Rosen loved it. And Tommy Unterberg was willing to pitch in.

At the end of April, Rosen wired Canion $1.5 million, more than any computer start-up had ever gotten on the basis of just a business plan.

Canion rented an office. He bought an IBM PC. He hired a staff. There wasn't time to buy furniture, so Canion brought some card tables from home. He set the telephone on an empty fruit crate.

The design engineer designed steel braces to hold the brain and disk drives in place.

The programming engineer began to crack the IBM memory.

The marketing man measured the space underneath an airplane seat and the space inside the trunk of a compact car.

When the prototype was finished in June, Ben Rosen called Jim Furneaux.

Rothschild agreed to invest another $150,000.

Other venture capitalists brought the total to $7 million.

Canion called a company-naming consultant.

The consultant sent over five possibilities.

Canion chose Compaq.

By August 1982, the IBM PC was clearly a success. It looked like IBM would sell almost as many PCs that year as Apple.

There was so much competition for shelf space that only the first company to piggyback the IBM PC would be a winner—and that meant that Compaq was racing time.

By November, Compaq PC was done. No one else was.

Canion scheduled a press conference. "Here it is," he said. He pointed to the cream-colored box. "The Compaq is twenty inches wide, sixteen inches deep and eight and a half inches high. The Compaq has a nine-inch screen. Like the IBM, it displays typewriter-style characters with serifs—plus graphs and maps. The Compaq can run all IBM programs; it weighs just twenty-eight pounds; it retails for $2,995." That was about the same price as the basic nonportable IBM with a black and white screen.

The orders poured in.

Compaq shipped the first computer in the middle of January 1983, almost a year to the day from the meeting with Rosen in Houston.

By then, half a dozen companies had unveiled their own IBM PC clones—and half a dozen more were rumored to have a clone in the works. But none of them seemed to work quite as well as the Compaq. None of the others could use every program written for the PC.

Compaq looked like a winner. But to keep customers happy, Compaq had to ship machines as soon as they were ordered. Compaq had to have a bigger factory. The one Canion had rented on Perry Road just couldn't handle the load.

Ron Canion called Ben Rosen. "We need $10 million. We've got to build a bigger factory," he said.

Rosen didn't have that kind of money. But a syndicate of investors might. Rosen called Jim Furneaux.

"Compaq needs $10 million," said Rosen. "Can you do a private placement?" A by-invitation stock sale to banks, insurance companies and pension funds. The minimum investment would be $100,000, and investors couldn't sell their stock for twenty-four months. Compaq was still too risky to sell to "public investors" with no strings attached; Compaq would not be ready to "go public" until the company had more experience—and at least one quarter of profits.

"Let's talk," said Furneaux.

"I'll be at the Personal Computer Forum in Palm Springs next week," said Rosen. "Let's sit down there."

Canion and Unterberg and Furneaux and Shelley Floyd, a Rothschild vice president who often worked for Furneaux, and Ben Rosen and his partner L. J. Sevin sat at the booth in the coffee shop in Palm Springs.

"We've got to talk about value," said Furneaux. He looked at Ben Rosen. "How much to you think Compaq is worth?" That determined what percentage of the company investors would buy for $10 million.

"One hundred and twenty million," said Rosen.

Furneaux frowned. "I think Compaq is worth closer to $90 million," he said.

Unterberg nodded. He thought so too.

"No," said Rosen. "Compaq is a winner. One hundred million."

"Compaq is the first non-IBM computer to meet the IBM standards," said Rosen.

"Compaq is better engineered than the competition," said Canion.

They kept talking.

Finally Furneaux nodded. "Okay, you've got it," he said. "The company is worth $100 million. We'll raise another 10 percent. Ten million."

"Okay," said Rosen.

Unterberg looked at Floyd. "You've got a month to sell that stock," said Unterberg. "Maybe two." He looked at his watch. "Let's break," he said. "There's just time for me to spend an hour by the swimming pool before I have to get back to the conference."

Floyd didn't spend a single hour by the swimming pool; she didn't make one conference session. She just drafted documents.

Jim Furneaux called Shelley Floyd into his office. "Put on your trench coat," he said. "You're going to do some espionage. What do dealers think about Compaq? What do suppliers say? How does the competition look at the company?"

Floyd visited a dealer. "I'm thinking of buying a computer," she said. "What do you recommend? Do you know anything about the Compaq?"

"Compaq is a great machine," said the man. "The best IBM standard computer on the market."

Floyd called a supplier. "I'm from a company that's considering entering into a relationship with Compaq," she said. "Does Compaq make its payments on time?"

"Oh, yes," said the man.

"What do other computer makers think of Compaq?" Floyd asked the Rothschild personal computer stock watcher. The stock watcher talked to competitors every day.

"Compaq is here to stay," said the stock watcher.

Jim Furneaux called. "Time to go to Houston for the due diligence," he told Floyd. Rothschild needed to investigate Compaq with sufficient "due diligence"; that way, it would have no legal obligation to cover investors' losses if Compaq went belly up.

The Rothschild team flew down the next day. A dozen lawyers were gathered around the table—Compaq had an outside counsel and a patent counsel; Rothschild had an outside counsel along with half a dozen accountants. A team of junior lawyers was sitting in the next room reading through Compaq board minutes. A team of junior accountants was reading through the invoices and counting the number of employees on the payroll.

"This is going to seem like a grilling," Furneaux told Canion. "But I'm just asking you the questions that investors are going to ask me."

"I'm ready," said Canion.

Floyd took a pack of Benson & Hedges out of her purse. She tapped the pack. "Are you sure that there is a demand for a portable personal computer?" she asked.

"Sure, I'm sure," said Canion. "Look at sales. We'll probably sell $5 million worth of computers this quarter."

"I think people are buying the Compaq as a novelty," said Furneaux.

"You don't spend $3,000 on a novelty," said Canion. "And that's not what our studies show. Before we made a single computer, we hired a market consultant to do focus-group studies on personal computers. He interviewed dozens of potential Compaq buyers. People who already have a personal computer see the value of having one that they can pack up and take on trips or put away in a snap if someone is coming to dinner. People who are looking for a computer see the advantages of a portable too. The only people who aren't interested in a portable are the ones who haven't ever considered buying a computer."

"Compaq doesn't have a sales force," said Furneaux. "Dealers aren't going to push your machine hard enough to beat IBM."

"We talked to the dealers," said Canion. "They said they push Compaq harder because they aren't competing with our own salesmen. Company salesmen can undercut dealer prices—and the dealers don't like that."

"You'll never have as many dealers as IBM does," said Floyd.

"We've got fifty-five already," said Canion. "We'll have seven

251

hundred by the end of the year." He paused. "We've got the big IBM dealers: ComputerLand, Sears, and Businessland. Those big IBM dealers don't want to depend on IBM for all their machines. If IBM decides to sell only through its own force—the way it sells all its other computers—the dealers will be left high and dry with nothing to sell." He looked at the vice president. "ComputerLand likes Compaq so much that the chain sells about half our machines."

"You're at the mercy of IBM," said Furneaux. "When IBM introduces a portable, Compaq is finished. IBM is relentless when it comes to stamping out competition."

"Everyone knows that IBM will introduce a portable," said Canion. "There's no question about that. A portable PC won't wipe us out. It will have different features—and a different price."

"It's going to be years before Compaq turns a profit," said Floyd.

"No," said Canion. "We expect to start making money during the second half of this year."

"Start-up companies usually begin to have big problems when sales pass the $100-million mark," said Furneaux.

"We expect $80 million of sales this year," said Canion. "As I said the day I founded Compaq, Compaq isn't a small company: Compaq is a large company in its formative stages. We've got a big-company accounting firm and a big-company ad agency and a big-company outlook."

Canion introduced the other Compaq executives to the Rothschild team.

"Compaq doesn't have much experience running a large company," Furneaux told the head of personnel.

"Not so," he said. "Together the top eight executives have 141 years of experience. There's not another start-up that can boast that."

"Don't you think that executives are going to leave Compaq for other companies?" asked the vice president.

"That's one thing we aren't worried about," said the head of personnel. "This company is in Houston, Texas, not the Silicon Valley. Our people are older; they've got families; they aren't looking for the road to Damascus."

"You'll never be a success with just one product," Furneaux told the head of product development.

"We aren't going to have just one product," the man responded. "We're working on three new products right now. We're going to have a whole family of products, just like IBM."

"That box doesn't look tough enough to be called portable," Furneaux told the design engineer.

The engineer laughed. "The case is made out of the same high-impact plastic that is used to make bulletproof windows and the face plates of space suit masks," he said. "It has been thoroughly tested. Before we okayed mass production, we had a lab test certify that the Compaq can withstand shock and vibration. The Compaq can withstand 40g of force."

Furneaux raised an eyebrow. The space shuttle had only had to survive 3g.

"We threw a Compaq against the wall," said the engineer. "We threw things at it. We burned the cover with a blow torch."

Furneaux laughed.

Canion took Furneaux's group through the Compaq factory. It looked shiny and efficient. Workers bolted the disk drives and brain boards to the steel frame; the frames rolled down silver conveyor belts to be boxed, tested and packed for shipment.

"Houston is a dangerous place to have a computer factory," said the vice president. "This building would be wiped out in a hurricane."

"So?" said the man. "We'd rent another building. The machinery on the assembly line isn't customized. Neither are the parts. If the factory were knocked out in a hurricane, we'd lose three weeks of production. Maybe less."

Furneaux flew back to New York. "Draft the sales memorandum," he told Floyd.

She drafted.

A couple of days later, Ron Canion called her. "Texas Instruments just sued us," he said. "They say that Compaq stole TI secrets."

"What?" said Floyd. She nearly dropped the receiver. A lawsuit was a disaster. Investors would steer clear of Compaq now.

But Furneaux told her not to worry. "Young companies get sued all the time," he said. "TI will settle. Investors won't even notice."

They didn't.

The orders poured in.

A bank wanted $250,000 worth.

An insurance company wanted $375,000.

A pension fund wanted $500,000.

Floyd even got a call from a French portfolio manager who wanted to invest $5 million but wasn't quite sure exactly what Compaq's product was.

By the end of February, the Rothschild "book" listed $20 million worth of sales. Compaq would have the money on March 19.

"Great job," said Tommy Unterberg. That was twice as much money as Compaq needed.

Rod Canion was glad that the money raising for the new factory was finally over. He wanted to work on product development, not convincing investors that Compaq would survive.

Then, in March, IBM unveiled a more powerful version of the PC with a Winchester disk memory—dubbed the "XT" for extended technology—and slashed the price of the PC. "We're not lowering our prices," Canion told his executives that spring. "We anticipated the cut. We've got to go all out on our XT." Compaq had been working on a powerful extended-technology portable "Plus" for just over a month. "There are rumors that IBM has a new product code-named 'Peanut.'" A home computer with a price tag under one thousand dollars. "There are rumors that IBM is working on a multiuser office system PC code-named 'Popcorn.' There are rumors that IBM is going to introduce a portable. We have to be ready."

The head of product development nodded. "We will be," he said.

"Compaq is becoming an industry standard," said the head of software development. "I've seen software boxes marked 'IBM or Compaq.' I keep getting calls from programmers who designed software on the Compaq, and then discovered that it didn't work on the IBM."

"Our dealer network will be up to seven hundred outlets by the end of the year," said the head of the sales department. "More than any of the other start-ups competing for the IBM market. And we get calls every day from new dealers. The dealers love us." The man showed the *Wall Street Journal*. "ComputerLand likes us so much that it took out a full-page ad to remind buyers that it does indeed offer the Compaq portable." The man passed Canion a page of numbers. "Sales are booming," he said. "Unit shipments are up to 11,100 for the first six months of the year. We're going to ship at least 50,000 in 1983."

"That means $18 million in sales for the quarter," said Canion. "Eighty million for the year."

"The dealers say that they can't keep the Compaq on the shelves," said the salesman. "They are turning away buyers."

"We need more money," said Canion. "We have to increase production. We'll need an even bigger factory than we thought. Buyers won't wait; buyers who get turned away now will opt for another brand of computer. We need to lock in the installed base now."

In June, Canion flew to San Diego for the semiannual Semiconductor Forum. At the preconference cocktail party, Rod Canion bumped into Jim Furneaux.

"We've got to talk," he said. "You told me that Compaq should think about selling stock next year. We need to sell stock sooner than that. We need to raise $100 million now."

Ever since the private placement, Jim Furneaux had been keeping a close eye on Compaq.

Things were looking good.

Furneaux was particularly impressed with the people Canion had hired away from other companies. In June 1982, Compaq had hired the production chief from Datapoint to handle manufacturing. Furneaux had known the chief for years, and he knew that the man was good—he would certainly ramp up Compaq's production to seven thousand units a month by December. In February 1983, Compac had signed on IBM's head of PC sales to run Compaq sales. Investors could no longer question whether Compaq knew how to sell its machines.

But by the end of June, Furneaux was worried. Compaq was doing better than ever, but the market was in trouble. There were too many personal computer makers, price cutting was getting vicious and retailers around the country were cutting back on brands.

Texas Instruments, Atari and Mattel, the three big makers of under-a-thousand-dollar "home" computers, had turned in big losses—and big management changes.

Osborne, maker of the first portable personal computer, was teetering. Orders were down. Half the work force was on furlough.

"Compaq's orders haven't dipped, and I don't think they will," Furneaux told Unterberg. "But selling stock is going to be a problem until the market picks up."

"Don't worry yet," said Unterberg. "We're talking about selling Compaq stock next year."

Then, at the end of June, Furneaux flew to San Diego for the Semiconductor Forum. He'd just ordered a glass of white wine, when Rod Canion tapped his shoulder. Canion told Furneaux that he wanted to sell $100 million worth of stock now.

Furneaux set down his glass. "That's going to be tough," he said. "The market is bad."

"Orders are way up," said Canion. "First-year sales are going to top $100 million. We think that that's a record year for a new company." He paused. "We need $100 million to keep up momentum."

"One hundred million is a lot of money to raise in this market," said Furneaux.

"But we've done in nine months what most start-ups do in nine years," said Canion.

"The problem isn't Compaq," said Furneaux. "The problem is the market. Investors have soured on computers."

Canion shook his head. "We've got to have a bigger factory," he said. "You've got to sell the stock." He paused. "I'm going to be in New York in July. Can you set up an interview for me with Rothschild?"

Furneaux frowned. Canion didn't understand that $100 million was impossible.

"Compaq is a great company," said Canion. "Investors love us."

It wasn't that simple. "I'll make you a breakfast appointment with Mel Lavitt," said Furneaux. Lavitt, L. F. Rothschild's head marketing partner. "If anyone can sell your stock in this market, Mel Lavitt can."

* * *

Mel Lavitt calls himself a "missionary." He's forty-six, tall and trim, with soft brown eyes and a curly beard. He wears a double-breasted suit, a gold tie pin and black tasseled loafers. Lavitt runs six miles in Central Park every night and sells stock the way an evangelist sells religion. Lavitt is a market man. When stock prices are up, he's exuberant; when they are down, he's depressed. He's not reserved; he's not understated; he never hesitates to tell a client what he really thinks. On a trip to Houston, Lavitt stopped to have his palm read by a Gypsy; she told him that he was creative.

Lavitt grew up in Denver and studied American civilization at Brown. He landed a job as an institutional sales trainee at Bear, Stearns & Company, but after three years moved down the street to C. E. Unterberg, Towbin. He thought that selling stocks in young companies would be more exciting than selling stocks in blue chips. It was. Soon Lavitt became the firm's sales partner—as well as the entire sales department. When Unterberg, Towbin merged with L. F. Rothschild & Company which already had several sales partners and a sales force, Lavitt was transferred to "marketing," where he taught the Rothschild salesmen how to sell stocks in companies whose names "began with Y or ended in X." Next Lavitt set up a department to position stocks in the minds of investors, and soon he made himself the world's leading expert on putting together a whistle-stop company sales tour guaranteed to make investors drool for stock.

"Compaq?" asked Lavitt when Furneaux called to set up a breakfast meeting with Rod Canion. "You know this is a bad time to sell stock. Raising that money for Compaq isn't going to be easy."

"Compaq is a good company," said Furneaux. "Compaq has good people and a good product. The stock will sell if we find the right angle."

"Maybe," said Lavitt. "I just might be able to sell Compaq if I can find the right appeal to the heart."

"Sit down with Rod," said Furneaux. "You'll find something. I'm counting on you."

"Tell me about the company," asked Lavitt when he and Canion sat down for breakfast in the dining room of one of the partners the following week.

Canion recited a quick history.

Lavitt frowned. The way Canion told it, the founding of Compaq came out dull. Yet Lavitt knew that the tale had all the elements of the classic start-up-in-a-garage adventure. "What makes Compaq special?" asked Lavitt.

"Special?" said Canion.

"What's different about Compaq from other companies?" prompted Lavitt.

"Well, there's a company spirit," said Canion.

"Yes?" said Lavitt.

"All the employees participate in the stock option plan," said Canion. "There's free coffee and soft drinks on every floor. Even the secretaries are proud of their employee number."

"What else?" asked Lavitt.

"We let the employees share in the enthusiasm," said Canion. "We have employee parties when there's a breakthrough. We show the employees video tapes of press conferences."

"And?" prompted Lavitt.

Canion droned on.

"You know, we need some computers in my department," said Lavitt. Sometimes talking about a specific project made an entrepreneur sparkle. "There are all kinds of things that I want to keep track of."

No luck. Canion answered in short, dull sentences.

Lavitt sighed. This was a cerebral company pure and simple. There just wasn't going to be an appeal to the heart. He'd have to talk to Furneaux about this. And to Tommy Unterberg.

"Let's go through what L. F. Rothschild will do to sell your stock to the public," said Lavitt. "We help you to write up a prospectus." An offering circular. "We put together a sales presentation with slides and speeches. We schedule a road show for you. That means half a dozen cities in Europe, half a dozen in America. You'll need to answer a lot of questions from investors."

Canion nodded. "I can handle that."

Lavitt sipped his coffee. Maybe.

Canion folded his napkin.

"I'll take you around," said Lavitt. They walked to "The War Room." "This is where we sell stock," he said.

Canion looked around. On the wall was a giant magnetic bulletin board marked like a calendar with squares for the days of the week facing the window. Lavitt explained that that was to help him keep track of the 600 events that Rothschild sponsored each year.

Lavitt and Canion walked out to the trading floor. Canion looked at the big green lighted screen on the wall; three and four letter stock symbols raced from right to left.

"We're doing an offering today," said Lavitt. Kolff Medical, the company that manufactured the first artificial heart, was being sold to the public.

Canion nodded. He looked at the traders. The whole room crackled with excitement. Canion was excited too.

"The stock just opened," said Lavitt. He pointed at the symbol "KOLF" on one of the salesmen's Quotron screens. "You'll be up there too someday."

"Well?" asked Jim Furneaux that afternoon.

"Tough sale," said Lavitt. "That man has no pizzazz. Quiet confidence, perhaps, but none of the usual table banging."

"You don't have to bang tables to sell stock," said Furneaux.

"Yes," said Lavitt. "But you know most computer executives are flashy. Steve Jobs goes to his press conferences wearing a tuxedo, blue jeans and tennis shoes." Jobs, the chairman of Apple Computer. "The only computer people who are really dull are the men at IBM. Rod Canion out-IBMs IBM."

"Maybe that's good," said Furneaux. "Investors are wary. You can tell them: 'Look, these guys aren't snake oil salesmen.'"

Lavitt paused. "That's good," he said. "I like that."

"It seems to me that stressing quiet, competent management is the best way to sell to investors who got burned on the flashy companies last winter," said Furneaux.

"That could work," said Lavitt.

"Could" was a little discouraging. But it was better than "couldn't."

At the end of July, Furneaux bumped into Canion at the American Electronics Associations conference in San Francisco.

"I enjoyed my breakfast with Mel Lavitt," said Canion.

"Great," said Furneaux. He didn't mention what Mel thought.

"I want to get going on that stock sale," said Canion. "We've asked E. F. Hutton to be your comanager." That had been Ben Rosen's decision. E. F. Hutton has seven thousand retail salesmen; Rosen figured that Hutton could sell a lot of stock to small investors.

Furneaux frowned. "We're worried that we won't be able to raise nearly as much money as you want," he said. "What is the absolute minimum amount of cash you could get by with?"

"Maybe $50 million," said Canion.

"That's still a lot," said Furneaux. "Investors think that Compaq is competing with IBM. They know that no one has ever beat Big Blue before."

"We have to have that money," said Canion.

"The market is bad," repeated Furneaux. "We may not be able to raise $100 million."

"If you can't sell stock, we'll have to come up with alternative ways to get cash," said Canion. "Maybe we should borrow the money from a commercial bank."

"If you borrow, you have to pay interest," said Furneaux. "Money we raise is interest-free. And it doesn't have to be paid back. Besides, the market could get worse."

"How soon can Compaq have your cash?" asked Canion.

"Raising money takes a long time," said Furneaux. "There are papers to draft. The SEC will sit on it for weeks. If we start working in September, we'll sell the stock in December. We'll finish just before Christmas."

Canion looked surprised.

Furneaux laughed. "We've done it before. The only time we have trouble selling is August. Investors are all on the beach."

"Call E. F. Hutton," said Canion. "We'll talk later."

That evening Furneaux cornered Tommy Unterberg and told him that Canion was thinking of getting the money from someone else.

"Compaq is a key client," said Unterberg. "If anyone sells Compaq stock, it will be Rothschild. Let me talk to Rod."

Unterberg called Canion that night.

Then he called Furneaux. "We're going down to Houston at the end of August," he said. "We'll cut a deal with Compaq."

Furneaux couldn't make that trip: he'd scheduled a vacation in Alaska that week.

Unterberg and Shelley Floyd, the Rothschild vice president who had worked on the Compaq private placement, would go instead. And a man from E. F. Hutton.

The three investment bankers met at La Guardia Airport the following Thursday morning.

There was a hurricane in Galveston headed toward Houston.

Floyd looked at the others. She turned the pages of her airline guide to find out when the last flight left Houston for New York. "Five-forty," she said.

The man from E. F. Hutton wrinkled his brow. "Do you think we should go?"

Unterberg looked at her. "You're right," he said. "If we get caught in the hurricane, we could be crushed like tin foil."

"Well," said the man from E. F. Hutton. "I guess I'll take the risk. Braving hurricanes is part of the job."

"I don't know," said Unterberg.

"We're investment bankers," said the man from Hutton. "We're risk lovers."

They boarded the plane.

The three investment bankers got to Compaq headquarters just in time for lunch.

Ben Rosen was already there.

It took all afternoon to settle the details.

Finally Unterberg and Canion shook hands: L. F. Rothschild would try to sell $100 million worth of Compaq stock by Christmas.

"We've got to hurry," said Floyd. "The last flight to New York leaves at five-forty. We want to beat the hurricane."

"I'm flying back to New York tonight too," said Rosen. "I've got a car. I'll give you a ride to the airport."

Rosen drove across Houston. He got to the airport so late he didn't have time to turn in the rental car. Rosen left it with the parking lot attendant and ran to the ticket counter.

The five-forty flight was still boarding.

The trip was choppy but safe.

But the next morning when Floyd tried to call Canion, the phone lines were down.

The hurricane had struck.

There were a hundred and one things to do—and hardly any time.

The lawyers had to draft the stock registration papers for the Securities and Exchange Commission. The sooner that was done the better; the waiting list was five weeks long.

The accountants had to go over the numbers. Fast. Normally a company has numbers ready forty-five days after the end of the quarter. This time the numbers had to be ready and checked and filed in twenty. The accountants weren't sure they could get it all done.

"Update your espionage," Jim Furneaux told Shelley Floyd.

She called a dozen Compaq dealers.

She called Compaq suppliers and Compaq watchers.

She told Furneaux that everything looked good.

Furneaux called Rod Canion.

"Sales are booming," Canion said. "We sold $4.9 million worth of computers in the first quarter, $18.0 million in the second quarter and we'll sell at least $35 million this quarter. It looks like we earned $4 million this quarter."

Furneaux called the head of the syndicate desk. "We're underwriting stock in Compaq," he said. "We're talking $100 million total. Can you sell the shares?"

"I don't know,' said the man. "Investors are pretty cool on computer stocks. Osborne just went bankrupt."

"Osborne wasn't like Compaq," said Furneaux. "Osborne wasn't a PC clone. Osborne wasn't even a fully functional machine. The Osborne didn't make sense for businessmen who have PCs at the office."

"Osborne made a portable personal computer," said the sales partner. "So does Compaq. That's as much as some investors care about."

Furneaux frowned. "Say the price of Compaq is $15 a share," he said. Investment bankers figure that they can't sell stock in a new company for less than $10 a share since big investors think cheap stocks aren't good quality; they can't sell for more than $20 a share since small investors think that's too expensive. "Can you sell 6 million shares? That's only $90 million total."

The man laughed. "Do you know how many orders you have to have to sell 6 million shares?" he asked.

Furneaux shook his head. He called Rod Canion. "There are a lot of rules about selling stock," he said. "As far as you're concerned, it boils down to this: be careful what you tell the press. The SEC gets nasty if it thinks you're trying to hype the stock."

"We have to talk to the press," said Canion. "We're going to announce the Compaq Plus on November 1." The more sophisticated verson of the Compaq. "Everything is set. The room at the Tavern on the Green is booked." The brick and glass restaurant on the edge of Central Park. "The invitations have gone out."

"I guess that will be okay," said Furneaux. "If the SEC asks, we can point out that the announcement was scheduled months ago."

"We'll only talk about the Plus, not the company," promised Canion.

"The press conference will change the deadlines," said Furneaux. "We can't file our prospectus before the conference because we have to mention the Plus in the documents—and it's bad policy to announce products in government filings. We can't file after the conference—reporters will ask about the financing and we'll have to tell them it isn't definite. That means we have to file just as the press conference begins. The documents need to get to the SEC before eleven on November 1."

At the beginning of September, one of Compaq's lawyers called Furneaux and asked him to come to Houston to go through the draft documents.

Furneaux called Shelley Floyd. They would both go.

The lawyers and bankers and accountants and Compaq executives met in a conference room at Compaq headquarters.

"Let me read off the risks," said a lawyer. He read twelve items.

"That's too many," said a second. "We can't have twelve risks."

"Isn't risk two subsumed in risk eight?" said another. "Can't we combine risks five and six?"

263

"Give me that list," said a third. "We'll fix this."

The lawyers argued.

Floyd stared. Did it matter how many risks Compaq listed?

"I've rewritten the list," said a lawyer late in the afternoon. "Six risks." He read them off:

"One. Business strategy. Compaq is dependent on IBM for technical specs. IBM could wipe out Compaq overnight by changing them."

Furneaux raised his eyebrows. IBM would also wipe out IBM by changing them. Seven hundred and fifty thousand people already owned PCs with the old specs; IBM couldn't abandon them.

"Two. Short operating history. Compaq has been making computers for less than a year."

"Three. Competition. There are a lot of personal computer makers. Some of them aren't going to survive."

"Four. Expansion. Compaq's success depends on increasing sales rapidly. There's a good chance that something will go wrong."

Furneaux frowned. Some chance, not good chance.

"Five. Product introduction. Compaq just unveiled a Winchester disk machine."

That didn't seem overly risky. Compaq had to have a second product. IBM already had a Winchester disk machine.

"Six. Dealer relations. Compaq depends on one dealer for half of its sales."

Furneaux nodded. The list sounded okay.

"I don't like risk three," said a lawyer. "That language isn't right."

"I think we ought to cut the list to five risks," said another. "Six risks is still too many."

The lawyers argued.

Furneaux stared at the ceiling.

"We're still at six risks," said a lawyer. "But we've redrafted them." He read the list.

"I don't like that wording," said a lawyer.

"Can't we get this down to five risks," said a second. "We can combine risks two and five."

"No," said a third. "Two and five are different. There are six separate risks."

Furneaux shook his head. Lawyers.

Furneaux and an associate flew down to Houston again at the end of October for a meeting to review punctuation.

The lawyers thought that the period ought to follow the quotation mark when a sentence ended with a quote mark. The investment bankers said that that wasn't good English. The lawyers didn't care about English.

The associate helped work out the last loose ends at the printer's. He had to make sure that everything was right: the right text, the right type face, the right amount of space between the "*L*" and the period in "L. F. Rothschild."

The proof was done at two in the morning. The last flight from Houston to Washington was long gone.

"The papers have to be filed in Washington by eleven tomorrow morning," said Furneaux from San Francisco. He'd left Houston after the punctuation meeting. "Charter a Lear jet. Send a lawyer to file."

A lawyer and the associate raced to the airport. They boarded the plane. It was stocked with champagne.

The associate raised an eyebrow. He wanted to sleep.

The jet touched down at Washington National Airport at eight-thirty Tuesday morning, November 1.

The lawyer caught a cab to the SEC. He pushed the papers through the window. The clerk stamped the time. Nine thirty-five.

The associate boarded the Eastern shuttle to New York. He got to the Tavern on the Green just after eleven o'clock.

The press conference had already started.

"This is the Plus," said Rod Canion.

Back in October, before the Plus was even finished, the market for technology stocks had begun to collapse. There were 250 different personal computer makers competing for the same business; now there was blood on the floor. Archives Inc., one of the first personal computer makers, was bankrupt; Osborne was bankrupt; Computer Devices was bankrupt. Texas Instruments had lost more than $500 million on home computers in just six months, and then pulled out of the business altogether. Even the giants were struggling. Digital Equipment Corporation announced that personal computer losses had pulled profits down 72 percent for the quarter; Apple profits were down 73 percent. Stock prices plunged. Apple fell from $62 share to $24; Victor Technologies skidded from $22 to $4¾.

The last thing investors wanted was new technology stock.

Mel Lavitt picked up the phone and dialed Jim Furneaux. "Look," he said. "I'm worried about this deal. I don't think that anyone can sell six million shares of Compaq stock, not at $15 a share; that's too many shares at too high a price. We need a strategy session," said Lavitt. "Meet me in Tommy's office."

Lavitt was sitting in the armchair facing Unterberg's desk when Furneaux strode through the door from the trading floor. The head of the syndicate department was there. So were two salesmen.

"Compaq is a key deal for this firm," said Unterberg. "Compaq is a high-profile company. Compaq is already a client. We're an investor. Our reputation is at stake."

Lavitt leaned back in his chair. "Look," he said, "maybe we're overestimating how hard this will be. I'm going to visit Compaq." Lavitt often visits companies before a stock sale. "I might just find the spirit of the company—maybe there's more pizzazz to Canion than I saw over breakfast."

Furneaux shook his head. He stared through the window at Brooklyn Bridge.

"Do anything you have to do to sell the company," said Unterberg.

Mel Lavitt flew down to Houston a couple of days later. He talked to Canion. He talked to the other top executives. He toured the plant.

As soon as he was back in New York, Lavitt called Jim Furneaux.

"I've got an idea," Lavitt said. "I want to send part of the sales team down to visit Compaq. That will make them think of Compaq as their company. That could be the key to making this deal a success."

"It's worth a try," said Furneaux.

Lavitt called the salesmen into a conference room. "You're going to Houston," he said. "You're going to visit Compaq."

"Why?" grumbled one. "We don't visit companies. What's wrong with Compaq?"

"Nothing's wrong," said Lavitt. "I want you to see what a great company this is."

Two weeks later, the salesmen boarded the plane to Houston.

They toured the factory. They had lunch with the top engineering team.

They met with Canion, and he explained what a floppy disk was, what software was. He carefully explained how to load a diskette into the slot. He demonstrated a program.

"What do you think that was all about?" asked a salesman on the plane ride home.

"I don't know," said the man in the next seat. "Compaq seemed like a great company to me."

On Saturday, November 6, Rod Canion flew to Geneva for the start of the road show. The European schedule was so tight that Rothschild had to charter a private plane. Mel Lavitt didn't come along—he explained that that wasn't his job—but Jim Furneaux did.

From the start, things went wrong.

The audience at the Hotel de Bergues in Zurich looked bored. "I thought they were going to fall into their soup," said Shelley Floyd, the Rothschild vice president, afterward.

The Zurich listeners didn't order any stock.

Neither did the investors in Paris or Amsterdam. They seemed more interested in the food, wine and cigars than the stock.

The meeting in London was at the Butcher's Hall. Furneaux clearly wasn't keen on the place: he told Canion that the technicians had once got upset when a Rothschild client tried to put a slide screen over the portrait of the Prince of Wales.

This time the chairs were hard, the food was awful and the investor reaction was worse.

The last stop was Edinburgh. The lunch was depressing. There were just five investors. And no orders in the book.

The U.S. tour was just as disastrous. Boston, New York, Chicago, Minneapolis, Los Angeles, San Francisco, Dallas, Houston— all quiet, hostile audiences.

By Thanksgiving, Canion had met hundreds of potential stock

buyers but Furneaux told him that there was not a single order in the book.

Mel Lavitt put the receiver in the cradle. Things were going from bad to worse. At the end of September, a *Business Week* cover story had proclaimed: "Personal Computers: And the Winner Is IBM." The article sent personal computer makers into a new sales frenzy. Kaypro offered buyers a free spreadsheet software diskette with a computer purchase; the Epson personal computer came with a free three-hundred-dollar printer. Victor Technologies offered students at Pepperdine University a one-thousand-dollar price cut on its computer, without success: students worried that they wouldn't get their deposits back if Victor went bankrupt before delivery. Only the IBM seemed to be thriving. Their most recent ad featured a pillow emblazoned with the company logo and the words "What most people want from a computer is a good night's sleep."

That was the main reason the Compaq sale wasn't going well.

But the road show hadn't helped. Lavitt had seen a performance in New York. It was B-plus at best—Canion was too stiff—it would take an A performance to get investors interested in this market. Lavitt didn't mention the problem to Canion though; he figured that that would just make Rod more nervous—and stiffer.

Lavitt started to call investors.

"Computers aren't on my list," said the first.

"Let me tell you about Compaq," said Lavitt.

"No," said the investor. "Not Compaq. Not for me. Not now."

"I don't buy companies that have been in business less than a year," said the next investor.

"Technology companies are risky," said another.

"Compaq is different," said Lavitt. "Its first-year sales will be close to $100 million."

"Compaq competes with IBM," said an investor.

"No," said Lavitt. "Compaq makes a complementary machine. Let me tell you about Compaq."

"No," said the investor. "Not Compaq. Not for me. Not now."

"There are a lot of IBM clones," said the investor.

"Compaq was the first clone on the market," said Lavitt. "It's the best."

"No," said the investor. "Not Compaq. Not for me. Not now."

One of the Rothschild salesmen called. "How much does the Compaq weigh?" he asked. "Is it lighter than the Panasonic? Investors keep asking me to compare the two machines."

A second salesman called. "How does the IBM stack up against the Eagle?" he asked. "What about the Corona? What about the Hyperion?"

Lavitt called Furneaux. "Investors keep asking about the competition," he said.

"I'll get you a spread sheet of specs," said Furneaux. Weight, footprint size, and number of expansion slots for Compaq and half a dozen competing machines.

"Looks great," Lavitt told Furneaux.

But spec sheets didn't sell stock, telephone calls did.

One investor ordered.

Then another.

The syndicate man from E. F. Hutton called. "Retail likes the stock," he said. "The orders are coming in."

But the institutional orders weren't.

By Thanksgiving, Lavitt's sales book showed orders for just three million shares. And all the sales were shaky. Orders could be canceled in a minute.

The orders trickled in.

It wasn't enough.

Lavitt would have to do something more. He called Rod Canion. "I'll meet you at Comdex," he said. Comdex, the biggest personal computer show of the year.

The Monday after Thanksgiving, Rod Canion was in the office putting the finishing touches on the agreement to buy land for the new headquarters. He looked over the building plans. He talked to the engineers about the next Compaq model, the lap computer.

On November 29, he flew to Las Vegas for Comdex. He and Mel Lavitt looked at the Panasonic personal computer, and at the Corona and the Eagle and the Hyperion.

"These aren't much competition," said Lavitt. "Most of them don't take any diskette that works in the IBM. Compaq is in a class by itself."

"I know," said Canion.

"But any competition makes investors worry," said Lavitt.

Canion nodded. Lavitt had said that time and time again. "We need that cash," said Canion. "If we don't expand the factory, we can't fill orders and we'll lose our edge. That could kill Compaq."

"I know," said Lavitt.

Mel Lavitt started to think sales would soon pick up. He figured that any fool who'd been to Comdex would know that the Compaq was the best personal computer around.

But things didn't get better after Lavitt got back to New York; they got worse.

"I want to cancel my order for Compaq," an investor told him.

"Cancel it?" said Lavitt.

"Yes," said the investor.

"What's wrong?" said Lavitt. "Compaq hasn't changed."

"I was at Comdex," said the investor. "I saw a lot of Compaq competitors. I don't want to make a bet until I know which machine is the winner."

"It's Compaq," said Lavitt.

"We'll see," said the investor.

The phone rang. It was another investor.

"Cancel my order for Compaq," he said.

"Cancel your order?" said Lavitt.

"IBM is tightening the screws," said the man. "The stock market is headed south. Technology stocks are dropping fast."

The phone rang again.

"Cancel my order for Compaq," said an investor.

"Why?" asked Lavitt. "What's wrong with Compaq?"

"Compaq is fine," said the investor. "But I'm getting out of stocks altogether. The market is down. I'm selling off."

Lavitt's phone rang.

"Cancel my order," said an investor. "Computers are off my list."

"Compaq is a great company," said Lavitt.

"Wrong industry," said the investor.

"Right company," said Lavitt.

270

"No," said the investor.

Lavitt put down the receiver.

He called Boston and San Francisco.

No orders.

London called. Cancellations.

Chicago called. Cancellations.

Lavitt counted the orders he had left: just 1.5 million shares. He had to sell six million. He picked up the phone. "I'm taking tentative orders at $14 a share," he told an investor. "Down a dollar a share."

"No thanks," said the man. "Compaq isn't on my list."

"What about at $12?" asked Lavitt.

"Maybe," said the man. "I'm good at $9."

Lavitt marked down the order. He called the next investor on the list.

The syndicate man from E. F. Hutton called.

"We may have to cut the price," said Lavitt. "The institutions aren't buying. I'm thinking of $12 a share."

"Retail is solid at $14 a share," said the man from Hutton. But there wasn't enough retail to buy the whole issue—and retail wouldn't buy unless "smart money" bought too.

Late that afternoon, Lavitt called Jim Furneaux. "No new orders at $15," he said. "But I've got some tentative orders at $14. I've got orders at $12 and $13 too. I even took one at $9."

"I don't know," said Furneaux. "Cutting the price signals to investors that no one wants the stock. That makes them sure something's wrong."

"I know," said Lavitt. "But we don't have much choice. There aren't enough orders."

"Looks bad," said Tommy Unterberg when Furneaux and Lavitt showed him the sales book.

"We have to cut the price," said Lavitt.

"Cutting the price could taint the company," said Unterberg. "It could make things worse."

"We don't have a choice," said Lavitt.

Unterberg looked at the book. He looked at Furneaux.

"We don't have much choice," said Furneaux.

"How's $12 a share?" asked Unterberg.

Furneaux looked at the order book. "Twelve is okay," he said. "Let me call Rod Canion."

Unterberg handed him the telephone.

Furneaux dialed. "Rod," he said. "The market looks bad." Furneaux talked about stock prices for ten minutes. He paused. "We're thinking about cutting the price to $12 a share," he said. "That means that Compaq will get $72 million instead of $90 million."

Canion sighed.

Lavitt took the receiver. "Rod," he said. "We can't raise more than that," said Lavitt. "No one is buying."

"Okay," said Canion. "I guess we'll have to cut back the expansion plans." He paused. "You said you wouldn't have a problem selling stock at Christmas. I hope you know what you're doing."

"We know what we're doing," said Lavitt. "The problem isn't Christmas, it's the market. The stock will sell at $12 a share."

"You had better be right," said Furneaux after Lavitt hung up. "We can't cut the price again. Investors will get so suspicious that they won't buy. Then we'll have to withdraw the issue—and Compaq might not be able to sell stock ever again."

"Compaq is now $12," Mel Lavitt told the first investor on his list. "Are you ready to order?"

"Didn't I say no at $15?" said the fund manager.

"Yes," said Lavitt. "But now the price is $12."

"So what's wrong?" said the manager. "How come you cut the price?"

"Nothing's wrong," said Lavitt. "The market changed."

"No," said the man.

Lavitt called another investor.

Lavitt looked at the order book.

Only 2 million shares sold.

Lavitt kept calling.

"I want to meet Rosen," said an investor late in the afternoon. Ben Rosen, the venture capitalist. "Maybe I'll buy after that."

"I'll set it up," said Lavitt.

"Can someone at Compaq answer my questions?" asked another investor.

"Rod Canion will call," said Lavitt.

Meanwhile, the market ticked up.

An investor called back. "I just talked to Rosen," he said. "Compaq is going to survive. I'll take some stock after all. Fifty thousand shares."

The phone rang again. "I just talked to Rod Canion," said another investor. "Compaq has a good marketing strategy. I'll take a hundred thousand shares."

That was good, but it still wasn't enough. Lavitt still had sold only 2.5 million shares. He called Jim Furneaux. "I can't get enough orders," he said. "We've got to pull all stops. Call every investor you know. Get orders."

Then he called Ben Rosen and Tommy Unterberg. "Call investors," he told them. "Get orders."

The orders trickled in.

The SEC cleared the stock on December 8. The issue would begin to trade first thing the next morning. All the shares had to be sold by then.

Lavitt looked at his watch. It was four o'clock. The stock market was closed.

"Come over to my office," Unterberg told Lavitt. "We've got to talk about the price." This was the last chance to change it.

Lavitt walked around the corner.

Furneaux was sitting in the green armchair facing Unterberg's desk. The head of the syndicate desk was there.

Lavitt handed Unterberg the order book.

"We've sold about 5 million shares," he said.

Unterberg nodded. "You've got a couple of hours," he said. "Can you sell any more shares?"

Lavitt looked at the order book once more. "Not at $12," he said.

Unterberg frowned.

"We've got to cut the price again," said Lavitt.

"How much?" asked Unterberg.

"A dollar a share," said Lavitt. "I could sell more stock at $11."

"Can you sell another million shares at $11?" asked Furneaux.

"I think so," said Lavitt.

"Let's cut the price," said Unterberg.

Furneaux dialed Compaq. "Rod," he said. "We're going over

273

the sales book one last time. "We've only sold 5 million shares at $12. That's just $60 million."

A little more than half of the $100 million that Canion had asked for in August.

"Mel Lavitt thinks that he can sell more stock if we cut the price," said Furneaux.

"How much more?" asked Canion.

"Mel thinks that he can sell six million shares at $11 a share," said Furneaux. A total of $66 million. "That's an extra $6 million."

"Okay," said Canion. "We don't have much choice."

Furneaux hung up. He nodded at Lavitt. "The price is $11," he said. "I hope you can sell those shares."

Portfolio managers who had said no at $15 and no at $12 started to say yes at $11.

At six o'clock, Lavitt called Jim Furneaux. "We sold the stock," he said.

"Great," said Furneaux. Furneaux called Ron Canion. "We've got your $66 million."

Canion was silent for a moment. Finally he spoke. "Break out the champagne."

Compaq stock traded up during the first few weeks after the company went public. Then in January 1984, the market for new issues collapsed and the price of Compaq slid to a low of $3.50 a share. As the market revived in the winter of 1985, Compaq stock rose up to $9 a share.

Its fluctuating stock price notwithstanding, Compaq was booming. First-year sales were a record $111 million, almost a third higher than Canion had predicted. Canion poured the profits back into the company. He launched a $20-million print and television advertising campaign and broke into Europe. In June, Compaq unveiled the DeskPro, a desk-top computer that boasted a more advanced—faster—microprocessor than the IBM. The DeskPro was even more popular than the Compaq; in the first six months, Compaq shipped fourteen thousand machines, and dealers couldn't keep the computer in stock. In March 1985, Compaq unveiled a computer telephone, and at the annual meeting in April, Canion announced a new machine that works like the IBM "Advanced Technology" PC. Compaq sales topped $329 million in 1984. By then, Compaq was firmly established as the number-one IBM standard machine clone with 5 percent of the personal computer market. And by 1986, Compaq was listed as a Fortune 500 company, making the list sooner after founding than any company in history.

In the spring of 1984, after IBM introduced its own portable personal computer, Compaq sales slowed at first, but not for long. The IBM portable was bulkier and heavier than the Compaq, and its screen was harder to read. Rod Canion is proud to have founded the only company to design a product that IBM couldn't build and market better.

Nineteen eighty-three was a record year for L. F. Rothschild too. The firm raised a total of $1.4 billion in thirty-seven public offerings. But the personal computer market collapse that had started in the fall of 1983 continued through 1984. By the beginning of 1985, there were just 150 personal computer manaufacturers, down from 200 at the beginning of 1984. L. F. Rothschild underwrote just eight offerings worth $102 million for first-time public companies. The market improved in 1985—and 1986 is looking up. In July 1985, General Felt Industries made a $200-million offer to buy L. F. Rothschild. The partners turned that down and announced that they would go public instead. In March 1986, Rothschild sold 7.7 million shares for $157 million.

The market slump depressed Mel Lavitt, but he and Tommy Unterberg stayed busy. There were private placements for Telematics, an electronic data switch manufacturer, and Gigabit, the maker of high-speed integrated circuits; stock offerings for Wyse Technologies, the video display terminal manufacturer, Software Publishing Corporation, designer of software for the first-time user, AST Research, a PC attachment maker, and Autodesk, marketer of engineering design software.

Jim Furneaux hardly knew that the market was off. In March 1985, he helped Compaq put together a $75-million debt offering. In May, he designed an innovative $215-million bond package for Intel: zero coupon notes, with rights to buy Intel stock at $40 a share (it was then trading at $28). At the end of August 1985,

Jim Furneaux resigned his Rothschild partnership to become a venture capitalist at Bessemer Investments in Boston. Now he spends all his time looking for another company as promising as Compaq.

(7)

Salomon Brothers

"We Don't Want to Be the Biggest, We Want to Be the Best"

"You want to sell the oil company?" asked Ira Harris. He leaned back in his swivel chair and pressed the receiver closer to his ear. "That might be damn smart." He stared through the window of his office at the Chicago skyline; the view from the Sears Tower was spectacular.

"We've got to do something dramatic," said Roger Briggs from his office on East Monroe six blocks away. "Esmark stock is at $26." It was March 1980; Esmark was well below the price it had been at the beginning of 1976. "To get the stock price up we have to get rid of our Swift meats subsidiary. We'll take a big loss on that—and to offset that, we'll have to raise cash by selling the oil subsidiary or selling Playtex. We could keep talking to Deutsche Bank about that investment they're thinking of making in Esmark."

Harris grunted.

"Selling the oil company looks like the best option," said Briggs.

"Maybe," said Harris. He tipped his cigar in the ashtray. "Selling the oil company would make sense. Esmark isn't a big enough company to be in the oil business. We both know you're never going to be one of the Seven Sisters. And oil isn't Esmark's kind of business anyway. You want to be in consumer products. If you get out of oil, you can expand there."

"We'll have a lot more flexibility without Swift," said Briggs.

Harris took a long green Don Diego cigar out of the box on his desk. He trimmed the tip and lit it.

"Oil deals are hot right now," said Briggs. "Shell bought Belridge in December for $3.7 billion. That's the biggest acquisition ever. The price came to $9.23 a barrel in the ground."

"With your oil in Texas plus your play in the Overthrust Belt, you've got what aggressive oil companies are looking for," said Harris. "That oil subsidiary might be worth $800 million."

"In that range," said Briggs.

Harris puffed on his cigar. "I like the idea of selling the oil company." He leaned back in his chair. "It makes more sense than selling Playtex. Playtex is a steady earner. It's got a lot of upside potential. Oil is cyclical." He paused. "It looks like earnings are near a peak, but who knows? You might get a higher price for the company if you wait."

"I know," said Briggs. "Everyone says that oil is at $32 a barrel on the way to a hundred. But Esmark needs cash now. We can't wait."

Harris shuffled the papers on his desk. His secretary walked in with a handful of pink telephone messages. Harris nodded at her to set them down. He started to sort through them. "There's another reason you can't fool around," said Harris. "You're vulnerable to a takeover."

"I know," said Briggs. The market value of Esmark stock is only $500 million. "Buying Esmark would be the cheapest way to buy our oil. That's why we need to sell the oil company fast."

Harris paused. "Okay, say you sell it for $800 million. You use $200 million to get rid of Swift. What are you going to do with the rest of the cash? You can't just sit on $600 million in cash." He paused. "We've talked before about buying back Esmark stock."

"We'll buy some stock," said Briggs.

"Who is going to buy Swift?" asked Harris.

"Some European company," said Briggs.

Harris raised his eyebrows. "We've been trying to sell Swift in the U.S. for years. What makes you think that the Europeans want the company?"

"A European company that wants to break into the U.S. food

market needs a good brand name," said Briggs. "Swift is a great name."

"True," said Harris. "But Swift doesn't have a good reputation as a company."

"Swift wouldn't be such a bad company without that union contract," said Briggs. "If we structure the deal right, the buyer can negotiate a new contract."

"If you have a buyer," said Harris.

"If the Europeans won't buy Swift, we'll sell the company to the employees," said Briggs.

"I don't know that the union wants Swift either," said Harris.

"Why not?" asked Briggs. "Unions have bought companies before. There's no reason the meat-packing union can't buy Swift."

"Just last month, the union refused to make wage concessions in order to keep a plant open," said Harris.

"This is different," said Briggs. "Keeping a plant open meant a couple of hundred jobs. Now it's a question of keeping the company alive. That is almost four thousand union jobs."

"The union might buy," said Harris. "It might not. If it doesn't, Salomon Brothers will think of someone who will."

Briggs grunted. "Put together some numbers for me," he said. "I want to know what Esmark's balance sheet will look like if we sell the oil company and Swift. Kelly wants to talk through the options tomorrow. There's a board meeting next week."

Harris flipped through his desk calendar. "Tomorrow is okay," he said. "We'll get someone cracking on the numbers right away."

Ira Harris is imposing. At forty-two, he is six foot one, weighs 235 pounds and has brown hair and glittery brown eyes. He wears dark-framed glasses and rumpled suits. For years, he chain-smoked cigars but stopped cold turkey in 1984; his kids said they didn't like the smell. Harris is one of the most successful deal makers in America, the man who matched Avis rent-a-car with Norton Simon, and oil tycoon Marvin Davis with Twentieth Century-Fox. He enjoys the trappings of success. He has a chauffeured limousine, a duplex in Chicago and a golf cottage in Palm Beach. Harris is a compulsive eater; his closet is stuffed with two sets of clothes, one to wear before, the other after, his annual visit to the La Costa health spa in Southern California. He loves spectator sports; he's been known to bring a television set to his box at Wrigley Field so he can tune in to a second game. Harris tends to see the bright side of things. One Christmas, he took the kids to Palm Beach for a week; it rained and the kids complained. "It's not so bad," Harris told them. "It's a hundred degrees warmer here than in Chicago."

Harris grew up in the Bronx. When he graduated from the University of Michigan in 1959, he decided to become a stockbroker and applied at thirty-two firms, but he was turned down by all thirty-two. He eventually landed a job at a one-office stockbrokerage company in New York and started selling mutual funds door-to-door in Manhattan. Two years later, he moved to a larger firm with a telephone-only sales force. He didn't seem destined for larger things.

As a fledgling broker, Harris had to find clients. One way he did that was by calling people who sent in information-request forms they clipped from the newspaper. One of Harris' forms came from a Fred Y. Presley. Harris called. It turned out that Presley was a sixty-seven-year-old financier whose hobby was running a night "school" to train young brokers to be portfolio strategists; Presley's favorite buys were so-called growth stocks like Polaroid and Xerox, companies that didn't make much income now, but would in twenty years. Soon Harris was Presley's prize pupil; he spotted a dozen growth picks and began to attract investing clients, mostly banks, pension funds and insurance companies.

In 1963, Harris' firm merged with a bigger one. The bigger firm sent Harris, then twenty-five, to Chicago to run the midwest operations. Harris orchestrated his first big merger a few years later: he paired up CNA, the giant insurance company, with Tsai Management and Research Corporation, the brainchild of the mutual fund pioneer Gerald Tsai. In 1968, Billy Salomon, managing partner at Salomon Brothers, offered Harris a partnership there. Harris leapt—and many Wall Street watchers said that the match seemed almost predestined. Harris and Salomon Brothers were cut of the same cloth: both were young, aggressive and innovative; and while Harris knew how to pick stocks, Salomon knew how to trade bonds.

"We don't want to be the biggest," says Salomon chairman John

Gutfreund, "we want to be the best." For almost 60 years, Salomon Brothers had been the trading upstart, the Wall Street house best known—and feared—for its daring. It was the first brokerage house to send stock and bond certificates by airmail, the first to offer a debt-for-equity swap, one of the first to sell mortgage-backed securities. Salomon stands by its clients: the firm underwrote the bonds for New York City long after every other house had politely refused. Salomon routinely bids so low on corporate bonds that even the most experienced competitors gasp. Salomon boasts talent, not tradition. The year Harris joined the firm as a partner, thirteen of the twenty-eight general partners, including Billy Salomon, had gotten their first Salomon job straight out of high school; one twenty-seven-year-old partner hadn't even gotten his high school diploma.

Arthur, Herbert and Percy Salomon began their work in the money brokerage business by working for their father's company. But in 1910, figuring they could make more money if they ignored Jewish tradition and kept the office open on Saturday, they formed their own company. At first, the brothers arranged overnight loans for big brokerage houses, but they quickly began trading short-term bonds as well. By the early twenties, Salomon Brothers dealt in Liberty bonds, Victory bonds, corporate bonds, foreign bonds and bankers' acceptances. Salomon opened regional bond-trading offices around the country, and pretty soon the firm began to itch to underwrite bonds, that is, guarantee the sale of new issues for a percentage fee.

In those days, companies gave their underwriting assignments only to a select group of polished and well-established underwriters known as "the Club": J. P. Morgan; Lehman Brothers; Goldman Sachs; and Kuhn, Loeb & Company. Upstart Salomon Brothers was distinctly not a member. But in 1933, Salomon got a break: after Congress passed a law saying that companies selling stocks and bonds had to file long disclosure forms detailing their financial health, the Club staged an underwriting boycott. Boycott notwithstanding, Swift & Company, the nation's largest meat-packer, needed money. Salomon agreed to sell $43 million worth of bonds for a fee of just $4 for each $1,000 bond, less than a quarter of the Club rate.

It was uphill from there. Salomon built up a bond underwriting clientele, opened a stock-trading desk and slowly forced its way into the stock sales business. In the late sixties, the firm had decided to branch into advising companies on what to do with the money Salomon raised by selling their bonds, so Billy Salomon, son of one of the founding brothers, hired a handful of investment banking specialists and changed the name of the statistical department to Corporate Finance.

Harris was one of the new hires. His first step was calling on clients to find out what kind of investment banking they needed. At the top of the list: Swift & Company, the meat-packer.

"We're pleased to be your investment banker," said Harris when he sat down with Don Kelly, the newly promoted chief financial officer. "Swift is Salomon Brothers' oldest investment banking client."

"You're not our investment banker," said Kelly. "You're an investment banker who has a relationship with Swift. From now on, we're handing out business on the basis of performance, and if you don't start performing, you're not going to get any. Salomon Brothers has never given us any advice on diversifying Swift. If we had listened to you, we'd still be a meat-packer with a lot of bonds out."

Harris gulped. "Well," he said. "We're trying to do more of that kind of work. That's why I was brought in. Let's talk about what you need."

Donald Kelly is quick-witted. He once introduced the company's industrial relations liaison, Debbie Kelly, no relation, as his daughter: "The family needed money," he explained, "so I put her on the payroll." He's down to earth. At fifty-seven, he is six feet tall, with twinkling blue eyes and thinning blond hair. He wears "*K*"-for-Kelly cuff links and crisp three-piece suits. He's a sharp strategist and a steadfast friend. He's unpretentious. Even after he was made president of Esmark (nee Swift), Kelly refused to hire a chauffeur, and drove himself to the office by seven every morning. Kelly unwinds on the golf course and with the boys at the bar. His favorite beer is Michelob.

Kelly grew up on the South Side of Chicago and left home after high school to work on construction jobs in Michigan and Texas. After a stint in the Navy, he set up shop as a data-processing consultant and, in 1953, got a job at Swift & Company for a salary of $125 a week, $65 less than the next best offer. He figured that a company that offered so little for a data processing expert didn't know anything about the subject, which meant that Kelly, the data processor, would move up the executive ladder quickly.

As it turned out, data processing wasn't the road to the top of old Swift & Company. Swift wasn't the sort of company that put much faith in data, or did much financial planning, but data processing turned out to be a good way to learn about meat-packing: Kelly spent fourteen years traveling from one Swift plant to the next, and soon he knew more about Swift and its problems than just about anyone at Swift headquarters. Kelly also knew that Swift wasn't going to change easily, but he had never been bashful about speaking his mind, so in 1967, he decided to tell his bosses what he thought.

For almost a hundred years, Swift & Company had been one of the world's proudest companies. In its heyday in the teens, Swift had had such a grip on grocery products—beef, lamb, veal, pork, chicken, turkey, butter, eggs, ice cream, cheese, soap, detergent, tin cans and cardboard boxes—that the Justice Department accused the company of trying to monopolize the food industry. Swift was the great meat innovator, the first company to ship prekilled cattle carcasses across the country in refrigerated railroad cars, the first company to use an assembly line—carcasses were hooked onto an overhead chain and pulled past a line of workers each of whom made just one cut. Swift's new packing processes were nothing short of revolutionary: the company lured millions of unskilled immigrants to Chicago, it turned the Texas plains into the meat basket of America, and it made fresh meat affordable for almost everyone; by 1979, beef consumption was up to 236.6 pounds per capita and meat-packers sold $41.3 billion worth of meat wholesale. Steak and potatoes had become as American as apple pie.

After Kelly joined the company though, Swift fell on hard times. Earnings had peaked in 1953, and the company got complacent. Other packing companies pioneered new methods of cutting, packaging and transporting meat. Other companies took the hard line with their unions. Swift just plodded along the old way. The factories were near antique. The "master contract" labor agreement said that all employees got the same wages and went on strike at the same time, irrespective of the local going rate.

In 1960, a former Swift butcher started a company called Iowa Beef Processors (IBP). Iowa Beef invented a packing technique called "boxing" beef, precutting shanks and sides at the factory and shipping them shrink-wrapped and crated. And Iowa Beef played tough. Iowa Beef squeezed the other packers' profits by bidding cattle prices up and slashing processed beef prices down; Iowa Beef attempted to bribe its way into the New York beef market, and Iowa Beef paid half the wages Swift did.

Iowa Beef should have scared Swift back to reality, but somehow it didn't. When IBP opened its big new "boxed"-beef plant in 1964, a low-level Swift executive was invited to tour. When the man got back to Chicago, he called his boss. "We've got problems," he said. "I just saw the Iowa Beef plant. It's sparkling, efficient and run like an Army camp. It's going to ruin us."

"Don't worry," laughed the boss. "Iowa Beef is pulling the wool over your eyes."

The man sent the boss a ninety-seven-point memo.

The boss didn't answer it, and neither did anyone else.

But the man was right.

Swift earnings continued to tumble. Swift became vulnerable to takeover. The rumors started.

Swift ignored them.

The calls from bidders came in.

Swift rebuffed them.

In 1967, Don Kelly, who was then controller, sent a memo to Robert Reneker, president, and son of Gus Swift's chief hog buyer.

"Swift has big problems," it said. "If the company doesn't fix them fast, it will go belly-up. Maybe by the end of next year."

Reneker called Kelly into his office. "What's this?" he demanded. He pointed at the memo. "How can we have all these problems? We made more money last year than we've made since 1953."

"That was the market, not the company," said Kelly. "Our stock price is low. We're cheap and vulnerable. We're going to get bought."

Reneker raised an eyebrow.

"Look what's happened to the other old-line meat-packers," said Kelly. "They've all been eaten." LTV had just bought Wilson Foods, United Brands bought John Morrell, U.S. Smelting & Refining bought Cudahy, and Greyhound bought Armour & Company. "You know Northwest Industries is hungry for Swift. So is Norton Simon." The chief executives of both companies had talked to Reneker about buying Swift.

"Well, what do you want to do?" asked Reneker.

"Close down unprofitable plants and diversify," said Kelly.

Reneker thought for a minute. "First make a study of the company," he told Kelly. "Find out what plants have to go. Then we'll remake our company."

By the late seventies, Swift had closed 334 money-losing units.

In 1969, when Kelly was just beginning to implement his program, he got a call from Ira Harris. That was when Kelly put Harris on notice that Salomon had to do a better job.

A couple of days after that, Harris called again. "Let's have breakfast," he said. "Let's talk about how Salomon Brothers can help Swift. Let's figure out what kind of a company you really want to run."

Harris and Kelly and Reneker met at Harris' office the next morning—and once a week for the next few months. By the end of the year, Harris had his marching orders: help make Swift into a consumer products conglomerate.

"Try to sell the fresh-meat-packing business," Kelly told Harris. "We've sold everything we could ourselves. We've dumped the soybean-milling company, the leather company, and 106 packing plants and sales offices."

"Don't you want Swift to be the core of your new consumer products company?" asked Harris.

"No," said Kelly. "Swift isn't making enough money. Meat-packing is a commodity business. Margins are low. The labor contract is killing us." He looked at Harris. "The only way we can get packing profits up is to get big concessions at the next contract negotiation. The union won't make concessions without a strike, and right now we can't take a strike. If the men who cut cattle carcasses walk out, so do the men who cure bacon and

285

ham—it's all one union. If we don't have bacon and ham for the supermarkets, we'll lose shelf space forever. And bacon and ham is where we make money, not carcass beef."

Salomon Brothers couldn't find a buyer for Swift fresh meats, but in 1975, Harris called with a diversification idea. "You like consumer products," called Harris. "What about International Playtex?"

"Ira," said Kelly. "You've got a lot of dumb ideas, but this is the best dumb idea I've ever heard. I don't know a goddamn thing about Playtex. I don't even know where the company's stock is listed."

"Playtex isn't listed," said Harris. "The stock isn't traded on any market. Playtex is part of Rapid-American." The private conglomerate headed by Meshulam Riklis.

"I know about Riklis," said Kelly. Riklis had a reputation for being smart—and slippery.

"I think Rick might be willing to negotiate," said Harris.

"Let's talk," said Kelly.

A month later, Kelly and Riklis met at Harris' house in Chicago on Sunday night. Hours later, they had a deal: Swift would buy Playtex for $210 million in cash, stock and notes.

Several months later, the men from Playtex made their first planning presentation. It was an eyeopener. The planners from Swift had always put Kelly to sleep; these planners were different, they had new ideas, new products, new strategies.

Kelly called Ira Harris. "Playtex is great," he said. "I want to buy more companies like that."

Soon Harris and Kelly began to line up a dozen attractive acquisitions: Jensen stereos, Almay cosmetics, STP oil, and Danskin leotards and tights.

That meant that it was time to change the name of the company: what Reneker and Kelly ran wasn't Swift the meat-packer anymore. Bob Reneker, chairman, hired a company name consultant.

"How about Esmark?" suggested the man after he'd read over a computer list. " 'Es' for Swift and 'mark' for quality."

"I like it," said Reneker. Then he called the staff into his office. "We're changing names," he said. "We're changing philosophy. We're making a clean break with the past." Reneker looked around the table. "We're moving headquarters." Out of the utilitarian offices on West Jackson Boulevard to an elegant suite in a sparkling silver skyscraper on East Monroe.

"We're severing the cord," said Kelly. He looked at the head of the public relations department. "We're throwing away the archives."

"We're what?" asked the man.

"Throwing away the archives," said Kelly.

The PR man gulped, and took the records home.

Kelly called the head of the Swift meats division. "We have a new name and a new philosophy," he said. "The way to make earnings consistent is to focus on marketing. Branded products will save us."

Esmark added a dozen branded products, but the profits didn't improve. The fresh-meat business was so bad that marketing profits looked like peanuts. Worse, Swift's new focus on marketing took so much time that internal controls went berserk: one year, Swift had more turkeys in inventory after Thanksgiving than it had had before. When newspaper reporters called for an update, Kelly, who'd been named president in 1973, said that Swift was a problem. The Esmark stock price sank.

Then came the straw that broke the camel's back. The chairman of Danskin refused to accept payment in stock when he sold his company to Esmark in 1979. Kelly had to raise the cash by selling commercial paper.

In March 1979, Don Kelly called Roger Briggs, the man who'd replaced Kelly as chief financial officer. "Rog," said Kelly. "We've got to do something. Swift fresh meats is killing Esmark."

"I've got some ideas," said Briggs. Briggs always had ideas. "Come on over to my office."

Roger Briggs is relentless. At fifty, he's a small, neat man with handsome, craggy features and dimples and twinkling blue eyes. Briggs is razor-sharp, and he's impatient; behind his back, he's called "the Pope." Yet he's so shy that he spends cocktail parties standing in the corner all by himself. He's a ham when he's with old friends: sometimes he's so expansive that he tells jokes about the stuffed-shirt investment bankers at Morgan Stanley, the most "white shoe" firm on the Street. He laughs that without Roger Briggs, Don Kelly would be "just a meat-packer."

Roger Briggs grew up in Old Greenwich, Connecticut, studied finance at the University of Miami in Florida and got certification as a public accountant. He worked for Price Waterhouse, the accounting firm, for ten years and then moved to Sterling Drug as controller. He tried a stint as portfolio manager at a mutual fund company, but that didn't turn out too well: Briggs did some calculations and decided that the fund was worth more as cash than it was invested in stocks and bonds, and he went to his boss with the good news. His boss was mad and Briggs knew he had to find another job. When a headhunter called Briggs in 1970 with a possible opening as controller at Swift & Company, Briggs was eager to talk. He met chief financial officer Don Kelly in a hotel room in Chicago. Kelly asked a couple of financial questions.

"That's it," said Kelly after half an hour.

"That's it?" said Briggs. "You don't have any more questions?" It had seemed like a very short interview.

"I'm done," said Kelly. "Interview's over." He stood up to leave.

"Why don't you stay for lunch?" asked Briggs.

"No thanks," said Kelly. "I've got work to do."

Kelly strode out of the room and Briggs thought maybe he'd bungled things. He hadn't. Kelly had decided to hire him on the spot; he called back the next day to offer him the job.

As controller, and later as chief financial officer, Briggs was responsible for lining up the money Esmark needed to build plants or buy companies. At first, that wasn't a big problem, but after a couple of years, the money got tight.

Briggs and Kelly had talked through the problems time and time again, but they couldn't agree on a way to get the stock price up.

In March 1979, just after the Danskin deal, Kelly called to talk again.

"We've got problems," said Kelly when he sat down on the white couch in front of Briggs' desk.

"I know," said Briggs. "Unstable earnings. Too much debt." He paused. "Our stock is undervalued."

"We're vulnerable," said Kelly. "A raider could buy us for less than it cost us to build the company. Buying Esmark is the cheapest way to buy Playtex—or the oil fields."

"We don't have any flexibility," said Briggs. "Our stock is so cheap that it doesn't make sense to use it to pay for acquisitions, assuming that someone will take it."

"We've talked this through again and again," said Kelly. "We've got to stop talking and act."

"We're agreed that we've got to get rid of Swift," said Briggs.

Kelly and Briggs were convinced that the price of Esmark stock was low because investors knew Swift earnings were erratic—Swift earned $81.1 million in 1974, $85.3 million in 1975, $58.1 million in 1976, $13.3 million in 1977, $40.2 million in 1978—and because investors were looking at Esmark as Swift the meat-packer instead of Esmark the conglomerate.

"Well, Swift isn't Esmark," continued Briggs. "Swift is two thirds of all Esmark sales, but just 10 percent of profits. It is a non-performing asset."

Kelly frowned. Clearly Swift was obscuring the rest of Esmark. Clearly the answer was to get rid of Swift. But how? "You can't sell Swift," said Kelly. "Ira Harris has been trying to sell Swift for years."

"You can't sell Swift whole," said Briggs. "That master union contract means that no one wants Swift. Maybe we can get around the contract by selling plants one at a time. If we close a plant and sell it, the master contract doesn't apply to the new owner."

Kelly nodded. That was true. "It might work," he said.

"Some of the plants could be profitable for another owner," said Briggs.

"They could," said Kelly. "But closing plants so that we can sell them is going to be expensive. We have to pay the workers severance and fund the pension and the medical plan. Getting rid of Swift is going to be expensive. It might run $200 million. Where are we going to get that kind of cash?"

"I've got some ideas," said Briggs. "But I'm more worried about selling the plants."

"No one in America is going to buy them," said Kelly. "Salomon has been begging companies to take them for years. And I'm not sure the Europeans will be interested either."

"The Europeans have bought a lot of American grocery store chains lately," said Briggs. "The Belgians own Food Town and Alterman's supermarkets; the French own Grand Union and Weingarten's; the Germans own A & P."

"That doesn't mean they want Swift," said Kelly.

"They've been buying food makers too," said Briggs. "Ovaltine, Baskin-Robbins, Howard Johnson, Bluebird meat, Ball Park franks and Alpo dog food." He paused. "Look," he said. "Some of the biggest food companies in the world are based in Europe: Nestlé, Unilever, United Biscuits. One of them might be interested. I'll make some calls."

Briggs was back to Kelly a couple of days later. "I just talked to a friend who's an executive at Deutsche Bank," said Briggs. Esmark had talked to Deutsche Bank about buying 4711, the German cosmetics company. "He says that the bank doesn't know anyone who wants to buy Swift, but that the bank might want to make an investment in Esmark itself, maybe $300 million in bonds. He wants you to go to Frankfurt to talk to the chairman."

"A Deutsche Bank investment could be the answer to our problems," said Kelly. "Three hundred million is enough to fix Swift up for sale and pay off some bank loans too."

Briggs set up a meeting.

Kelly flew to Frankfurt at the beginning of November. He talked to the chairman of Deutsche Bank. Then he called Roger Briggs. "Deutsche Bank is definitely interested in that investment," he said. "I think we ought to have some outside consultant put together a study on just how much Esmark is worth."

"That's easy," said Briggs. "Investment bankers call me every week to tell me what they think Esmark is worth. I'll have one of them write up a brochure."

"Call Ira Harris," said Kelly. "This is a job for Salomon Brothers."

Briggs picked up the phone. "Deutsche Bank is interested in buying some Esmark bonds," he told Harris. "We need a piece of paper that explains why Esmark is a good investment."

"Okay," said Harris. "We'll get that started right away." Harris hung up. He buzzed his secretary. "Who's free to do some legwork on Esmark?" he asked the head of Corporate Finance when the man got on the line.

"How about Ken Wilson," said the Corporate Finance man.

"Great," said Harris. He'd never met Wilson, but he'd heard that Wilson was sharp.

Kendrick R. Wilson III is hard-working. At thirty-three, he has gray hair, green eyes and a ruddy complexion. He's never quite neat: his collars are darned, his socks don't match, his shirttails are untucked. Wilson's desk is stacked high with documents, and he never gets to the bottom of his pile of pink telephone slips. He works so hard that the rarely sees his wife and two blond daughters: he's out of the house by six every morning so he can get his battered Honda from northern Westchester to lower Manhattan before the traffic gets too thick; he's rarely home by eight. Wilson plays golf but not well; he fly fishes. He'd rather be sailing.

He's a native of New Jersey. When Wilson started at Dartmouth in 1965, he wasn't particularly serious or responsible. His college leadership positions included vice president of the ski patrol and social chairman of his fraternity. Then, after his junior year, Wilson volunteered for Viet Nam. He trained as a ranger and paratrooper and led Green Beret missions in Nam and Cambodia—and returned to Dartmouth a changed man. He became a model student and graduated with flying colors. He worked at Bankers Trust Company for a year, went to Harvard Business School and landed a job in New York as an associate at Smith Barney, Harris Upham & Company, a small investment bank. In its heyday, Smith Barney had been among the best on the Street, but soon after Wilson got there, it lost momentum, and key executives. Three years later, Wilson got an offer from Salomon Brothers. A couple of friends had left Smith Barney for Salomon, and Wilson liked what he heard. In 1978, he too made the leap. Wilson was so junior that he didn't get an office, just a desk in the bullpen right behind a partner's secretary. He did what he was told, mostly legwork for partners raising money for big companies, particularly banks. Occasionally he worked on other kinds of companies too. He happened to be free when Harris called to find a man to do a study for Esmark.

"What kind of study?" asked Wilson when Harris called. Wilson was a little surprised that Harris was giving him this job. Wilson wasn't based in Chicago, he didn't know Harris personally, he didn't know much about Esmark. "What do you want me to look at?"

"Call Briggs," said Harris. "Briggs will explain what he wants."

When Wilson called, Briggs didn't mention the possibility of Deutsche Bank buying $300 million worth of bonds. "I want an assessment of how much Esmark is worth," he said. "Piece by piece."

"What do you mean, 'piece by piece'?" asked Wilson.

"Pretend each subsidiary is a separate company," said Briggs. "How much would Esmark get by selling the companies?"

Wilson was silent. He'd never done a study like that before, so Briggs' "answer" didn't seem like an answer at all.

"I want it in February," said Briggs.

"Okay," said Wilson. He didn't see how he could finish before March. "Can we pin down just what you want?"

"I already told you what I want," said Briggs.

"Well, yes," said Wilson. He asked a couple of questions.

Briggs didn't say much more, but Wilson got the impression that Briggs thought that the sum of the pieces of Esmark was worth more than the whole. Apparently Briggs wanted confirmation of that on Salomon Brothers letterhead.

"I'm going to need a lot of numbers," said Wilson. "I can't break the company into pieces without knowing what each subsidiary earns."

"Call the subsidiaries yourself," said Briggs. "I don't have those numbers."

"Okay," said Wilson. He put down the receiver and headed to the Salomon Brothers library. He spent days studying the Esmark numbers. Finally he made out a list of questions for the subsidiary managers.

The managers didn't have the right numbers either.

Wilson estimated.

"I've got sales," he told Briggs a week later. "I've got reported profits. But I still need more detail. I need real subsidiary profits. I need plant-by-plant balance sheets. I can't figure values without knowing subcompany-by-subcompany profits."

Briggs grunted. "I'll get you some estimates," he said.

Wilson was just starting the first computer runs in early January when Roger Briggs called again. "I want to see your study next week," he said.

"But..." Wilson began. He had been shooting for finishing up the first week in February.

"You've been working for two months," said Briggs. "I want to see some results."

Wilson gulped. He guessed he could finish in a couple of days if he went flat out. "How's Monday?" he asked. "I'll have to work all weekend to be done by then."

Briggs snorted. "Get it done," he said.

Wilson spent both Saturday and Sunday in his office crunching the numbers and writing the text of the report. He finally finished just after midnight Sunday, got a couple of hours sleep at his desk and caught the seven o'clock flight to Chicago.

He lugged the study into Briggs' office. "Here it is," he said. He was proud of it: two fat black volumes filled with chart after chart of comparisons, graph after graph of earnings, page after page of painstaking analysis.

Briggs didn't look impressed. He flipped through a couple of pages. "I just want the bottom line," he said. "How much is each part of Esmark worth?"

Wilson started to explain the methodology.

Briggs turned to the summary page.

Wilson looked at Briggs. He looked at the book. He started to read off the summary numbers. "I made estimates of how much each subsidiary is worth as a going concern," said Wilson. "And of how much each is worth closed down." He ticked off the numbers:

Estech, the chemical subsidiary that makes fertilizer, cartons and boxes, and dental equipment: $350 million to $400 million.

International Jensen, maker of car stereos and home high-fidelity equipment: $125 million to $150 million.

International Playtex, maker of Playtex bras, Round-the-Clock panty hose, and Danskin tights: $500 million to $600 million.

Vickers Petroleum Corporation, the oil driller and gas station operator: $610 million to $770 million.

STP Corporation, maker of STP oil additives: $50 million to $75 million.

Swift & Company, the meat processor: $300 million.

Total value of Esmark: between $1,220 million and $1,580 million, $55 and $71 share, triple the current stock market price.

"That sounds about right," said Briggs. "It's about what I expected." He closed the binder and set the two volumes next to his "In" box. Wilson had the feeling that Briggs thought that he could have done the whole thing in about half an hour, right off the top of his head.

"Now you've got to figure out what to do about Swift," said Briggs. "I'm thinking of getting rid of the fresh-meats division. I think I can turn processed meats around."

"You mean close it?" asked Wilson.

Briggs scowled. "Sell it, close it, give it to the union," he said. "Whatever gets me the most money."

Wilson shrugged.

"I want it done soon," said Briggs. "And I don't want any ——ing around." He looked at Wilson.

Wilson just stared. How was *he* going to sell Swift fresh meats?

"Call John Copeland," said Briggs. Copeland, the president of the fresh-meats division. "Copeland is going to help you."

Later that afternoon, Wilson called. He didn't have any good ideas. He hoped that John Copeland did.

John Copeland is conscientious. At fifty-seven, he's big, with strong features and stiff black hair and brown eyes. Copeland is proud. He wears custom-tailored suits and shiny shoes. He belongs to the Chicago Club and the Union League Club, and he plays executive tournament golf. Yet he's not elegant; he's not graceful; he's not good with words. Although he's lived in Chicago for twenty years, he's got a soft southern accent, and soft southern charm.

Copeland grew up in Louisiana and started college at Louisiana State. In 1943, he volunteered for the Army in World War II and after V-E Day headed back to the States to finish up his degree in accounting. One Thanksgiving, Copeland went with his wife and baby boy to Sioux City, Iowa, to visit his wife's parents. There happened to be a big Swift meat-packing plant in town, and Copeland drove over to the plant and filled out a job application form. Later that day, he got called back; Copeland started to work at

Sioux City that February. Copeland had been hired as a management trainee, but his first job wasn't managing at all—it was grading beef. He stood on the cutting floor next to a packer with a chain saw; after the packer sliced the whole beef carcass in half between the twelfth and thirteenth ribs, Copeland studied the cross section of the muscle; the more marbling, the higher the grade.

After a couple of months, Copeland was transferred to the marketing department, and soon he was an aide to a key vice president. As Swift & Company, that was a sign that you were on the way, and Copeland was: by 1965, he was head of the lamb and veal division, and the next year he was named vice president in charge of all beef, pork, lamb and veal production. Eight years later, John Copeland was made president of the fresh-meats division. Once that had been the third most powerful position in the company; the head of fresh meats reported to the president and the chairman—and fresh meats was what Swift was all about. Nineteen seventy-three though was the year that Kelly got aggressive about diversifying, and the hierarchy at the company had changed. Swift was just a part of Esmark, and a part that was going to be less and less important to Esmark profits every year; the head of the packing division wasn't regarded as the heir to the chairmanship, not any more.

Copeland had seen the Iowa Beef threat coming, but when he tried to warn his boss, the man just laughed. By the time Copeland was running Swift fresh meats eight years later, it was too late to catch up. Copeland closed plants, but he couldn't boost profits. In April 1976, Don Kelly called to say that he wanted Copeland to meet the man he'd just hired as president of Swift, a marketing executive from Colgate Palmolive.

At their first meeting, Copeland gave the marketing man two lists of plant names on his napkin, the money-losing ones and the profitable ones. "You've got to close a lot of plants," he said.

The marketing man took the napkin, asked for a follow-up memo and later closed four of the money-losing plants. Next thing Copeland heard, the marketing man had launched Soup Starter soup mixes and Sizzlean breakfast strips. There was never another mention of the list, or the problems in the fresh-meats division. Instead, the more Copeland got to know the marketing man, the more sure Copeland was that Swift wasn't going to survive.

In January 1980, just about the time Roger Briggs called Ken Wilson to say that it was high time that he finished up his study, John Copeland called Don Kelly. "I'm thinking about going to the union with a proposal about the Clovis, New Mexico, beef plant," he said. "We're going to demand competitive wages. We're going to demand that we cut the payroll. We're going to offer bonuses to workers who will leave now. Esmark is going to have to foot the bill. It could cost as much as $3 million." He read the proposal.

"That makes sense," said Kelly. "I'm behind you."

"You know as well as I do that the union hasn't been receptive before," said Copeland. "They may turn this down."

"It's worth a try," said Kelly.

Copeland flew down to Clovis at the beginning of February. The union turned him down cold. As soon as he got back to Chicago, Copeland called Kelly. "They said no," said Copeland.

Kelly swore. Then he called Roger Briggs. "The union turned down the proposal at Clovis," he said. "That's it. I'm closing down the fresh-meats company. How much can I get if I sell the plants?"

"Maybe $300 million for all of Swift," said Briggs. "That's what Ken Wilson just told me." Briggs looked at the two Salomon Brothers binders in his "In" box. "Who knows what you'd get for just fresh meats."

"I'm going to try," said Kelly. "We'll sell Swift fresh meats to the union. We'll figure out something."

"Salomon Brothers is working on that," said Briggs. "Why don't we get the Swift guys in the loop."

"Good idea," said Kelly. He called the marketing man. Then he called Copeland. "I want to see you first thing tomorrow morning," he said. At the marketing man's office.

"Okay," said Copeland. He couldn't imagine what Kelly wanted, but he didn't ask. He'd find out soon enough.

Kelly and the marketing man were waiting when Copeland got to the meeting the next morning. "Bill has resigned," Kelly told Copeland. The marketing man. "Esmark is going to dispose of fresh meat-packing in one way or another."

Copeland was silent for a minute. "What do you man, 'dispose of'?" he finally asked. "You can't get rid of fresh meats just because the union said no at Clovis. We knew they were going to say no."

"I'm not sure how I'm going to dispose of fresh meats," said Kelly. "I'll do what works. Right now, I just want you to put together a company that can manage itself." Swift fresh meats didn't have a legal department or a personnel department or a treasury department; Kelly couldn't sell Swift without that. "I'll try to sell that company. I'll try the Europeans. I'll try the union."

"Do you really think you can convince the union to buy those plants?" asked Copeland. "They aren't even willing to make wage concessions."

"If the union won't buy fresh meats," said Kelly, "we will pull the plug."

Copeland stared.

"Ken Wilson from Salomon Brothers is handling this," said Kelly. "He'll be in touch."

Later in the afternoon, Roger Briggs strolled into Don Kelly's office. "I think we ought to sell the oil company," he said.

Kelly raised an eyebrow. "Sell the oil company and get rid of fresh meats?" he asked.

"Our oil company is never going to be a major," said Briggs. "We can't compete with a Mobil."

"True," said Kelly.

"Oil prices are up," said Briggs. "And oil companies are selling for fancy prices. This may not be the perfect time to sell, but selling the oil company is a better way to get the cash we need to fix up Swift for sale than making a deal with Deutsche Bank."

"True," said Kelly. "Have you talked to Ira about this?"

"Not yet," said Briggs. "I wanted to talk to you first."

"Call Ira," said Kelly. "Set up a meeting."

"What do you think about selling the oil company?" asked Don Kelly when he and Roger Briggs sat down with Ira Harris and Ken Wilson the next day.

"You don't have much choice," said Harris.

Wilson read off some numbers.

By the end of the afternoon, it was settled. Esmark would get rid of both the oil company and the fresh-meats division. Ron

Freeman, the Salomon Brothers oil and gas partner, would auction oil. Ken Wilson would put together a plan to dispose of Swift. Ira Harris would oversee the entire project.

A week later, Wilson and Freeman flew down to the oil company headquarters in Wichita, Kansas.

When they returned, Wilson called Roger Briggs. "We think we can get in the neighborhood of $700 million for the oil company," he said.

"Bullshit," said Briggs. "Someone from Lazard just called me and said that he could sell it for $1.4 billion." Lazard Frères is another investment bank. "If you can't get me $1.2 billion, you can forget it."

Wilson told Harris about Lazard.

Harris called Freeman.

"What's this about Esmark's oil company only being worth $700 million?" demanded Harris.

Freeman started to explain why he had made that estimate.

"You had better look again," said Harris. "I want to know why Lazard thinks that the company is worth twice as much as we do. If we are going to stand by our number, we had better be right."

After he talked to Harris, Freeman took a second look at the oil company. He called Wichita. It turned out that the oilmen had forgotten to mention some of their reserves when Freeman had visited. The company was worth a little more than a billion dollars.

Wilson called Briggs with the revised figure.

"Great," said Briggs. "I guess I don't have to use Lazard after all. I'll talk to Ira."

Harris called Wilson a couple of days later. "Freeman is starting an auction for the oil company," he said. "You finish up that plan to sell Swift. Let's have it ready right away. Roger gets impatient."

Wilson put down the receiver. He couldn't believe he was supposed to be figuring out how to sell Swift: Salomon had been trying to sell Swift for five years, and he'd only been on the job for one year. He got out his two-volume Esmark study and looked at the numbers. Briggs had made it clear that he thought that selling to the union was the best alternative. Wilson dialed John Copeland's number. "I need a list of all the Swift plants," he said. "I want to know why each plant isn't competitive and whether

298

each plant can be made competitive. We need to pick out the ones to close and the ones that can stay open."

"I'll get that to you right away," said Copeland. That was an easy request; Copeland had been making lists like that for years.

A couple of days later, Copeland called back. "Most of the beef plants are in bad shape," he said. "The wages are too high. The plants aren't so bad; we'd make money with a competitive contract."

That didn't help Ken Wilson. "Numbers?" he asked.

"Sure," said Copeland. "The one boxed-beef plant we've got is profitable. We struck a deal with the union. We'd keep the plant instead of selling to Iowa Beef if the union made concessions."

Wilson jotted down the numbers. "Pork?"

"The pork plants make money," said Copeland. "Iowa Beef doesn't pack pork, and the other companies that do pay pretty much the same wages we do."

Wilson jotted down the earnings estimates.

"Our one lamb plant makes money," said Copeland. "The one broiler plant would be competitive if the wage rate were slashed in half."

"What about the sales units?" asked Wilson. Many of the Swift sales units were really grocery warehouses, and they were losing money.

"We can close most of those," said Copeland. "Our big customers buy through headquarters anyhow."

"Okay," said Wilson.

"Listen," said Copeland. "This is what I think we have to do." He read off a list of plants and branch houses. "That's the way to make a profitable company."

"Let me run it through the computer," said Wilson.

Wilson did some preliminary calculations. Then he called Copeland. "This is better than I'd expected," he said. "It looks like we can make a profitable company. But I need some help. I have to figure out what these profit numbers will be after the union has made its concessions. So I want you to estimate how many concessions the union will make."

"Let's do it plant by plant," said Copeland. "The local wage rate is different in each city." Copeland ticked off estimates.

Wilson noted them on the margin of his plant list. "I've got to play with these numbers," said Wilson. "I'll call you back when I've run these through the computer."

"How's Swift going?" asked Roger Briggs a couple of days later.

"Okay," said Wilson. He didn't want to admit that he was having trouble. "Making a company isn't easy," he said. "I can't just string together the profitable plants and say that that's a company. A company like that makes money—but it doesn't make business sense. Every time I close a plant, it turns out that that plant supplied some sales unit that I wanted to keep open. Every time I close a sales unit, it turns out that I've left a plant with no place to sell its output."

Briggs didn't say anything.

"I've called John Copeland twenty times now," said Wilson. "Every time I think I've figured out a way the plants can work as a company, he has some new reason that they can't."

Briggs grunted.

"I'll get it right," said Wilson. "I just need some time."

By the end of May, Wilson thought he finally had it.

Copeland thought so too.

Wilson called Briggs. "We've got this union sale worked up," he said. "Esmark isn't going to get a lot of cash out of this. You're going to end up *giving* the union the plants—and the problems."

"Read it," said Briggs.

First, Wilson read off the list of plants that he'd just checked with Copeland. Then he read the proposal. "Esmark sets up a Swift fresh-meats company that owns the assets of the fresh-meats division. The union buys 63 percent of the stock of that new company for $135 million."

"Just $135 million?" said Briggs. "The company is worth $260 million."

"The union doesn't have any cash," said Wilson. "The union has to borrow the money to do this. I called some commercial banks. I talked to our buy-out guy. He's says that $135 million is the max the union can borrow for this. That's why you are only going to sell the union 63 percent of fresh meats. Esmark keeps 37 percent."

Briggs didn't say anything.

Wilson kept reading. "The new fresh-meat-packing company

will pay dividends on its stock just like any other company, and the union will use its dividends to pay back its $135-million loan." He paused. "As part of the deal, Esmark is going to pay pension benefits to union members who worked for fresh meats when fresh meats was part of Esmark," he said, "and the union is going to make wage concessions so that the new fresh-meats company is competitive."

"Good," said Briggs. "Sounds good."

Wilson sighed. He'd done it.

After Wilson hung up, Briggs called John Copeland. "Wilson gave me the proposal. I want you to present it to the union."

"I'm not sure that the Swift fresh-meats sale is going to work," said Copeland. "The company that Wilson and I put together makes sense, but that company can't make money without wage concessions, and this union doesn't make concessions."

"The union has a choice of making concessions or losing everything," said Briggs. "If the union doesn't make concessions, Don Kelly is going to close Swift. This is our last proposal."

"I'll give it a try," said Copeland.

Copeland called a lawyer in Washington. "I know you're on good terms with the union," he said. "I'm going to propose that the union buy Swift fresh meats. Can you give me a hand?"

"Sure," said the lawyer. "I'll make an appointment for you with the union president."

At the beginning of June, John Copeland flew to Washington to present the Esmark proposal to the union president. He sat in the union man's office and read through the term sheet that Briggs had given him. "Esmark is being generous," said Copeland. "Esmark is giving you two thirds of the new meat-packing company. In exchange, Esmark wants the new company to have a chance to survive, and that means that you have to make wage concessions."

The union president shook his head.

"This company can't survive without wage concessions," said Copeland. "Iowa Beef pays its workers half as much as we pay yours. Esmark is ready to close the company down." He looked at the union president.

The union president shook his head. Clearly he didn't believe that.

"I'm serious," said Copeland. "Look what just happened at

Armour. The union refused to make concessions, and the company closed three of its four packing plants. If Esmark closes Swift fresh meats, 3,350 of your members will lose their jobs."

"It's against my philosophy to own companies," said the union president. "But I'll take a look at this."

"I need an answer by next Wednesday," said Copeland. The Esmark board was scheduled to meet on Thursday morning to approve the plan. "If you don't accept this offer, Esmark is going to close down Swift fresh meats completely. Kelly is set on that."

The union president didn't say anything.

Copeland stood up to leave. There didn't seem to be anything more to say.

As soon as Copeland got back to Chicago, he pulled out his file of plant-by-plant financials. He called the Swift finance man into his office. "Put together a small meat-packing company that would be profitable even without union concessions," he said. Don Kelly would surely be able to sell that company—to Europeans, maybe, or even to Americans—and Copeland wanted to be ready just in case the union president said no.

The union president called Swift's Washington lawyer again a week later. "I want to talk," he said. "I'll see you Monday." Three days before the board meeting Don Kelly had scheduled to decide what to do with Swift fresh meats.

The lawyer called Copeland. "The union man wants to see you," said the lawyer.

"I'll be out on the first plane," said Copeland. The union man must have decided to accept the proposal. Why else would he want to see Copeland?

Copeland flew to Washington, D.C. and caught a cab to the lawyer's office on K Street. "He's at the union headquarters," the lawyer's secretary told Copeland. "He left you a message." She handed Copeland a sheet. Copeland read: "The union president called. He said he wanted to see me immediately, alone. Wait here. I'll call you when he's ready to see you."

Copeland sat down to wait. It was three o'clock. He looked through the window of the office at the union headquarters across the street. Surely the lawyer would call soon.

The lawyer didn't call.

Copeland kept waiting.

Finally at about six o'clock, the lawyer walked into the office. Copeland looked at him. By now, Copeland was sure that the answer was no. He didn't want the news. "Well?" he asked.

"The union turned you down cold," said the lawyer. "The president said he won't negotiate. He doesn't want to see you at all."

Copeland shook his head. "Doesn't he understand that Esmark is going to *close* Swift fresh meats?" asked Copeland. "Doesn't he understand that this was the last offer?"

The lawyer shook his head. "The president doesn't believe that Esmark is going to close Swift," he said. "He says that you are just trying to palm your mistakes off on the union."

Copeland shook his head. "It's all over," he said. "Esmark is going to close Swift. I know Don Kelly. That was Kelly's best offer."

"I know," said the lawyer. "I'm sorry."

Copeland called Kelly with the bad news.

The next morning when Copeland got back to Esmark headquarters, Kelly was sitting at his desk talking to Esmark executives about closing Swift. "I gave the union a chance," he said to Copeland. "We can't do any more than we've done. I'm closing Swift."

"Don," said Copeland. "I want one more chance. I had the finance people at Swift put together some numbers assuming we don't get labor concessions. They say we can create a profitable company out of Swift fresh meats. There are some good plants. And we might be able to get around the union contract. There has to be a way that Esmark can sell part of fresh meats and break the master agreement."

"No," said Kelly. "Your proposal won't work. The union won't cooperate. I'm closing Swift."

"I've put together some numbers," said Copeland. "I strung together all the profitable plants to make a company. The company doesn't make much beef—that's disappointing because Swift has always been known as a beef-packer—but the nonbeef parts of Swift are profitable."

Kelly frowned.

"Just take a look at these numbers," said Copeland. He held out a page of calculations. "Five years ago, Swift fresh-meats division earned $33 million not counting plant-closing costs. Swift is an attractive company."

Kelly pushed the sheet away. He didn't have time for Copeland's numbers. "We're closing Swift," he said. He was so steamed up about the union and so upset that he had to close Swift that he wasn't really listening. "I'm going to lunch." He put on his jacket and strode out.

Copeland went back to his office. He called a staff meeting. "This is the worst morning of my life," he said. "Esmark has decided to close Swift." He looked at the other executives. "I know you'll be able to find other jobs, but it won't be the same. I've done everything I could. It wasn't enough."

No one said much. No one believed Copeland.

After the meeting, Copeland walked the three blocks to the Chicago Club on East Van Buren Street for lunch. He sat by himself. When he finished lunch, he went downstairs to the lounge on the mezzanine and ordered a straight Canadian Club. Then he had another. Earlier he'd just been depressed; now Copeland was mad.

"Hi, John," said a voice.

Copeland looked up. It was another Swift executive.

"Can we talk?" said the man.

"Sure," said Copeland.

"Were you serious this morning when you said that Kelly was going to close Swift fresh meats?" asked the man.

Copeland nodded.

"For sure?" asked the man.

Copeland nodded again. "I've put together a new proposal to make Swift salable," said Copeland, "but Kelly won't look at it."

The executive thought for a minute. "Why don't you go sit in the big conference room next door to Kelly's office? Kelly is a sociable fellow. Pretty soon Kelly will come out to see what you're doing. Then you can convince him to give Swift one more chance."

"That's a good idea," said Copeland. "I'll do that." He looked at the Swift man. "You come with me," he said.

The two executives walked down Wabash to Esmark headquarters on East Monroe Street. They sat in the conference room. Kelly was still at lunch.

After half an hour, Don Kelly wandered in. "What are you doing in here?" he asked.

"Waiting for you," said Copeland. "I want to show you the numbers that the Swift financial people put together."

"Is this what you were talking about this morning?" asked Kelly. He hadn't caught the fact that the financial people had done it. That was different.

"Yes," said Copeland.

Kelly felt badly about closing Swift fresh meats, and he'd had lunch by himself to think over the decision. Lunch had calmed him down, and he was ready to listen to a way to keep the company open. "I'll take a look," he said. He sat down.

Copeland handed Kelly the numbers.

Kelly read carefully.

When Copeland finished, Kelly nodded. "Maybe this can work," he said. "I'm willing to give this a try. I'm keeping processed meats, but you can have fresh meats." He called the president of the processed-meats division into the strategy center. "Do you want any of the plants from the Swift fresh-meats division?" asked Kelly.

"No," said the head of processed meats.

Kelly looked at Copeland. "We'll give this a try," he said. "I'll have Salomon Brothers put together a brochure on the company. The Europeans might be interested. I'll make one last try to find a buyer for Swift fresh meats."

Roger Briggs called Ken Wilson later that afternoon. "Put together a sales brochure on Swift fresh meats," he said. "We're going to sell that company."

"Okay," said Wilson. "But I think you're being a little optimistic about the possibility of a buyer."

"Write the brochure," said Briggs.

"Yes," said Wilson. "I just don't want to waste too much time."

"Someone is going to buy this company," said Briggs. "I need a brochure."

While Wilson worked on the brochure, Ron Freeman, the Salomon oil and gas partner, auctioned off the oil company. It seemed clear that a buyer would pay top price if he got just the parts of the company he wanted, so Freeman broke the subsidiary into three separate companies and held three auctions. Petro-Lewis won the small drilling company for $27.6 million; Total Petroleum (North America) won the refining and marketing operations for $347 million; Mobil bid the high $760 million for the TransOcean oil and gas fields.

The Mobil money went straight to Esmark's shareholders. The other $300 million of cash would pay for taxes and expenses—and for fixing Swift.

In July, when Wilson finished the brochure, Kelly took it to Europe to show to potential buyers. No one was interested. They'd heard about Swift and its problems.

"I've got a new idea," Briggs told Kelly in August after Kelly got back from Europe. "Let's sell the company to the public."

"You think the public wants to own Swift fresh meats?" said Kelly. He didn't think so.

"Why not?" asked Briggs. "Swift fresh meats will be a profitable company after we spend $200 million to fix it up for sale."

"It isn't a profitable company now," said Kelly. "Everyone knows that."

"Esmark will pay to close plants and fund the pension," said Briggs. "We'll sell the company as plants instead of a company—and that will break the master contract. Swift will be competitive. Salomon Brothers won't have any trouble selling the stock."

"I don't know," said Kelly. "I think it will be a tough job."

Briggs grunted. "We're running out of alternatives," he said.

"Okay," said Kelly. "If you think the public will buy, I'm willing to sell."

Kelly called John Copeland. "We're going to spin the company off to the public," said Kelly.

Copeland could hardly believe that. "What are you going to call this company?" asked Copeland.

"Anything you want," said Kelly.

"Swift," said Copeland. He had to have the name.

"No," said Kelly. "You can't have the Swift name. Esmark is keeping that. We're keeping the branded, processed products."

"We don't have much chance of surviving without the Swift name," said Copeland. "People buy our meat because it's Swift. Employees work for us because it's Swift."

"I'll think about it," said Kelly.

Kelly called back a couple of hours later. "You can keep the Swift name for the company, but not for consumer products," he said. "Esmark is keeping the sausage and bacon plants and we are going to keep using the Swift name on those products."

"The name for the company is all I need," said Copeland. He paused. "From now on, Swift fresh meats will be called Swift Independent."

Later that afternoon, Roger Briggs called Ken Wilson. "No luck in Europe," he said.

Wilson's heart sank.

"I've decided that you're going to sell Swift Independent to the public," said Briggs. "I figure you can get maybe $50 million for half the stock."

Wilson was speechless.

"It will be easy for you," said Briggs. "You know Swift fresh meats inside out."

"I'm not sure we can sell the stock," repeated Wilson. "Not in this market."

"Of course you can sell the stock," said Briggs. "That's your job: selling stock."

"Investors don't like meat-packers," said Wilson. "They've heard Don Kelly say that Swift was in trouble so many times that they'll never buy."

"Don't worry," said Briggs. "This won't be the same Swift. Esmark is going to fix the company so it is profitable before you sell it. Esmark will close the money-losing plants and assume the severance and pension payments."

"I'm not sure that investors are going to believe that," said Wilson. Clearly Briggs didn't understand how much investors didn't like Swift. Just the Swift name was going to make it hard to sell the stock. "Investors are going to be skeptical that Esmark really solved the obsolete-plant problem. And besides, closing plants doesn't change Swift management."

Briggs didn't say anything.

Wilson could almost feel Briggs glaring at him over the telephone.

"Small investors will love the stock," Briggs finally said. "Swift is a company they've heard of. The price will be right. It will sell out in hours."

"Maybe," said Wilson. "Let me talk to our syndicate man," he said. The Salomon Brothers syndicate desk was in charge of putting together the group of banks to underwrite and sell the stock. "He'll know what investors will buy. He has a good feel for the market."

"I want you out here tomorrow," said Briggs. "We're having a meeting to talk about how we're going to get Swift ready for you to sell it."

"I'll be there," said Wilson.

Wilson put down the receiver. He shook his head. Then he dialed the syndicate man and told him Briggs' plan.

"Come on," said the syndicate man. "You're pulling my leg."

"I'm serious," said Wilson.

"It can't be done," said the syndicate man. "There's nothing the Street likes less than stale meat."

Wilson paused. "Ira wants us to bust our ass for this deal."

The syndicate man hesitated. "Well," he finally said. "Something can be done."

The next morning, Wilson flew out to Chicago for a meeting with Briggs in the Esmark board room.

"How much stock do you think you can sell?" asked Briggs. "Fifty million? Sixty million?"

"I'm not sure we can sell any stock at all," said Wilson. "My syndicate man says that the Street won't buy Swift."

"You need to sell at least half the shares," said Briggs. "We'll keep at least 20 percent of the stock. That will show that we believe in Swift."

Wilson nodded. The accounting rules said that if Esmark owned half of Swift Independent, then Esmark had to count all of Swift profits—or losses—as if they were Esmark profits. If Esmark owned between 20 and 50 percent, it counted just that percentage of Swift earnings. Below 20 percent, Esmark could count as earnings only the dividends Swift paid, if any.

"Esmark has to come out of this with $30 million," said Briggs.

Wilson shook his head. He still didn't think he could sell the stock. "I've got to work on this. I'm not sure that this is going to sell."

Briggs stared at him. "Will you have the numbers ready next week?" he asked.

"Next week?" asked Wilson. He'd been thinking of next month. "I'll try. It's going to be a lot of work."

"You've already got a proposal," said Briggs.

"That was the union proposal," said Wilson. "That assumed union concessions. This is different. I can't assume any concessions. I can only include the profitable plants. Esmark is going to pay the closing costs on the others." He paused. "Or that's what you keep telling me."

"What do you need to sell a company to the public?" Briggs asked. "What kind of numbers do you think it takes to sell a meat-packer?"

Wilson thought for a minute. "Three years of historic profits and an up quarter." Wilson had to work out a way for the new Swift Independent to show those profits. Swift fresh meats, as it currently existed, didn't have even one year of historic profits.

Briggs nodded. Obviously he thought that Wilson could get his three years of profits and his up quarter by massaging the numbers.

Wilson guessed that he didn't have much choice.

Ken Wilson was sitting at his desk adding up the numbers on his calculator when John Copeland called three weeks later.

"I've been working on the company," said Copeland.

"Oh?" said Wilson.

"I've been putting together a staff," said Copeland.

"That's good," said Wilson.

"I've got some preliminary estimates on overhead," said Copeland.

"Great," said Wilson.

"I've picked out the board of directors," said Copeland. "I'll read you the list." He read: Dolph Briscoe, the former governor of Texas; Martin Emmett, president of Standard Brands; Howard Dean, president of Dean Foods; Donald Jacobs, dean of the Northwestern business school; Roy Kottman, of Ohio State's agriculture school; George Dalferes, a Washington lawyer, and Roger Briggs of Esmark.

"Sounds good," said Wilson. Having prestigious directors would make it easier to convince investors to buy the stock.

"I've also had an idea," said Copeland. He paused.

"Oh?" said Wilson. He was sure Copeland had some scheme that would change all the number crunching that he had done.

"You've been talking about closing plants," said Copeland.

"Yes," said Wilson. Something in the way Copeland said that made Wilson positive that Copeland was going to wreck the numbers.

"Well, I want to reopen some plants," said Copeland.

"What?" said Wilson.

"Some of the plants that you're closing would be profitable if the union made wage concessions," said Copeland.

"I know that," said Wilson.

"I'm going to reopen those plants as part of this new company," said Copeland. "I'm going to open them at competitive wage rates."

"Are you sure that's going to work?" said Wilson. "The union refused to make concessions at Clovis in February. The union refused to buy the company in June. What makes you think that the union is going to make concessions now?"

"The union has made concessions before," said Copeland. "The union made concessions when we sold our pork plant in North Carolina to Dinner Bell Foods: the plant closed on Friday as Swift and opened Monday as Dinner Bell with the same workers at half the wages."

"I'm not sure the union is going to see Esmark selling a plant to Swift Independent quite the same way," said Wilson.

"We've got some good beef plants in the Midwest," said Copeland. "They could make money if we had a better labor agreement."

"Have you talked to the union about this?" asked Wilson.

"Yes," said Copeland. "I just saw the union president."

"What did he say?" asked Wilson.

"Well," said Copeland. "I told him that the beef plant in Guymon, Oklahoma, is scheduled to be closed but that I thought we ought to reopen it as part of the new company. He didn't seem very enthusiastic."

Wilson waited.

"He said that he wished that I'd just close the plant and walk away from it," said Copeland. "But I said that I would do everything to keep that plant open. And I will." He paused. "When you finish off the numbers for Roger Briggs, make sure to include that plant."

"How I am supposed to estimate wages?" asked Wilson.

"Just use the going rate," said Copeland. "Eight dollars an hour."

"Okay," said Wilson. He called Briggs. "Copeland wants me to include that beef plant in Oklahoma," said Wilson. "The one that's closed. He thinks he can get the union to agree to eight dollars an hour."

"Isn't that the going rate in Oklahoma?" asked Briggs.

"Copeland says so," said Wilson.

"Count it in," said Briggs.

"I hope he gets the concessions he wants," said Wilson. "This company I'm putting together isn't like anything that really exists."

"You said you wanted three years of historic profits and an up quarter," said Briggs.

"I know," said Wilson. "I know."

Wilson redid the numbers.

Copeland called. "I've been looking at the plant financials again," he said. "There are two more plants that could be profitable if we got concessions." He named them. "Count those in too. I'm going to reopen them with competitive wages."

Wilson shook his head. "Okay," he said. He redid the numbers again. Then he called Copeland. "I'm coming out to Chicago," he said. "I've got to finish these numbers."

"Come on out," said Copeland.

Wilson flew out to Chicago a couple of days later. The two sat in the board room next-door to Copeland's office. Wilson lit a cigar. "I need estimates of corporate overhead," he said.

"Like what?" asked Copeland. Copeland had spent the past two months trying to figure out how much it would cost to run Swift Independent. The staff was hired; the board of directors appointed; the estimates were in. Copeland knew them like the palm of his hand.

"Headquarters rent," said Wilson.

"We're going to keep the offices right here," said Copeland. "Rent's the same as before." The two floors of the building on West Jackson that Swift & Company used as headquarters were simple and functional; there wasn't an Oriental rug outside the elevator the way there was at Esmark headquarters. "We don't need frills," said Copeland. "No flowers at the reception desk. No art collection on the walls."

311

"Are you going to have a corporate plane?" asked Wilson. "How much is that going to cost?"

"No plane," said Copeland. "If we absolutely have to have a plane for some meeting, we'll rent one."

"How many lawyers are you going to have?" asked Wilson. As part of Esmark, Swift didn't have lawyers on staff; when it had a legal problem, Swift borrowed a lawyer from Esmark's team of twelve.

"Three lawyers," said Copeland. "A general counsel plus two assistants."

"I hope that's enough," said Wilson. "How much are you going to pay them?"

Copeland made an estimate.

"Finance staff?" asked Wilson.

"Treasurer, assistant treasurer," said Copeland. He gave Wilson an estimate for those salaries.

"Have you lined up your bank credit?" asked Wilson. Swift had always "borrowed" from Esmark when it needed cash. "What's the interest rate going to be?"

"You're not going to believe this," said Copeland. He smiled. "I got the money for less than Esmark used to charge me."

Wilson raised his eyebrows.

"Esmark was making money off us," said Copeland. He shook his head.

"What about insurance?" asked Wilson. That had always come through Esmark's insurance subsidiary.

"I lined up a policy," said Copeland. He paused. "Esmark overcharged me on that too." Wilson scribbled down the numbers for annual premiums.

"I've got a couple of other questions," said Wilson. He read down a list.

Copeland gave him the numbers.

"Thanks," said Wilson. He ran them through the computer. Then he called Copeland. "It looks like maybe this company can be profitable. Maybe we have a shot at selling the stock after all."

Copeland didn't answer. Of course Swift Independent could make money; of course the investment bankers could sell the stock. Swift Independent was a fine company. These investment bankers

312

amused him: all they seemed to do was sit in the board room smoking cigars and ask him to figure out off-the-wall numbers.

"It looks good," Wilson told Briggs from New York the next morning. "I just ran the numbers through the computer. The company is going to make a profit."

"Three years of historic profits?" asked Briggs.

"Three years of historic profits," said Wilson. "And an up quarter."

"I knew you could do it," Briggs said.

A couple of hours later, when Wilson was all but finished with the report, he looked up. The head of the corporate finance department was stomping down the corridor toward him. Wilson grinned hello.

The man glared.

Wilson put down the page and turned off his calculator. He couldn't imagine what he'd done wrong, but clearly whatever it was was horrible.

"Get into my office," said the department head when he got to Wilson's desk. "The screening committee is meeting right now to decide on whether or not to sell that Swift fresh-meats stock. You've got to make a presentation."

"The screening committee is voting on this?" asked Wilson. That wasn't possible. The Salomon committee was supposed to vote on whether to handle a stock sale for a new client before anyone started doing the number crunching. Had Swift Independent been a new client, it would almost certainly have been turned down. Since Esmark, an important long-term client, was selling Swift, the usual rules didn't apply. It hadn't occurred to Wilson that the screening committee would ever look at the deal.

"That new partner on the committee just found out about Swift," said the head of the corporate finance department. "*He* called this meeting."

Wilson followed the head of the corporate finance department down the hallway. Four partners were sitting sternly around the table in the partner's office.

The head of the corporate finance department sat down. Wilson explained that Esmark wanted to sell Swift to the public.

"Esmark shouldn't be doing that," said the head of the corporate finance department. "Meat-packing is an entrepreneurial kind of business. Esmark ought to sell the company to Swift's management team."

Wilson shook his head. John Copeland didn't have the money to buy Swift, and besides, Roger Briggs had been the one who decided to sell to the public in the first place.

"I'm not sure meat-packing is entrepreneurial," said another partner. "Selling Swift to the public might have some merit."

Wilson nodded. As far as he was concerned, Salomon Brothers didn't have any choice.

"We've got to be reasonable about this," said the new partner who had called the meeting. "How much stock are we talking about?"

"Fifty million dollars' worth," said Wilson.

"That's a lot of stock for a new company," said the partner.

"I know," said Wilson. "Swift Independent is a big company."

"Are you sure that the people running Swift Independent can run a big company?" asked the partner.

"Well, no," said Wilson. "They've never run a company. I guess that's the biggest risk to Swift Independent's surviving."

"What are the other risks?" asked the partner.

"Swift might not be able to reopen all the plants it wants to at competitive wages," said Wilson. "Overhead might run a lot more than Copeland thinks."

The partner asked some more questions.

Wilson answered. He wanted to tell the partner that sensible though his questions were, they were pointless. If Salomon Brothers didn't do this deal, the firm would lose an important client.

The partner kept asking questions. "We have to think about this," he said when the meeting broke up.

Wilson walked back to his office. He shuffled the papers on his desk. The numbers were done, and the papers were all ready to go, but he needed the go-ahead from the committee.

A couple of days later, the new partner strolled into Wilson's office. "Put together a memo on that screening committee meeting," he said.

"Okay," said Wilson. That sounded bad. What was he going to do with a memo?

"This deal looks okay as long as we're very careful about the numbers," he continued. "You have to double-check everything. And you have to remind Roger Briggs about Esmark's responsibilities to Salomon Brothers and to Swift Independent."

Wilson nodded.

"Esmark has to follow through on its promises to Swift," said the partner. "Esmark has to indemnify Salomon Brothers. Esmark has to understand that we can't underwrite a company that doesn't have a clean report for the accountant. And we won't sell the stock unless it is priced right."

"Okay," said Wilson. He'd already done most of that; it was standard policy, and Briggs wasn't going to like being reminded.

"Send me a copy of the memo when it's done," said the partner. "And read it to Briggs on the phone."

"Okay," said Wilson. He could leave out a couple of the points when he read the list: he knew it would annoy Briggs, and besides, he figured Harris would have left it out himself.

"Thanks," said the new partner. He stood up to go.

Wilson watched the partner walk down the corridor toward the office. Then Wilson turned back to his papers. He was almost finished. At the end of the week, Wilson wrote the memo. He called Roger Briggs. He read the memo. He didn't mention the indemnity.

Next Wilson called the partner in charge of the entire equity department. "We need to have a meeting to talk about selling Swift fresh meats," he said.

"Get down here," said the head of equity.

Wilson walked downstairs to the trading floor. The head of equity was waiting in the big conference room. The syndicate man was with him.

The head of equity looked at Wilson. "So you want to sell stock in a meat-packer," he said. "Okay. But I don't let our clients get their fingers burned. Is this company going to go bankrupt?"

"No," said Wilson.

"Tell me what could go wrong," said the sales partner.

"The union might not make concessions," Wilson said. "Management might sink under the new burdens; hog and cattle prices might jump through the roof."

The head of equity nodded. He looked at the syndicate man. "Tell me why we won't be able to sell the stock," he said.

"No one wants stock in a company that had low cyclical earnings—and a history of problems," said the syndicate man.

The head of equity nodded again. He switched on the speaker phone and dialed Roger Briggs at Esmark.

"Hi, Roger," yelled the head of equity. "I've just been talking to Kenny Wilson and our syndicate man about this Swift offering." He paused. "We've thought it through very carefully and we want to go ahead. Wilson is on the deal. The syndicate people say it can be done. I'm all for it."

Wilson squirmed. He certainly wanted Swift Independent to survive as a company, but *he* couldn't promise anything.

The syndicate man blanched. *He* didn't think Salomon Brothers could sell this stock.

The head of equity grinned. *He* was sure that Wilson and the syndicate man could do this.

"Great," said Briggs. He'd been sure that the investment bankers would come to their senses and get enthusiastic about selling the stock.

After the call to Briggs, Wilson pulled the syndicate man aside. "What do you really think about this stock?" he asked.

The syndicate man frowned. "There's nothing the Street likes less than stale meat," he said.

Wilson went back to his office. Briggs had said that Esmark would add two investment banks to manage the sale. Maybe one of them would have an idea. He dialed the top syndicate man at E. F. Hutton.

"Fresh meats?" said the man. "Fresh-meat-packing? How in the hell do you think you're going to sell that?"

Wilson raised an eyebrow. He dialed the head of syndicate at Goldman, Sachs.

"Meat-packing?" said the man. "That stock isn't going to sell."

Wilson looked out the window. They were right. He had to talk to Roger Briggs. He picked up the phone. "I need to see you," he said when Briggs got on the line.

"About what?" asked Briggs.

"Oh, just to confirm some details on the offering," said Wilson.

316

Briggs paused. "Can't we do that on the phone?" he asked.

"No," said Wilson.

"Well, okay," said Briggs. "It had better be important." He marked down an appointment for seven the next morning.

Wilson flew out to Chicago. He went out to dinner at Gene & Georgetti's to fortify his nerves. While he sipped his Scotch and water, he made a list of questions for Briggs. The possibility of selling much less than $50 million worth of Swift stock was the last item on the list.

Briggs was already in his office when Wilson arrived the next morning. Briggs seemed to be in a foul mood. "You called this meeting," he snapped. He looked at Wilson. "What the hell do you want?"

"I've got a list of ten questions," said Wilson. He pulled out his cocktail notes.

Briggs glared.

"I need to borrow the Esmark plane to visit the packing plants for due diligence," said Wilson.

"Take the plane," said Briggs. "You didn't come in here at seven in the morning to ask me that."

"Well, no," said Wilson. "I need some other things."

Briggs scowled.

Wilson read off the next eight items on his list. Nothing important.

Briggs tapped his fingers on the desk.

"I'm not sure that we can sell $50 million worth of stock in a meat-packer," Wilson said finally. "We might have to cut the total."

"What?" snapped Briggs.

"I'm not sure that we can sell half the stock in the fresh-meats company at any price," said Wilson.

"Bullshit," said Briggs. "I'll bring in Morgan Stanley." Morgan Stanley then handled more stock issues than any investment bank in the world. Morgan Stanley was Salomon's number-one rival. Briggs knew that. "I'll call right now," he said. He reached for the phone.

Wilson swallowed. "Okay," he said. "We'll give it a try." He paused. "It might be less than $50 million though."

Briggs just scowled.

Wilson flew back to New York that night. First thing the next morning, he called Harris. If Salomon Brothers was going to sell this stock, Harris had to convince the syndicate people to give it their best effort. "I've finished up the prospectus on Swift Independent," he said. "I'm ready to finish up the due diligence and file with the SEC." He paused. "The company looks great. I'm having a little trouble getting the syndicate man excited about the company. He keeps talking about 'stale meat.'"

A few days later, Wilson's phone rang. It was the treasurer of Esmark.

"I just saw your brochure," he said. "I've decided that I want to buy Swift Independent. I'm putting together an offer to do a leveraged buy-out of the company myself." He was planning to buy Swift with a bank loan secured by Swift's own assets.

"You're doing what?" asked Wilson. "You're going to make an offer for Swift Independent?"

"Yes," said the treasurer. "I'm going to resign my job and run the company. What do you think?"

"How much are you going to pay?" he asked.

"Maybe $100 million," said the treasurer. "I don't have the money yet. I just wanted to tell you before I told Briggs."

"Thanks," said Wilson. He put down the receiver. He called the syndicate man. "You're not going to believe this," he said.

"Try me," said the man.

"The treasurer of Esmark is going to make an offer for Swift Independent," said Wilson. "He thinks he can pay $100 million."

"One hundred million is a lot of money," said the syndicate man.

"I know," said Wilson. "When I told Briggs that we could sell half of Swift Independent for $50 million, I was being very optimistic. I think we'd be lucky to sell it for $40 million."

"We've already started to take orders," said the syndicate man.

"If Briggs wants to negotiate with the treasurer, we'll have to pull the stock offer. We can't be selling to the public and talking to an investor at the same time."

Wilson nodded.

"But if you pull the offer, you won't be able to start it again.

318

Investors will assume that there's something wrong with the company."

"I know," said Wilson. "I know."

The phone rang; Wilson grabbed the receiver. It was Roger Briggs.

"I just talked to our treasurer," said Briggs. "He's going to make an offer for Swift Independent."

"I've heard," said Wilson. It sounded like Briggs was sniffing victory.

"This is great," said Briggs. "I told our lawyer to put together some bidding rules. Maybe we'll get a couple of other offers. When investors find out that there are other offers for Swift, they'll snap up the stock."

"It isn't going to work that way," said Wilson. "If investors find out about the other offer, they won't buy the stock. They'll assume that this other, better deal is going to go through and they'll find something else to buy. If the deal falls apart, investors will think it was because there was something wrong with the company— and they won't buy. And besides, it isn't ethical to try to sell the company to the treasurer of Esmark and the public at the same time. If you are negotiating with the treasurer, then you have to stop taking orders from investors."

Briggs didn't say anything.

"If you stop taking orders now, you may not be able to get any when you start again," said Wilson. "Investors are going to be suspicious. They are going to assume that there is something very wrong with Swift if the treasurer of Esmark wouldn't buy it."

Briggs didn't say anything.

"You've got to choose one or the other," said Wilson.

"Maybe you're right," said Briggs. "I'll have to think about this."

"But remember, it's going to be hard to get this stock sale going again if you stop now," said Wilson. "As my syndicate man says, 'there's nothing the Street likes less than stale meat.'"

Briggs didn't respond.

A couple of days later, John Copeland picked up a rumor that Esmark's treasurer was going to bid for Swift Independent. Copeland hoped it was just a rumor. Then just as Copeland was stepping into his cab to get the airplane home from the Esmark annual meeting in Kansas City, the treasurer of Esmark ran up to him. "I'm putting together a bidding group," he said. "I hope you'll stay on to run the company."

Copeland scowled. "I'd heard that you were doing this," he said. "I was surprised that I hadn't heard it from you. I don't think it will work."

Copeland got in the cab. He flew back to Chicago.

A couple of days later, Copeland heard that an investment banker in Chicago was making a bid for Swift too. Copeland figured that now there would be a flood of "leveraged buy-out" proposals. He called Roger Briggs. "I don't think that a leveraged buy-out is a good idea," he said.

"We're selling Swift to the highest bidder," said Briggs. "If you want to make your own bid, you've got twenty days."

Copeland called Ken Wilson. "You know there are two bids out for Swift Independent," he said.

"I've heard," said Wilson.

"Briggs told me that I have twenty days to put together a bid," said Copeland. "I'm lining up some financing. If anyone buys this company, it is going to be me."

Wilson sighed. Now there were going to be three bids.

"I don't think this is a good idea," said Copeland. "I think that this company ought to be publicly owned. Maybe if we get into the act, we can get the whole idea of a leveraged buy-out stopped."

"I hope so," said Wilson.

"Why don't you talk to Briggs?" said Copeland.

"I have," said Wilson. "But I'll try him again."

Wilson called Briggs. "Are you going to go through with these LBO bids?" asked Wilson. "I don't think any of those groups is going to be able to put together the money to pay for Swift Independent. A bird in the hand is worth two in the bush."

"I've looked at these LBOs," said Briggs. "I agree with you. "I've decided to sell the stock to the public after all."

Now it was up to Salomon Brothers to sell the stock. If that could be done.

* * *

The syndicate man put together a group of ninety-five brokerage houses to share the underwriting risk. Most of the big investment banking firms refused to join, but if Briggs was right and the stock appealed to small investors, that wouldn't matter; the small banks had plenty of small customers. Wilson arranged for Copeland to make a whirlwind eighteen-city tour of the country—to meet with stockbrokers and large potential investors—and went along to make sure that the meetings went smoothly.

"You aren't going to believe this," Wilson told the syndicate man when he got back from Atlanta, the last stop on the tour.

"Try me," said the man.

"The investors were wild about Swift Independent," said Wilson. "I think we're going to be able to sell the stock after all."

The syndicate man laughed. "Sometimes I like to be wrong," he said.

Wilson nodded. He called one of the New York salesmen. "How's it going?" he asked.

"There's a lot of interest," he said. "No firm orders yet."

"Good," said Wilson. He put down the receiver. The phone rang. It was the top salesman in Chicago.

"The Firestone pension fund wants 125,000 shares," he said. "Solid."

Wilson called the syndicate man. "We just got our first firm order," he said. The phone rang again. It was the salesman in New York.

"The Morgan Bank wants shares," he said. "So does Manufacturers Hanover. So does Chase Manhattan."

"Great," said Wilson.

The salesman in London called. "I've got orders from fifteen banks," he said. "More than 200,000 shares."

Pretty soon there were more orders than shares of stock. The sales period was over.

On April 21, the day before SIPCO stock began to trade, Wilson and Copeland met with the syndicate man and the New York salesmen in the big conference room off the trading floor to set the selling price.

The syndicate man got out his order book. "We're oversold," he said. "We've sold 440,000 more shares of stock than we'd planned to issue."

Wilson nodded.

"The price is still $15 a share," said the syndicate man. "Okay?" He looked at Copeland.

Wilson nodded again.

"Let's call Briggs," said Wilson.

They called. "We've sold 2.75 million shares," said Wilson. "Half the stock."

"For how much?" asked Briggs.

"Forty-one million dollars," said Wilson.

Briggs grunted. He'd known that the stock would sell.

The next morning, Ira Harris called Ken Wilson. He talked about the orders. "And they told us it couldn't be done," he said.

Wilson laughed, but he didn't say anything. There wasn't anything to say.

Swift Independent was a big success. First Copeland wrung big concessions from the meat-packing unions. Then he began to expand the fresh-meats product line with new cuts and finer grading. He bought and renovated beef plants in Des Moines, Iowa, and Hereford, Texas; he bought and renovated pork plants in Worthington, Minnesota, as well as Huron, South Dakota, and St. Joseph, Missouri. Next Copeland expanded into processed meats— outside the master contract—under the Tender Pride beef and the Tend'r Lean pork labels. In 1983, Copeland sold the Swift Independent chicken plant to Gold Kist; the plant had never been a moneymaker, and Swift didn't have a big enough base in the chicken business to keep fighting.

The stock price soared. On January 14, 1982, a little more than six months after the first stock sale, Swift Independent began to trade on the American Stock Exchange. Someday, Swift Independent may trade on the New York Stock Exchange along with the other large American companies.

Now that he is past sixty, Copeland is getting ready to retire. He has named a successor to fill his shoes after he leaves, and he spends less and less time at the office. Copeland now tries to make four golf tournaments each year, and he's proud that his company made it.

* * *

As Briggs predicted, selling Swift fresh meats made the price of Esmark stock soar. By December 1981, eight months after selling Swift, Esmark shares hit $50 each. A year later, after a two-for-one split, the price was $56½.

At first, other businessmen couldn't believe what Kelly had done. "How do you handle being chairman of a $3-billion company instead of a $6-billion company?" asked one.

"Easy," said Kelly. "I just stand in the $3-billion corner at cocktail parties."

Esmark didn't stay a $3-billion company for long. In 1982, Kelly bought Jhirmack shampoos and Discwasher Inc. The next year, he made a run at Purex and a bid for Stokely-Van Kamp. Profits ticked up. Kelly talked about retiring. Then in the summer of 1983, he struck a deal to buy Norton Simon, maker of Hunt tomato sauce, Wesson oil, Max Factor cosmetics and owner of Avis rental cars, for $1 billion. A year after that, Kelly sold Esmark to Beatrice—Tropicana Orange Juice, La Choy soy sauce, and Samsonite luggage—for $2.6 billion, $60 a share, one of the largest nonoil mergers on record.

The sale left Kelly out of a job, but he and Briggs quickly formed their own company, Kelly, Briggs & Associates, to buy and manage consumer-products companies. In early 1986, Kelly, Briggs bought Beatrice.

Kelly says he has no plans to retire. Ever.

Selling Swift to the public was the first in a long string of successful underwriting deals for Salomon Brothers. By 1983, Salomon Brothers, the outsider, had became the biggest underwriter in the business, with twice the volume of Morgan Stanley, the traditional leader. And Salomon remained on the cutting edge. It introduced car-loan-backed securities and money multiplier bonds. In 1983, the firm traded more than $1 trillion worth of stocks and bonds, and ranked near the top for brokering corporate marriages and currency swaps.

By 1983 though, Salomon Brothers was no longer independent.

In August 1981, a team of partners, including Ira Harris, sold Salomon Brothers to the Phillip Brothers commodity empire for $550 million. At the time, that looked like top dollar—a premium of $250 million over book—but as Salomon profits soared in 1982, partners grumbled that they had been short-changed. That plus a dismal year for commodities made the marriage unhappy and Salomon chairman John Gutfreund soon ousted Phibro chairman David Tendler to consolidate control. Profits remain high, the bonds Phibro used to pay the Salomon partners have tripled in value, and Gutfreund insists that the future is bright.

So does Ira Harris, although he won't be part of it. After fifteen years as a Salomon partner, and five years as a member of the firm's executive committee, Harris decided he had had enough. Although he resigned both posts, he still makes more deals than ever from his Salomon office in the Sears Tower. And he's lost fifty pounds.

In January 1984, Wilson was elected a Salomon Brothers partner. He's got an elegant office all his own instead of a desk in the bullpen and a staff of half a dozen associates. Although Wilson still works hard, he has finally got time for his wife and girls, weekends if not evenings. He's waiting for the day that his girls are old enough to hear the tale of how their daddy helped save the world's greatest meat-packing company.

(8)

Drexel Burnham Lambert

"And You Thought You Were Too Small for Drexel Burnham"

"We just got subpoenaed on Phillips," said John Sorte.

Paul Higbee laughed.

"Our lawyer called this morning," said Sorte. He leaned back in his chair. "He said that he'd just got a notice from Phillips demanding all the documents on Mesa's bid in our files and asking the person most involved in the situation to give a deposition. So he called me."

"Well, yes, Mesa's your client," said Higbee. "If anyone here has talked to Boone, it's you." He walked across the office and sat down in the armchair in front of Sorte's desk.

"I told his lawyer we'd like to be involved in Phillips," said Sorte. "We're keeping an eye on the deal. But we haven't even talked to Boone. We don't have any documents. There's nothing to depose me about."

"Did he believe you?" asked Higbee.

"Of course he did," said Sorte. "But Phillips won't. Everyone thinks Drexel is involved since we raised money for Pickens during the Gulf fight."

Higbee looked at the Gulf deal memento on the corner of Sorte's desk: a tin of Gulf oil embedded in a lucite cube.

"Even the *Journal* thinks we're involved," said Sorte. He shuffled through the stack of papers on his credenza until he found the

December 6, 1984, front section. "It implied that we were already rounding up financing so Boone can get control of Phillips."

Higbee looked at the article. He tossed the newspaper into Sorte's "In" box. "What do you think is going to happen?"

"We're rooting for Boone," said Sorte. "I called him to wish Mesa good luck."

"Sixty a share is a high price to pay for Phillips," said Higbee.

"Boone knows what he's doing," said Sorte. "He called it right on Cities Service and General American and Gulf."

"Phillips is different," said Higbee. "Boone is talking about a leveraged buy-out."

"You never know," said Sorte. "Maybe this time he'll be able to negotiate a friendly merger. Maybe he won't need money to make a hostile offer."

"I don't know," said Higbee.

"If negotiations don't work out," said Sorte, "Boone knows he can call Drexel."

John Sorte is unpretentious. At thirty-seven, he is five feet ten, with green eyes and sandy blond hair. Sorte can be snide—and snappy—he doesn't tolerate fools well. His office is stacked knee-deep in papers: Sorte is scheduled to move down the hall in six months, and it seems like a waste of time to put the documents into the files. Sorte lives on Manhattan's Upper West Side, but he tries to spend weekends with his wife and three-year-old son Bradley at their house in Lakeville, Connecticut. Summers mean sailing his Sunfish on Lake Wononskopomuk: winters, skiing at Butternut. He's always on the job; Sorte has lost track of the number of times he's been called out of town to do a deal after he'd dressed for a black-tie dinner.

Sorte's an Air Force brat. He grew up in Europe and Albuquerque, New Mexico, and majored in chemical engineering at Rice University. But after spending two college summers working at Texaco's New Orleans office, he quickly decided that working for an oil company wasn't for him. Sorte had to get special permission to work past five o'clock, and no one would listen to his ideas; there didn't seem to be a place for achievers. Sorte headed to the Harvard business school, and when he got his M.B.A. in 1972, he landed a job at Shearson, Hammill. He worked on corporate finance, sometimes for oil and gas companies. Two years later, Fred Joseph, Shearson's chief operating officer—the man who'd recruited Sorte to Shearson—left to become head of investment banking at Drexel Burnham Lambert. Joseph kept calling Sorte, and in 1980, Sorte too made the leap. Drexel seemed to offer more opportunity, as well as more money.

"And you thought you were too small for Drexel Burnham," trumpet the newspaper ads. Drexel Burnham Lambert is untraditional. The firm isn't interested in courting blue chips and winning commodity underwritings. Instead, Drexel focuses on high-fee creative—and sometimes controversial—deals for clients that are less than household names: "high yield"—aka junk—bonds for Green Tree Acceptance, puttable common stock for Arley Merchandising, subordinated Yankee bonds for Swan Brewing. Drexel helped Sir James Goldsmith buy and liquidate Diamond International; it financed Saul Steinberg's abortive raid on Walt Disney Productions. Drexel has the largest junk-bond trading operation of any firm in the world, the largest leveraged-buy-out-financing group, the largest noninvestment-grade commercial paper operation. In 1984, Drexel underwrote more securities than any other firm except Salomon Brothers. Its wheeling and dealing has made Drexel the second-largest private investment bank on the Street— just after Goldman, Sachs—and the most feared. Among Drexel's more aggressive clients: T. Boone Pickens of Mesa Petroleum, Oscar Wyatt of Coastal Corporation, Carl Lindner of Penn Central, Jay Pritzker of Hyatt Corporation, and Carl Icahn of Icahn Capital.

I.W. "Tubby" Burnham, scion of the Harper bourbon distillery fortune, founded Burnham & Company in 1935. The height of the Depression was hardly an auspicious time to open a brokerage house, and Burnham & Company struggled for fifteen years. By 1950, Burnham had a trading department, an underwriting department and a distinctly second-tier list of corporate clients. Then in 1973, Drexel Firestone, the old-line investment banking house that had once been part of the J. P. Morgan empire, went up for sale. Buying Drexel would catapult Burnham into the top bracket of Wall Street banks. Tubby Burnham worried that the Burnham name would tarnish the Drexel, but he decided to try. In March 1973, Burnham bought Drexel for $10 million. A year later, Drexel Burnham bought an ailing "research boutique" controlled by the Banque Bruxelles Lambert and changed the firm's name to Drexel Burnham Lambert.

The Drexel-Burnham marriage quickly hit the rocks. Thirteen of Drexel's blue-chip clients moved their accounts in less than a year. The Drexel bankers refused to talk to the Burnham bankers, and morale was low.

Then, in 1975, Fred Joseph, the charismatic new head of the corporate finance department, sat all the bankers down. "We've got to make ourselves special," he said. "We're not going to keep any clients unless we can offer something that the competition can't." That something would be special services for small, medium-quality firms like Texas International and Golden West Homes.

In 1977, Drexel found another niche. Since 1975, Drexel Burnham had had the largest junk-bond-trading desk on the Street. In those days "junk" meant "fallen angels" like Lockheed and International Harvester, but Joseph realized that investors who bought traditional junk would also buy high-yield bonds issued by speculative young companies with no credit history or credit rating who offered high interest rates. One thing led to another. In 1980, as interest rates soared to 21 percent, Drexel enticed investors with securities redeemable in either cash or silver. Profits soared. But Drexel still wasn't mainstream. The big action was in mergers. Goldman, Sachs and Morgan Stanley seemed to have that business locked up.

Drexel was underwriting just $1 billion worth of junk bonds a year when John Sorte signed on as a partner—the total for 1983 was $14 billion. At first, Sorte worked on general corporate finance problems, including oil and gas. Then, at the beginning of 1984, he was offered the job as head of the oil and gas department.

Sorte was still trying to decide if he wanted the job when he got a call from Mike Milken, the head of the junk-bond-trading desk.

"I've been talking to Boone," said Milken. Boone Pickens, chairman of Mesa Petroleum. "He's interested in raising money to pay for his Gulf Oil bid. Maybe we can do a financing. It might not be a good idea, but if it is, we're talking about big dollars. It's worth a trip to Amarillo." Mesa headquarters.

Sorte caught the next flight.

T. Boone Pickens is provocative. At fifty-seven, he has watery blue eyes and thinning blond hair. He's charming and clean-cut. He wears conservative suits, lunches on takeout hamburgers and pays Mesa $2,000 an hour when his wife borrows the company Falcon 50. Pickens is a workaholic. He's on the job at least twelve hours a day—sometimes Saturday—and has twelve telephones in his Amarillo, Texas, town house. Pickens plays golf and racquetball, doesn't smoke, drinks moderately and snacks on Granny Smith apples. He unwinds by riding horses on his 14,000-acre ranch or stalking quail on the Texas plains. In 1980, Pickens earned $7 million, more than any other CEO in America. Boone watchers say his goal is to be governor of Texas.

A native of Holdenville, Oklahoma, Pickens majored in geology at Oklahoma State and in 1951 landed a job as a junior geologist at Phillips Petroleum. After four years, Pickens resigned; he was frustrated with the Phillips bureaucracy. He sank his $1,300 Phillips savings plan refund check into a new 1955 Ford wagon and set out on his own as an oil wildcatter. A year later, he got backing from a couple of Amarillo businessmen—$2,500 in cash and a $100,000 credit line—and formed Petroleum Exploration Inc. In 1959, he sank $35,000 into Canadian properties, and five years later, Pickens consolidated his holdings into Mesa Petroleum. Pickens had a knack for timing. Mesa bought Hugoton Production before anyone knew Hugoton owned a stake in the largest natural gas field in the continental United States. Mesa sold its U.K. and Canadian production just before those governments passed laws which made American ownership unattractive. Mesa profits soared: $5 million in 1974, $42 million in 1978, $126 million in 1983.

Pickens got high marks from oil company watchers for how he managed Mesa, and the better Mesa did, the more disgusted Pickens became with the way other oil executives were running their companies. Most majors were pumping out more oil each year than they were finding; they were in effect liquidating themselves.

329

Liquidating was okay as long as the shareholders got the benefit, but instead of putting their earnings into higher shareholder dividends, many companies squandered their cash on money-losing refining and marketing departments and on high-risk low-payoff domestic exploration. Pickens hadn't done that. In 1979, he had put Mesa's oil and gas reserves into a special royalty trust owned by the shareholders. The revenues from those fields went directly to the Mesa shareholders.

At first, Pickens just talked about poor oil company management. Then he started to move.

In June 1982, Pickens bid $45 a share for Cities Service, America's nineteenth largest oil company, and perhaps its worst managed. Pickens lost out to Gulf—Gulf later backed down and Cities sold out to Occidental Petroleum—but in the process Pickens cleared $31.5 million.

Pickens made a mental note about Gulf management and moved on to the next name on his list: General American Oil. By December, Mesa owned 7.5 percent of GAO and had bid $40 a share for the rest.

A couple of days after Pickens made the bid, he got a call from his investment banker. "There's a white knight surfacing for General American," said the man. "But it doesn't want to make an offer unless you approve it."

"I'm not going to approve," said Pickens.

After lunch, the investment banker called again. "The white knight is going to bid," he said.

"Who is it?" asked Pickens.

"Phillips," said the banker. "Call Bill Douce." The chairman of Phillips. "He's hunting in Georgia. Here's the number."

Pickens called that night.

"Boone," said Douce. "Phillips is going to bid for General American. We thought a lot about doing this and we almost didn't."

"If you've got to bid, you've got to bid," said Pickens.

"We've done some investigating," said Douce. "Mesa can't pay more than $40 a share. Phillips is going to bid $45. We'll buy you out."

Pickens and Phillips negotiated. Douce agreed that Phillips would buy back the Mesa stock for $45; Pickens agreed not to buy any GAO stock for five years.

Phillips bought General American.

Pickens earned $43.6 million.

He didn't sit on the cash for long. In February, Pickens began to buy stock in Superior Oil. The brother and sister who controlled the company had been feuding for years. Their fight bubbled over. Takeover rumors swirled. The stock soared. In September, Pickens sold for a profit of $31.6 million.

Pickens had always been brash. Now he got brasher. He formed the Gulf Investors Group partnership and after several months of skirmishes bid for Gulf Oil, the smallest of the Seven Sisters.

Gulf didn't think it had a problem.

But Pickens was dead serious. His only worry was lining up financial muscle, but one of the investors in his Gulf bidding group was a Drexel client. "Why don't you talk to Mike Milken?" suggested the man. Milken, the head of the Drexel junk-bond-trading desk.

Pickens met Milken in Los Angeles.

"We might be able to do something for you," said Milken. "Someone from corporate finance will come to Amarillo to talk."

Milken called John Sorte.

Sorte flew to Texas the next day.

He thought the Pickens proposal made sense, and soon Drexel had lined up commitments from investors to buy $2.2 billion worth of Gulf Investors junk bonds.

It turned out that Pickens never used the money.

At the beginning of March, Chevron bought Gulf for $13.2 billion, the largest takeover in history. Gulf shareholders earned $6.5 billion. The Pickens partnership made $760 million.

By then, Pickens was already putting together a $2.1-billion war chest. At the end of the Gulf fight, Sorte helped Pickens raise $300 million by selling bonds to Penn Central, the holding company controlled by raider-investor Carl Lindner. Then in the summer, Sorte put together a Drexel-sponsored $500 million in notes.

While Sorte lined up the money, Pickens looked down the list of the top twenty oil companies for his next target. He considered Sun. He considered Mobil. He considered U.S. Steel, parent of Marathon Oil. Finally Pickens settled on two companies, Unocal and Phillips Petroleum.

Unocal, like most oil companies, seemed poorly managed. Chairman Fred Hartley was three years past retirement. Pickens had always looked down on Hartley.

Phillips had a mediocre exploration record; almost half its stock was owned by institutions, which would be quick to sell to a high bidder. Pickens thought Phillips might even welcome him: Bill Douce, the chairman, was scheduled to retire on April 30, 1985; and Phillips' base in Bartlesville, Oklahoma, was just down the road from Boone Pickens' hometown.

At the end of October, Pickens and two other oil investors got together to form Mesa Partners to buy stock in Phillips and Unocal.

William Douce is determined. At sixty-five, he has wire-framed glasses and a jaunty grin. On the wall of his office is a portrait of Douce in a cowboy hat and caption: "There were a helluva lot of things they didn't tell me when I hired on with this outfit." Douce is tough, some say dictatorial. "Sometimes I'm wrong," he explains, "but I'm never uncertain." He's a member of the Masonic Lodge, the Shrine, the Theta Tau engineering fraternity and the First Presbyterian Church of Bartlesville. The all-purpose affirmative he uses at least five times a day: "You bet." He's a bird hunter: pheasant, duck and quail.

Douce is a native of Caldwell, Kansas, and majored in engineering at the University of Kansas. When he graduated in 1942, Douce landed a job at the Phillips refinery at Borger, Texas. Three years later, he was transferred to Bartlesville and made a supervisor in the refining department. In 1955, Douce got his "big break": he moved to New York to manage the East Coast introduction of Phillips' revolutionary new Marlex plastic, the material used to make Hula-Hoops.

It was up and up after that. Douce worked his way to the top of the Phillips Chemical Company. Then in 1971, he was named one of the three Phillips executive vice presidents, and was promoted to president in 1974. Six years later, Douce was named chief executive. Two years after that, he was chairman.

The Phillips that Douce inherited was plagued with problems. In the mid-seventies, Phillips had been caught with a multimillion-dollar political slush fund; the company chairman pleaded guilty to violations of federal election laws and paid a fine. In 1977, the

Phillips Bravo well blew out and spewed oil into the North Sea for eight days. Three years later, the Phillips refinery in Borger, Texas, exploded. Then one of the legs of the Alexander Keilland platform snapped; 123 people were killed when the rig capsized into the North Sea. While company disasters made headlines, Phillips drilled dry hole after dry hole.

At the end of 1981, Douce embarked on a massive rehabilitation program. He shut down thirteen chemical plants and closed the Kansas City refinery. Douce sold a refinery in Great Falls, Montana, two synthetic rubber plants in Borger, and carbon black factories in Australia and Colombia. Douce put the Nose Rock uranium mine on hold. He cancelled the strategic minerals program. At the same time, Douce slashed the payroll by seven thousand, saving $100 million a year, cut capital expenditures from $2.6 billion in 1981 to $1.4 billion in 1983, and pushed for better drilling results. Although the field Phillips found off the Ivory Coast turned out to have less oil than expected, Phillips found a 500-million-barrel field at Point Arguello off the coast of California. That wasn't enough new oil to satisfy Douce, but it was a start. Phillips kept looking.

At the same time, Douce expanded. In 1982, he orchestrated the $1.2-billion purchase of General American Oil; a year later, he shook hands on the $1.7-billion acquisition of Aminoil, the R. J. Reynolds subsidiary.

Phillips was "in lean and fighting form," but the stock price didn't respond. Until June 1982, Douce didn't worry about that. When Boone Pickens bid for Cities Service, oil companies suddenly became hot takeover targets and Phillips was at the top of every stock watcher's hit list.

Bill Douce started to worry.

A couple of months later, in the fall of 1982, Douce bumped into Boone Pickens at an oil industry conference in Palm Springs. Douce and Pickens were old friends; they'd worked together on the board of the American Petroleum Institute, even hunted quail together. "Boone," said Douce. "When are you going to bid for Phillips?" He laughed. "If you make the right offer, we might take it."

Pickens shook his head. "I'm not going to bid for Phillips." Not now anyway. He was already looking at General American.

Douce was glad to hear that Pickens wasn't about to strike. But maybe someone else would.

Douce asked his investment banker to fortify the company against attack.

In the spring of 1983, Joseph G. Fogg III of Morgan Stanley flew to Bartlesville to make a presentation to the Phillips board. Fogg recommended three charter amendments, aka shark repellents—proposals designed to discourage companies from launching raids. The board agreed to only one of the amendments: the "fair price amendment." A rule that said two thirds of the shareholders had to approve any merger except an all-cash deal at the right price.

In October 1984, two years after Pickens had said he wasn't interested in Phillips, Douce picked up the word that Pickens was looking at Phillips.

That seemed like nonsense, but someone was clearly buying.

Douce had his people investigate. Pickens seemed to be buying stock in both Phillips and Unocal. So was a Houston money manager named Fayez Sarofim. Sarofim was the big buyer. By the end of November, he seemed to have almost 8 million shares of both Phillips and Unocal.

Douce called Joe Fogg at Morgan Stanley.

The president of Morgan Stanley called Sarofim. "Why are you buying so much Phillips stock?" he asked.

"For my institutional clients," said Sarofim.

The Morgan president suspected that Sarofim was working in cooperation with Pickens, but there was nothing he could do.

At the beginning of December, Douce flew to Spain for a J. Ray McDermott drilling company bird-hunting expedition. Fred Hartley of Unocal was also there.

The shooting was good.

Hartley was afraid Pickens was about to raid Unocal.

Douce joked about which one of them would have to dash to Madrid and gun up the Gulfstream.

The oil executives had just finished dinner at ten-thirty on Tuesday night, December 4, when Douce got a message that Bartlesville was on the phone.

He walked into the other room to take the call.

"Listen to this," said the Phillips treasurer. He read a Dow Jones wire:

Mesa Partners, a Texas general partnership made up of affiliates of Mesa Petroleum and Wagner & Brown of Midland, Texas, said it intends to make a cash tender offer for at least 15 million shares of Phillips Petroleum at $60 a share. Mesa Partners added that it is seeking financing to tender for an additional eight million shares. Mesa Partners said it currently owns 8.8 million shares of Phillips or 5.7% of the company. If the partnership acquires 23 million shares through its tenders, ownership would increase to 20.6%.

"I'll be in Bartlesville tomorrow," Douce told the treasurer. He walked back into the dining room. He looked at Hartley. "Relax," said Douce. "I'm it."

Boone Pickens had spent the weekend working out the details of the Phillips offer.

"We're going to make an offer for Phillips and at the same time solicit consents for a new board," Pickens told his takeover team after hours of brainstorming at the Helmsley Palace Hotel in New York. "That will put the company in a squeeze. If the directors start to wreck the company to scare us off, the shareholders will side with us to throw out the board. The question is price."

Pickens finally decided that $60 a share was high enough to keep all but the biggest oil companies from bidding; and Pickens was assured at least $150 million in profits if another company did come in.

"We'll file as soon as we get the papers ready," said Mesa's chief financial officer. The Pickens offer wasn't formal until the disclosure documents were filed at the Securities and Exchange Commission. Filing set the clock ticking: Pickens could buy in twenty business days.

There was only one worry: Mesa had promised a year ago not to buy General American stock for five years. And Phillips owned General American. It was just conceivable that Phillips would get a court to say that the General American contract forbade Mesa from buying Phillips stock.

"That agreement doesn't mention Phillips," said Pickens' lawyer. "We'll file in Delaware to get a declaratory judgment that the

335

agreement doesn't apply to Phillips. The odds that we'll win are seventy-thirty." Mesa was incorporated in Delaware, and the Delaware courts tend to understand business issues.

Two days after Pickens announced Mesa Partners' bid for Phillips, the lawyer called.

"Phillips just sued us in Oklahoma for breaking the GAO standstill," he said. "The judge issued a temporary restraining order to keep us from commencing a formal offer. But we don't have to worry. We've got a very strong case."

The next night, Joseph Flom, the ace takeover lawyer from Skadden, Arps, Slate, Meagher & Flom, called Boone Pickens. Flom wasn't representing Phillips or Mesa, but he was friends with both Pickens and Douce. "Are you interested in selling your stock back to Phillips at a premium?" asked Flom.

"Absolutely not," said Pickens. That was greenmail, a practice that was legal but highly controversial. "We're interested in an LBO." A leveraged buy-out, a deal in which Mesa Partners would buy Phillips with bank loans secured by Phillips assets.

The Mesa team talked strategy all weekend.

Joe Flom, the lawyer-intermediary, called again on Monday. "Phillips isn't interested in an LBO," Flom told Pickens. "But the company has some properties that Mesa might want. Would you be interested in swapping your block of stock? It will be an attractive price." The market price of the block.

"No," said Pickens. He thought "attractive" meant less than the Phillips properties were worth, and that was totally unacceptable. That was greenmail.

All along, Pickens had expected Phillips to resist his offer, but he hadn't expected the kind of resistance he got. Their tactics were awfully underhanded.

Phillips hired a detective to investigate rumors that Pickens was illegally tipping off members of the Amarillo Country Club about his bids. As far as Pickens could tell, all the man did was harass Pickens' family.

Phillips sued Pickens in Oklahoma for violating the GAO standstill and for the alleged tip-offs, formally called "insider trading." Initially the court ruled for Phillips. Pickens fumed. He hadn't violated any agreements. He hadn't tipped off anyone.

Phillips lined up two wholesalers to file a class action suit on the grounds that a Pickens takeover would hurt their business; Phillips paid the wholesalers' legal bills and indemnified them against losses.

The town of Bartlesville worked itself into a frenzy. The Chamber of Commerce held an anti-Pickens "crisis forum." A local store printed hundreds of "Boone Buster" T-shirts. The First Baptist Church organized a two-week round-the-clock prayer vigil. The public school system encouraged children to write postcards to President Reagan about Pickens' bid. More than three thousand postcards arrived in Washington. Phillips employees belted out a new song:

> There's gonna be a meeting at the old town hall tonight.
> And if they try to stop us, there's gonna be a fight.
> We're gonna get our company out of this awful fix.
> 'Cause we don't want to change our name to Pickens 66.

"If I buy Phillips, my wife and I will move to Bartlesville," said Pickens. "There won't be any massive layoffs. Mesa has just 660 employees. Phillips has 29,000. There isn't much job overlap."

Bill Douce had flown from Spain to new York via Bartlesville the day after the Pickens announcement crossed the wire. For days now, he had been holed up in a suite at the Helmsley Palace Hotel plotting to save Phillips.

"The Pickens offer is no good," said Joe Fogg, the investment banker. "Boone is offering cash for just 15 percent of the stock. It isn't clear what he's going to do after that. If he buys the rest of the stock, it probably won't be in cash. The shareholders won't profit from this."

Douce nodded.

"Pickens is interested in the Mesa shareholders," said Fogg. "He doesn't care about the Phillips shareholders or the Phillips employees or Bartlesville. And we've got our backs to the wall. Some of the things that we'll have to do to protect the shareholders will make the institutions mad. Institutions like takeovers." Institutions owned about half of Phillips stock.

"Our best defense is probably the General American standstill," said Marty Lipton, the takeover lawyer from Wachtell, Lipton, Rosen & Katz. "We've got a good chance of winning the case. If we win, we'll stop Pickens in his tracks."

"Look at all the alternatives," said Douce.

By the end of the week, when the rumors were swirling, Fred Hartley of Unocal called. He had just gotten back from the McDermott hunting trip. "The word is rampant that there is going to be a marriage between Phillips and Unocal," said Hartley. "I want you to know it didn't start with me."

"It didn't start with me either," said Douce. Buying Unocal might make Phillips too big for Pickens to swallow, but it didn't make a lot of business sense.

Douce took the elevator down to the lobby.

Boone Pickens was waiting to get on. He looked like he had just been jogging. "Hi, Bill," said Pickens. He reached out to shake hands.

"How's things?" asked Douce. He hadn't expected Pickens. Douce had assumed that Pickens was staying around the corner at the Waldorf-Astoria; that's where Pickens had lived during the Cities fight.

Pickens grinned. The elevator doors closed.

"The courts have blocked Mesa for now," said Marty Lipton when the Phillips team sat down on December 14. By then, Phillips had filed half a dozen lawsuits; they'd tried to subpoena Drexel, but John Sorte, the partner on the Mesa account, insisted that Drexel wasn't involved. "But that could change; the courts could still rule for Pickens on appeal. We need to talk about defenses."

"Morgan Stanley has looked at a lot of alternatives for Phillips," said Fogg. "A white knight. A defensive acquisition. A self-tender. Buying back the Pickens block. We considered a leveraged buy-out of Phillips, but we couldn't line up the bank financing. We looked at buying Mesa. That doesn't make sense. Mesa is over-priced." Besides, Mesa Petroleum didn't control the Phillips shares, Mesa Partners did—and Phillips couldn't buy Mesa Partners: it was a partnership. "We've been looking at a recapitalization."

Offering to buy back shares of stock with newly printed bonds. "That might get rid of Pickens, but it will leave the company vulnerable. There won't be much stock left on the market. A raider could buy the company cheap."

"Why don't we do an exchange offer and put half of the remaining shares in a trust for employees," suggested Lipton.

Phillips would offer to exchange stock for a package of debt securities; each shareholder could decide whether or not to send in his stock. "The employees could pay for those shares with wage concessions. If half the stock is in an employee trust, then a raider can't buy control without the okay of the trustee. And the trustee would only sell if the price were right."

"We can afford to buy 70 percent of the stock for notes worth $77 a share," said Fogg.

"We'll have to sell $2 billion worth of assets," said the president of Phillips. "We'll cut the capital-spending budget. We'll cut expenses."

"If we do an exchange offer for 70 percent of the stock, we won't be able to sell commercial paper," said the chief financial officer. "We'll have to line up a bank loan. Our debt rating will drop from AA to BB. The bonds will be junk bonds."

"The only alternative is a recapitalization and I don't think that's wise," said Lipton. "A recap has to be approved by the shareholders, and the soonest you can schedule a vote is February. Phillips would be a sitting target for two months. The arbs own 8 percent of your stock." The traders who make money buying and selling takeover stocks. "They'd sell if some company tried to make a low raid. Besides, if Pickens opposes the recapitalization, the shareholders might not pass it."

A 70 percent exchange offer seemed like the best alternative.

The board approved the terms at the meeting December 16, but Lipton and Fogg decided not to call Pickens until they had heard the final decision on the standstill case. The GAO suits had been consolidated in Delaware, and on Thursday, December 20, the court decided that the standstill between GAO and Mesa did not apply to Phillips.

"We've got to negotiate with Pickens," said Fogg. "Now he is free to make an offer, and if he makes an offer, we've got just twenty days and no good alternatives. We've got to think of a way to get him to go back to Amarillo without bidding."

Douce nodded.

"The odds are good that if we settle with Pickens, no one else will come in," said Fogg. "None of the oil companies are interested. Phillips is too big for a raider like Carl Icahn or Irwin Jacobs. If Pickens pledges to vote with us, being a sitting duck for two months while we wait for the shareholder vote on our recapitalization isn't a big worry anymore."

That was good.

"We don't need to implement the plan we talked about at the board meeting," said Fogg. "I think Pickens will settle for less than 70 percent. He wants out. He's been burned by the backlash in Bartlesville. Stock watchers say he overbid. Oil prices are down. I think we could get rid of Pickens by buying back just 30 percent of the stock."

"Let's try," said Douce.

Fogg called Joe Flom, the lawyer who had tried to start negotiations before.

Flom set up a meeting the next night. Fogg and Lipton were representing Phillips. The Mesa chief financial officer negotiated for Mesa Partners.

"We're looking at a recapitalization," said Fogg.

The Mesa CFO nodded.

"Do you want to be stopped out now?" asked Lipton. Did Mesa want Phillips to buy its block of stock?

"No," said the CFO. He wasn't interested in greenmail.

"We're going to buy 30 percent of our stock for notes with a face value of $60 a share," said Fogg. "We're going to sell 35 percent of that stock to an ESOP." An employee stock ownership plan.

The two teams talked through the details.

"What's this package worth?" asked Mesa's chief financial officer. Clearly $60 a share for 30 percent of the shares was worth $18 a share. What the remaining 70 percent of the shares would be worth after the buyback wasn't certain.

"Fifty-three a share," said Fogg. He showed the CFO a page of calculations.

"The only rule we're working under is that you won't be a continuing shareholder," said Lipton. "We will buy all your shares."

"We're not selling our stock to Phillips," said the Mesa CFO. That looked like greenmail. "But we'll sell it to Morgan Stanley." At the same $53-a-share price that the other stockholders got. That wasn't greenmail. "Morgan Stanley can do what it wants with the shares."

That was okay with Phillips.

The meeting broke up.

"It wasn't a negotiating session," the CFO told Pickens when the Mesa team caucused. "They just showed us what they'll do if we don't settle."

"They could easily change the $60 a share in notes to $60 a share in cash," said Pickens. "That would beat our offer. The ESOP will make Phillips bulletproof. If they implement that plan and we don't sell them our stock, we can't win."

The CFO called Fogg after midnight. "We're willing to talk," he said. "This plan might be acceptable if you change some of the terms. You'll have to buy 50 percent of the stock in notes. You'll have to buy $1 billion more of it with cash."

"We're within striking distance of an agreement," said Fogg. "We'll send over a draft tomorrow morning."

When the Mesa CFO read the draft, it wasn't what he thought Fogg had agreed to. The text said that Phillips would buy 30 percent of its stock for debt; the agreement would be interpreted under Oklahoma law. Mesa Partners would get $53 a share in cash.

The Mesa CFO called Fogg. "Forget it," he said. "If this is what you call negotiating, we don't want to be part of it. We thought you were talking more than 30 percent. We find this Oklahoma law clause offensive." Mesa hadn't been treated well in Oklahoma courts: Phillips had sued Pickens there for violating the GAO standstill clause.

"You don't have to negotiate," said Fogg. "We're willing to keep on fighting." Fogg hadn't thought anything was settled on the phone the night before; he thought he and the CFO had just been trading ideas. The Oklahoma courts hadn't even been mentioned.

"We're packing," said the Mesa CFO.

Fogg called an hour later. "We'll drop the Oklahoma clause," he said. "We're waiting if you want to negotiate."

The Mesa CFO headed to Fogg's office.

The two teams argued all day.

"I don't understand why you're being so tough," Flom told Pickens late in the afternoon. "You're getting $53 a share in cash."

By midnight, Mesa and Phillips had agreed to a buyback of 38 percent of the stock. Everything was settled but the fine print.

First thing Sunday morning, Bill Douce called Boone Pickens to make sure he felt they were close to an agreement. Then he called the Phillips directors and told them to fly to New York.

Pickens called Douce early in the afternoon. "We've cleared up all the details," he said.

"Come up to my suite," said Douce. "Let's visit."

Pickens came.

The Phillips president and chief financial officer walked in. Pickens walked over to shake the president's hand. The man took off his coat and hung it up. He looked at Pickens. He hesitated. Finally he shook. Then he walked into one of the bedrooms.

Pickens and Douce sat down.

They chatted about quail hunting. They talked about the rumors that Pickens was going to run for governor of Texas.

"You hurt Phillips, Boone," said Douce. "You made us load up with debt."

"I helped the shareholders," said Pickens.

Douce was silent for a minute. "Why did you bid for Phillips, Boone?" he asked. "You told me two years ago you weren't going to."

"I didn't promise anything," said Pickens.

Douce shook his head. "You know, Boone, if you and your wife had lived in Bartlesville for six months, you probably would have won their hearts. But I don't think you would have lasted six weeks."

The Phillips board approved the Mesa Partners settlement that night. Late Monday afternoon, Christmas Eve, Douce flew to Bartlesville for a press conference. Then he flew to Kansas City to spend Christmas with his daughter and her husband. He slept well that night for the first time in almost a month.

The battle was over.

* * *

"Happy New Year," said Ivan Boesky. He twisted the telephone cord.

"Happy New Year to you too," said Carl Icahn.

"I hear you're involved in Phillips," said Boesky.

"I bought some stock," said Icahn.

"The recap plan that Phillips just announced is a bad deal for shareholders," said Boesky. "If the employees own 30 percent of the company, Phillips will be takeover-proof. No one will ever make a bid." The employees would never sell their shares to a raider. "Phillips is ripe for a proxy fight."

Icahn raised an eyebrow. He'd heard that Boesky had 3 million Phillips shares. "Proxy fights generally don't work," said Icahn. "And besides, proxy fights aren't my style. It's always more powerful to have a lot of stock and do a tender."

"Someone has to do something about Phillips," said Boesky.

"I know," said Icahn. "There's got to be a tender. I can put up $400 or $500 million."

"I might join you," said Boesky.

"You'd have to put up $150 million," said Icahn.

"That's too much," said Boesky. "I'll put up something."

"Well," said Icahn. "I'm still not sure I'm going to do anything. If I do, I'll probably be on my own. I don't like partnerships."

Carl Icahn is contentious. At forty-nine, he is six feet tall, with flashing brown eyes and dark wavy hair. He's a topnotch chess strategist; for years, he was obsessive about poker. Icahn leads the good life: he lives on a thirty-eight-acre estate in Westchester, travels in a private plane and drives a maroon stretch Cadillac limo and a silver Mercedes 500. He's a corporate raider par excellence— and proud of it: the reception area of his New York office is decorated with framed annual report covers of companies he has beaten. Icahn is zealous, single-minded and candid. "I'm not a Robin Hood," he says. "I buy stock in a company to do something."

Icahn grew up in middle-class Bayswater, Queens, the son of a small-time lawyer. He was the first graduate of Far Rockaway

High School to go to Princeton. After he got his philosophy degree in 1957, Icahn headed to medical school but quit after two years: studying sickness made him a hypochondriac. He landed a job as a trainee at the Dreyfus Corporation, made $50,000 in the 1961 bull market and lost everything when prices collapsed a year later. He sold his car to make ends meet and decided never to stake his earnings on the stock market again. He spent the next few years jumping from one small options house to another, and in 1968, he borrowed $400,000 from his uncle to form Icahn & Company, an options and arbitrage boutique.

Ten years later, Icahn had made more than $100 million. But the game was getting crowded. Icahn decided that instead of betting money that someone else would launch a corporate raid, he would launch the raids himself. He would find an undervalued company and then threaten a proxy fight or takeover. That seemed like a no-lose strategy: either the company would perform, or it would sell out to a white knight bidder, or it would buy back Icahn's stock at a premium.

Icahn bought 5 percent of Tappan stove for $8 a share and made $10 a share when Electrolux bought the company a year later. He wrestled with Dan River textiles, drove Marshall Field into the arms of BAT Industries, greenmailed American Can, and forced Chesebrough-Pond to buy the polymer plastics division of Icahn-controlled ACF.

When Icahn read about the Phillips recapitalization plan, he smelled business.

On December 27, just four days after Pickens struck his deal with Phillips, Carl Icahn started to buy Phillips stock.

Irwin Jacobs, the raider-investor, called from Minneapolis. "I'm getting involved in Phillips and I'm buying stock," he said.

"You do what you want," said Icahn.

"The Phillips plan is a bad bet for the shareholders," said Jacobs.

"No kidding," said Icahn.

"The price of the stock is going to go way down," said Jacobs.

"Yeah," said Icahn.

On Sunday, December 30, Ivan Boesky, the biggest arbitrageur on Wall Street, called Carl Icahn to talk about Phillips.

Jacobs and Boesky and a dozen other arbs kept calling Icahn to talk about Phillips. Icahn kept buying stock and thinking.

"Why don't you talk to Drexel?" Boesky suggested when he called.

"Maybe I will," said Icahn. "When I make up my mind."

John Sorte flew to Hawaii for two weeks of vacation on December 26. Since Mesa wasn't going to buy Phillips after all, Pickens wouldn't be needing Drexel to raise cash.

Just after New Year's, Paul Higbee, Sorte's deputy in the oil and gas department, called.

"We're thinking of doing something on Phillips," said Higbee. "The market doesn't like the recap plan." Phillips stock had dropped $10 a share the day after the announcement. One company watcher had labeled it the "Phillips Phizzle"; the *New York Times* estimated that traders had lost $100 million on the deal. "This looks like an opportunity for us. Phillips is worth at least $53 a share and the recap plan is worth less than $45. Phillips is putting the plan up for a shareholder vote. We've got two months to find a buyer."

Sorte nodded. Phillips was certainly an opportunity, but he wasn't sure for whom. Most of Drexel's traditional oil and gas clients wouldn't be interested. Mesa couldn't bid. Coastal was thinking of making a bid for American Natural Resorces. Occidental Petroleum was negotiating a merger with Diamond Shamrock.

"We've put together an LBO proposal," said Higbee. "We're making up a list of companies and investors to call. If we find a new bidder for Phillips, is that going to be a problem for Mesa?"

"I can't see why," said Sorte. "Mesa's signed a standstill. If there's a bid higher than $53 a share, Pickens can tender."

By the time Sorte got back from Hawaii, the papers were ready. Sorte looked over the numbers. He looked at the list of potential bidders.

"There's one thing I want to make clear," said Fred Joseph, the head of the investment banking department, when Sorte and the other corporate finance partners sat down to talk through the plan. "We're not going to get involved in greenmail. Whoever wants our help has to sign a letter promising not to sell any Phillips stock back to Phillips except on the same basis as every other shareholder."

Sorte nodded. Drexel had been criticized for financing greenmail. Boone Pickens was being accused of greenmailing Phillips.

"Let's go," said Joseph.

The head of the mergers and acquisitions department started to make calls. He tried a leveraged–buy-out group in New York. The group was interested, but the talks bogged down.

The M&A man left a message with the Pennzoil chairman's secretary. He called Lazard Frères, Pennzoil's investment bank.

Pennzoil didn't call back. Neither did Lazard.

What about Phillips management? The M&A man called Phillips' investment bank. No call back.

Then Ivan Boesky called. "What are you doing about Phillips?" he asked. "There are values there. Phillips is an opportunity."

"Look at this," said Boone Pickens. He pointed to the stack of newspaper clippings on his desk. "Now that Phillips stock has dropped $10 a share, we're being charged with greenmail."

The Mesa chief financial officer thumbed through the articles.

The *New York Times*: "The decline in Phillips stock undoubtedly sullied Mr. Pickens' reputation in the arbitrage community. Yesterday arbitrageurs said that they felt let down by the Texan. They asserted that at $53 a share, Mr. Pickens would be bought out at a price that could be significantly above what the other shareholders will receive."

The *Dallas Morning News*: "'I have heard people say they will never do another of Pickens deals again,' said a Dallas oil company watcher. 'But that's emotions taking over.'"

Barron's: "It's a clear case of red and greenmail, in keeping with the season. Boone barrels out of Bartlesville, practically swathed in cash, leaving Phillips' other shareholders green with envy and scarlet with rage."

And many more.

"We have to do something," said Pickens. "Phillips has to get the value of the plan up. We've got to stop this greenmail talk."

"We have to be careful," said the lawyer. "We've got an agreement with Phillips to support the plan."

"We can still make an informal suggestion," said Pickens. "We can propose an LBO at $53 a share. Phillips wasn't interested when we brought up the idea before, but with the stock at $45 a share, they might have a different feeling."

Agreed.

Pickens dictated a letter:

Dear Bill:

I am sure that you are as surprised as I am that the agreement for Phillips' recapitalization has been so misunderstood and so maligned. Our agreement has been incorrectly characterized as one which will significantly weaken Phillips and as greenmail by Mesa Partners. We entered into the agreement based on the belief that the program you proposed would significantly increase values for all shareholders. Towards that end, there are alternate courses which could accomplish our mutual objectives. You and your board might wish to consider a leveraged buy out at $53 a share. In that event, I want you to know that Mesa Partners is prepared to cooperate fully.

I trust that you will accept this letter in the constructive spirit in which it is offered. If you would like to discuss this more fully, I'd be pleased to visit with you.

Pickens waited.

No reply.

The rumors started. Jacobs was buying. Icahn was buying.

Finally Douce's letter arrived.

Dear Boone,

While we are also surprised that the proposed recapitalization plan has been misunderstood by the public, we continue to believe that the plan is in the best interests of Phillips and its stockholders. Without discussing the issue of whether your letter is consistent with the provisions of Section 12 of our agreement, we look forward to your support of the plan and your favorable vote at the shareholders' meeting.

Bill Douce had spent the first two weeks of January calling Phillips shareholders to talk about the recap plan and boning up on corporate raiders.

347

He read up on Carl Icahn and Irwin Jacobs.

He read about Sir James Goldsmith and David Murdock and Ivan Boesky.

Douce wasn't too worried. It would take $9 billion to buy Phillips. Icahn couldn't borrow that much. Neither could Jacobs. And Joe Fogg knew that Pennzoil wasn't interested.

Then on January 7, Bill Douce got the letter from Boone Pickens.

When Douce read it to Marty Lipton, Lipton frowned. "We've already agreed that a leverage buy-out doesn't make sense," said Lipton. "A recapitalization is the best alternative."

"Isn't Pickens supposed to support the recap?" asked Douce. This letter wasn't very supportive.

"Yes," said Lipton. "In public."

Douce nodded. They'd remind Boone.

At the end of the week Douce sent Pickens a reply.

Then he flew to the Phillips ranch for two days of hunting.

Boone Pickens called. "There are all kinds of rumors," he said. "Jacobs is buying. Icahn is buying."

"I've heard," said Douce. He'd had a couple of telephone messages from Carl Icahn, but Joe Fogg had told him not to call back. Fogg didn't want Icahn to get the idea that Phillips would negotiate.

"You've got to do something," said Pickens. "Phillips is vulnerable. You ought to consider a leveraged buy-out. Mesa will help you raise the money."

"We're not interested in an LBO, Boone," said Douce. "We think the recap plan is the best thing for the shareholders. We think that the recap plan will pass."

"Bill," said Pickens. "You have to do something. You're playing with the big boys now."

"I thought you were a big boy, Boone," said Douce.

Carl Icahn stared at the *New York Times* headline:

"Phillips Opposed by Jacobs."

Then he skimmed the story. Irwin Jacobs owned a block of Phillips stock; he would vote against the recap plan. Icahn dialed Minneapolis. "What are you going to do?" Icahn asked Jacobs. "Are you going to make a tender offer?"

"What are *you* going to do?" Jacobs asked Icahn.

"I don't know," said Icahn.

"Why don't you come out and say something?" asked Jacobs. "Why don't you come out against the deal?"

"When I am ready to do something, I will do it," said Icahn.

Ivan Boesky called Carl Icahn again a couple of days later.

"What about Phillips?" asked Boesky. "Why don't you talk to Drexel? Drexel has an LBO plan."

"I've decided not to get involved," said Icahn. "I've stopped buying."

Phillips stock dropped to $43 a share.

Icahn started to buy again. Maybe he would get involved after all.

Then, a Morgan Stanley partner called Icahn. "I understand you are buying Phillips stock," he said. "I don't think you realize what you're getting into."

Boesky called again. "You ought to talk to Drexel," he said. "Drexel has put together an LBO for Phillips."

"Maybe," said Icahn. "I'm not ready to commit."

But he kept buying.

By January 4, Icahn had more than 4 million shares.

Icahn dialed Leon Black, head of Drexel leveraged–buy-out group, and Icahn's investment banker.

"What's on your mind, Carl?" asked Black.

"Phillips Petroleum," said Icahn. "I'm thinking about doing a deal."

Leon Black is roguish. At thirty-four, he is six feet three, with wavy brown hair and brown eyes. He spends weekends hunting antiques and romping with his one-year-old son Benjamin, but he has no hobbies, no diversions. "I like what I do," he explains. Still, he admits that it would be nice to be able to buy a series of concert tickets and be able to attend more than one or two of the events.

Black grew up in New York City and majored in philosophy at Dartmouth. He toyed with the idea of becoming a writer but, to the chagrin of his professors, decided that he had to make money instead. When he finished at the Harvard business school in 1975, he landed a job as a consultant at Peat Marwick Mitchell. After a one-year stint as the assistant to the publisher of *Boardroom Reports*, Black lined up an interview at Drexel Burnham Lambert; investment banking looked exciting, and Drexel seemed to be the place for someone on the fast track. Black spent three years doing legwork for corporate finance accounts. Then he decided that it was time to establish his own niche. He convinced his bosses to let him set up a financing group to target the cable television business. Between 1981 and 1983, he logged fifteen deals worth $1.5 billion, all with new Drexel clients. Black was named a partner—his four-year apprenticeship was the shortest on record—and given a new assignment: leveraged buy-outs. Black put together the $600-million buy-out of Days Inns, the $635-million buy-out of Blue Bell clothing (Wrangler jeans and Jantzen swimming suits), and the $1.35-billion buy-out of Northwest Industries. Black also helped Metromedia go private. By then, Black's department was the number-one factor in the buy-out business with $4.5 billion worth of deals in 1984, more than ten times the volume of the closest competitor.

In the summer of 1984, Carl Icahn called Drexel to arrange a refinancing of his $300-million buy-out of ACF. Black lined up $523 million, enough to pay off the $225 million of old debt and leave a $300-million war chest. Icahn didn't have a new target in mind, and during the fall, Black and Icahn talked on and off about possible companies. Nothing seemed quite right.

In late December, Icahn called Black to say that he was thinking about Phillips.

Black didn't think that meant anything. Icahn thought about a lot of companies. Black flew to Saint Moritz for two weeks of vacation.

Just after Black got back, Icahn called again. Now he owned 5 million shares of Phillips, and he wanted to do something.

"I don't think we're representing anyone else on Phillips," said Black. "I'll get back to you." Black called the head of the M&A department to find out what was going on with the Phillips proposal.

"We don't have a buyer," said the man. "Icahn is on our call list, but we weren't sure that he wanted to try something this big."

350

Black called Fred Joseph, executive vice president and head of investment banking.

"Icahn is fine," said Joseph. "But remember that we decided to try Phillips only if we could get a written promise that there wouldn't be greenmail."

Black called Icahn.

"I'm not going to greenmail," said Icahn.

"Why don't you come down here and talk?" said Black.

"No," said Icahn. "We'll meet at my office." Tuesday, January 29.

Black called John Sorte. "Icahn is interested in Phillips," said Black. "He's got about 5 million shares."

"I'm thinking about launching a proxy fight," said Icahn when he sat down with Black and Sorte on Tuesday. Now Icahn owned almost 7.5 million Phillips shares; he'd just bought 2.7 million shares from Ivan Boesky.

"That's okay," said Sorte. "But it doesn't make a lot of sense unless you present shareholders with an alternative."

They talked.

"I'll get back to you," said Icahn.

Black called Icahn the next morning.

There was a meeting that day. There was a meeting Thursday.

By Friday, Icahn had made up his mind. He would launch a proxy fight and make a friendly offer for Phillips. Donaldson, Lufkin & Jenrette, the brokerage house whose oil company watcher had called the recap plan the "Phillips Phizzle," would help line up votes against the plan. Drexel would raise the cash for the Icahn bid.

Black and Sorte caught a cab to Icahn's office for a strategy meeting late in the afternoon.

"I'm going to offer $55 a share," said Icahn. Drexel estimated that Phillips was worth as much as $65 a share. "Fifty-five a share in cash for half the shares, $55 in notes for the rest."

The price seemed right.

The bankers and Icahn talked about tactics for several hours.

"We need a letter committing Drexel to raise the money," said Icahn late in the afternoon.

A Drexel lawyer shook his head. "No," he said. "We can't

351

commit to raising money. That's underwriting. But don't worry. We can raise the cash."

"So why can't you commit?" asked Icahn.

Black looked at the lawyer.

The bankers and lawyers argued.

"We will write a letter saying that we're confident that we can raise the cash," suggested the lawyer.

"That's not enough," said Icahn.

"A letter is a very strong statement on Wall Street," said Sorte. "The institutions will know that if we say we can raise the money, we can."

Icahn rolled his eyes.

They argued for hours.

"A friendly deal isn't going to work," said Icahn. "Fifty-five a share is a steal. It's too cheap." Phillips had already turned down Pickens' offer of $60 a share.

"I don't know if we'll be able to finance a hostile offer," said Black. "It might take us a month to raise $4.5 billion if the bid is hostile. You can't wait a month to announce your bid. The shareholder meeting is February 22."

"A hostile offer is the only way I have a chance for the company," said Icahn. "We are going to have to go hostile."

Sorte looked at the Drexel lawyer. "Can we make an offer before financing is lined up?" he asked.

The lawyer thought. "I don't see why not," he said. "You can make the offer conditional on getting financing." No one had ever tried that before.

The meeting broke up late in the night.

Icahn and Black and Sorte were on the phone with each other most of the day Saturday. By midnight, Icahn had agreed to a letter.

Sunday night, Black drove into New York from his house in Weston, Connecticut, for a meeting in the DLJ board room.

"I've changed my mind," said Icahn. "I need something better than a letter saying that you're confident. That isn't strong enough."

"We can say we're highly confident," said Black.

They talked.

"No," said Icahn near midnight. "A letter isn't enough."

Black raised his eyebrows.

"If you can't give me a commitment, you can forget about the offer," said Icahn.

Black couldn't give a commitment.

The meeting broke up.

Black called Sorte. "Carl changed his mind," he said. "No bid."

First thing Monday morning, Black and Sorte both went to a Drexel Corporate finance committee meeting.

Black got to his office just after eleven.

Carl Icahn called. "I've been thinking," he said. "Maybe a letter that says you're highly confident is enough. Get up here. Let's talk."

Sorte and Black caught a cab.

"We'll need a commitment fee of 1 percent," said Black. Icahn would have to pay investors who agreed to buy bonds, whether or not Icahn won Phillips. "One half a percentage point for Drexel. One half a percentage point for our clients." That was the going rate.

"No," said Icahn. "That's too much money. With my name and reputation, you are not going to have trouble raising the money. You will raise it easy."

"One percent," said Black.

"Forget it," said Icahn.

Icahn called Mike Milken, the head of the Drexel junk bond sales department in Beverly Hills. "For Chrissakes," said Icahn. "You can do this deal and there should not be any problem. One percent is too high a commitment fee. I want you to be my partners."

Milken called Leon Black.

"We're willing to cut our fees and be a partner," Black told Icahn later in the afternoon. "But we can't cut the fees for our clients."

"Maybe we can work something out," said Icahn.

"The fee will be half a percentage point," said Black. "One quarter for Drexel. One quarter for our clients. Drexel gets 25 percent of your profits."

"Half a percentage point is okay," said Icahn. "Ten percent of profits."

Black tried to negotiate.

Icahn wouldn't budge.

Just after four, Icahn called Joe Fogg. "I'm going to make a proposal," said Icahn. "I'll be at your office at five."

"Come on over," said Fogg.

But first there were the papers to draft: Icahn's letter to Phillips, Icahn's no-greenmail letter to Drexel, the Drexel engagement letter, the term sheet.

Icahn was running late. At half past five, Icahn buzzed his secretary. "Call Fogg," he said. "Tell him I've been delayed. I'll be there at six."

The teams kept working on the papers.

At seven-thirty, everything was almost done. Icahn buzzed his secretary. "Call Fogg," he said. "Tell him I'm out the door."

An hour later, Icahn was still working on the text of the letter. He buzzed his secretary. "Better call Joe Fogg," he said. "Tell him I'm not quite out the door yet, but I'll be there soon."

"I'm not calling," said the secretary.

"What?" said Icahn.

"I've already embarrassed myself," said the secretary. "You call."

Icahn called.

By nine o'clock, the papers were finally done.

Icahn took the elevator down to the lobby and walked the six blocks down Sixth Avenue to Morgan Stanley headquarters in the Exxon Building.

Joe Fogg was waiting.

Icahn handed him the letter.

Fogg skimmed it.

Icahn owned 7.5 million shares of Phillips. Icahn thought that the recap plan was worth $43 a share. Icahn proposed that he put together an LBO of Phillips in which shareholders got $55 a share in cash or stock. If Phillips didn't accept the Icahn offer or change its offer so that it was worth $55 a share by February 6, Icahn would solicit proxies against the recap—and force the LBO by offering to buy the stock directly from shareholders. Icahn would not accept greenmail.

"Well?" asked Icahn.

"What kind of experience have you had running an oil company?" asked Fogg.

"None," said Icahn. "But I want current management..." He stopped. "I didn't come over here for an interview. What difference does it make what I know about oil companies? I'm offering good money for Phillips."

"We'll have to release this to the public," said Fogg. "We'll get back to you."

Bill Douce had been busy since Boone Pickens had interrupted his hunting trip to say that the "big boys" were buying Phillips. He had been on the phone trying to convince shareholders to vote for the recap plan. He had talked to employees about the ESOP. He had talked to Joe Fogg.

On Monday, February 4, when Douce was at the lodge after a day of quail hunting, Joe Fogg called.

"Carl Icahn just made an offer for Phillips," said Fogg.

Douce could guess what Icahn had in mind. "I'll be in New York tomorrow," he said. A day before the hunting trip was scheduled to end.

Fogg called again half an hour later. This time Marty Lipton, the takeover lawyer, was on the line. So were Phillips' president and chief financial officer.

"We're going to have to respond to the proposal," said Lipton. "We'll need to make out a list of questions."

"Icahn has set a deadline of Wednesday afternoon," said Fogg. "We don't have much time."

"I'll call a board meeting," said Douce. "You get the questions."

Douce was in New York Tuesday afternoon. By then, the lawyers had already sent a list of questions to Icahn. The deadline for the answers was five o'clock.

The answers arrived by messenger just before the deadline.

Douce read them through.

"These aren't satisfactory," said Lipton.

They were short. They were evasive. Icahn seemed to be making a lot of promises that Douce didn't think he could keep.

The board met at Wachtell, Lipton that afternoon.

"Icahn's proposal clearly isn't a good deal for shareholders," said Fogg. "The price is too low. We think Phillips is worth $60 to $75 a share. Besides, Icahn's offer isn't certain. I don't think he can line up financing, no matter what Drexel says."

"What can we do?" asked Douce.

"The best alternative is to sweeten the recap plan," said Fogg.

"We are suggesting that you issue 'fair value' rights to protect the shareholders from bids," said Lipton. Stockholders would get one right per share—a note that could be exchanged for a one-year Phillips bond worth $62 if someone bought 30 percent of Phillips; if the recap plan was defeated, the rights would protect Phillips against a bid below $62 a share; the rights would expire if the plan passed.

The directors talked.

Finally they agreed: Phillips would pay shareholders an additional $3.32 a share in preferred stock. Phillips would give all shareholders special "fair value" rights.

"The rights are risky," said Fogg. "Institutions might call them a poison pill." A special kind of stock that dramatically increased the price that a raider had to pay for a company. "Institutions don't like pills. Still, I think we'll win. We are offering shareholders a good deal."

John Sorte caught a cab up to Icahn's office as soon as Icahn called to say that Phillips had sent over a list of questions—Leon Black was in Chicago negotiating another buy-out. Sorte didn't like the idea of a list: no one ever sends written questions. When one company proposes to buy another, the investment bankers sit down and talk things through.

Sorte skimmed the sheet.

15. Who will manage the company if your proposal is accepted? What experience do you or they have in managing a major integrated international oil company?

16. Will you liquidate the company? What asset sales do you contemplate to pay down indebtedness? What do you anticipate will be the timing of such sales or the amount realized?

17. What plans do you have concerning capital expenditures by the company?

18. What are your plans concerning the company's arrangements with its jobbers, suppliers, etc.?

19. Do you plan to maintain a major headquarters operation in Bartlesville?

"This looks like the questions that they asked Boone during the lawsuit," said Sorte. "With some additions by committee."

Icahn laughed.

"Clearly Phillips is going to turn us down," said Sorte. "They're going to use our answers as ammunition for their press releases."

"We've got to answer," said Icahn. "They're hoping we don't."

"They'll probably just sweeten the recap plan to look like $55 a share to make us go away," said Sorte.

"Yeah," said Icahn.

The Phillips press release arrived late Wednesday afternoon.

The board had indeed sweetened the recap plan—Phillips said by $3 a share, but it looked more like $1 a share to Sorte—and it had adopted a poison pill.

"That was a risky move," said the head of the Drexel M&A department. "Institutions don't like these things. They make companies hard to take over—and big shareholders like to get takeover premiums for their stock."

"The pill might not be legal," said the Drexel lawyer. The Delaware court had just ruled that pills adopted as part of an overall antitakeover strategy were legal, but this pill was different: it was directed against a single shareholder, Carl Icahn.

"We've got to respond," said Icahn.

Black and Sorte and the head of the Drexel M&A department and Icahn brainstormed.

Finally they decided to swallow the pill.

That made sense.

If Icahn bought another 25 percent of Phillips, then all the shareholders, including Icahn, would have the right to exchange their stock for a note worth $62 a share, $19 a share more than Icahn thought he'd get from the recap.

"I'll have to raise my price," said Icahn. Phillips had sweetened its recap price. "I'll bid $57 a share for 25 percent of the stock."

The team drafted a letter and sent it over to Morgan Stanley by messenger.

Sorte and Black and Icahn went home.

The other bankers headed to Le Cirque, the three-star restaurant at the Mayfair Regent, for dinner with lawyers from Skadden, Arps, Joe Flom's firm. They chatted about the poison pill.

357

"Icahn's proposal won't work," said one of the Skadden lawyers. "I don't care what the press release says. Marty's pills kill when swallowed."

Bill Douce was puzzled by Carl Icahn's newest proposal. Icahn wanted to swallow the pill. Clearly Icahn didn't understand how the pill worked.

The Phillips bankers and lawyers sat down at the conference room table to draft a reply:

Dear Mr. Icahn,

As the enclosed press release states, we find your letter setting forth your new intended tender offer difficult to interpret. As we read your letter it would appear that you think that the new Phillips rights would provide that a person who acquires 30% or more of Phillips common stock would have the right to exchange his common stock for the senior notes. This is not so.

We suggest that you might want to review the supplementary proxy material prior to making further proposals to take over or bust up Phillips. We also suggest that you reconsider the now improved recapitalization plan. We believe that its value is so close to the values you seem to find that you would not really wish to attempt to force the bust up and liquidation of Phillips and the resultant hardship to the thousands of employees who would be thrown out of work, all for the purpose of your making a few dollars more profit on the stock you bought during the past few weeks. Phillips is acting responsibly and responsively to the interests of its shareholders. We hope that you too will act responsibly.

Leon Black couldn't believe that Phillips had written that letter. It was nasty—and it was unfair. Icahn had promised not to bust up Phillips.

Icahn tossed the letter aside. "Let's talk strategy," he said.

They talked.

"You'll have to make your offer conditional on the board repealing the poison pill," said Sorte.

Icahn nodded. "We'll solicit consents and elect a new board of directors." The same technique that Boone Pickens had tried before. "I'll go on the board. So will Al." Al Kingsley, Icahn's number two. "Black. Sorte." Plus someone from DLJ.

The team kept talking.

"Okay," said Icahn late Friday night. "I'm going to make an offer for the whole company. I'll raise the cash price to $60 a share." To stampede the stock into Icahn's hands. "The securities will be worth $50 a share." The blended price would be $55 a share, just as in the first offer.

"We'll talk tomorrow," Icahn told Black when the meeting broke up.

"Sure," said Black. He'd call Icahn in the afternoon.

First thing Saturday morning, Icahn dialed Black in Connecticut. No answer.

Icahn dialed Black in New York.

No answer.

Icahn dialed Sorte in Connecticut.

"The temperature is sixty degrees," said a recorded voice.

Icahn slammed down the receiver. He dialed Sorte in New York.

"Hello," said Sorte. He looked at the clock. Seven A.M.

"What's that number you gave me in Connecticut?" yelled Icahn. "It's the goddamn weather."

"That's not the weather, Carl," said Sorte. "That's a monitor in the house. It's hooked to the heating system."

Icahn was silent for a moment. "Where's Leon?" he asked. "We've got to talk."

Black was probably sleeping. "I'll get him," said Sorte. "He'll call."

"Okay," said Icahn.

Black finally called at noon. "We've got to renegotiate fees," he told Icahn. "This is looking bleak. The commitment fees will have to be higher."

"No way," said Icahn.

Black and Icahn negotiated.

"We were talking about a friendly deal when we set those fees," said Black late in the afternoon. "This is very hostile."

Icahn hung up. Ivan Boesky, the big arbitrageur who lived down the road, was coming for dinner.

"I might want to join you," said Boesky when the family sat

359

down at the table. Boesky had bought 4 million shares since Icahn launched his fight; he was considering contributing some of his stock to the equity that would remain after Icahn's LBO of Phillips.

"You know, I am pretty much of a lone wolf in this stuff," said Icahn. "If you want to join me, we might be able to work something out." If Boesky joined, it wouldn't help Icahn much: everyone knew that Boesky had stock and was already planning to vote it against the recap plan. "It would have to be a couple of hundred million dollars."

"Let's talk," said Boesky.

Sorte and Black came into New York on Sunday night for a meeting at Icahn's law firm.

Ivan Boesky was meeting with his lawyers in an empty conference room. Boesky was trying to figure out if he could get involved legally.

Icahn and his team talked through strategy.

Boesky called Icahn into his meeting.

"I can't help," Boesky told Icahn. "My lawyers say there isn't a way."

"Okay," said Icahn. It didn't make much difference.

Icahn and Boesky walked into the Drexel strategy meeting.

"Hi," said Boesky.

"Hi, Ivan," said Black.

The bankers chatted with Boesky for a few minutes. Boesky left.

The team kept talking for hours. Icahn agreed to raise the commitment fee to Drexel's clients to three-eighths of a point, and to give Drexel 20 percent of his profits.

"We can't make Boone's mistake," said Sorte. "He announced that he was going to make an offer, and Phillips blocked him in the courts. Boone never did make his proposal formal. We've got to get an offer out before Phillips can stop us."

"If we can get an ad in the paper, we're okay," said one of the lawyers. "Once we've run the ad, the offer has officially commenced."

Sorte didn't get home until three-thirty in the morning.

Monday, Carl Icahn called Irwin Jacobs. "I hear you sold most of your stock," he said. If Jacobs had sold his proxies too, Icahn had probably lost votes.

Jacobs was noncommittal. "You know how I feel about this situation," said Jacobs.

"I understand completely, Irwin," said Icahn. Jacobs had kept the proxies and would vote with him.

Then Icahn opened the *New York Times*. "Pickens Attacks Phillips Poison Pill," read the headline. Icahn buzzed his secretary. "Get me Boone Pickens," he said.

"Before you say anything," Pickens began when he answered, "I have to tell you that I will report anything you tell me back to Douce."

"I hope you do," said Icahn. He talked about the Phillips offer for a few minutes. "I saw what you said about the pill. Phillips has broken its agreement with you. You can sell your shares." Maybe to Icahn.

"I don't see it that way," said Pickens. "I've got an obligation."

Pickens called back a couple of hours later. "Maybe you ought to talk to Douce," he told Icahn.

"I don't see any point in that," said Icahn. "I've talked to his investment bankers."

Black and Sorte walked into Icahn's office with the tender-offer documents. Icahn read them through one last time.

The team talked strategy until midnight.

"Let's see how the story looks in the *Times,*" said Icahn.

That seemed like a good idea. Sorte sent his assistant out to get a paper.

"Icahn Revises His Bid," read the headline. "Traders Unimpressed."

Bill Douce stared at the headline. Boone Pickens was criticizing the recap plan again. Pickens had told the *Wall Street Journal* that he didn't like poison pills, that they were "designed to entrench management."

"Can't we sue him?" Douce asked Lipton.

Lipton looked at the newspaper. "I don't think so," he said. "Pickens is just criticizing the pill. The pill wasn't part of the package Pickens approved. For the record, Pickens still supports the recap plan."

"But not in fact," said Douce.

Lipton shook his head. Suing Pickens now wouldn't help anyway.

The telephone rang.

It was Boone Pickens. "I've been talking to Carl," he said. "I think you should talk to him about his proposal."

About his LBO. "No," said Douce. "I already told you we don't want to do an LBO." Pickens just wouldn't give up.

"I think you should talk," repeated Pickens.

Douce wouldn't commit.

He wasn't worried yet. Icahn had made a fool of himself trying to swallow the poison pill. A dozen major newspapers had written feature articles on Bartlesville—and how disastrous it would be for the town if Icahn won Phillips.

Over the weekend, though, Douce started to hear rumors that Icahn was going to make a tender offer. If Icahn did, Phillips would have to respond.

No offer Monday.

No offer Tuesday.

Then just before midnight Tuesday night, someone bought a *New York Times*. Icahn had taken out a tender-offer ad.

The battle was on.

Phillips sued Icahn for misleading investors.

The strategists caucused to write ad copy.

"What about 'Where's the beef?'" suggested Joe Fogg. "That will tell people that the Icahn offer isn't really there."

"No," said Douce. "We're keeping on the straight and narrow."

"We've got to say something," said Lipton.

They talked.

Finally they chose a headline: "Is Icahn for Real?"

"We're losing credibility," Leon Black told Carl Icahn on Wednesday. "We've got to line up some of the commitments. That's the only way to make the traders believe your offer."

"Did you see the Phillips ads?" asked Icahn. "'Is Icahn for Real?' When are we going to be able to run ads?" Phillips had gotten an Oklahoma judge to bar Icahn from communicating with Phillips stockholders through the mail, newspapers or any other method.

"The only way we can fight back is to line up your money," said Sorte.

"Okay," said Icahn.

The question was how much. "The more the better," said Black.

"If we raise $2 billion, your offer has real credibility," said Sorte. "That's about as much as we can raise in forty-eight hours." Icahn had scheduled two key meetings with institutional shareholders in the next two days.

"We can raise $2 billion by then," said Black. "The commitment fee will be a half a percent."

"I'm not sure," said Icahn. Two billion would cost him $10 million. "I can't afford to pay more than $7 million. If the recap plan is not defeated, my offer is void. Paying for commitments now could be throwing money away."

"What about $7.5 million," said Sorte. "We'll raise $1.5 billion."

Icahn couldn't make up his mind. Maybe he should spend $10 million and go for $2 billion of commitments.

"We can get you $2 billion," said Black. "We can get you more."

Icahn thought. "No," he finally said. "Seven and a half is as far as I'm going." The Drexel high-yield bond department spent Thursday calling.

The next day, Icahn met with institutional shareholders at the University Club in New York. "I've got some of my commitments lined up," he said. "I'll be making an announcement tomorrow."

The money managers cheered.

After the meeting, Carl Icahn called John Sorte.

"We've got $1.5 billion in commitments," said Sorte. "The offering was oversubscribed. Don't announce the numbers until we have signed telexes."

"I may want to raise the price," said Icahn. "Especially if they sweeten the recap again. I don't want to be stuck because of these commitments. I don't want to have to run back to everybody for permission."

"I don't think that will be a problem," said Sorte. "If you raise the price, you'll have to increase the equity you put in, but raising won't be a problem."

"I want to be sure," said Icahn. "Raising could be very important to me."

"Let me talk to our lawyer," said Sorte. He called back a few minutes later. "As far as I'm concerned, you can raise the price of the tender as long as you get the cash with subordinated money."

The signed telexes were in by the middle of the afternoon. Icahn announced that he had accepted $1.5 billion in financing.

Drexel and Icahn spent the weekend sorting through the telexes.

About three o'clock Sunday afternoon, Black drove to Icahn's house in Westchester.

They talked strategy.

They drafted an ad. The order barring Icahn from talking to shareholders had finally been lifted on Friday.

"Let me do this," said Icahn. He and Black had argued about the text.

Black walked across the room. He picked up the copy of Icahn's Princeton philosophy thesis.

Icahn wrote ad copy.

Black read philosophy.

"We need to talk about additional financing," said Icahn late in the afternoon. "We'll talk tonight." At the meeting at Icahn's lawyer's office in New York.

Black went home for dinner at six. Then he drove to New York City.

"Do we want to line up more commitments?" asked Icahn when the strategists were seated around the table.

"We could probably raise another $1.5 billion in time for the meeting," said Black. The shareholder meeting was scheduled for Friday.

Icahn frowned. That would cost him another $7.5 million.

"Do we need to release the names of buyers?" asked Sorte. "They don't want to be harassed by Phillips."

"I don't think so," said one of the lawyers. "You don't have to publish the names of your banks when you make an offer. Bond buyers ought to be treated the same."

The meeting broke up.

First thing Monday morning, Ivan Boesky called Carl Icahn. "Why don't you line up the rest of the commitments?" asked

Boesky. "I think Drexel could do it. So do the other arbs."

"Well, I don't know if I am going to do that," said Icahn. "You guys all say that, but it's my money that I am putting up. What happens if I put up all this money and Phillips sweetens the deal substantially?"

"I will help," said Boesky. "I will put up some of the money."

"I'm not sure that I want to do this as a group," said Icahn.

Carl Icahn called Leon Black.

"Do you want to go ahead on the additional commitments?" asked Black. "We've got to get started."

"I've got enough," said Icahn. "I can win the shareholder vote with the commitments I've got."

Bill Douce was worried.

On Friday, February 15, Icahn had announced that he had $1.5 billion worth of financing commitments. Phillips had sued for the names of the backers, and on Tuesday, Icahn went public.

"This is some list," said Joe Fogg when he saw the list. The Belzberg brothers, Saul Steinberg, Steve Wynn, Larry Tisch, Meshulam Riklis.

"Carl Lindner isn't here," said Lipton. "Neither are Fred Carr or Jimmy Goldsmith."

"Drexel's still got some dry powder," said Fogg. Drexel could easily raise more money.

The outlook for the vote on the recap plan wasn't good.

Half a dozen big shareholders had come out against it.

Irwin Jacobs announced that he had sold his 4.5 million shares on the market but had kept the proxies. He would vote the proxies with Icahn.

Harrison Goldin, comptroller of New York City, announced that he would vote the Big Apple's 334,600 shares against the plan.

Capital Group, the largest shareholder, seemed to be leaning toward Phillips. "There doesn't seem to be an alternative to the recapitalization plan," the executive vice president told the *Wall Street Journal.* "If it's voted down, you could end up with a wild crap shoot."

"The proxy cards are coming in," said the proxy solicitor. "They

365

don't look good. I've never seen so many management cards marked no. You've got to get a majority of yes votes to win. An abstention counts as a no. Right now it looks close."

If Phillips lost, the company would have to come up with a new plan. And if there was a new plan, Douce wanted to be damn sure that it satisfied the shareholders.

"I've been talking to the arbs," said Joe Fogg. "I hear that Icahn is losing stomach for the fight. He doesn't want to own Phillips."

"We'll put a feeler out after the meeting," said Douce.

Douce called the shareholder meeting in Bartlesville to order at ten o'clock, Friday, February 22. It was pouring rain outside.

A man from the California state teacher's retirement plan— 124,650 shares—stood up to explain why he'd voted against the plan.

A shareholder from New York stood up and criticized the plan.

"I'm Frank Cale, a retiree living in Bartlesville," said the next man. "I'd like to ask these gentlemen what they expect a company like Phillips to do when these people that are so greedy for money come in and try to take over a company with the prospect of tearing up the city. I've got faith in Phillips, and I think these people need a little more faith."

Another retiree stood up. "If this thing is voted down, does it mean the destruction of Bartlesville?"

"No," said Douce. "If it's defeated, the company will continue to operate just as we were before all this started. The company is not going to die, and we're not going to go out of business."

"We're just as vulnerable to takeover," said the retiree.

"We are vulnerable to takeover, as we've always been," said Douce. "That isn't recent."

"There have been two attacks so far," said the retiree. "There will be more."

"Yes, sir," said Douce. "There might be."

Al Kingsley, Icahn's number two, stood up. Icahn had been so worried about security at the shareholder meeting that he sent his team to Tulsa on a private jet; Icahn had booked the entire top floor of the Westin Hotel at Williams Plaza—the Icahn team wasn't staying at the Hotel Phillips in Bartlesville—and hired half a dozen armed security guards. "Let me first say that we also love Bartlesville," said Kingsley. "We love all the employees and Phillips Petroleum. We're not against Phillips Petroleum. What we are against is the recapitalization plan. The headquarters will remain in Bartlesville. We don't want to bust up or break up Phillips. What we do want to get is fair value for our shares."

"I'd just like to ask that Icahn man over there why they got into this company just a little over a month ago and are now trying to say that this plan is no good," said a shareholder. "Why didn't they just stay out of the company?"

"I've served on a board of directors of a large oil company and I've seen it sold," said a stockholder who had been a director of Skelly Oil. Getty had controlled Skelly for fifty years. "I've seen what happens to the shareholders. I've seen what happens to the employees, the communities, and it has not been good. These people who have come in and acquired stock within the last few months are not your real shareholders. All they want is an extra dollar or an extra quarter. I hate to use this word, but we call them prostitutes."

"The proxy solicitors think we won," said John Sorte when he sat down in Carl Icahn's office.

"Phillips left the polls open," said Leon Black. "They must be trying to drum up more votes."

"Yeah," said Icahn.

"If we've won, we're going to have to line up the rest of the commitments," said Sorte. "It will be easier to sell the bonds if we have an equity partner, someone who can put up another $500 million. Maybe someone with oil know-how."

Icahn nodded. "Make the calls."

Late Saturday afternoon, Leon Black called Carl Lindner, the savvy raider who controls Penn Central. Penn Central had invested $300 million in Mesa to help with its Gulf bid; now Penn Central had some free cash. And Lindner was interested.

John Sorte called Marvin Davis, the oil tycoon. Davis was interested.

Another Drexel partner called Sir James Goldsmith, the British investor who bought and liquidated the Diamond International forest products company. Goldsmith was interested.

The head of the Drexel M&A department called Pennzoil. Pennzoil still didn't call back.

Sunday afternoon, Joe Fogg called Carl Icahn. "Let's talk about what kind of recapitalization plan you want," he said.

Icahn called Leon Black. "Phillips is ready to negotiate."

Black and Sorte caught a cab to Icahn's office at four-thirty Monday afternoon for a strategy meeting. Fogg was scheduled to arrive at half past five.

They knew what they would ask for: a value of $55 a share, a promise that Phillips would drop the ESOP, and payment of Icahn's expenses.

"We're thinking about reworking the recap plan," said Fogg when he sat down in Icahn's office. "What do you need?"

Icahn listed the points.

"How much are your expenses?" asked Fogg.

Icahn thought: $7.5 million of commitment fees, at least $10 million Drexel fees, at least $3 million of legal fees. "Off the top of my head, $20 million," he said. "Maybe $25 million."

They talked about the recap plan.

"I'm not sure we can get to the value you want," said Fogg. "We can't get to $55 a share in this format. The more value we give to shareholders by swapping stock for bonds, the less the remaining stock is worth."

Sorte frowned. "Of course you can get the value of the package up to $55 a share," he said. "Phillips is worth more than $65 a share."

"Not without doing an LBO," said Fogg. "Not without selling off major assets. We aren't going to liquidate the company."

"If you can't figure out a way to get that value to the shareholders, Drexel can," said Black. "We'll sell some bonds for Phillips and use the cash to support the price of the stock."

Fogg blanched. "There is no way that Drexel is going to issue junk for Phillips," he said.

"That's an interesting statement for a firm that just opened a junk-bond-trading desk," said Sorte. Morgan Stanley just had. With fanfare.

"That's a different part of the firm," snapped Fogg.

Sorte raised an eyebrow.

"Let's move on," said one of the Phillips bankers. "Phillips is not going to issue junk bonds. Phillips isn't that kind of a company."

The bankers talked.

Finally Fogg stood up to leave. "Sit tight," he said. "We'll get back to you."

"What?" asked Icahn. "Are you saying you think we're going to do nothing while you dream up new variations on your poison pill?"

Fogg was silent.

"You're crazy," said Icahn.

Fogg sat down again.

Icahn and Fogg argued.

Finally they shook hands: Phillips would initiate no hostile moves until a settlement was reached; neither would Icahn.

Bill Douce didn't understand quite what had gone wrong, but Phillips would clearly have trouble getting the votes for the recap plan. Joe Fogg insisted that that didn't mean that Phillips had lost its independence too.

"Icahn seems to be ready to talk," said Fogg on Monday night. "We need to settle the new terms."

The Phillips team met in Bartlesville on Wednesday to do that.

"We've been through the shareholder vote routs," said Douce. After talking to shareholders for two months, Douce had a clearer idea what they needed.

"An exchange offer makes sense," said Fogg. A tender offer for debt; since Phillips wouldn't put the new plan up for a shareholder vote, the company would have to drop the ESOP and the shark repellents; those had to be approved by shareholders. "That will make it clear to the stockholders that our plan is a better deal than Icahn's."

The only question was what kind of debt to offer shareholders— and how much.

The strategists talked. Finally they agreed that Phillips would offer to buy half its stock with notes worth $62 a share; Phillips would raise the dividend from $2.40 a share to $3.00 a share, and Phillips would give shareholders $4.09 a share in preferred stock. Phillips would sell $2 billion of assets to raise the cash for that.

"Icahn wants his expenses," said Fogg. "He says he's spent $20 million to $25 million."

"Zero is too much to pay Icahn," said the president of Phillips.

"We'll give him up to $25 million," said Douce. That was what Phillips had paid Pickens.

Fogg nodded.

"I'll schedule a board meeting for this weekend," said Douce. He looked at Fogg. "You call Icahn."

Carl Icahn flew from New York to Washington on February 27. Congressman Tim Wirth had invited him to testify on takeover policy before the House subcommittee on securities law. Boone Pickens was also on the panel. So was Fred Joseph, the head of investment banking at Drexel. So was Charles Kittrell, an executive vice president of Phillips Petroleum.

Wirth called the hearing to order.

"Carl Icahn is a predator out for a fast buck," said Kittrell. "This takeover is an abuse of the free market. We are up to our eyeballs in this ruckus. I'm not painting Mr. Icahn as a black hat, though I'd like to, but his techniques are to make a fast buck without responsibility to shareholders, employees and communities."

Icahn rolled his eyes. "I'm not a Robin Hood," he said. "But I really believe in what I'm doing. A lot of people with the money to do what I'm doing don't want to get into these things because you start reading about yourself in the newspaper. I used to read that I'm a gangster. Now they say I'm not real. I look at myself in the mirror every morning, and I think I'm for real."

"Placing a going-out-of-business-sale sign on a profitable concern for short-term gain is not appropriate public policy," said Kittrell. "The Icahn bid threatens jobs, exploration, research, philanthropic activities. It diverts management attention from running the company."

"Mergers don't divert management from running companies,"

said Pickens. "They divert management attention from hunting and fishing camps."

"This takeover is an abuse of the free market," said Kittrell.

"I'm a friend of the shareholder," said Icahn. "I tried to call when I bought the stock, but they were on the golf course. There have been gag orders against me, just for making a bid that I thought was fair. Kenny Rogers should write a ballad about me."

"You view yourself as a friend of the shareholder the same way that Custer was a protector of Indians," said Mike Synar, the congressman from Oklahoma.

"Phillips is suffering from two problems afflicting American business," said Icahn. "Mediocre managers and bloated bureaucracies. The only way you can get some of these guys off the golf course is to start a tender offer."

Kittrell exploded out of his chair. "I take offense at that accusation. We made $810 million last year. We replaced our oil and gas reserves. Our bureaucracy is pretty effective."

Somebody asked about the stockholder vote.

"I don't know why it takes you so long to count the vote," said Pickens.

"Holding the polls open a week after the vote was supposed to close is undemocratic," said Icahn. "This is a Soviet-style election."

"Marvin Davis just called to say he isn't interested," Leon Black had told Carl Icahn just before Icahn flew to Washington. "Davis is pessimistic on oil prices. Carl Lindner at Penn Central is cool. I had breakfast with Jimmy Goldsmith this morning. He's going to the Bahamas for vacation, but he wants you to sit down with his deals man."

"I'll do that Thursday," said Icahn. As soon as he got back.

The meeting with the Goldsmith team went well.

The next day, the *New York Times* reported that Icahn was talking to Goldsmith. Drexel confirmed the rumor, hoping that would keep the pressure on Phillips.

By then, Drexel was convinced that the shareholders had voted down the recap plan.

Thursday afternoon, Icahn called Black. "I just talked to Joe

Fogg again," he said. "Fogg is coming here this afternoon."

"We're putting together a new recap plan," said Fogg when the two teams sat down in Icahn's office. "We're trying to work out something that will address your concerns. There's a board meeting scheduled for tomorrow. Sit tight."

Icahn rolled his eyes. "My bankers are pushing me to do something," he said. "I don't know if I can hold them back."

"Sit tight," repeated Fogg.

Fogg called Icahn again on Saturday morning. "The board meeting has been rescheduled for Sunday," he said.

Icahn called Black. "The board meeting is Sunday," he said.

Fogg called Sunday afternoon. "We need a meeting," he said. "Five o'clock."

"We'll be there," said Icahn. He called Black. Black called Sorte. Sorte wasn't in. He was at the law office working on the papers for another deal.

"We've put together a new package," said Fogg when Black and Icahn sat down in the conference room at Morgan Stanley that evening. "We're going to tender for 50 percent of Phillips. We'll pay with notes worth $62 a share."

Icahn didn't look convinced.

"We've already put out the press release," said Fogg. "You have two choices. You can drop your proxy contests and negotiate a settlement with us. Or you can fight."

Icahn stood up. He and Black would talk.

"That package is worth about what they claim," said Black.

"We can't win," said Sorte. He'd gotten to the meeting at a little after seven. "We're offering $60 a share. Phillips is offering $62. They're making a self-tender. Their offer closes before ours does."

"We've got a chance," said Icahn. "We're offering cash."

They talked.

"Okay," Icahn told Fogg at eight-thirty. "I'm ready to negotiate."

Fogg and Icahn sat down in a small conference room.

"First, we'll settle the standstill," said Fogg. An agreement to buy any Phillips stock or help someone else buy it. "We want an agreement with you and an agreement with Drexel promising not to get involved in Phillips for twelve years."

"That's ridiculous," said Icahn. "The most we're giving you is two."

Fogg and Icahn argued.

At eleven-thirty, they shook hands.

"I got you a good deal," Icahn told Sorte and Black when the team caucused. "Five years for Drexel. I'm signing a standstill for seven."

"Five is too long," said Sorte. "We don't want to sign a standstill at all. The only standstill we've ever agreed to was two years."

"I got you the best deal you're going to get," said Icahn.

"No," said Sorte. "Each standstill sets a precedent for the next. We'll negotiate this ourselves."

"Okay," said Icahn. He shrugged.

Sorte and Black walked into the negotiating room.

"We'll listen," said Fogg. "But we'll only negotiate with Carl."

"We don't want to sign a standstill," said Sorte.

Lipton shook his head. "We need a standstill from Drexel more than we need one from Icahn."

"Five years is too long," said Sorte. "It sets a terrible precedent."

Fogg looked at Lipton. They had told the Phillips board that the longest standstill Drexel would sign was one year.

Black and Sorte left the room.

Icahn and Fogg negotiated.

By twelve-thirty they had a deal. Drexel would sign on three years.

That left just expenses to settle.

"We'll give you up to $25 million," said Fogg.

"That's not enough," said Icahn. "I've spent $32 million."

Fogg raised his eyebrows. That wasn't possible. Icahn was making up expenses.

"I deserve to get reimbursed for what I spent," said Icahn.

"The ceiling is $25 million," said Fogg. The Phillips board had been reluctant to authorize that much.

Fogg and Icahn argued. They couldn't agree.

At midnight, the teams caucused.

Lipton called Douce at his suite in the Helmsley Palace. "Icahn is holding out for $30 million in expenses," he said. "The board set a ceiling at $25 million. Can we raise?"

"I could go to $30 million," said Douce. He paused. "But I'm not going to. Twenty-five million is the maximum."

"They won't give me more than $25 million," Icahn told his team. "I think I spent $30 million."

"Let's add up the numbers again," said Black.

They added.

"It's only $28 million," said Sorte.

Icahn frowned. He walked back to the negotiating table.

Fogg wouldn't budge.

Neither would Icahn.

The teams caucused again at one-thirty.

"Carl," said Sorte. "It's clear that Fogg can't go above $25 million. That must be what the board gave him."

"It's not worth breaking a deal for this," said Black.

Icahn walked back to the negotiating table.

He argued.

Fogg wouldn't budge.

At three in the morning, Icahn threw up his hands. "All right," he said. He had gotten a good deal for the Phillips shareholders; he had made $52.5 million for himself. "Twenty-five million."

The Phillips exchange offer went as planned: more than 91 percent of the stock was tendered for the $62-a-share note package. But the deal turned out to be a disappointment for shareholders; when oil prices collapsed in early 1986, Phillips stock sank to less than $10 a share. By then, Phillips was operating on a stiff austerity plan. Almost a third of the workforce had been laid off; the executive dining hall now serves the same food as the employee cafeteria; intercompany mail is delivered just twice a day. Phillips is still trying to sell assets to pay down its debt, but that's hard to do in a buyers' market. And the interest costs really hurt: Phillips paid $3.2 billion in interest in 1985, up from just over $1 billion in 1984.

Bill Douce retired on April 30, 1985. He took his wife to Europe—he even bought her a ticket home on the Concorde although he doesn't think the supersonic flight is worth the price—and keeps busy. He's got more time for hunting, more time for his family and time to watch T. Boone Pickens.

Boone Pickens didn't sit on his Phillips profit for long. Even before the Phillips-Icahn fight was over, Pickens had launched yet another corporate raid. On Valentine's Day, Mesa Partners announced that it owned 7.9 percent of Unocal but that it was just an investor. Unocal launched a fierce anti-Pickens campaign. Pickens called John Sorte. The day after Easter, Mesa offered to buy half of Unocal for $54 a share, $6 a share over market. Unocal struck back with an offer for 70 percent of its stock in senior notes worth $72 a share; Mesa Partners was excluded from the bid. Pickens was sure that the offer was illegal, but, in a surprise decision, the Delaware Supreme Court ruled that excluding Pickens was legal. Though Pickens lost that fight, Mesa earned $83 million on its Unocal stock in the second quarter of 1985, and Unocal earnings were just $120 million that quarter, down $60 million from 1984, mostly because of the cost of fending off Boone Pickens.

John Sorte hardly saw his family during the Pickens fight, but lately he's had more time. The Delaware ruling means that for the present, investors like Pickens and Icahn can't win—the Securities and Exchange Commission is putting a new law on the books reversing the Delaware decision—and that means that Sorte is once again putting together traditional oil company underwritings. He misses the merger action.

Carl Icahn didn't rest on his profits either. In late May, after making more than $24 million in a quick fight with Uniroyal, Carl Icahn announced that he owned 10 percent of TWA and would bid $18 a share for the rest. Texas Air Corporation, owner of Continental, Texas Air and New York Air, topped Icahn with a bid for $23 a share, but Icahn kept buying until he owned 45.5 percent of the stock. Icahn eventually bought TWA, but it looks like this was more trouble than it was worth. In March 1986, the flight attendants went on strike and airline watchers predicted that the carrier would soon go bankrupt.

The big hostile takeover deals prompted an outpouring of bad publicity, and prompted Congressman Tim Wirth to call Drexel executives to Washington to testify on the benefits of junk bonds and takeovers. The publicity notwithstanding, Drexel has remained the premier house for the second-tier company. In 1985 Drexel ranked fifth in underwriting. Drexel helped Sir James Goldsmith win control of Crown Zellerbach forest products. In May 1985, Fred Joseph, the executive vice president who built Drexel's investment banking department into a powerhouse, was named vice chairman and chief operating officer. Joseph said that under his guidance, Drexel would keep doing what it does best. With a lower profile.

The pace hasn't slowed for Leon Black. Just after Icahn shook hands with Phillips, Black was promoted to cohead of the mergers and acquisitions department and moved his office from the seventh floor to the eighth. Black helped Icahn plot strategy in the Uniroyal and TWA fights. At the end of August, Black went on vacation in the south of France. He says he deserved it.

Notes and Sources

The text of *Behind Closed Doors* is based primarily on personal interviews. I have used quotation marks to indicate dialogue that the participants at each meeting remember having been said. The quotations fairly reflect the substance and flavor of what the participants told me was said; they do not necessarily indicate the exact words used.

In addition to the extensive interviewing, I also consulted press clippings concerning each deal and read proxy statements, depositions, annual reports and public relations department publications. What follows is a list of key interviews and written sources.

Introduction

Books and Articles: *The Day the Bubble Burst: A Social History of the Wall Street Crash of 1929* by Gordon Thomas and Max Morgan-Witts (Garden City, N.Y.: Doubleday, 1979); *The Guilded Age*, edited by H. Wayne Morgan (Syracuse, N.Y.: Syracuse University Press, 1963); *The Era of Theodore Roosevelt and the Birth of Modern America* by George E. Mowry (New York: Harper & Row, 1958); *America in the Twenties: A History* by Geoffrey Perrett (New York: Simon & Schuster, 1982); *FDR: Launching the New Deal* by Frank Freidel (Boston: Little, Brown, 1973); *J. P. Morgan* by Stanley Jackson (New York, Stein & Day, 1983); *The Money Lenders* by Anthony Sampson (New York: Viking, 1981); *Once in Golconda: A True Drama of Wall Street 1920–1938* by John

Brooks (New York: Harper & Row, 1969); *The Transformation of Wall Street* by Joel Seligman (Boston: Houghton Mifflin, 1982); *The Great Crash* by John Kenneth Galbraith (New York: Avon, Anniversary Edition, 1979); *The Bankers* by Martin Mayer (New York: Ballantine, 1974); *Famous Last Words on the Dalliance of Banks in Commerce 1817–1935: A Brief Chronology of the Recurring Imprudent Behavior Which Led to the Passage of the Glass-Steagall Act*, edited by E. F. Hutton (New York: Securities Industry Association); "Scapegoat of the Crash: Charles E. Mitchell, Congress and the Roosevelt Administration" by Thomas F. Huertas and Joan L. Silverman (paper presented at the American Historical Association, December 29, 1983); "Money at Risk: Financial Institutions Are Showing the Strain of a Decade of Turmoil" by Tim Carrington and Daniel Hertzberg (*Wall Street Journal*, September 5, 1984).

Bank of America

Interviews: Richard Cooley, William Pettit, Stan Carlson, Randy James, Roy Henderson (Seafirst); Harry Mullikin (Westin Hotels); Lee Kimmell, Ken Wilson, Dick Barrett (Salomon Brothers); Lee Prussia, Robert Frick, Steve McLin, David Coulter, Gene Conatser, Irv Gubman, Mike Romanchek, Helmut Loring (Bank of America); Joe Wender (Goldman, Sachs).
Books and Articles: *The Biography of a Bank* by Marquis James and Bessie James (New York: Harper & Row, 1954); *Firstbank: The Story of the Seattle-First National Bank* by Shelby Scates (Seattle: Seafirst Public Relations, 1970); daily press clips (July 1982 to June 1983) from the *Wall Street Journal*, *New York Times*, *Seattle Times* and *Post-Intelligencer*, *San Francisco Chronicle* and *Examiner*, *American Banker*, *Time*, *Newsweek*, *Fortune*, *Forbes*, and *BusinessWeek*; "The Cooley Years—A Legacy of Innovation and Growth" (*Wells Fargo News*, January 5, 1983); "Budging the Giant: At BankAmerica Corp. a New Regime Strives to Reverse Declines" by Victor Zonana and Kathryn Christensen (*Wall Street Journal*, May 20, 1982); "The Logical Leader" by John Merwin (*Forbes*, November 8, 1982); "Bank on the Leader" by Chris Barnett (*Continental Magazine*, February 1983); "Bank of America: Can the World's Largest Bank Regain Its Competitive Edge?" by Roger Skrentny (*California Business*, June 1983); "BankAmerica in Search of Itself" by Robert Bennett (*New York Times*, October 30, 1983); "Stirring a Giant: BankAmerica Corp., Seeking a Turnaround, Seems to Gain Ground" by Victor Zonana (*Wall Street Journal*, January 27, 1984).

Morgan Bank

Interviews: Tom Kellogg, Barbara Austell, Breck Denny, Brian Weight, John Olds, John Lane, Irene King, Gordon Nelson, Vinod Genveja (Morgan Bank); Mike Dacey, David Smith, Jim Reynolds, Tom Gallagher, Al Brittain, David Beim, Bill Austin, Jim Reilly, Tom Hardy, David Beers (Bankers Trust); Rick Schile, Roger Matthews (Allied); Richard Williams (International Monetary Fund).

Books and Articles: *The House of Morgan: A Social Biography of the Masters of Money* by Lewis Corey (New York: G. Howard Watt, 1930); *The Morgan Houses: The Seniors, Their Partners, and Their Aides* by Vincent Carosso (Tarrytown, N.Y.: Sleepy Hollow Press, 1981); *Some Comments on the Morgan Bank* by Longstreet Hinton et al. (New York: Morgan Guaranty Trust, 1979); *The Changing Times of Bankers Trust Co.* (New York: Bankers Trust, 1978); *The Seven Sisters: The Great Oil Companies and the World They Shaped* by Anthony Sampson (New York: Viking, 1975); *The Money Lenders* by Anthony Sampson, (New York: Viking, 1981); *History of Royal Dutch Shell* by Dr. F. C. Gerretson, 4 vols. (London: E. J. Brill, 1953–57); *Enterprise in Oil* by Kendall Beaton (New York: Appleton-Century-Crofts, 1957); Salomon Brothers, *Petroleum Monthly* (January 1982 to December 1984); Morgan Guaranty, *World Financial Markets* (February 1982 to November 1983); Bankers Trust Company, *Energy Viewpoint* (August 1981 to December 1983); *Indonesia: Economic Update 1984* (Republic of Indonesia, Department of State for National Development Planning); OPEC daily press clips (July 1982 to March 1983) from the *Wall Street Journal, New York Times, Time, Newsweek, Fortune, Forbes, BusinessWeek*; "Thomas W. Lamont, Banker, Dies at 77 in Florida Home" (*New York Times*, February 4, 1948); "Why Blue Chips Bank on Morgan" by John Carson-Parker (*Fortune*, July 13, 1981); "The Wealth and Aura of Morgan" by Robert Bennett (*New York Times*, April 10, 1983); "Morgan Guaranty Takes Aim at Wall Street" by Scott McMurray (*American Banker*, July 8, 1983); "Inside the Morgan Machine" by Susan Wittebort (*Institutional Investor*, July 1985); "Bankers Trust Takes on Wall Street" by Gary Hector (*Fortune*, January 9, 1984); "Bankers Trust: Leaner and Luring the Big Money" by Robert Bennett (*New York Times*, August 3, 1980); "Bankers Trust Goes Wholesale into the Corporate Sector" by Arlene Hershman (*Banking World*, August 1983); "Bankers Trust's Winning Gamble" by Arlene Hershman (*Dun's Business Month*, May 1983); "Bankers Trust Strives to be a Merchant Banker" by Scott McMurray (*American Banker*, July

25, 1983); "Wholesale Banking's New Hard Sell" (*BusinessWeek*, April 13, 1981); "Sanford's New Banking Vision" by Robert Bennett (*New York Times*, March 17, 1985); "OPEC's Unruly Members" (*Fortune*, August 9, 1982); "OPEC's Heavyweights Are Ready to Cut Prices" (*BusinessWeek*, February 14, 1983); "The Decline and Fall of OPEC" by Henriette Sender (*Dun's Business Month*, March 1983); "The Crumbling of a Cartel" by William Marbach (*Newsweek*, March 21, 1983); "The Emperor with No Clothes" by Charles Alexander (*Time*, March 21, 1983); "OPEC Knuckles Under" by Charles Alexander (*Time*, March 28, 1983).

Citibank

Interviews: Bill Rhodes, Walter Wriston, Harry Heneberger, Tom Huertas (Citibank); Guy Huntrods (Lloyds); Leighton Coleman, Steve Darst (Morgan Guaranty); Toni Geyelin, Kathleen Donovan (Chase Manhattan); Bob Londono (Chemical); Bruno Nucci (Bankers Trust); Rick Bloom (Bank of America); Susan Segal (Manufacturers Hanover); Keiji Fuji (Bank of Tokyo); Sandy Tilman (Arab Banking Corp.); Michael Rossi (Wells Fargo); Dennis Wright (Continental Illinois); Afonso Celso Pastore, José Serano (Brazilian Central Bank); Jacques de Larosière, Ted Beza, Bill Dale (International Monetary Fund).
Books and Articles: *Debt Shock: The Full Story of the World Credit Crisis* by Darrell Delamaide (Garden City, N.Y.: Doubleday, 1984); *The Mexican Rescue* by Joseph Kraft (New York: Group of Thirty, 1984); *Brazil: A Strategy for the 1980s* by Bryce Ferguson (New York: Citibank Public Affairs Department, December 1981); daily press clips (June 1983 to January 1984) from the *Wall Street Journal, New York Times, Financial Times, Journal of Commerce, Fortune, Forbes, BusinessWeek*; "Citicorp's Daring Bid for the Consumer" by Carol Loomis (*Fortune*, May 24, 1980); "The Money Machine" by John Brooks (*New Yorker*, January 5, 1981); "Inside Citicorp" by Robert Bennett (*New York Times Magazine*, May 29, 1983); "Walt's Triumphant Farewell" by Cary Reich (*Institutional Investor*, July 1983); "The Champion of Citi" by Peter Field and Nigel Adam (*Euromoney*, October 1983); "Has Delfim Worked His Last Miracle?" by Nicholas Asheshov and Cary Reich (*Institutional Investor*, August 1980); "Querem a Cabeca de Delfim (E Por Que Figueiredo Não Entrega)" (*Veja*, August 31, 1983); "How They Tried to Rescue Brazil" by Nigel Adam (*Euromoney*, October, 1983); "Is Time Running Out for Brazil?" by Lenny Glynn (*Institutional Investor*, April 1984).

Goldman Sachs

Interviews: Geoff Boisi, Ken Brody, David Leuschen, Chris Flowers, Bob Freeman, Steve Friedman, Todd Bergman (Goldman, Sachs); Phil Wallach (Occidental Petroleum); David Murdock (Pacific Holdings); Charles Waidelich (Cities Service); James O. Boisi (Morgan Guaranty); Martin Lipton, Peter Hein (Wachtell, Lipton, Rosen & Katz); Bruce Wasserstein (First Boston); Henry Breck, Tom Hill (Lehman Brothers).

Books and Articles: *"Our Crowd"* by Stephen Birmingham (New York: Harper & Row, 1967); *The Remarkable Life of Dr. Armand Hammer* by Bob Considine (New York: Harper & Row, 1975); daily press clips (June–September 1982) from the *Wall Street Journal, New York Times, Los Angeles Times, Tulsa Tribune, Time, Newsweek, Fortune, Forbes,* and *BusinessWeek*; "A Pace Setter in Investment Banking for 75 Years" by Merryle Stanley Rukeyser (*Finance*, January 25, 1945); " 'Let's Ask Sidney Weinberg,' " by Robert Sheehan (*Fortune*, October 1953); "Directors' Director" by E. J. Kahn (*New Yorker*, September 8 and 15, 1956); "Big Blocks Make More of a Splash" (*BusinessWeek*, January 15, 1966); "Diversification's Marriage Brokers" (*Forbes*, February 15, 1967); "Mr. Wall Street to Mark his 100 Years at Goldman, Sachs" by Robert E. Bedingfield (*New York Times*, November 18, 1967); "Goldman, Sachs Celebrates Its First 100 Years" by E. M. Christner (*Finance*, December 9, 1969); "Takeovers: Goldman, Sachs for the Defense" by Julie Connally (*Institutional Investor*, November 1977); "The Pacifist: Goldman, Sachs Avoids Bitter Takeover Fights but Leads in Mergers" by Tim Metz (*Wall Street Journal*, December 3, 1982); "Nice Guys Finish First" by Jack Egan (*New York*, November 14, 1983); "Inside the Goldman, Sachs Culture" by Beth McGoldrick (*Institutional Investor*, January 1984); "How Goldman, Sachs Grew and Grew" by Irwin Ross (*Fortune*, July 9, 1984); "Goldman's Rise in Real Estate" by Fred R. Bleakley (*New York Times*, June 17, 1985); "The New Generation of Investment Bankers" by Beth McGoldrick (*Institutional Investor*, March 1985); "A Player in the High Stakes Game of High Finance" (*Wharton Alumni Magazine*, no date); "The Capitalist Connection" by James Cook (*Forbes*, April 28, 1980); "The Riddle of Armand Hammer" by Edward Jay Epstein (*New York Times Magazine*, November 30, 1981); "Armand Hammer Talks About Daumier, Lenin, van Gogh, Brezhnev, Renoir and Reagan" by Milton Esterow (*ARTnews*, December 1982); "Occidental is Trying to Sell Beef Unit" by Stephen Sansweet and Betsy Morris (*Wall Street Jour-*

nal, August 28, 1984); "Unrealized Dreams: Occidental Petroleum Hasn't Always Thrived from East-Block Deals" by Scot Paltrow (*Wall Street Journal*, August 30, 1984; "The Uneasy Peace at Occidental" by Winston Williams (*New York Times*, September 9, 1984); "Wall Street Stunned as Shamrock Cancels Giant Occidental Merger" by Robert Cole (*New York Times*, January 8, 1985); "Behind the Balk at Shamrock" by Fred R. Bleakley (*New York Times*, January 9, 1985).

Continental Illinois

Interviews: Fred Florjancic, Dennis Wright (Continental Illinois); John Payne (Morgan Guaranty); Taylor Wagenseil (Citibank); Harold Dietz (Irving Trust); Carter Evans (Chemical Bank); Bill Repko (Manufacturers Hanover); Art Schoen (Bankers Trust); Maureen Kelly (Bank of America); Lou Zircher, Ernie Charon (Chase Manhattan); Don Lennox, Jim Cotting, Bob Lannert (International Harvester); David Schulte, Diane Baker (Salomon Brothers); Andrew Sage, Ralph Hellmold (Lehman Brothers). Articles: daily press clips (March 1981 to September 1983) from the *Wall Street Journal, New York Times, Forbes, Fortune, BusinessWeek*; "Shaping Chicago's Top Bank" by Robert Bennett (*New York Times*, September 28, 1981); "On the Offensive: Behind Homely Image of Continental Illinois Is an Aggressive Bank" by Paul A. Gigot (*Wall Street Journal*, October 15, 1981); "Toil and Trouble at Continental Illinois" by A. F. Ehrbar (*Fortune*, February 7, 1983); "Troubled Bank: Continental Illinois, Its Safety Net in Place, Ponders Next Hurdles" by Jeff Bailey et al. (*Wall Street Journal*, May 16, 1984); "Chilling Specter at Continental" by Robert Bennett (*New York Times*, May 20, 1984); "Banker Uncle Sam: Possible Nationalizing of Continental Illinois Raises Many Questions" (*Wall Street Journal*, July 19, 1984); "Anatomy of Failure: Continental Illinois, How Bad Judgements and Big Egos Did It In" by Jeff Bailey et al. (*Wall Street Journal*, July 30, 1984); "The Rise and Fall of Roger Anderson" by Steven Strahler (*Crain's Chicago Business*, January 14, 1985); "International Harvester's Story: How a Great Company Lost Its Way" by Barbara Marsh and Sally Saville (*Crain's Chicago Business*, November 8 and 15, 1982); "The Strike that Rained on Archie McCardell's Parade" by Carol Loomis (*Fortune*, May 19, 1980).

L. F. Rothschild

Interviews: Tom Unterberg, Belmont Towbin, Mel Lavitt, Jim Furneaux, Andy Malik, Shelley Floyd, Chris Swenson, Michelle Preston, Marcia Roth, Elizabeth Burke, Susan Reiner (L. F. Rothschild, Unterberg, Towbin); Rod Canion, Jim Harris, Bill Murto, Jim D'Arezzo, Sparky Sparks, Steve Flannigan, John Gribi (Compaq); Ben Rosen, L. J. Sevin, Robin Grossman (Sevin Rosen); Richard Giles, Phil Pettit (E. F. Hutton); Ed Marsten (Bracewell & Patterson); L. John Doerr (Kleiner, Perkins, Caulfield & Byers).

Books and Articles: *Engines of the Mind* by Joel Shurkin (New York: Norton, 1984); *The Little Kingdom* by Michael Moritz (New York: Morrow, 1984); *RELease 1.0* (formerly *The Rosen Electronics Letter*) by Esther Dyson and Ben Rosen (New York: Rosen Research, December 12, 1983; March 8, 1983; January 6, 1983; January 19, 1983; August 24, 1981); daily press clips (January 1981 to December 1983) from the *Wall Street Journal, New York Times, Fortune, Forbes, BusinessWeek*; "L. F. Rothschild: A Lift from High Tech Issues" (*Pensions & Investment Age*, March 29, 1982); "Going Wild Over Going Public" (*BusinessWeek*, December 6, 1982); "Tracing the Roots of L. F. Rothschild, Unterberg, Towbin" by Dennis Weintraub (*Computer Systems News*, October 3, 1983); "Money Merchant: In Venture Capitalism Few Are as Successful as Benjamin Rosen" by William Bulkeley (*Wall Street Journal*, November 28, 1984); "Newcomers in Personal Computers Have Trouble Breaking into Market" by Bob Davis (*Wall Street Journal*, February 18, 1983); "What's New About This Boom" by Irwin Ross (*Fortune*, May 30, 1983); "IBM's Personal Computer Spawns an Industry" (*BusinessWeek*, August 15, 1983); "Personal Computers: And the Winner is IBM" (*BusinessWeek*, October 3, 1983); "Caveat Emptor: Shakeout of Producers of Personal Computers Makes Buyers Nervous" by William Bulkeley (*Wall Street Journal*, November 25, 1983); "The Tinkerings of Robert Noyce: How the Sun Rose on the Silicon Valley" by Tom Wolfe (*Esquire*, December 1983); "Making a Mint Overnight" by Alexander Taylor (*Time*, January 23, 1984).

Salomon Brothers

Interviews: Ira Harris, Ken Wilson, Ron Freeman, Jay Higgins, Bill Rifkin, Ed Olsen, Tony Brooks, John Gutfreund, Jay Elsas (Salomon Brothers); Donald Kelly, Roger Briggs, Ed Harrison, Karl Becker (Esmark); John Copeland, Doug Gray, Richard Knight, Richard Jaracz (Swift Independent).

Articles: daily press clips (May 1981 to May 1982) from the *Wall Street Journal, New York Times, Chicago Sun-Times* and *Tribune, Time, Newsweek, Fortune, Forbes, BusinessWeek*; "Fast and Canny Traders" (*BusinessWeek*, June 27, 1964); "Living It Up in a 'Salomon-Sized' World" by Carol Loomis (*Fortune*, April 1970); "William R. Salomon: Investment Banker of the Year" by James P. Roscow (*Finance*, December 1970); "Salomon Brothers: In Step with the Times" (*Investment Dealers' Digest*, November 10, 1971); "Salomon: The Spectacular Debut of an International Upstart" by Cary Reich (*Institutional Investor*, January 1978); "A Maverick Pushes into Wall Street's Club" (*BusinessWeek*, April 3, 1978); "Ira Harris: Chicago's Big Dealmaker" (*BusinessWeek*, June 25, 1979); "The Morning After at Phibro-Salomon" by Carol Loomis (*Fortune*, January 10, 1983); "Pigs, Purses and Project Redeployment" (*Forbes*, March 1, 1973); "Tough Numbers Man Sets Up the Esmark Derby" (*Fortune*, April 1977); "Esmark's Chief Looks Ahead" by Kenneth Labich (*Fortune*, October 3, 1983); "Esmark's Kelly Isn't a Retiring Kind of Person" by Herb Greenberg (*Chicago Tribune*, July 31, 1983); "To Engineer Slick Deals, Esmark's No. 2 Man Combines Timing, Finesse and Intimidation" by Meg Cox (*Wall Street Journal*, June 24, 1981).

Drexel Burnham Lambert

Interviews: John Sorte, Leon Black, Bob Linton, Fred Joseph, Chris Anderson, David Kay, Jay Bloom, Herb Bachelor (Drexel Burnham Lambert); Carl Icahn, Al Kingsley (Icahn Capital); Joe Morrow (Morrow & Co); Mark Belnick (Paul, Weiss, Rifkind, Wharton & Garrison); T. Boone Pickens, David Bachelder (Mesa Petroleum); Alan Stephenson, Philip Geltson (Cravath, Swaine & Moore); Bill Douce, Pete Silas, Glenn Cox, Paul Endacott (Phillips Petroleum); Joe Fogg, John Wilson (Morgan Stanley); Marty Lipton, Jim Fogelson, Paul Vizcarando (Wachtell, Lipton, Rosen & Katz).

Books and Articles: *Phillips: The First 66 Years* (Bartlesville, Okla.: Phillips Petroleum Public Affairs, 1983); daily press clips (December 1984 to March 1985) from the *Wall Street Journal, New York Times, Washington Post, Los Angeles Times, Chicago Tribune, Bartlesville Examiner-Enterprise, Amarillo Globe Times, Tulsa Tribune, Time, Newsweek, Fortune, Forbes, BusinessWeek*; "Drexel Burnham Lambert Finds a Niche" by Linda Sandler (*Institutional Investor*, October 1981); "The Firm that Fed on Wall Street's Scraps" by Joel Dreyfuss (*Fortune*, September 3, 1984); "Drexel Burnham Finds Self in Heady Company" by Linda Grant (*Los Angeles Times*, March 11, 1984); "Drexel Burnham: The Street's Fastest Growing Investment Bank" by Ed O'Toole (*Investment Dealer's Digest*, September 11, 1984); "At Drexel, a New Chief's New Problems" by Winston Williams (*New York Times*, May 26, 1985); "The New Generation of Investment Bankers" by Beth McGoldrick (*Institutional Investor*, March 1985); "High Times for T. Boone Pickens" by John Greenwald (*Time*, March 4, 1985); "It's Time To Make a Deal" by Joseph Nocera (*Texas Monthly*, October, 1982); "Boone Pickens, Company Hunter" by Peter Nulty (*Fortune*, December 26, 1983); "The Biggest Knockover: T. Boone Pickens and the End of Gulf Oil" by L. J. Davis (*Harper's*, January 1985); "Playing for Keeps: T. Boone Pickens" by Joe Rhodes (*Dallas Times Herald*, March 25, 1984); "Why Gulf Fell: What's Behind the Biggest Corporate Takeover" (*BusinessWeek*, March 19, 1984); "Into Turbulence: The Flight Plan of T. Boone Pickens" by Jonathan Lansner (*Pittsburgh Press Sunday Magazine*, April 29, 1984); "Texas Oil Man Has Pioneer Spirit" by Raad Cawthon (*Atlanta Journal-Constitution*, June 10, 1984); "T. Boone Pickens: The 'Deal-Maker' Whose Foes Call Raider and Friends Call Easy Pickens" (*Tulsa World*, August 12, 1984); "Why Boone Can't Lose" by Joseph Nocera (*Texas Monthly*, April 1985); "Mixed Signals: Mesa Petroleum's Chairman Hints About a Takeover" by Tim Metz and Charles F. McCoy (*Wall Street Journal*, November 27, 1984); "The Lone Wolf of Wall Street: Why Carl Icahn Relishes the Hostile Takeover" by Adam Zagorin (*Manhattan, inc.*, October 1984); "Carl Icahn's Calculated Bets" by Colin Leinster (*Fortune*, March 18, 1985); "Battle Tactics: Carl Icahn's Strategies in His Quest for TWA Are a Model for Raiders" by William Carley (*Wall Street Journal*, June 20, 1985).

I would like to thank the following public relations liaisons for their assistance: John Keane, Ray Tomin (Bank of America); Art Merrick, Katie Weiss (Seafirst); Helen Braun, Jack Morris, Laura Dillon (Morgan

Guaranty); Robin Wakeman, Tom Parisi (Bankers Trust); Chris Pagano (Allied); Dick Howe (Citibank); Joan Horvich (Goldman, Sachs); Gordon Reece (Occidental Petroleum); Carol Rhyne (Continental Illinois); Annette DeLorenzo (International Harvester); Marcia Roth (L. F. Rothschild); Ken Price (Compaq); Phil Thomas (Esmark); Bill Dillman (SIPCO); Mel Adams (Salomon Brothers); Ann Hartog, Naomi Rosenfeld (Drexel Burnham); Dan Harrison (Phillips); Warren Vieth (Mesa).

H O P E L A M P E R T was born in Boston, Massachusetts, and raised in San Francisco. A graduate of Harvard University, she covered Wall Street for *Newsweek* magazine for two years, reporting on stories including the Braniff Airways bankruptcy, the Drysdale affair, and the Vatican bank scandal, before writing her first book, *Till Death Do Us Part: Bendix vs. Martin Marietta*. A prize-winning journalist, Miss Lampert has written for the *New York Times Magazine, Manhattan, inc.*, and *The Washingtonian* and currently covers American business for the London *Observer*. She lives in New York City.